Fallen Bodies

THE MIDDLE AGES SERIES

Ruth Mazo Karras, General Editor
Edward Peters, Founding Editor

A complete list of books in the series is available from the publisher.

Fallen Bodies

Pollution, Sexuality, and Demonology in the Middle Ages

Dyan Elliott

PENN

University of Pennsylvania Press

Philadelphia

Copyright © 1999 University of Pennsylvania Press
All rights reserved
Printed in the United States of America on acid-free paper

10 9 8 7 6 5 4 3 2 1

Published by
University of Pennsylvania Press
Philadelphia, Pennsylvania 19104–4011

Library of Congress Cataloging-in-Publication Data
Elliott, Dyan, 1954–
Fallen bodies : pollution, sexuality, and demonology in the Middle Ages / Dyan Elliott.
p. cm. — (The Middle Ages series)
Includes bibliographical references and index.
ISBN 0-8122-3460-X (cloth : alk. paper). —
ISBN 0-8122-1665-2 (pbk. : alk. paper)
1. Sex — Religious aspects — Christianity — History of doctrines — Middle Ages, 600–1500. 2. Demonology — History of doctrines — Middle Ages, 600–1500. I. Title. II. Series.
BT708.E43 1998
261.8′357′0902 — dc21 98-29858
CIP

For Paul Strohm

Contents

Acknowledgments

A NUMBER OF PEOPLE have contributed to this project. Many thanks to David Brakke, Peter Brown, and Elizabeth Clark, whose patient responses to my often importunate questions helped me thread my way through the unfamiliar ambages of late antique thought. John Efron pointed to opportune analogues in the Jewish tradition. Charlotte Schoell-Glass provided stimulating parallels informed by her own discipline of art history. Barbara Newman and Mary Baine Campbell offered careful readings of Chapters 2 and 6 respectively. Miri Rubin drew my attention to relevant materials from her own work on host desecration. Peter Jelavich gave the manuscript an energetic reading and was an important resource for discussing its wider implications. In addition, I am most appreciative of the encouragement I received from Ruth Karras and Jerry Singerman of the University of Pennsylvania Press.

I also have been the beneficiary of generous institutional assistance. I am exceedingly grateful to Indiana University and the Institute for Advanced Study in Princeton for their support of this undertaking. The National Humanities Center provided a productive environment for its final stages.

Different parts of the book initially were aired in various public forums. "Sex in Holy Places" was presented at the University of Minnesota (March 1992). The Newberry Library was an especially formative venue in this respect, since my work on nocturnal emissions, the basis for Chapter 1, was first vetted there (March 1994), as was its companion study on female sexuality (February 1997), which became the basis for Chapter 2. I am grateful to Mary Beth Rose, then director of the Newberry's Center for Renaissance Studies, for these opportunities. The workshop on women and religion in the Middle Ages at the University of Groningen (October 1995) first prompted me to revisit the thorny problem of the priest's wife (Chaps. 4 and 5). I would like to thank Anneke Mulder-Bakker and Peter Hatlie, who were responsible for organizing this event. The questions raised by these different groups often permitted me to turn critical corners in my thinking. Earlier versions of two of these chapters have appeared elsewhere. "Sex in Holy Places: An Exploration of a Medieval Anxiety" (Chap. 3) was published in the *Journal of Women's History* 6,3 (Fall 1994); "Pollution, Illusion, and Masculine Disarray: Nocturnal Emissions and the Sexuality of the Clergy" (Chap. 1) has more recently appeared in *Constructing Medieval Sexuality,* ed. Karma Lochrie et al. (Minneapolis: University of Minnesota Press, 1997). I would like to thank the respective publishers for permission to use these works.

Finally, my deepest debt is to my colleague and partner, Paul Strohm, who has read this manuscript more times than either of us would like to remember. Each reading invariably brought improvement (whatever the cost to the authorial ego). I also discovered, to my chagrin, that he is virtually incorruptible: he will not say something is right when it's not—no matter what blandishments or threats a particular appellant may use. What's right in this book is very often due to him; what remains wrong has much to do with my residual recalcitrance. But in all its rightness and wrongness, this book is for him.

Abbreviations

AA SS	*Acta Sanctorum*. Paris: Victor Palmé, 1865–.
AB	*Analecta Bollandiana*. Brussels: Société des Bollandistes, 1882–.
ACW	*Ancient Christian Writers*. Westminster, Md.: Newman Press, 1946–.
BHL	*Bibliotheca hagiographica latina antiquae et mediae aetatis*. 2 vols. Subsidia hagiographica no. 5. Brussels: Société Bollandistes, 1898–1901; and *Bibliotheca hagiographica latina: Novum supplementum*. Ed. H. Fros. Subsidia hagiographica, no. 70. Brussels: Société Bollandistes, 1986.
BS	*Bibliotheca Sanctorum*. 12 vols. and index. Rome: Città nuova editrice, 1961–70.
CCCM	*Corpus Christianorum, Continuatio Mediaeualis*. Turnhout: Brepols, 1966–.
CCSL	*Corpus Christianorum, Series Latina*. Turnhout: Brepols, 1953–.
CSEL	*Corpus Scriptorum Ecclesiasticorum Latinorum*. Vienna: F. Tempsky (et al.), 1866–.
DMA	*Dictionary of the Middle Ages*. 13 vols. New York: Scribner, 1982–89.
DS	*Dictionnaire de spiritualité*. Under the direction of Marcel Viller et al. 16 vols. Paris: Beauchesne, 1937–95.
DTC	*Dictionnaire de théologie catholique*. Ed. A. Vacant et al. 13 vols. Paris: Letouzey et Ané, 1930–50.
EETS	*Early English Text Society*. London: Trübner (et al.), 1864–.
FC	*Fathers of the Church*. New York: Cima, Fathers of the Church (et al.), 1947–.
LNPNFC	*A Select Library of Nicene and Post-Nicene Fathers of the Church*. New York: Christian Literature Co. (et al.), 1887–92; rpt. Grand Rapids, Mich.: Eerdmans (et al.), 1952–
MGH	*Monumenta Germaniae Historica*. Hanover: Impensis Bibliopolii Hahniani (et al.), 1826–.

NCE	*New Catholic Encyclopaedia.* 14 vols. and index. New York: McGraw-Hill, 1967.
PG	*Patrologiae cursus completus . . . series Graeca.* Ed. J.-P. Migne. 162 vols. Paris: J.-P. Migne, 1857–66.
PL	*Patrologiae cursus completus . . . series Latina.* Ed. J.-P. Migne. 221 vols. Paris: Garnier Fratres and J.-P. Migne, 1844–64.
SC	*Sources chrétiennes.* Paris: Editions du Cerf, 1940–.

Introduction

THIS BOOK IS PURPOSEFULLY SITUATED on slippery and shifting terrain. Its central concerns are twofold. First, it attempts to reveal aspects of the clerical intelligentsia's reinterpretation of inherited sexual and religious traditions within the altered conditions of the high and later Middle Ages. Out of necessary deference to tradition, this reinterpretative effort frequently employed obfuscation, subterfuge, and disavowal. Second, the work as a whole suggests various forms of sullen self-maintenance by which the past resisted eradication and even reasserted itself within the very discourses intended to effect its suppression. Certain discursive zones attract attention to themselves by their extremes of repetition or emotional intensity, revealing the persistence of a sensitivity that is noteworthy even when one grants the intractability of past discourses. Rather than confirming existing or newly promulgated areas of belief, these zones evoked a mixed or irresolute response, and their affective product was anxiety in the beholder. For the western church, ritual pollution, sexual regulation, and the status of the demonic were three areas within which such irreducible and anxiety-producing kernels were carried forward, even within the stream of rationalizing high medieval discourse. These particularly obdurate zones resist neat reconceptualization. Instead of gradually differentiating themselves in ways amenable to the resolution of interpretative difficulties, such areas became increasingly interconnected as the Middle Ages progressed.

Early Christianity is frequently contrasted with Judaism for its cavalier attempt to dispense with many of the complex taboos that differentiated the pure from the impure in social and cultic life.[1] But, as with many attempted revolutions, this was a partial one at best. The human body, frail and corruptible, would continue to be a locus of concern that would serve to prolong and extend pollution fears. Thus, in the words of Mary Douglas, "the spiritual intentions of the early Church were frustrated by spontaneous resistance to the idea that bodily states were irrelevant to ritual."[2] This resistance was differentially applied. Recent work by scholars such as Peter

Brown, Dale Martin, Elaine Pagels, and Aline Rousselle has compellingly suggested the ways in which reproductive and erotic impulses were regarded with escalating suspicion in early Christian circles.[3] In fact, Christian sexual taboos would in many ways amplify the concerns latent in their Jewish prototype. The imperative of sacerdotal purity is perhaps the most conspicuous example. According to the Book of Leviticus (15.16), conjugal intercourse constituted a temporary impurity for the priest. But the Christian adulation of chastity enhanced this stricture considerably.[4] Already by the fourth century, the bishops of Rome were calling for an entirely celibate clergy.[5]

The distance between the pure ideal and the inevitability of an impure reality—the pure being constantly impugned by transgressions in both deed and thought—was the space within which the symbolic terrain of the demonic world was constituted.[6] The possibility of demonic incursion into human affairs was fostered by a broadly accepted theological understanding of the propinquity of the human and demonic realms. By virtue of original sin, the human body was fallen—rendered irretrievably impure from the outset and thus vulnerable to onslaughts of demons, who were perceived as inherently the enemies of purity. Faced with the challenge of bridging the gap between an impossible ideal and its flawed human expression, Christian commentators could hardly ignore the explanatory resource afforded by a constant demonic presence.

Humanity's doomed battle against the powers of defilement is exemplified in the predicament of woman, perceived both as self-contaminating (thus in a sense already a casualty of the diabolical war against humankind) and as a source of contagion to others. The implacability of pollution taboos surrounding the female body is especially demonstrable in the tensions generated over menstruation, which will here be used as an exemplar for the extent of pollution anxiety's grim hold. Myths surrounding menstruation were ancient and ubiquitous. According to classical tradition, the blood itself was believed to possess uncanny powers that could alternately destroy or heal—an association that automatically linked woman's body with supernatural forces.[7] Moreover, as Mary Douglas and others have suggested, a state of defilement was fundamentally linked with the sacred, since both conditions were contagious, dangerous, and circumscribed by numerous prohibitions.[8] Menstruation was thus quintessentially possessed of qualities that would foster ambivalence toward women—an ambivalence that was frequently marked by rituals of separation and purification. In the Hebraic tradition, the Levitican isolation of the menstruating woman was grounded on the conviction that the woman was unclean. She required purification when the danger she presented subsided, but until that time her uncleanness was a source of contamination that could be easily communicated to others (Lev. 15.19–24). Not only was she off-limits for sexual relations, infractions against this rule being punishable by death (Lev. 20.18), but those who came into contact with her must likewise be purified.[9] The process of giving birth also reduced the woman to a state of menstrual impurity (Lev. 12.1–7).

Christ ostensibly broke with this tradition. The very act of healing the woman with flux (Matt. 9.20; Mark 5.25) demonstrated relative indifference to the Levitican taboos, since the bleeding woman's very touch, even confined as it was to Christ's garment, would have rendered him unclean.[10] This attitude is in keeping with Christ's relocation of concerns over purity to the inner person, emphasizing the polluting nature of sin. Thus he is reported to have said:

> There is nothing from without a man that entering into him can defile him; but the things which come from a man, those are they that defile a man. . . . For from within, out of the heart of men, proceed evil thoughts, adulteries, fornications, murders.[11]

The question of menstruation and its incumbent uncleanness is not mentioned by Paul, so his precise attitudes were unclear. Yet in most areas, Paul would persevere in the abrogation of Judaic law's preoccupation with physical uncleanness.[12]

By the third century, however, evidence suggests that Christian communities were themselves stigmatizing menstruating women. The *Didascalia,* which attempted to refute these practices, spoke with contempt of the superstitious beliefs—apparently advanced by the women themselves—that menstruation put the Holy Spirit to flight.[13] Certain authoritative interventions intended to counteract specious prohibitions also occurred in the West. In a letter attributed to Gregory the Great addressed to Augustine of Canterbury, the author attempts to allay a series of anxieties that turn on the potential of bodily emissions to pollute sacred precincts—concerns that parallel those outlined in Leviticus.[14] The treatment of the menstruating woman is typical of the letter's general strategy. As a concession, she should not be prohibited from entering a church, "for this natural overflowing cannot be reckoned a crime." Even so, menstruation is cast as an infirmity, with womankind likened to the woman afflicted with flux who was healed by touching the garment of Christ. Applying this logic to the situation at hand, the author argues that the menstruating woman should not be forbidden to enter a church nor even to receive communion. Nevertheless, this concession was qualified by various contingencies. It was possible, for example, that the woman would judge herself as unworthy of communion.

> It is the part of noble minds to acknowledge their faults to some extent even when no fault exists, for an action is often itself faultless, though it originates in a fault. So when we are hungry it is no sin to eat even though our hunger is the result of the sin of the first man. A woman's periods are not sinful, because they happen naturally. But nevertheless, because our nature is itself so depraved that it appears to be polluted even without the consent of the will, the depravity arises from sin, and human nature itself recognizes its depravity to be a judgement upon it; so mankind having wilfully committed sin must bear the guilt of sin though unwillingly. Let women make up their own minds.[15]

Thus the impulse that stimulated the women referred to in the *Didascalia* to perceive themselves as ineligible for communion, a tendency derided as both overscrupulous and misguided by the third-century legislator, is actually commended by the later authority. Similarly, although ostensibly denying the quasi-menstrual pollution surrounding the afterbirth of a woman, maintaining that a woman would be within her rights to enter a church to give thanks immediately after her delivery, "Gregory" does acknowledge that the process of giving birth is in some way vitiated by two past faults. First, the pleasure that is almost invariably present in the act of conception is considered sinful, even though it was a result of the concupiscence to which humanity was prey as a consequence of the fall. Second, woman's pain in birth is related to the curse God visited on Eve (Gen. 3.16).[16] In this way, the author justifies his retention of the Levitican ritual of purification after birth. Yet, by the reasons he adduces, woman, even though free of personal sin, nevertheless becomes a compelling image for original sin and the fallen condition of the human body—an image of woman that would remain available throughout the Middle Ages.[17]

This palpable dismissal, demurral, and ultimate reinstatement of pollution taboos in revised form—enacted in miniature in the letter to Augustine of Canterbury—is a constant pulse in the history of Christianity. For instance, the efforts of "Gregory" were undercut by the very explicit concerns with ritual purity expressed in penitential literature that sought to bar the menstruating woman from partaking of communion or even entering a church.[18] In a similar vein, a woman who entered a church in advance of the Levitican stipulations was forced to do penance.[19] By the late eleventh century, when the first liturgies for the rite surrounding the purification of the mother after parturition appeared, this ceremony had evolved into a full-blown penitential ritual involving the complete prostration of the mother while reciting the penitential psalm *Miserere mei* (Ps. 50). Such ritualized gestures certainly increased the sense of the innate sinfulness of birth, possibly moving the woman's condition even closer toward a perception of active sinfulness.[20] Similarly, an eleventh-century blessing, designed for a woman's room after parturition, invokes God's protection against evil spirits, to which her condition makes her especially prone. Over the mother, the priest would intone:

> I commend in holy and singular custody to you [God] the soul and body of your servant, and all her thoughts and acts that you may protect her from evil spirits, that she should never cross over into their power—neither now nor in the future.[21]

The ominous phrase "neither now nor in the future" suggests that woman's ongoing susceptibility to such unsavory influence was as inescapable as her own body.

Perhaps the most compelling measure of the persistence of the pollution beliefs associated with women's physiology was the continued effort to separate the Virgin Mary from all such sources of contamination. The Virgin was widely believed to have been spared not only the pain of parturition but also the polluting effects of afterbirth. Although the theologians of the high Middle Ages were reluctant to commit themselves to the Virgin's freedom from the taint of menstruation, fearing lest they sever her from humanity altogether, there were still energetic attempts to effect a salutary distance.[22] According to Thomas Aquinas (d. 1274), for example, while the hot lust of ordinary intercourse draws the menstrual blood down to the woman's genitals for purposes of conception, the blood used in the conception of Christ never visited these lower regions. On the contrary, the operation of the Holy Spirit brought completely pure and untainted blood directly to the Virgin's womb.[23]

The main focus of this work is the high and later Middle Ages, the period that offers some of the most complex and intricate restagings of this pattern: an ostensible relaxation of pollution concerns, accompanied by their prolongation at other expressive levels or their reinstitution by other means. For instance, attention was deflected from physical pollution by the revived emphasis on intention and conscious culpability as the vector for impurity—a transition explored in Chapter 3, "Sex in Holy Places." Moreover, a theological refurbishment of the sacraments made them theoretically impervious to many of the ancient conditions of ritual impurity as well as to the personal sinfulness of the officiating priest—developments attending the rise of eucharistic piety (discussed in Chap. 5). And yet, these chapters suggest that a psychic price remained to be paid for this apparent dispensation. The very relaxation of pollution concerns generated considerable anxiety, while theoretically moribund prohibitions continued to enjoy a covert and almost eerie afterlife.

Often the ancient taboos were reinstated through other avenues, those against the menstruating woman again being a case in point. In his discussion of the Levitican prohibitions, the thirteenth-century William of Auvergne, doubtless influenced by the new influx of medical knowledge that characterized his age, tends to reify the corrupting influence of the menstruating woman. So great is her contagion that her very gaze leaves a stain of filth on a mirror. Conception during menstruation, moreover, results in irreparable harm to the fetus.[24] But William also builds on the association between menstruation and idolatry that was forged in the Hebrew Bible and became ubiquitous in Christian exegesis.[25] Thus he argues that the Levitican discussion of menstrual uncleanness was also historically conditioned by women's erstwhile conviction that their monthly cycle made them lunar favorites—leading to their idolatrous worship of the moon with offerings of menstrual blood. He also alleges that witches made many monstrous things with menstrual blood.[26]

In other words, to buttress the retention of taboos surrounding menstruation, William—one of the earliest scholastic writers to show intense interest in diabolism and witchcraft—aligns women and their polluting potential with the diabolical realm. But even when biological women were not explicitly evoked, the potent metaphors of female pollution were used to feminize and discredit those perceived as spiritually suspect. Nicholas of Lyre's fourteenth-century *Postilla* on the *Glossa ordinaria* moralizes that the woman with flux is the soft and effeminate individual ("homo mollis et effeminatus") who perseveres in his or her sin.[27] The thirteenth-century monk Caesarius of Heisterbach would feminize the Jews—who in the course of the high Middle Ages would come to be increasingly associated with the diabolical—by alleging that Jewish men were subject to a debilitating flux of blood on Good Friday.[28]

Woman's bond with the diabolical was not solely contingent on the unsavory potentials of her polluting body but was multiply determined. From a biblical standpoint, Eve's initial coalition with Satan inaugurated humanity's fall. As is well known and will be explored further in the present work, this transgression casts a long shadow for both its pivotal "historical" quotient and its metaphoric potential. Chapter 2 ("From Sexual Fantasy to Demonic Defloration") further demonstrates that woman, biologically and hence morally inferior, represented a node of vulnerability for Christendom at large, and thus would continue to be viewed as especially susceptible to demonic influence.[29]

Both demons and women were also considered explicit harbingers of ritual pollution, a perception sustained and extended in several of my chapters. Chapter 1, "Pollution, Illusion, and Masculine Disarray," examines clerical efforts to disavow and distance themselves from their own fantasy lives, especially as epitomized in their association with nocturnal emissions. "The Priest's Wife," a two-part study that comprises Chapters 4 and 5, traces some of the unpredicted psychological ramifications of the institutional war against women, who were perceived as polluting the ministers of the altar. In these two cases, which involve both involuntary and voluntary sexual misdemeanors, the quest for ritual purity invites the priestly participants, and other commentators on their struggle, to invoke mechanisms of repression. Repression, in turn, fosters a turbulent unconscious, in which favorable conditions prevail for a solidification of women's association with the diabolical realm.[30]

The introduction of psychoanalytic concepts such as "repression" has never been extensively accepted in the community of historians—and yet the alternative strikes me as unthinkable. The argument is still sometimes made that terms such as repression, or indeed the entire concept of the unconscious, should be held in abeyance in order to avoid anachronism or in deference to the medieval clergy's own conscious aims. But such a response would be misguided, I believe, since it ultimately leads to flattening out the medieval psychic landscape by confining its description to the vocabulary in which medieval thinkers were accustomed to describe themselves. The inescapable consequence of this self-restriction on the part of the modern historian would be to promote interpretations that medieval authors would themselves "approve." The identification and description of such interpretations is, of course, vital to the understanding of the late medieval horizon and indispensible to the historical enterprise. But the refusal to acknowledge impulses, motives, and fantasies incompatible with medieval self-understanding would constitute an unacceptable avoidance of our interpretative responsibility. My own effort to come to terms with the complexities of medieval psychic processes is limited to certain specific cases, rather than seeking a more ambitious explanation of the "medieval psyche" itself. But in these specific cases I do indeed rely upon certain—often tacit—theoretical underpinnings, which I will engage briefly here.

In a formulation with considerable relevance to the medieval demand for a ritually pure clergy, Freud argues that repression occurs when social and ethical norms attempt abridgment or effacement of a libidinal instinct.[31] The repressed instinct, barred from the conscious mind, is consigned to the unconscious, where it becomes attached to an ideational representative—some object available within the contemporary symbolic order.[32] This representative will, in Freud's words, "proliferate in the dark," associating itself with whatever material it comes in contact with and thus creating fantasies of frightening and seemingly alien power.[33] The return of these repressed elements to the conscious mind can occur only when the ideas or images are sufficiently distorted that they can elude the censorship of the conscious mind, as would be the case with dreams or visions.[34] If we apply some of these insights to the situation of the western clergy, their frequently distorted perceptions of women, which emerge in the course of antifeminist polemic, may be perceived as the result of a similar process. The requirements of clerical celibacy entailed a repression of libidinal instincts, particularly heterosexual ones.[35] Gathering force in the unconscious, the banished instincts broke through into the conscious mind as hideous and predatory fantasy women—whose images, as we will see, especially abound in the high and later Middle Ages. The return of these repressed desires to consciousness is contingent on their distortion, whereby they are altered in such a way that they are no longer recognizable as objects of desire.[36] Therefore, in a certain sense, the images that return have been so successfully fused with the demonic that they are no longer perceived as mere women and thus, in their repugnant guise, are no longer subject to the censorship that would accompany objects of libidinous desire.

Although I do not consider myself a "psychoanalytic historian" as such, I do regard the concepts of repression (as a basis for subsequent distortion) and the unconscious (as a place where a transformative labor of resymbolization is accomplished) as contributing to the explanatory effort I have undertaken. Indeed, aspects of Freudian thought, most markedly its attentiveness to relations of past and present in its recognition of the past within the present, seem to me particularly and even uniquely compatible with the historical enterprise. My hope is, in turn, that the work at hand will open new perspectives on the ever-present, and yet inexorably progressive, link between women and the demonic.

This union between women and the demonic, itself the product of repression and fear, is never neatly deployed, even by those who testify most vociferously to its existence. Indeed, pivotal authors such as Peter Damian, William of Auvergne, and John Nider, who could justly be described as leading contributors to the tradition that advanced the link between women and the demonic in the high and later Middle Ages, seem least in control of the linkages and other effects their writings produce. Under the cover of reform-oriented or rationalist and quasi-scientific enterprises, their writing actually serves as a vehicle for a painful return of repressed symptoms, together with the turbulence and anxiety that accompany the entry of repressed concepts into language.[37]

The demonic host also reveals itself as a repository of repressed instincts in its capacity as a dark surrogate for humanity. As frequent instigators of sin, especially sexual sin, the demons were constantly available to Christendom at large, and the clergy in particular, as repressed "doubles."[38] Nor was the medieval clergy entirely insensible of such points of identification with the demonic world. From a theological standpoint, humanity was understood to have been created as a substitute for the angels who fell from heaven.[39] Yet it too, like the demons, would fall in its turn. While Christ's salvific role would ensure that the elect would eventually be restored to a prestigious condition parallel to the one experienced by the angels, demons — as counterweight — would continually seek to affiliate humankind with their own darker (and arguably more germane) destiny. Thus, similarly debased, humans and demons become readily interchangeable. Demons enacted or at least appeared to enact sexual transgressions that were forbidden to their human counterparts. Periodically, we find humans being substituted for demons in various exegetical efforts. What came to be the accepted reading of Genesis 6.2 is a case in point. The biblical text describes how the sons of God, originally construed as fallen angels, bred with the daughters of men and thus engendered a race of giants. As we will see, Augustine reinterpreted this controversial biblical passage as connoting holy men who fell from chastity. Similarly, Nicholas of Lyre would allegorize the sons of God as evil clerics and the daughters of men as the lusts of the world. Their union would, in turn, engender a deluge of vices in the laity.[40] The same spirit of substitution animates the deep play apparent in Chaucer's Wife of Bath's Tale, which opens with the Wife's satirical acknowledgment that the incubus has been supplanted by the friar:

Wommen may go saufly up and down.
In every bussh or under every tree
Ther is noon oother incubus but he.[41]

Behind the teasing suggestion that the friar is but a sorry substitute for the incubus is the more startling assertion that the incubus was always only a "stand-in" for the friar.

Although the demonic realm was an arena in which many of the clergy's repressed desires were enacted, upon condition of their disavowal, circumstances propitious for a conscious and purposeful reconfiguration and redeployment of the demonic could (and did) arise. "On Angelic Disembodiment and the Incredible Purity of Demons," the last chapter in this work, accordingly treats a major theological initiative to create a substantial distance between humans and demons—a distance that seemed necessary for refuting heretical perceptions of humanity's kinship with demons. This initiative resulted in a shift from an image of a lascivious and even sexually depraved demon to an austere and entirely spiritual entity—a creature disgusted by humanity's sexual vices. Yet, as innovative as this reconstruction of the demon might be, it is nevertheless continuous with the tradition of demons as doubles. Demons and humans have simply changed places. Rather than humans looking on in horror at the sexual excesses of demons, it is the demons who are horrified by the flagrant acts of humans.

This book does not profess to be a history of pollution, sexuality, or demonology. In fact, it is not intended as a linear history at all. The various chapters were generated by particular problems that, I believe, reveal pivotal aspects of the workings of medieval society's inner life. This orientation around specific problems inevitably means that certain topics suffer. There is, for example, no sustained discussion of menstruation beyond the few remarks in this introduction, though the subject often comes up in the context of a given problem.

The various issues engaged in this work had different ways of recommending themselves to me. For instance, the medieval attention to nocturnal emissions and clerical wives as possible threats to ritual purity initially drew these issues to my notice. But medieval concerns also presented themselves through more covert routes. Sometimes an anomalous detail, though presented authoritatively, nevertheless failed to pass itself off as part of an inherited tradition, signaling the alloy of deliberate innovation. For instance, the statement that demons are repelled by "unnatural vice," which seems first to have surfaced among thirteenth-century theologians, struck me in this way. On further examination, this detail emerged as symptomatic of the much larger theological attempt at drawing firmer boundaries between the natural and the supernatural. This division, moreover, underwrote aspects of a new ideology for the persecution of deviance, which was deployed along complex and ever-widening frontiers.

This book embraces the conviction that the superficially marginal is often imaginatively (and hence ideologically) central. As Carlo Ginzburg and others have shown, it is precisely in the anecdotal, the incidental, the idiosyncratic, that we often find the keys to unlocking much larger issues.[42] One of my working assumptions is that many of the clues to past conundrums are displaced into different discursive registers. Sometimes this displacement is deliberate. In the course of these chapters, for example, the exemplum will emerge as a veritable treasure trove for suppressed concerns that were probably generated by, but could not find expression in, more formal theological forums. Thus, at a time when canonists and theologians were calling for the payment of the conjugal debt regardless of the circumstances, the exemplum tradition would garner graphic evidence of suppressed, but hardly vanquished, pollution taboos that argued the opposite (see Chap. 3). In this instance, these different venues permitted an uneasy coexistence of both new and old codes. But sometimes the interaction between different discursive registers staged a more lethal challenge to doctrine, albeit more obliquely couched. Thus at a time when theologians had ostensibly proved that the Host was impassible—both untouched by external outrages and impervious to human sinfulness—the exemplum tradition would articulate widespread fears of sacramental inefficacy in the face of sacerdotal impurity (Chap. 5). Similarly, as theologians were formally stressing the obdurate malice of the devil and his legions, proving once and for all their ineligibility for redemption, the exemplum tradition would posit some plausibly repentant demons (Chap. 6). Not only does this image of repentance covertly challenge the verdict of divine, and necessarily ecclesiastical, judgment but it resonates with contemporary heretical assumptions.

Although modern historians have frequently looked to the exemplum tradition as an index of "popular culture" or a point of mediation between high and low culture, I assume no such clear divisions.[43] Even if such neat distinctions were conceptually viable, proof of their existence could not reasonably be sustained due to the multiple reworkings, and hence effacement, of such boundaries in written tradition.[44] My own movement among different registers—be they theological, hagiographical, canonistic, pastoral, historical, literary, or heretical—reflects a view of their necessary interrelationship and ultimate interdependence. This interdependence is conditioned by mutual participation in an enlarged imaginary system that is, in turn, immanent in its diverse cultural expressions and imparts a basic coherence to medieval culture. This is not to be taken as an uncritical acceptance of the earlier Marxist view of society as an analytical "totality," particularly if this concept is strictly understood in terms of its implicit historical telos.[45] Nor, at another totalizing extreme, am I at all persuaded by current idealizations of a "Christian Middle Ages," which tend to presume social harmony at the expense of discord.[46] The coherence to which I refer is not premised on a sense of consensus or even a stable set of shared assumptions. In fact, the integrity of the imaginary system is especially apparent in its tensions, conflicts, contradictions, and ambivalences as they resonate with and speak to one another. Thus orthodoxy would formulate anxious questions about divine judgment that only heretics dared to answer. Similarly, what is presented as a local superstition surrounding the Host emerges as an expression of the most despairing of theological fears.

Although the various chapters might appear to address discrete problems (and in fact each chapter could be read separately), the book as a whole demonstrates the ways in which these issues resist separate treatment and interpenetrate one another. Subjects such as the pivotal role of the Gregorian Reform, the implications of transubstantiation, or concerns over supernatural miscegenation—to name a few—will be revisited on different occasions from varied perspectives throughout this work. The chapters themselves move thematically to different arenas for these shared concerns, proceeding from the microcosm to the macrocosm. Thus, "Pollution, Illusion, and Masculine Disarray" (Chap. 1) focuses on the bodies of men; "From Sexual Fantasty to Demonic Defloration" (Chap. 2) treats the bodies of women; "Sex in Holy Places" (Chap. 3) concerns sacred space; "The Priest's Wife" and "Avatars of the Priest's Wife" address institutional purity (Chaps. 4 and 5); and "On Angelic Disembodiment and the Incredible Purity of Demons" (Chap. 6) concerns the boundaries between the natural and the supernatural world.

The book is further united by a common set of preoccupations, which presuppose many of the historical and ideational patterns outlined above. Individually, the chapters explore the different facets through which the impossible quest for purity, be it personal or institutional, created a pocket of vulnerability that was ever susceptible to hostile penetration by the agents of defilement. The work in its entirety, moreover, advances our understanding of how this very vulnerability was coextensive and ultimately complicit with the rise of witchcraft charges.

1

Pollution, Illusion, and Masculine Disarray

Nocturnal Emissions and the Sexuality of the Clergy

A box full of clothes — if left for long — will putrefy. So it is with our thoughts if we don't perform them corporeally.

— Evagrius of Pontus[1]

IN HIS *MORALIA* Gregory the Great (d. 604) discusses some of the more insidious ways in which the devil afflicts God's holy people. Although making little headway during their waking hours, the devil is nevertheless permitted to fill the minds of the saints with filthy thoughts in sleep. But Gregory also prescribes a remedy, one that precociously anticipates Freud's theory of sublimation. A person must overcome these anxieties by raising the mind to higher things. Thus he glosses the biblical verse "So that my soul rather chooseth hanging and my bones death" (Job 7.15):

What is designated by the soul except intention of the mind, what by the bones except the strength of the flesh? Everything which is hung is beyond a doubt raised from lower things. The soul therefore chooses hanging so that the bones die, because when the intention of the mind raises itself to the heights, all strength of the outer life dies within.[2]

To stay with Freud for a moment, it is safe to say that Christian ascetics may have longed for sexual sublimation, but they generally had to settle for repression, with the attendant problems suggested in the epigraph. The presence or absence of erotic dreams, especially those culminating in ejaculation or "pollution" (to use the medieval term) represented for the would-be ascetic the sad distance between aspiration and actuality, providing a sensitive gauge for clocking the relative success or failure of disciplinary efforts to gain mastery over the body. The problem of such emissions also provided one of the rare occasions for theologians and pastoral counselors to speak frankly about the male's sexuality and body, by which I mean that these discussions could and did occur divorced from any reproductive telos. Here I should add that despite efforts of doctors and the occasional theologian to make pollution an equal opportunity offense for men and women, the discourse was inescapably framed around masculine embarrassments, particularly those of the would-be celibate ascetics and priests who were preoccupied with the way in which physical impurity impinged on ritual activities.[3]

Autoeroticism, whether voluntary or involuntary, would seem to frustrate attempts at historicization. Hence, Eve Kosofsky Sedgwick's article "Jane Austen and the Masturbating Girl" argues that masturbation "seems to have an affinity with amnesia, repetition or the repetition compulsion, and ahistorical or history-rupturing rhetorics of sublimity."[4] Likewise with nocturnal emissions; even the external disciplinary ramparts erected against such shadowy occurrences seem to argue for a transhistorical dimension. For example, the unflagging presence of prayers warding off pollution in the compline service is an indication that, at least on the ritualistic level, pollution never ceased to be a concern throughout the Middle Ages. But the level of intellectual and probably emotional engagement with this subject was temporally uneven. Nocturnal emission was a matter of considerable concern until the time of Gregory the Great, received only the most routine treatment (mainly in penitential literature) from the seventh until the twelfth century, and thereafter commanded increased attention until the end of the Middle Ages. The intensification of discourse in pastoral and theological circles in the later period is the primary focus of this chapter. However, the urgency of the later discourse was predicated on the all-too-effective efforts at repression in the early Middle Ages. And to this "first wave" of concern I first briefly turn.

The patristic age set the stage for later discussions of nocturnal emissions by framing three interlocking problems: the extent to which such emissions inhibited participation in ritual; the way in which pollution could be transformed into an occasion for self-examination; and the determination of the degree of culpability of the individual. Ritualistic interests could be said to constitute the seminal category. Attention to ritual purity raised the question as to whether a person so stained should abstain from the Eucharist—as a recipient, of course, but especially as a celebrant. This was a very real concern in the early church, when pollution taboos ran high. Both the *Didascalia* and the *Apostolic Constitutions,* for example, reacted against this level of rigor in the Syrian church.[5]

Although a potential liability from a sacramental standpoint, such emissions had possibilities from the perspective of ascetical training, which developed into a second nexus of concern. Spiritual directors turned to pollution and its attendant circumstances as a possible index to the relative strength of the passions and, conversely, to the progress of the soul's ascent. This stratagem is especially clear in the symptomatologies of John Cassian (d. 435) in the West and John Climacus (d. 649) in the East. Cassian, for example, posited an ascending scale of chastity with six gradations. In the first stage, the monk does not succumb to the assaults of the flesh while waking; in the second, his mind does not linger over voluptuous thoughts; in the third, the sight of a woman no longer inspires lust; in the fourth, the waking body is immune to even the most simple movements of the flesh; in the fifth, the mind is no longer flustered by writings that discuss reproduction. By the sixth and final stage, a monk is impervious to sexual temptation while asleep. To demonstrate the last stage, which is extremely rare, Cassian invokes the exceptional purity of a singularly graced monk with the appropriate name of Serenus. His stable and enduring purity was the result of a visionary evisceration in answer to his earnest prayers for perfect chastity.[6] Cassian also proffers practical advice against pollution. The diet must be strictly regulated and the intake of water reduced so that the bodily humors become sluggish and slow.[7] He also recommends that one cover the kidneys with lead, as the touch of metal inhibits the "obscene humors." If this level of abstemiousness and care is faithfully pursued, the monk should not be troubled by nocturnal emissions more than three times a year.[8] Occasionally, however, the devil's malice will stimulate gratuitous pollution just prior to communion to forestall the reception of the sacrament, as was the case of one monk. In this instance, the only way to break the vicious cycle was to receive the Host.[9] But to play it safe, the monk should never go to sleep after evening services because the devil, ever jealous of purity, would almost inevitably sully him with pollution.[10] Similarly, John Climacus, whose *Ladder of Divine Ascent* outlines the thirty precarious rungs that constitute the ascetic's ascent to God, envisages a program similar to Cassian's:

The beginning of chastity is a refusal to consent to evil thoughts and occasional dreamless emissions; the middle stage is to be free of dreams and emissions even when there are natural movements of the body brought on by eating too much; the completion of chastity comes when mortified thoughts are followed by a mortified body.

To his mind, the best strategy against pollution is to fall asleep while saying the "Jesus Prayer."[11]

The third discursive strand that bridges both questions of ritual purity and the impetus to self-examination concerns the degree of culpability inherent in nocturnal emissions. Athanasius (d. 373), hostile to the overscrupulousness of monastic culture, was the first to argue that such experiences were sinless, since they were involuntary and required by nature, pragmatically enlisting the support of medical authorities to buttress his contention.[12] Clearly, Athanasius was advocating a much more forgiving approach than either the impersonal taboo that had governed many early eucharistic discussions or the ascetic program of self-examination. But Athanasius's resolution only addressed the raw physicality of ejaculation—an occurrence that was, in fact, merely an epiphenomenon of a much more complex process: the dream.[13] Augustine (d. 430), however, was less willing, or less able, to divorce orgasm from its dream context, thus offering one of the more nuanced contributions to the issue of culpability. Book 10 of the *Confessions* reviews classical theory regarding the way in which the mind stores in the memory various images that have been abstracted by the senses.[14] This leads to a frank but angst-ridden discussion concerning the problems arising from memories of his sexual past. By pondering the vexed relations between sexual memory, erotic dreams, culpability, and selfhood, Augustine offers an arresting instance of the link between shame and identity formation that has been posited by developmental psychologists:[15]

When I am awake [these memories] obtrude themselves upon me, though with little strength. But when I dream, they not only give me pleasure but are very much like acquiescence in the act. The power which these illusory images have over my soul and my body is so great that what is no more than a vision can influence me in sleep in a way that reality cannot do when I am awake. Surely it cannot be that when I am asleep I am not myself, O Lord my God? . . . And why is it that even in sleep I often resist the attractions of these images, for I remember my chaste resolutions and abide by them and give no consent to temptations of this sort? Yet the difference between waking and sleeping is so great that when, during sleep, it happens otherwise, I return to a clear conscience when I wake and realize that, because of this difference, I was not responsible for the act, although I am sorry that by some means or other it happened to me.[16]

Augustine would seem to be at least partially enacting what one theorist describes as the "Thank God, it was only a Dream" syndrome, wherein the awakened dreamer feels authorized to dismiss the content and certainly the outcome of fantasies as an interruption in the regular program rather than an expression of real desire.[17]

Augustine's solicitude for his defamiliarized sleeping self ("I am sorry that by some means or other it happened to me") might, under other circumstances, have encouraged him to develop a theory of personal complicity with aberrant mental images equivalent to what we now term the unconscious. Yet, as becomes clear from his other works, Augustine raises these questions in order to suppress them once and for all.[18] Master of the interior that he was, Augustine mobilized his full theological genius around the problem of disowning the realm of dream-fantasy, thence forestalling the examination of its contents. In so doing, he definitively broke with the classical tradition of oneirocriticism, which subjected every aspect of dreams to painstaking analysis. Indeed, if the dream book of Artemidorus is any indication, erotic dreams elicited particular scrutiny.[19]

Augustine first distanced the realm of unconscious fantasy by his invocation of concupiscence—the inevitable and unruly consequence of original sin, operating as an impersonal chaos theory but affecting the individual in a deeply personal manner. Concupiscence created a tragic estrangement between the spirit and the body: "it is because it was to Him [God] that we refused our obedience and our service that our body, which used to be obedient, now troubles us by its insubordination." Like static interfering with a clear transmission, concupiscence inhibited the body's reception of and ready compliance with the commands of the higher spirit. Not surprisingly, the genitals were the site of greatest affliction: "It is no wonder that everyone feels very much ashamed of this kind of lust; hence, these organs, which lust in its own right, if I may so speak, sways or allays in defiance of the will's decision, are properly called *pudenda*."[20]

Second, Augustine's *Literal Meaning of Genesis* points to the necessary symbiosis of image, thought, and speech, suggesting the ways in which these could lead to "no-fault arousal" in sleep: "Now if the images of these corporeal things, which I have necessarily thought of in order to say what I have said, were to appear in sleep as vividly as do real bodies to those who are awake, there would follow that which in waking hours could not happen without sin."[21] The dreamer is free from sin, however, since the will is immobilized or bound during sleep.

Third, and finally, Augustine exculpates the sleeping state by pointing to the realm of the demonic, an area that already loomed large in the *Sayings* of the desert fathers and from this font had made considerable inroads into Cassian's work.[22] Augustine provided lurid and compelling descriptions of the body's susceptibility to demonic infiltration through the senses: "This evil thing creeps stealthily through all the entrances of the senses: it gives itself over to forms, it adapts itself to colors, it sticks to sounds, it lurks hidden in anger and in the deception of speech, it appends itself to odors, it infuses taste." As Augustine emphasizes elsewhere, such besiegement had dire effects on the thought process: "[Demons] persuade [men] . . . in marvellous and unseen ways, entering by means of that subtlety of their own bodies into the bodies of men who are unaware, and through certain imaginary visions mingling themselves with men's thoughts, whether they are awake or asleep."[23] On at least one occasion, Augustine even enhanced demonic power considerably by arguing that the devil actually read minds, supplementing the more common view (to which he also subscribed) that the devil's perspicacity was predicated on his grasp of subtle body language that was imperceptible to mere mortals.[24] Thus, for Augustine and his successors,[25] unwelcome sexual fantasies were the unsolicited and unwilled work of demons who penetrated the human senses, accessed the images stored in the memory, and came up with illusions so potent, so familiar, yet so diabolically vitiated that not only was the dreamer without guilt (provided he did not consent to these images) but the actual content of these dreams did not warrant scrutiny.[26]

The suppression of the dream landscape was confirmed in the celebrated letter attributed to Gregory the Great written in response to a series of questions posed by the later Augustine of Canterbury. This is a key text for the West, uniting the three strains of inquiry discussed above. Thus "Gregory" uses culpability, determined through careful self-examination, as a touchstone for resolving questions of ritual purity. The ninth and last question is, "Can anyone receive the Body of the Lord after an illusion such as is wont to occur in a dream; and if he is a priest can he celebrate the holy mysteries?" In his response, "Gregory" discerns three types of nocturnal emissions. Two are relatively innocuous: those occurring "through a natural superfluity or weakness" are pronounced guiltless and thus not considered impediments to ritual; those resulting from a superfluity brought on by gluttony do carry a taint, but do not absolutely bar participation in or celebration of the Eucharist if it is an important occasion, such as a feast day—provided that the individual was not entirely overwhelmed by evil imaginings (*turpi imaginatione*). If a substitute celebrant can be found, however, the author advises the besmirched priest to abstain from celebrating, although not from receiving. However, emissions resulting from evil waking thoughts are more serious and need to be broken into their several stages to be understood adequately:

> For all sin is committed in three ways, namely by suggestion, pleasure and consent. The devil makes the suggestion, the flesh delights in it and the spirit consents. It was the serpent who suggested the first sin, Eve representing the flesh was delighted by it, and Adam representing the spirit consented to it: and when the mind sits in judgement on itself it is necessary to make careful distinction between suggestion and delight, between delight and consent.[27]

It is only the consent of the spirit that constitutes a completed sin, which would be an absolute bar to the sacrament.

The Augustinian-flavored focus on the will reduced dream-imagery to depersonalized figments produced by the devil. Analysis, never leveled at the dream proper, was reserved for determining the degree of the dreamer's complicity or resistance. Significantly, by Gregory the Great's time, the word "illusion," designating demonic interference in a dream, had become intrinsically linked with erotic subject matter and probable pollution, an association that invariably cast a pall over efforts to analyze any dream.[28] This fusion resulted in what Jacques Le Goff has designated a "repression of dreams," associated with the repression of sexuality.[29] We can see this dual repression at work in multiple liturgical contexts. The famous "Ambrosian" prayer at compline beseeches: Let dreams and the fantasies of the enemy recede far away; and suppress our enemy; lest we pollute our bodies.[30] Evening prayers, dubiously attributed to Alcuin (d. 804), ask that fantasies and beautiful apparitions be held at bay and that the supplicant's chaste members, timorously entrusted to bed each evening, rise as clean temples of the Holy Spirit, prepared to do God's work.[31] Likewise, the celebrating priest prays for the "humor libidinis" to be extinguished in him.[32]

The positive side of this repression was that the potential for individual responsibility, and thus guilt, was greatly reduced. There was a tendency to see all emissions as practically interchangeable pollutions (in the generic sense of the word) that could be scrubbed away in much the same way as the dirt in a room. And, in point of fact, the ritual to reconcile a church defiled by various unsavory emissions like the shedding of blood or the spilling of seed treats the church much like a person in need of scrubbing. Thus the priest and the congregation pray: "Take away from us, Lord, we beseech, all our iniquities, that we may merit to approach spots purified in your name with pure minds." The consecration, said by the bishop, asks God to restore "what either negligence pollutes, or anger commits, or drunkenness stimulates, or passion [*libido*] subverts," all of which are attributed to the "jealousy of the ancient serpent," which the ceremony seeks to extinguish.[33] Occasionally, the penitentials do impose greater penalties on a nocturnal emission abetted by consent: hence a passage from *Excerpts from a Book of David* isolates "he who willfully has become polluted in sleep," which Pierre Payer takes to mean someone who went to sleep desirous of such an experience.[34] Similarly, Rudolph, bishop of Bourges, in his disciplinary *capitula* of 866, slaps on extra penance for the priest that knowingly abetted his fantasy life by dwelling on filthy thoughts while awake.[35] But the provoking fantasy no more necessitated analysis than the "obscene humor" that issued from the unwitting cleric's loins.

Although the patristic period successfully repressed the full complexity of the problem of pollution, the high Middle Ages saw the repressed return, trailing six hundred years of symptoms in tow. If we are to believe Jacques Lacan, the repressed always returns retroactively, in conjunction with the historical perspective requisite for interpretation. Hence, in the words of Lacanian interpreter Slavoj Žižek:

> The Lacanian answer to the question: From where does the repressed return? is therefore, paradoxically, From the future. Symptoms are meaningless traces, their meaning is not discovered, excavated from the hidden depth of the past, but constructed retroactively—the analysis produces the truth; that is, the signifying frame which gives the symptoms their symbolic place and meaning.[36]

In the high Middle Ages a new set of historically defined circumstances rendered previously repressed phenomena impossible to ignore. The first of these new circumstances was the effort to reform the church by developing a ritually pure clergy.[37] Intrinsically linked to this reform was the development of a formal sacramental system, enhanced by a new emphasis on the Eucharist. And thus, despite the fact that Cassian's association between the malice of the devil and unwarranted pollution just prior to communion had become something of a commonplace by the high Middle Ages,[38] the heightened premium placed upon the Eucharist worked to exacerbate concerns about pollution. The official promulgation of the term *transubstantiation* at Lateran IV (1215) is in many ways a veritable celebration of the wonder-working powers of a newly purified—and hence newly vulnerable—clergy.[39] In this context, Paul's imprecations against the foolhardy who receive the body of Christ unworthily, hence eating and drinking to their own condemnation (1 Cor. 11.29), assume new and still more dire implications. Authors like Vincent of Beauvais would apply this text directly to the problem of nocturnal emissions, urging the sullied priest to confess prior to celebrating Mass. One who rashly approaches the sacrament while still implicated in the snares of sin is polluted by the body of Christ in direct proportion to the degree of culpable taint.[40]

The second circumstance was the rise of the penitential forum. Through the mandatory imposition of auricular confession on the laity—also an innovation of Lateran IV—pollution fear was transmitted like a virus from the clergy to the laity.[41] The potential for the laity's progressive sensitivity to such matters becomes apparent when comparing two English confessors' manuals. Robert of Flamborough's early thirteenth-century manual, completed prior to Lateran IV, seems to regard nocturnal emissions as undifferentiated stains that can be erased by sufficient penance. Thus a person who receives the sacrament after such an occurrence is assigned seven days on bread and water.[42] Thomas of Chobham's *Summa for Confessors,* however, roughly contemporary with Robert's work but written shortly after Lateran IV, distinguishes among seven kinds of nocturnal emissions with varying degrees of culpability, hence calling for a higher level of self-examination.[43] Pastoral sources would continue to encourage this heightened awareness. The late thirteenth-century John of Freiburg, who incorporated many of the sophisticated insights of Dominican theologians into confessional discourse, reaffirms that nothing is sinful when reason is bound. Yet he introduces the sobering notion that a nocturnal emission might be symptomatic of mortal sin if the waking thought that led up to it was mortally sinful.[44] By the fifteenth century, the Dominican theologian John Nider had further refined his analysis of this issue by applying scholastic discussions of interpretative consent: when the will's exercise of rational judgment is suspended due to delectation, such deliberate suspension is nevertheless tantamount to a mortal sin.[45]

The fifteenth-century theologian John Gerson's contribution is especially notable, since he saw fit to devote several treatises to this and related problems. Indeed, his introduction to the work *On the Knowledge of Chastity* suggests that the preoccupation with seminal emissions eddied out beyond men to women, beyond the privileged zone of the confessional to alternative discursive venues, and beyond the sleeping to the waking state:

> I wrote a few things earlier about preparation for the mass under ten considerations, the occasion taken principally from the subject of nocturnal pollution. Lately, however, I've been asked about pollution that seems to occur while one is awake—something that especially disturbs timorous consciences in different individuals of both sexes. I was able to consider these matters [from their accounts occurring] both inside and outside of confession.[46]

The contagious viscosity of this paranoia is in many ways a tribute to the inquisitional tactics of the confessors. Gerson was himself something of a virtuoso in this respect. Strategically advising the confessor to move from the general to the specific, Gerson directs him to begin with matters involving little or no blame, "because if the sinner wishes to lie and flee, he will often be overtaken by such things that naturally happen to all, or [at least] the opposite is very rarely found; if he immediately denies those things it is clear that he is afraid to speak of more serious matters."[47] The priest, who is cautioned not to make a stern face, might then proceed to a more direct inquisition:

> "Friend, do you remember ever in your childhood, around ten or twelve years, that your penis or shameful member was erect?" If he says no, he's immediately convicted of a lie and that he wishes to flee and fears to be caught. . . . If he should confess that it is so, again the confessor should say, especially if the [penitent] is young: "Friend, was that indecent? What therefore did you do so it would not be erect?" . . . If he does not want to answer, it should consequently be asked more plainly: "Friend, did you not stroke and rub your penis in the way boys do?"[48]

Nor should the confessor be deterred by the fear of putting wicked thoughts in the innocent penitent's head, a misgiving often expressed in earlier confessors' manuals. Because of the "corruption of nature" (*ex corruptione naturae*), boys of three or four are already inclined toward masturbation because of a certain unfamiliar itch that accompanies erections.[49]

Yet the therapeutic effort to discover and diagnose sins was not without danger to the practitioner. As Gerson was aware, the penitent-patient's sexual confessions could infect the priest-doctor sufficiently to provoke pollution. Hence Gerson reassured the potentially abject priest that pollutions resulting from carrying out spiritual responsibilities were sinless, although he did volunteer directions for hearing confession that were designed to keep sexual arousal at a minimum. The confessor, averting his gaze from the speaker, should assume a posture least conducive to stimulation — be this standing, kneeling, or even full prostration. He should limit himself to terse and controlled speech, which was more easily accomplished the better prepared the penitent was for confession. If the sinner was ready "to vomit forth the entire virus willingly" (*sponte totum virus evomere*), fine and good. If, however, the penitent was excessively inhibited by shame and the sin required painstaking extortion, this put the confessor at greater risk. But it was always safer to hear confessions *after* one had celebrated Mass.[50]

Female penitents presented a particular challenge for Gerson. So anxious was he to spare the priest the anguish of pollution that in one vernacular sermon he saw fit to alert women to their possible role as passive temptresses. Thus he raises the delicate question: if a woman was certain that her confession would sexually arouse the priest — particularly if she was guilty of erotic thoughts involving him — should she confess elsewhere?[51] Gerson reluctantly resolves this problem with an affirmative answer: she should go to another confessor, even if her usual priest refuses to grant her leave. A similar awareness of the priest's inadvertently truant imagination doubtlessly directed Robert of Flamborough's much earlier prophylactic reticence. Operating under the assumption that the average priest had not attained Cassian's fifth stage of chastity (wherein reading about sex was a matter of indifference), Robert anticipates and blocks the potential eroticism of the written word. He urges that "sins against nature" should be extorted with extreme caution, "but the way of extorting should not be written down."[52]

Despite its attendant dangers, the confessional nevertheless had the potential for providing Christendom with a forum in which its fantasy life might be scrutinized, as confessors trained the analytical spotlight inward. Such introspection would be in keeping with the contemporary revival of interest in dreams, especially apparent in secular letters.[53] The clergy, however, limited culpability to conscious intention, which corresponded with the Augustinian identification of self with consciousness and will. This led to renewed efforts to exculpate the polluted individual and to put distance between the dreamer and what Freud would call the work of the dream. There were exceptions: the twelfth-century Hildegard of Bingen, for instance, regarded the erotic movements of the sleeping body as implying consent of the soul—a perception that might be psychologically damaging in its own way, but one that argued well for the examination of fantasy.[54] But encyclopedist Vincent of Beauvais was much more representative of prevailing views. Inspired by Aristotle's *On Sleeping and Waking,* Vincent argues that nocturnal emissions do not occur at the order of the soul (*non ad animae imperium*). Through his deployment of Augustine, he asserts the impossibility of thinking certain thoughts in sleep without becoming aroused.[55] We have also seen how the Dominican John of Freiburg concurred, asserting that nothing should count as sin if reason is bound. Following the lead of Thomas Aquinas (d. 1274), John further asserts that a pollution that begins and ends in sleep by no means constitutes a sin. Indeed, he points out that Thomas was prepared to disregard a waking pollution provided that the fantasy began in sleep.[56] John Gerson similarly advanced that since fantasies are produced without our consent, they are sinless. Although granting that some bodily fluids can pollute the spirit, others only simulate corruption, "just as is the case in sordid or impure dreams, when it is not a sin but a similitude of sin."[57] This attitude authorized most theologians to discount the content of the dream. Matthew of Cracow's *Concerning the Manner of Confession and Purity of Conscience*—a late thirteenth-century treatise that enjoyed considerable authority, since it circulated under Aquinas's name—was typical. It advised that in the course of confession, "nothing ought to be said about the dream itself because there is no fault there." He did, however, concede that thoughts leading up to a dream or the delight inspired by the dream after the fact were potentially culpable.[58]

Gerson would initially appear to be something of an exception in this respect, in one sermon actually encouraging the penitent to reveal the content of dreams. Moreover, in another context he uses the *visio* (one of several subgenres of a dream, according to the various schemata for classification) to talk about pollution.[59] Yet these avenues for fuller investigation—for better or for worse—are limited in their effect and basically consistent with the principle of denial enunciated earlier. Thus he only argues for the revelation of the dream's contents in order to direct the confessor to the sin that preceded the dream. The dream itself, however, is of no intrinsic interest.[60]

Gerson's evocation of dreams for the purpose of discussing the problem of pollution in his *On Preparation for the Mass,* while on the surface more analytically promising still, is ultimately symptomatic of even greater repression. The ninth consideration he cites is that, in the event that one fails in his preparations for the sacrament, God will help him rise. To demonstrate this principle, Gerson evokes a nameless man's dream of being cast into a toilet (*in cloaca*). The man clings to the supporting stick lest he be cast further into the excrement, but loses hold due to the terrible stench. When he prays to God, however, he again catches hold of the stick. Gerson explains: our conscience is a clean toilet filled with daily excrement. The stick is our own industry in rising upward. The more we raise our eyes to God, the more successful we are in distancing ourselves from the excrement. Excrement also plays a central role in the second exemplary dream. The tenth consideration of the same treatise features a dream of Celestine V (d. 1296), originating in his autobiographical writings.[61] According to Gerson's version, which retains the basic contours of the original, Celestine ascended to a marvelous royal court, only to be humiliated when the ass he was riding voided its bowels on the road: "The most pure man was horrified and detested not this iniquity but this pollution [*hanc non iniquitatem sed inquinationem*]." But a voice from the throne assured Celestine that the court could not be contaminated by his irrational and fat ass (*suus asellus corpulentus et irrationalis*), which voided itself unconsciously and by necessity.[62] Celestine's dream was in response to a specific appeal to God about his own worthiness to celebrate the Eucharist after experiencing a pollution, even as Gerson's rendition was specifically prompted by certain priests' scruples over performing Mass after being polluted by a "night dream."[63] In either case, the ready substitution of infantile dreams of defecation for the erotic dreams of adults—of excrement for semen—is disturbing. And it is with this anecdote that Gerson concludes his treatise.[64]

But, if the content of the fantasy was frequently unexamined and unexaminable, its consequences could not be ignored. Even if the sinful potential of nocturnal emission could be neutralized by insisting on the absence of intention, clerical purity was still at a premium. Thus most authorities continued to abide by the counsel against celebrating Mass after nocturnal emissions unless so required by some compelling reason such as danger of scandal—the position articulated in the letter to Augustine of Canterbury and attributed to Gregory the Great.[65] Moreover, as seen above, this same letter demonstrated the extent to which masculine identity was overinvested in the will and its exercise of reason: "It was the serpent who suggested the first sin, Eve representing the flesh was delighted by it, and Adam representing the spirit consented to it." Thus the occurrence of involuntary pollution posed a severe challenge to masculine pretensions. Gerson is sensitive to the limits of the will and warns against the dangers of overscrupulosity, arguing that excessive abstinence and attention can be counterproductive and can, in fact, stimulate pollution. Thus he urges the superior to "be not over just" (Eccles. 7.17) because "he that violently bloweth his nose bringeth out blood' (Prov. 30.33).[66] He also evokes the analogy of someone obsessed with not properly attending to the recitation of the canonical hours, who finds that this concern results in useless and inattentive repetition. Gerson advises that the confessor *not* permit this recalcitrant penitent to repeat his hours as penance.[67]

Even as efforts to consolidate masculine identity through emphasis on rationality could lapse into irrational obsession, likewise too rigorous a focus on the unruly masculine body could have the undesired effect of dissolving it into a feminine one. In keeping with the discursive idealization of sexual "apatheia" and perhaps even the androgyny current in some early Christian circles, past authors had made moves toward validating a passionless expulsion of masculine seed that might well be described as "quasi-menstrual." In Cassian's sixth and most auspicious degree of chastity, for example, a person would purge himself of extra humors without titillation. But the total lack of affect in this description is disconcerting: the perfect individual was just as likely to ejaculate while waking as while sleeping, in prayer as in bed, in a crowd as alone, nor would he perceive it as the kind of secret that he would hide from other men or that would make him blush.[68] Although Cassian was frequently utilized in various theological treatments of pollution and chastity in the high Middle Ages, this passage was rarely invoked.[69] With the revival of medical discourse and the quasi-medical expertise of confessors such as Gerson (who frequently consulted doctors for information about bodily emissions),[70] cognoscenti would have found too many similarities between Cassian's notion of perfect chastity and the involuntary emissions and general effeminacy associated with physical conditions like gonorrhea. According to the classical physician Soranus, whose influence continued into the later Middle Ages, gonorrhea entailed frequent emissions without sexual arousal. He also prescribes the same remedy for this ailment that Cassian had advised for nocturnal emissions—a leaden plate.[71]

But the danger of slippage into femaleness remained uneasily at the margins of the discourse. Medieval medical authorities, such as the eleventh-century Constantine the African, explicitly link frequent nocturnal emissions with a colder, moister, and hence weaker, more feminized seed. Not surprisingly, the sower of such seed tends to engender daughters.[72] Likewise, Gerson's *On Preparation for the Mass* cannot avoid an onslaught of female images and analogies in its discussion of whether a priest who has experienced a nocturnal emission should perform Mass. Sifting carefully through the various levels of consent, Gerson's basic intention was, as suggested above, to allay the fears of the overscrupulous and exculpate any but the most complicit dreamers—an old agenda, employing familiar material. Gerson draws on the exegetical tradition, so extensively employed by Gregory the Great, in which the menstruous woman is seen as a type of sinner.[73] But Gerson explicitly aligns this imagery with masculine pollutions, an association invited by the very similar treatment of men's genital discharges (of the nonseminal variety) and women's menstrual and nonmenstrual genital bleeding in Leviticus 15. Even so, this alignment has the potential for wreaking havoc with conventional gender boundaries.[74] Gerson initially compares the dreamer to the menstruous rags of sin referred to in Isaiah 64.6, sending him, as did Gregory in the case of sinners or unclean women, to the fountain of the house of David (Zech. 13.1). The celebrating priest is then likened to the woman with flux:

> You suffer bleeding and cannot be cured by doctors, namely by your exercises; touch with complete faith along with the hemorrhaging woman—Martha, according to Ambrose—the fiber of Jesus's clothing. Namely touch the most holy host so that you will be purged.[75]

Gerson thus offers a cure similar in nature to the one reported by Cassian as successful for the monk consistently prevented from receiving the sacrament by untimely pollutions: to put this demonic perturbance to flight by receiving the sacrament. Although there is nothing remarkable or new about this counsel, it was nevertheless being proffered in a very different religious culture than that of Cassian. Hence Gerson's already transgressive use of conventional imagery leads directly into a discussion of the mystery of transubstantiation. He first ventriloquizes the complaints of those who think it revolting that Christ's body should enter "our stinking stomachs" (*foetulentum stomachum nostrum*), and then counters with the fact that Christ consented to be preserved in the maternal viscera for nine months and endured the skin of afterbirth—a material of unrivaled powers for pollution, inspiring unparalleled horror.[76]

To recapitulate Gerson's thought: the priest is first likened to a menstruating woman through his contact with the Christ/Host; then, more obliquely to the Virgin Mary for harboring Christ in his stomach. (The first time Gerson touches on this subject he uses the word *venter,* which can be translated as stomach or womb.) He also argues that nature will find a way to expel its filthy liquid (*foedum humorem*), using the example of a lactating mother: "It is evident in women who have recently given birth whose paps are dry when milk is not elicited but otherwise [milk] is always ready to flow."[77] But Gerson was not content simply to vindicate nocturnal pollution by virtue of its inevitability. Argumentatively salvaging as much as he can from an unpropitious situation, Gerson maintains that pollution wins merit for whoever suffers it unwillingly. The image he uses to emphasize this point is striking. He compares the resisting victim of pollution to St. Lucy, who assures her would-be violator: "If you corrupt me against my will, my chastity will be double-crowned."[78]

The many-gendered crossings of Gerson's torturously feminized clergy give new meaning to Augustine's initial portrait of the divided self, vitiated by demonic interpolations and unpredictable fluxes. Yet one final dimension of the discourse on pollution remains to be discussed. In the high Middle Ages the intimate enemy (namely, erotic thoughts and their physiological consequences), unexamined and repressed internally, was ultimately externalized and began to walk abroad. This eventuated in the dramatic emergence of the demon lover in ecclesiastical culture—a figure that was probably never absent from folk tradition and would now enjoy an extended life in venues as disparate as the witch trials and romantic fiction. The learned preoccupation with demons was in many ways a byproduct of scholasticism, the methodological refinements of which ushered in a higher degree of credulity among its practitioners. As Jeffrey Burton Russell has suggested, efforts to contend rationally with the natural world had the effect of forcing more and more inexplicable phenomena into the realm of the demonic.[79] The change from earlier centuries is striking. In the eleventh century, Burchard of Worms actually assigned penance to individuals who erred by crediting such tales:

> Do you believe what certain individuals are accustomed to believe: that there are certain wild women whom they call women of the woods (*sylvaticas*), who they say are corporeal, and when they wished would show themselves to their lovers, and they say that [these women] would enjoy themselves with [their lovers] and again (when they wished) would hide themselves and disappear? If you believed [these things], [you should do penance for] ten days on bread and water.[80]

In contrast to Burchard's stigmatization of such beliefs, the conviction that supernatural creatures (now designated as demons) sexually consorted with humans was generally maintained in learned circles of the thirteenth century. Indeed, leading scholars would rise to the challenge of explicating the most intricate nuances of the apparitional corporeality of demons and how this impinged on their sexual practice.[81] The concurrence of this later affirmation of sexual congress between demons and humans with the pollution fears generated by the scholastic discourse on transubstantiation was probably no mean accident. Both sets of beliefs conveyed a new preoccupation with materialization and immediacy. The emphasis on the actual presence of Christ in the sacrament of the altar might be seen as reinforcing the insistence on the actual presence of demons polluting the minister of the altar.

From the standpoint of a preoccupation with demonic love as well as a heightened degree of credulity in these matters, the thirteenth-century Caesarius of Heisterbach's *Dialogue on Miracles* is representative of the age. Caesarius was a Cistercian monk; most of his anecdotes portraying men beset by amorous succubi (or women beset by their male counterparts, incubi) concern professional celibates of various stripes. Although Caesarius's fascination with the realm of the demonic is manifest, the nature of his investment is, I would argue, often inflected or even concealed. For example, Caesarius tells of a certain scholar named John who, upon learning that he had slept with a succubus, "replied with a strange word, which modesty forbids me to repeat, scoffing at the devil, and no whit disturbed."[82] Thus Caesarius ends his anecdote abruptly and opaquely, resisting any possible impulse to interpret or moralize. This superficially relaxed attitude might suggest that demons were more a locus of entertainment than anxiety. Likewise, a subsequent, rather clipped account of an incident involving a nocturnal emission might be interpreted as indicating a parallel detachment. A monk in Caesarius's house developed an embarrassing itch after he had forgotten to say the single psalm that had been assigned to him as penance for a wet dream. The itch disappeared the moment he said the psalm.[83]

These two relatively truncated anecdotes never name repressed and volatile material directly, nor should we expect them to do so. Their presentational strategy is to treat such materials as unexceptional and uncontroversial, and the reader becomes complicit with this strategy by accepting the story's surface reassurances. A third and more narratively suggestive anecdote, however, offers the conflation of demon lover and wet dream within a single frame. It demonstrates the way these two phenomena, united by repression, were situated at the crossroads of desire and fear. The lay brothers of the Cistercian order were taking a midday rest in the dormitory one summer. A certain brother saw the devil in the shape of a Benedictine nun making the rounds of the various beds. Pausing at some and hurrying past others, she eventually stopped at a particular one. She placed her arms around the neck of the bed's sleeping occupant, kissed him, and then vanished. When the onlooking brother rushed to his confrère, "he found [him] fast asleep indeed, but lying in a fashion that was both immodest and exposed."[84] The violated brother died within three days.

The tale is provided with a clear analogue. In this subsequent episode, a waking monk watched while the Virgin Mary went from bed to bed in a monastic dormitory, blessing each sleeping monk. She turned away from one, however, who, when informed about the occurrence the next day by the vigilant brother, admitted that he had been sleeping in a careless fashion. Caesarius's informant for the tale was unclear, however, as to the exact nature of the monk's transgression—whether he had removed his belt, taken off his shoes, or undone his tunic—the point being that these symptoms of laxness would have been in violation of the rule.[85]

Both tales highlight the monastic tradition's perception of the bed as a zone of danger, implicit in the Benedictine rule. Benedict was very particular about the manner in which his monks should sleep. All monks were to be in the same room, if possible, while maintaining separate beds. They must be fully clad in their robes, which must, in turn, be fastened. Moreover, a light must burn all night in the room. Youngsters should not be permitted to sleep alongside one another but should be interspersed with their elders. Monastic authors, such as Peter Damian (d. 1072), would further censure those who lingered in bed, even on what was seemingly the most innocent pretext. Thus Peter tells of a monk who, due to an alleged infirmity, habitually said compline in bed. He was eventually exposed by the very demon he was attempting to exorcise for his shameful masturbatory practices, occurring under the cover of prayer.[86]

The two anecdotes of Caesarius, although partaking of these interpretative underpinnings and so striking in their common form, are still most clearly united in their binary division. Each story is but one half of an integral unit and flagged as such by the author, who cross-references each of the related tales in the telling. The deliberate separation of these two mirror-episodes sets the stage for the fracturing of the image of woman, which is at the heart of each narrative. Woman's bifurcated representation as demonic nun and celestial Virgin is analogous to what psychoanalysts describe as "splitting," wherein a child divides the world into good and bad, beginning with the mother's breasts. This radicalization (and oversimplification) is initially resorted to as a defense mechanism against feelings of guilt, ambivalence, and anxiety—feelings that, in a medieval context, would arise from the tensions generated over clerical celibacy. Nevertheless, splitting is a doomed strategy, since it occasions even more anxiety, ultimately resulting in neurotic behavior.[87]

However counterproductive in the long term, the splitting operative in these two related anecdotes is temporarily enabling insofar as the process facilitates a pivotal distance between the monks and the lay brethren—the protagonists of the two separate stories. The monks are visited by the Virgin Mary: one is unworthy, but the majority prove worthy of her blessing. The frightening and sexually voracious nun is the lot of the lay brothers: she fastens on one unfortunate but lingers over the beds of many. Thus the secondary splitting of male subject, attendant on the initial division of the female object, permits a clerical audience to distance itself further from the implicit sexual content of the visions.

Both visitations are further riven by a final and purposeful fracturing. The person who actually experiences the illusion is not the sleeper but the waking, watching brother—a condition under which the sleeper is additionally estranged from the potentially disturbing content of the dream. The visions themselves, however, operate as interpretative elaborations of what the sleepers either are or, equally important, are *not* experiencing in their dreams. The lay brother, lying in an unseemly position, is dreaming about the Benedictine nun, and this results in his death. The situation of his monkish counterpart, although handled much more gently, is essentially parallel. Also lying in an unseemly position, and thus forfeiting the coveted blessing, he presumably was *not* dreaming about the Virgin. He was, in fact, dreaming about the Benedictine nun.

The nun, then, metaphorically and technically the dark lady by virtue of her status and her habit (*monialis nigri ordinis*), is at the center of both phantasmic narratives, whether this be implicitly or explicitly so. She is quite literally a dream come true, and on the most obvious level represents the rejected heterosexual alternative implicit in clerical celibacy. But if we were going to subject this material phantasm to more rigorous analysis, any semblance of a heterosexual matrix suddenly dissolves. We soon learn that such figures are not just the object of fantasy but are themselves the materialization of fantasy. They are constituted entirely from surplus semen. Elsewhere, when speculating on the demonic paternity of the Huns, the magician Merlin, or the English kings, and whether such individuals will rise on the day of judgment, Caesarius volunteers: "'I have heard about this question from a very learned man; he says that demons collect all wasted human seed, and from it fashion for themselves human bodies, both of men and women, in which they become tangible and visible to men.'"[88] Nor is Caesarius completely unjustified in his assessment. More celebrated thinkers, such as Aquinas, also argue that demons can produce certain natural effects on the human senses because of their diabolical manipulation of seeds.[89] The authors of *Malleus maleficarum,* the notorious fifteenth-century inquisitorial manual directed against witchcraft, would dangerously narrow this inquiry by asking explicitly whether the seeds gathered from nocturnal emissions can be used by a demonic incubus to impregnate a human woman. Their answer is probably not, unless the devil knew that there was sufficient generative virtue in the seed. Our inquisitors are more inclined to follow a different but equally invasive line, perhaps first enunciated by Aquinas. Thus a demon would first pose as a succubus, garnering the unsuspecting human male's seed, next would transport it at dizzying speed (so none of the heat of its generative virtue would be lost), and then would shapeshift into a male-seeming incubus. In this form it would impregnate a woman.[90]

And so the succubi and incubi of the high Middle Ages possess no fixed sexual identity. The prefixes of the words are the key to their situational gendering: the incubus lies on top; the succubus lies underneath. This etymology is implicit in John Nider's discussion of demonic paternity in his *Formicarium,* the first significant work on witchcraft: "[A demon] is not able to generate offspring of its own but of the man for whom it made itself a demon succubus." The same message hovers as a damaging subtext to the inflected comment in Nider's confessor's manual when he compares a husband having sex on the bottom to a "demon succubus."[91] Ironically, however, it is precisely the unstable sexual identity of the predatory demon stalking the cleric that makes this scenario a compelling *figura* for the cleric subjected to unwelcome emissions.

The occasion of involuntary ejaculation, and its phantasmic accompaniments, opens the way to anxious acknowledgment of gender turmoil held at bay by original and inadequate acts of stabilization and exclusion. The clergy had attempted to create a female-free zone premised on a body that was hermetically sealed by ascendant male reason. Women reentered through the fissures in body and soul. The fantasy women that return to our sleeping clerics are masculinized monsters that lure the clerical world toward the witch hunts. Family and lineage are repressed, and the sleeping cleric—menstrual in his weakness and preyed upon by quasi-women constituted from wasted seed—dreams of a possible better human future for the wasted seed at the end of this illusion. Demonic seed-swapping also attacks the very core of paternity and even identity in so lineage-conscious a patriarchy. The mutating gender of the demon lover signals the clergy's bewildered sexual orientation. Finally, the dissolution of the priest's gender identity in the course of demonic illusions elevates pollution fears surrounding the Eucharist to an entirely different plane by challenging not simply the purity of the clergy but also its claims to unalloyed masculine ascendancy. This is a critical anxiety, since transubstantiation was fast becoming the central mystery of the faith, threatening to displace the incarnation and its heterosexual core. For transubstantiation was based on the ineluctable stability of gender identity—a male cleric handling the body of a male God.[92]

2

From Sexual Fantasy to Demonic Defloration

The Libidinous Female in the Later Middle Ages

FROM THE TIME OF AUGUSTINE, the genitals' noncompliance with the will was the most compelling example of the postlapsarian body's revolt against reason.[1] This paradigm of unruliness was supposed to pertain to both sexes. But since Augustine's observations were apparently based on the genitals' irrational movements, and were therefore more evocative of phallic folly, the female instance was very much at the margins of his concerns. The treatment of nocturnal emissions is a case in point. Although theoreticians such as Albert the Great (d. 1280) granted that both women and men had night pollutions, female emissions never received the same emphasis as male.[2] As suggested in Chapter 1, this not atypical indifference to female experience was compounded by an absence of sacramental consequence in the case of female pollutions. Unlike priests, who were obliged to perform the Mass at predictable intervals, women were invariably communicants as opposed to celebrants. If they had any doubt about their worthiness to partake of the sacrament, they could easily abstain.

Nevertheless, this explanation masks several important asymmetries, resulting from differences in argumentative purpose as well as contemporary constructions of a gendered physiology. The discursive logic framing wet dreams was exculpatory in nature, founded upon the palliation of masculine embarrassments and the furtherance of clerical goals. Emphasis invariably fell upon the passivity and ultimate sinlessness of the clerical sufferer. For example, the predisposition to a nocturnal emission might be incurred by a previous sin, such as gluttony, since overeating purportedly built up excess humors in the system.[3] In the course of the dream proper, the sleeper's will was bound and he or she could not consent to the sexual images witnessed.[4] Since clerical authorities tended to subscribe unequivocally to the Augustinian view that all sin was voluntary, a dreamer could therefore not sin.[5] Moreover, these same authorities were at pains to emphasize the impossibility of a person's thinking certain thoughts while asleep without having a physical reaction.[6] Whereas the male was perceived as functionally the active party in heterosexual copulation, in the course of a wet dream he was passively held in thrall by his biology or even victimized by demons or by demonically inspired thoughts. Thus, if we were to look for an analogy between the sexes, the inadvertently polluted cleric actually had less in common with a woman whose erotic imaginings resulted in pollution than with a menstruating woman. Both the male who was polluted in a dream and the menstruating woman, though by no means considered sinful in themselves, were construed as representative of humanity's fallen state.[7]

Yet, despite the way in which nocturnal pollution may be perceived as radically "feminizing" the male by its analogies with menstruation, gender symmetry breaks down over the question of sexual fantasy. Although woman was inherently self-polluting by virtue of her reproductive system, which functioned as an omnipresent token of humanity's original guilt, she remained ineligible for the exculpatory argument when it came to possible pollution in any way associated with sexual arousal. In distinction from the medieval view of the potentially resistant male, the perspective on female eroticism was founded upon a conviction of woman's essential complicity in the pursuit of sexual pleasure. Passive in heterosexual intercourse, woman was nevertheless more highly sexed and ultimately seen as supremely engaged, indeed in a certain sense "active," in imaginative exercises—particularly those of a libidinous nature. In fact, woman's active imaginative power was considered to be so potent that it became a crucial key for understanding perceptions of sexual difference. The female imagination, moreover, was impinged on by both body and soul, with important consequences for female physiology and spirituality.

This chapter examines some implications of these overlapping configurations for women's precariously constituted sexuality in theologically inflected writings, particularly of the thirteenth century. I place particular emphasis on a Dominican ambiance, since those authorities were at the forefront of the scholastic Aristotelianism that theorized the widespread belief in women's greater lust, thus bringing it into sharper focus.[8] Moreover, the high profile of Dominicans as papal inquisitors would ultimately ensure a transmission of these views into their rationalization of women's role in witchcraft.[9]

The Female Libido and the Mechanisms of Conception

Vincent of Beauvais's encyclopedic miscellany, *The Mirror of Nature* (between 1247 and 1259), provides us with an excellent vantage point from which to observe what the various authorities who were available to learned circles — be they scientists, theologians, or philosophers — had to say on questions of female sexuality.[10] In particular, *The Mirror of Nature* conveniently summarizes much of the material in support of the familiar argument for women's heightened libidinousness. At several strategic junctures, Vincent points out that women were not only more lustful than men but more lustful than all female animals with the possible exception of the mare.[11] He also appeals to William of Conches (d. ca. 1154), whose argument for the existence of the female seed had important implications for women's greater lust.[12] William is attempting to disprove some theorists who deny the existence of female seed on the basis of rape victims. According to these skeptics, women were known to have resisted their attackers and nevertheless become pregnant, which argues against a female ejaculation. (And, in keeping with what Thomas Laqueur has dubbed the one-sex model, which aligns female physiology, and thus experience, with that of the male, these same scholars had trouble disassociating the expulsion of seed from pleasure.[13]) In response to these allegations, William contends that, even if the act is initially displeasing to the victim, the frailty of the female flesh ultimately gains the upper hand. Thus the rational will is overcome by the natural will, and a victim of a rape emits her seed and becomes pregnant.[14]

Vincent also addresses women's libido directly in a chapter that is rubricated "Why women are more fervent in coitus than men." Here again, William of Conches is enlisted to explicate some of the seeming contradictions of women's greater lust:

> Since, moreover, women are naturally frigid and humid, how does it happen that a woman is more fervent than a man in lust? I answer that it is harder to light a fire in wet wood, but it nevertheless burns longer and more intensely in it. Thus the heat of lust in a woman who is naturally more humid burns longer and more intensely.[15]

Furthermore, the cold womb yearns for and delights in the man's hot seed—a phenomenon that William compares to the way in which serpents are wont to enter the mouths of sleepers. In contrast with the single pleasure of a man's ejaculation, woman enjoys a twofold pleasure in coitus, both expelling and receiving seed. Finally, all other animals refrain from coitus after conception except woman, who becomes more ardent. William explains this in terms of humanity's unique possession of memory, coupled with the ability to project into the future. Hence a woman remembers past delights and desires future ones, while the level of her natural ardor is raised by the presence of a fetus.[16]

Ancillary support is enlisted to buttress this contention about female sexual appetite. Vincent cites an anatomical work that relates that woman's greater lust is rooted in her complexion, the cold wetness of which is compared with denser metals. Thus iron, though slower to ignite than gold, burns more virulently, eliciting greater agonies when applied in torture. The nervous aspect of the female complexion ensures that every sensible nerve is desirous of repletion through contact with sperm. But only the lower nerves of the uterus are moistened and sated, while the upper nerves are unabated in their titillation. Finally, Vincent also cites patristic corroboration. Jerome (d. 420) argues that women are inclined to hide the fact of their menstruation from their husbands out of a reluctance to abstain from sexual intercourse. Similarly, Gregory the Great (d. 604) reviles women who refuse to nurse their children out of a desire to remain sexually active.[17]

Vincent further demonstrates how female libidinousness may be read through medieval theories of vision, which cast the individual as the object of impressions. Thus Augustine argued that all physical bodies leave imprints of their shape on the soul.[18] Moreover, according to Avicenna, the delight resulting from a beautiful sight is experienced not in the instrument of vision but in the soul itself.[19] The way in which vision, enhanced by the female sexual appetite, sent a sympathetic current between body and soul is evinced by two anecdotes reiterated on a number of different occasions by Vincent. The great orator Quintilian was said to have defended a certain matron who, having gazed upon an image of an Ethiopian, gave birth to a black child. Hippocrates also allegedly saved a woman who gave birth to a child that resembled neither parent by urging that her bedroom be searched for a vindicating picture, which was fortunately found. Nor are such tales limited to the classical tradition. After many years of service to his difficult father-in-law Laban, the biblical patriarch Jacob requested that his payment should consist of all the spotted lambs subsequently born to the flock (Gen. 30.32). He then proceeded to manipulate the odds in his favor by peeling the bark from rods (so they seemed speckled) and placing them in front of the flock's drinking trough in the expectation that the ewes would be mounted while drinking. Vincent, who tells these stories to explain some of the disparate ways that resemblance works as well as to warn pregnant women lest they gaze at certain animals (such as apes), adds that Jacob's experimentation in genetics is supported by Jerome's own observations about herds of Spanish horses.[20]

Several complementary theories are advanced as explanations. Jacob's success is "from the effect of longing and looking which [causes the ewe] to draw the colors and images of things seen in the fervor of extreme lust into herself."[21] This is corroborated by a passage from Augustine arguing that an avid gaze is not simply limited to sight but affects the whole body of a creature, citing the way a chameleon's entire body changes color. The tender malleability of the fetus makes it particularly prone to registering its mother's desire.[22]

A gloss on Aristotle additionally provides four reasons for resemblance in the fetus: the agent power (the seed), heat, strength, and the power of the imagination.[23] The glossator is certainly aware of conception as a zone of contestation between various forces: "In the first place, like tends to engender like, if its own [generative] power is able to conquer. If not, however, the other power which dominates will assimilate its progeny to itself."[24] But the gendering of the forces struggling for mastery is, at first glance, rather muffled when compared with the competing two-seed view of conception. In contrast, Thomas of Cantimpré (d. ca. 1270), a contemporary of Vincent's and an unabashed two-seeder (arguing that those who deny the existence of a female seed clearly lie), portrays conception as follows:

> The male and female sperms are at cross purposes, as Galen says. The purpose of the male sperm is to shape in the likeness of him from whom it was separated unless something else prohibits it. The purpose of the female sperm is to attempt a shape in the likeness of her from whom it separated.[25]

Even so, the Aristotelian gloss is potentially as deeply conflicted with regard to tensions over gender dominance as the two-seed position, though perhaps not as explicitly so. Not only seed but heat and strength were associated with the male's contribution as well. Yet it is largely through the imagination, and the various influences acting on it, that the female's generative presence is felt. And thus at a time when the Aristotelian one-seed theory of conception was possibly gaining over the Galenic two-seed,[26] female influence was nonetheless grimly present in the most untamed and unpredictable way: the imagination.

The Imagination, Sensuality, and Spirituality

In order to describe the activity of the imagination, Vincent turns to the anonymous *Book Concerning the Soul and Spirit,* employed extensively in the thirteenth century, which describes how the imagination, in conjunction with the corporeal senses and the power of sensuality, was considered as much a power of the body as of the soul.[27] The imagination was largely dependent on the senses for material. The senses, in turn, were thought to derive from a fiery power arising from the heart, which was purified in the brain, and then, when deployed outward, resulted in the five zones of sensitivity, which apprehended the external world. That same power of sensual perception (relaying its impressions of the outside world) would be withdrawn inward to the fantasy chamber and then led further backward to create the imagination. Though positioned in such a way that it touched the rational soul, the imagination nevertheless retained a corporeal aura.[28]

> And thus the imagination is a likeness of the body, conceived by contact with bodies through the senses of the body and led inwards through the same senses to the purer part of the corporeal spirit and impressed on it. Namely on the peak of the corporeal spirit and in the depths of the rational—it informs the corporeal and touches the rational.[29]

Despite the imagination's indebtedness to the corporeal senses, the relationship is not a direct one, but abstract and derivative. Bodies may leave imprints of their shape on the soul in their absence. Yet the mind is frequently deceived by the similitude of things through impaired judgment.[30] Nor is the imagination's repertoire restricted to what had actually been experienced, as the content of dreams would argue.[31] Finally, as the examples of the ill-begotten babes of misglancing matrons suggest, the imagination could be randomly impressionable—even dangerously so. Certain checks were, of course, implemented to control these potentially errant powers. For instance, according to Vincent's own view, sensuality was held in check by reason, fantasy by intellect.[32]

Women—deeply but mysteriously implicated in the reproductive process, deemed overly sensual and purportedly deficient in both reason and understanding—were naturally considered more imaginative. Some of the physical ramifications of women's heightened imaginative powers have already been mentioned with regard to questions of conception. A mother's ardent gaze made an impression on her imagination which, in turn, impressed itself on the fetus. Impression is also a figure for William of Conches's understanding of the normative formation of a fetus—only in this instance the mother's body is the agent of the impression. The womb itself is likened to a mint for coins that contains seven cells. Each of the cells is impressed with the shape of a human, a multiplicity that would in theory permit a woman to have several different sexual partners in close proximity and conceive more than one child by different fathers.[33] A modified version of this view is later found in Albert the Great, who argues that a woman can receive two or more impregnations and retain them, if they are in relatively close succession. Thus an adulterous matron was exposed when she bore two sons, one resembling her husband and the other her lover.[34]

Female impressionability also has important spiritual implications—some of which contemporaries may have perceived as positive, some negative, but many settling into an ambivalent gray zone that defies strict categorization. From a devotional standpoint, spiritual writers, such as Richard of St. Victor (d. 1173), described the imagination as the handmaiden of Rachel, who was the traditional symbol of the contemplative life. Spiritual directors of the high and later Middle Ages attempted to harness the imagination, perhaps particularly the female imagination, by structuring meditation around events in the life of Christ.[35] These imaginative exercises were believed to have a potentially profound impact on the holy person's body—the most famous example probably being Francis of Assisi (d. 1226), whose meditation on Christ's passion resulted in his reception of the stigmata. But the theologian Thomas of Cantimpré, in particular, bears witness to many miracles of devotional somatism: thus a pilgrim to the Holy Land was so deeply moved by the site of Christ's sufferings that he died on the spot from ruptured entrails; Thomas claims to have seen with his own eyes how the sign of the cross was inscribed on the breast of a monk; a woman in Brabant similarly received a wound in her side from meditating on the crucifixion; a pagan tyrant, tantalized by his Christian captive's avowal that he carried the crucifixion in his heart, ripped him open only to discover the instruments of the passion.[36]

As the work of Caroline Walker Bynum has shown, this kind of intense somatic response to pious meditations is especially characteristic of female spirituality. Women mystics, already "ultra-embodied" by virtue of their gender, partook of a mind-body symbiosis so compelling that they came to represent the humanity of Christ, both through self-identification and to the community of the faithful at large.[37] The external and miraculous consequences of this association were often dramatic. Though Francis may have been the most famous of stigmatics, there were far more female stigmatics than male in the later Middle Ages.[38] Likewise Thomas of Cantimpré's apocryphal tale of heathen torture as a mechanism for revealing the instruments of the passion in the heart of a Christian man receives perhaps its final form with Clare of Montefalco (d. 1308). Interpreting literally Clare's oft-repeated claim that she bore the cross in her heart, the nuns of her community performed an ad hoc postmortem on the day after Clare's death in order to reveal the anticipated marvel. Not only did Clare's heart contain an effigy of the crucifixion with all the instruments of the passion (replete with minute details, such as the five sinewy thongs on the scourge that smote Christ), but her gall bladder contained a miraculous triune stone representing the Holy Trinity.[39]

By the later Middle Ages, contemporaries had found ways to explain such miraculous somatic capacities in terms of the latent proclivities of the female body. Thus the fifteenth-century John Gerson argues on the basis of complexion that women are more inclined to the concupiscible path in spiritual matters, as evidenced by the compassionate nature of their soft hearts and their propensity for contemplation.[40] In the late fifteenth century, Peter Pomponazzi (d. 1525) took Augustine's discussion of the impact that the mother's meditation had on her fetus one stage further, synchronizing women's remarkable spiritual capacities with their physiology. Hence he speculates on the possibility of a meditating mother imposing the instruments of the passion on the fetus.[41]

The female imagination, working through female physiology, ultimately blurs the boundaries between active and passive. With regard to the female mystic, divinely wrought physical changes are ostensibly impressed on her passive form. Indeed, any active effort to simulate celestial markings, such as stigmata, would be the worst kind of sacrilege, though one that purportedly occurred not infrequently in the later Middle Ages when fictive claims of sanctity proliferated.[42] But, although passivity was in many ways the best assurance of the authenticity of miraculously wrought somatic changes, the female mystic was active in preparing the way for divine inscriptions through her ascetical practices and especially her ardent meditations—meditations that were assisted by physiological considerations (such as a concupiscible complexion) working in conjunction with an active imagination. In this sense, the appearance of the stigmata or similar markings represented a successful collaboration between God and his chosen mystic and was recognized as such. Hence Article 57 of Clare of Montefalco's process of canonization advances "that those things she saw or otherwise apprehended through her corporeal senses, she reflected [*reflectebat*] and applied to compassion and conformity and imagining of the passion of Christ."[43] Authentic displays of somatic grace could not exist in a spiritual vacuum.

A similar conflation of passive and active modes, so characteristic of female spirituality, was also believed to pertain to female reproductive processes. For instance, the matron who looks awry at the moment of conception can alternately be described as passive receptor and active impressor. If the fetus is construed as just another part of her body, the woman's somatic response to a visual stimulus is simply reactive. But, when the fetus is perceived as an entity unto itself, the mother's imagination emerges as the active agent in conception. Moreover, the seven-celled matrix that stamps the shape of the fetus, already mentioned by William of Conches, particularly accentuates female agency. One need not look far to find varied and even polarized analogies for the womb's activities. On the one hand, it parallels the effect of pious imitation, whereby the internalization of a holy model is likened to the impression of a seal on soft wax.[44] On the other hand, this process could just as readily be compared with the way in which the devil registers himself on the human imagination.

The same imaginative qualities that distinguish women as potential objects of supernatural privilege render them susceptible to unsavory influences. Thus William of Auvergne (d. 1249) argues that, just as the heightened impressionability of the female soul makes women more prone to true visions and revelations, so are women equally susceptible to superstition. He cites belief in the "good women" (former fairies who had devolved into demons in the scholastic period) who go from house to house at night and also in baby-eating *strigae* as examples of female folly.[45] Indeed, the odds are weighted in favor of imagination as a locus of contamination insofar as this particular power of the soul, so closely aligned with the senses, is the one most vulnerable to demonic influence. Thus when William speaks of the manner in which demons afflict holy men, he asks, "How could they do this if they did not have entrance to their souls and if they did not have the power of painting thoughts in their imagination and perhaps in their intellectual power?"[46]

Although Vincent of Beauvais subscribes to the general consensus in according the devil limited access to the soul and no access to the mind, he agrees that the devil can enter the imagination on the crest of bodily humors. Having gained access to the imagination, he imprints images by a process likened to that of reflection: "it is just like a mirror if moved in a [second] mirror. The impressed form in the one [the devil] ends up in the other [the human soul]. The soul, however, will believe that these [images] were formed in itself alone because of the evil spirit's violent attachment to it." Evil thoughts would, in turn, arise from these diabolical impressions.[47]

And so the devil's power over the soul depends largely on the impression his suggestions make on the imagination: "the devil can be compared to a baker because mixing himself with the body, he lights the soul by his suggestion as if an oven, yet he doesn't enter, but stays outside like a baker."[48] The image of the oven is, in itself, subtly encoded as female insofar as the medical tradition perceived the womb as an oven, designed for baking the excess moisture from the fetus.[49] Moreover, the woman's imagination, particularly prone to demonic cooptation, possesses the same facility for making impressions on external bodies that we have hitherto seen exercised only internally (influencing her own body or the fetus). The externalization of this process receives an in-depth treatment with regard to the witch's alleged power of fascination in the fifteenth-century *Malleus maleficarum*. The prototypical example of what came to be seen as a quintessentially female ability is the deleterious glance of the menstruating woman. But this wayward and questionable power was also believed to have a potentially more deliberate and focused analogue:

Thus if anyone's spirit be inflamed with malice or rage, as is often the case with old women, then their disturbed spirit looks through their eyes, for their countenances are most evil and harmful, and often terrify young children of tender years, who are extremely impressionable.[50]

It stands to reason that resistance would likewise reside not merely in the rejection of demonically tainted imaginings but also in a healthy mistrust of all imaginative endeavors. If this be the case, then women, functioning as both subjects and objects of medieval imaginative discourse, would be doubly stigmatized. Not only were women multiply associated with enhanced imaginative powers, but the ascetical tradition articulated in the *Lives of the Fathers* suggests that the images of women, diabolically insinuated or not, frequently peopled the imagination of aspiring celibates of many stripes.

From Masturbation to Mental Defloration

The penitential literature of the early Middle Ages suggests that masturbation was a vice to which both men and women were prone, yet more attention seems to have been paid to masculine propensities in this period.[51] A possible shift is discernible in the early eleventh century, when penitential authorities such as Burchard of Worms displayed a more equitable division of attention between male and female autoeroticism.[52] In a similarly inclusive vein, Peter Damian (d. 1072) reported a miracle of the Virgin involving the release from purgatory of a woman who was guilty of what seems to have been mutual masturbation with other girls during her adolescence.[53] But only with thirteenth-century scientific assertions about women's biologically enhanced lasciviousness were women clearly identified as especially susceptible to this practice. Albert the Great's discussion of prepubescent and pubescent girls exemplifies this tendency:

[With the first signs of puberty] a girl then also begins to desire coitus, but she does not emit [seed] in her desire: and the more she has sex, or even rubs herself with her hand, the more she wants sex, because through such rubbing the humor is gathered but not emitted, and with that humor, heat is attracted: and, since the female body is cold and suffers from a closure of pores, it does not quickly emit the seed of coitus: and this is the reason that certain girls around the age of fourteen are not able to be satisfied by coitus and then if they do not have a man, they nevertheless mentally dwell on having coitus with a man, and often imagine male genitals. And they rub [themselves] very often with their fingers or other instruments until, with the [seminal] paths widened through the heat of rubbing and coitus the spermatic humor goes out, with which the heat departs: and then their groins are tempered and they are then made more chaste.

Then the flux of menstruation also occurs and their pollutions are multiplied, both sleeping and waking: and then they press their legs together by folding one across the other, and so one part of the vulva scratches the other, because delectation and pollution arise from this.[54]

Although this chapter of Albert's work is devoted to puberty in both sexes, it offers no parallel discussion of masturbation for males. The emphasis on female autoeroticism is, moreover, linked with woman's greater sex drive by a seeming tautology: young women masturbate because of their appetite for sex, which is fostered by their masturbation. "They have extended their [seminal] paths by the heat of rubbing and they are made wider and are filled with humor: and also the memory of coitus then excites the appetite."[55] Even so, Albert concedes that some select women have never experienced a nocturnal pollution or a pollution of any kind and remain chaste all their lives. (In fact, a witness in Clare of Montefalco's near-contemporary process of canonization suggests a parallel or even greater degree of miraculous closure in deposing that he learned from Clare's doctor "that Clare possessed within herself so great a lock [*clausura*] to her virginity that she was not able to do or emit those things which women commonly do or emit—even without the help of another creature.")[56] Albert's scientific explanation of such physiological reticence has the effect of withholding approval from women whose nighttime chastity is a simple effect of disposition, while maintaining suspicion of their daytime activities:

It happens that some women are never polluted in their dreams nor do they emit the seed of coitus due to some disposition of the complexion—as we said already earlier. And this happens more often in women than men because their bodies are less porous and the seed of coitus does not leave them except through extensive rubbing.[57]

This rationalization for a woman's inadvertent freedom from nocturnal emissions diminishes her quotient of implied virtue considerably.

Thomas of Cantimpré, a one-time student of Albert, relates a series of anecdotes concerning the sin of masturbation—a sin in which both sexes were implicated. Yet his presentational strategy, leading with some lurid instances of female self-abuse, tacitly suggests that women were especially susceptible to this form of pollution. Thus Thomas alleges that while he was working as a confessor in the episcopal camera, a grief-stricken woman admitted that when she was masturbating in her bedroom, she heard a demon positioned between her bed and the wall shout "si, si, si" (which she interpreted as an interjection of indignation). Another woman confessed to Thomas that when she was in the process of polluting herself, a demon contemptuously goaded her on, assuring her that she would pay dearly in the next life for this particular pleasure. A third, who spent many years in a convent feigning holiness, received posthumous censure from a diabolical sow and its black piglets. The porcine demons entered the cloister where she was buried, dug up and dismembered her body, and spread her entrails through the entire length of the cloister.[58] In contrast to these three instances, two of which he learned from the offenders themselves, only one example of a male masturbator is presented.[59]

Despite a woman's innate propensity to this vice, masturbation destroyed all claims to even nominal virginity.[60] But this very awareness of female frailty supplied the mortar for the construction of a western cult of virginity.[61] Indeed, as Albert the Great would have it, "incorruption is eminently present in that which is particularly able to be corrupted." With regard to the designation of virginity as an angelic lot, Albert further cites the *Glossa ordinaria* to the effect that virginity in a corruptible body is loftier than angelic chastity, since the virgin has to struggle against corruption, while an angel does not.[62] Thus the veneration of "true virgins"—those who were mentally and physically intact, being polluted neither at the hands of men nor at their own—would be all the greater. And these perceptions would also be sharpened and extended by renewed efforts to locate sin in an individual's intention—a tendency beginning with Abelard (d. 1142), but one that soon eddied out and literally revolutionized the Christian world.[63]

The emphasis on intentionality had both positive and negative ramifications for the spiritually ambitious woman. It could be extremely enabling: the female vocation was strewn with obstacles like forced marriage; even consecrated virgins were not safe from defilement.[64] Beset by such potential depredations, female chastity could reside in a tacit or expressed granting or withholding of consent to a constrained act. This was by no means a new insight. In the patristic period, Augustine had countered the rhetoric extolling the virtues of intact virginity and its corollaries (I am thinking particularly of Jerome's approving list of violated matrons or matrons, who, fearing violation, ended their own lives[65]) by arguing that a forcibly violated woman, who never consented to the act, remained essentially undefiled. At times, this view leads Augustine to liken the former virgin's physical violation to the wound incurred in the course of a martyr's passion.[66]

And yet, the female soul was believed to be relentlessly permeated by her body. In no way exempt from the physiological misogyny of his day, Augustine perceived rape as a potential source of intense pleasure. The virgin's susceptibility to this pleasure was something of an inevitability, considering her truant body. But she could experience pleasure and yet remain unstained, provided she did not consent to this pleasure. Mental complicity with the act, and not the act itself, was thus the ultimate source of violation. A truly unwilling sufferer may escape stigmatization, even while experiencing derivative pleasure:

> An attack on one's body may inflict not merely physical pain, but may also excite carnal pleasure. If such an act is perpetrated, it does not compromise the virtue of chastity, to which the sufferer clings with an iron will; it merely outrages the sense of shame.[67]

The projection of undesired pleasure on the unfortunate victims of rape is doubtless one the most offensive applications of Augustine's theory of concupiscence, that most telling symptom of the fallen human body. When he further likens the constrained pleasure accompanying rape to the sexual stirrings that occur in sleep, the analogy is sadly inadequate—not least of all because of its reliance on a male paradigm of nocturnal emissions.[68] The comparison, moreover, further associates uncontrolled concupiscence with the sleeping male versus the waking female.

Having reopened the attractive but unreliable portal of intentionality, the clergy seemed determined that as few women as possible should pass through. Ecclesiastical authorities either persisted in being less forgiving than Augustine throughout the Middle Ages or denied altogether that a woman could withhold her consent from pleasure: a woman who had been raped could not be veiled as a virgin. This not only was the letter of canon law but was corroborated by theologians, such as Thomas Aquinas (d. 1274), who reasoned that "because it is especially difficult that in such delectation some movement of pleasure should not arise, on that account the Church, which cannot judge inner things when the woman is outwardly corrupted, should not veil her among virgins."[69] This view was reinforced on other occasions in the writings of Thomas—perhaps most particularly when he resolved that even God cannot entirely repair the pristine integrity of a former virgin.[70] Other kinds of evidence also imply that intentionality made insufficient inroads into women's spiritual life. Barbara Newman's recent analysis of the literature aimed at the formation of religious vocation demonstrates how in the twelfth and early thirteenth centuries the specter of intact virginity, and its extreme fragility, still tended to limit women's spiritual horizons.[71]

Even so, numerous indications from the high Middle Ages suggest that virginity was coming to be perceived more as a mental state than a physical one.[72] This was an immense boon to a spiritually upwardly mobile matron such as Margery Kempe, whose thwarted desire for chastity was assuaged by Christ's assurance that she was as beloved to him as any maiden.[73] From the standpoint of women's purported imaginative powers, however, the emphasis on intentionality could also be turned against women by enlarging their capacity for complicity in desire and multiplying the threats to chastity. Thus, as the fetishization of intact virginity tended to recede, the dangers of self-pollution became more pronounced. This heightened concern paralleled the renewed anxiety over wet dreams among the clergy—an anxiety accompanying the emphasis on transubstantiation and associated with the corresponding fear that a potentially sullied priest might actually handle God. But, as I suggested in the introduction to this chapter, an important difference separates these seemingly analogous situations: the polluted cleric is asleep and thus usually blameless; the female virgin is awake and hence much more prone to censure. One could almost say that women willfully chose what men only dreamt of.

Waking pollution could take many forms. An area of increased concern was the effect of sexual fantasies on an individual's chastity. The kind of mental corruption envisaged here was again by no means new in its general contours. Jerome's famous letter to the virgin Eustochium had decried virgins only technically deserving of the name, while Isidore of Seville (d. 636) had similarly cautioned that a virgin in body alone received no reward in the afterlife.[74] Women had traditionally been, and would continue to be, the preferred targets of such concerns. The twelfth-century Aelred of Rievaulx's rule for recluses, for example, although still very intent on an intact hymen, recognized that the battle to maintain chastity must be waged along more subtle fronts as well: "But also without the company of another's flesh virginity is commonly corrupted, chastity violated, if a very strong heat striking the flesh subdues the will and rapes the members." The devil, moreover, ever the enemy of chastity, is seen as raising the temperature of the virgin's body by day and infesting her thoughts by night.[75]

Thirteenth-century scholastics were prepared to specify with a greater degree of exactitude the moral and physical repercussions of succumbing to the lure of such carnal thoughts. Once again, these discussions were oriented around the situation of female virgins: men were introduced into the discussion, if at all, only as poorly integrated analogues. Thus Aquinas describes three kinds of corruption that could assail a woman's virginity: the first is purely physical; the second, which consisted in the release of seed, was both physical and spiritual; the third was a sensation produced from one of the many passions that coursed through the body and was likewise physical and spiritual. Only the first kind of corruption—physical violation by an external agent—is peremptorily dismissed as not corresponding to the individual's virtue. In contrast, the second and third are treated as the very moral substance of virginity, since a person could choose to accept or reject these sensations. So female defloration is configured within a consensual framework, thus ultimately rendered an act of the will.[76]

The recasting of physical integrity as a largely mental construct presents new challenges for women, especially apparent in Albert the Great's attentive and quasi-clinical analysis of virginity and the loss thereof. At the outset, technicalities like the hymen are brushed to one side by Albert: if, for instance, it were pierced by a sword, virginal integrity would not suffer. Rather, emphasis is placed on a fantasy life that is aided and abetted by the will.

> I emphasize "by the will" because sometimes a person deliberates about coitus, making the genitals and other parts inclined to concupiscence with the intention and zeal of exciting the heat of concupiscence and delighting in it, and corruption follows such thoughts with the flowing of the filthy humors and the completed pleasure of coitus. And I say that such a person loses her virginity since that completed pleasure corrupts the body.[77]

He then goes on to deny that there is such a thing as corruption of the mind alone. If this kind of pleasure is pursued deliberately, "the spirits are extended to the genital members in an act of pleasure and the person begins to be completely delighted and to be polluted through the imagination just as through the deed."[78] Albert's reasoning is superficially grounded on the premise of gender equity: since men experience no actual division of the flesh in the loss of their virginity, the hymen should not be perceived as the main signifier of female virgins. But this ostensibly gender-blind criterion raises the stakes considerably, being ultimately more prejudicial to women in proportion to the manner in which female chastity was more severely mandated than male. Moreover, in Albert's view, a virgin who is polluted through her sordid imaginings cannot recoup her losses through penance.[79] Nor can such a woman be veiled as a virgin without a special dispensation from the bishop. Even with such a license, she would not receive the full "truth" of the sacrament of veiling. Albert's begrudging lenience, barely countenancing the veiling of a sullied virgin at all, is premised on a free-wheeling biblical exegesis: thus Jacob and other patriarchs married not only free women but also slaves. Solomon took not only queens but concubines to his bed as well, et cetera.[80] The implication is clear: the fallen virgin, her integrity in tatters, did not qualify for a proper veiling, even as she would never attain the full status of *sponsa Christi*. She thus would not be held in the same esteem by the celestial bridegroom as were the true brides who had preserved themselves for his embrace. Yet this lesser order of woman might still bring him gratification through a kind of concubinage.

But Albert's rigor in this area was exceptional. Thomas of Cantimpré observes that many were even of the opinion that if a woman lost her virginity but retained her hymen she could nevertheless regain her virginal status, provided she experienced true contrition and undertook penance. Eventually, Thomas would go on to endorse this position—one that was also supported by Albert's more famous student, the other Thomas. Even so, Thomas of Cantimpré is perhaps sufficiently ambivalent that he decides to include Albert's view as well—even if (as he says) it sounds odious:

> Namely, in no way should she be reputed a virgin whom a flux of concupiscence polluted in carnal delight of the senses, while her reason was stupefied—even if she retained the sign of her chastity intact, uncorrupt, and whole.[81]

The situation became more vexed as the Middle Ages progressed. John Gerson subscribed to the seemingly less rigorous position, arguing that a woman corrupted by thoughts alone could have her integrity restored by penance.[82] He was also quick to reassure anxious laypersons who solicited his opinion that the so-called medial humors (those that leave the genitals unbeknownst to individuals until they find telltale traces in their clothes and to which women were especially prone) do not constitute sin.[83] Gerson was nevertheless preoccupied, even morbidly so, with the potential for mental defloration. Thus he would argue in his *On the Knowledge of Chastity* that the "fumosity" of spirits can cause a titillation that results in corruption, independent of any seminal discharge.

But if virginity is truly corrupted through the fullness of delight from such things without any flow of seed, according to the opinion of certain masters, alas for sorrow, for it is stupefying to think in how few [individuals] virginity would remain—unless perhaps the lack of sufficient rational judgment would excuse this in boys and girls.

As we later learn in the same treatise, Gerson was reluctant to exempt ostensibly unlikely categories for sexual activity: a eunuch can deflower a virgin; prepubescent boys and girls inflame each other; the frigid or bewitched engage in wicked excesses in desperate attempts at self-arousal precisely because they cannot achieve an orgasm.[84] With these bizarre external threats assailing individuals who were functioning at a low sexual ebb, woman was left with little hope of defending herself against the internal machinations of her libidinized self.

The Demon Lover

Both woman's sexual capacity and her breadth of imagination made her the perfect partner for the demon incubus—a figure that had been a part of orthodox tradition from the patristic period. Augustine had tentatively lent credence to tales of demon lovers, arguing that the evidence of their female victims was too prolix to ignore. Still he made no final pronouncement: "I would not dare to decide on evidence like this, whether or not certain spirits, embodied in the kind of aerial substance, whose force we can feel when it is fanned against our bodies, are subject to the passion of lust and can awake a responsive passion in women."[85]

Augustine had hesitated over the question of whether demons "with their aerial substance" received any satisfaction from sexual intercourse with mortals. Thirteenth-century scholastics, however, resolved this question in the negative. Demons lacked bodies and thus could not experience pleasure.[86] They also, necessarily, lacked gender. From a certain perspective they could be construed as ideal lovers, since their main concern was to give pleasure to their partner. Hence they only assumed appropriately sexed bodies in order to seduce and corrupt humans and, for this purpose, could theoretically appear as a male-seeming incubus or a female-seeming succubus. William of Auvergne drives this point home by arguing that, were demons actually capable of feeling lust, they would hardly resort to mortals, since they could assume much more beautiful forms in accordance with their angelic nature.[87]

In the thirteenth century, woman's susceptibility to incubi was often tacitly understood as opposed to explicitly stated, generally being communicated through the sheer numbers of instances alone. Thus *The Dialogue on Miracles* by the Cistercian writer Caesarius of Heisterbach (d. 1240) offers multiple anecdotes that turned on this form of female weakness, and only then assures the reader that men as well as women endured this supernatural harassment, suffering incursions by female-seeming succubi.[88] But much of the theory explaining woman's special susceptibility was already in place. William of Auvergne links woman's receptivity to every kind of supernatural visitation, including the incubus, with the greater impressionability of her soul.[89] By the fifteenth century, John Nider, whose writings were of central importance to the development of a learned discourse on witchcraft, is much more forthright in his statement that women were more frequently afflicted by demon lovers than were men—though they were also more inclined to imagine that they were afflicted when they were not. He then goes on to say that male vulnerability was, in distinction, expressed less through external assault than through inner incapacity, resulting in impotence.[90]

The incubus and the succubus operate differently in religious narrative. Often a succubus is introduced into the tale so that the holy man can resist it—the classic case being, perhaps, from the life of St. Anthony.[91] His holy will and, hence, his virility are affirmed by his resistance. As I argued in Chapter 1, the male who succumbs to the sexually aggressive succubus is often peculiarly feminized, ultimately wasting away as a result of this supernatural contact. Thus, the demon succubus stalking the sleeping cleric was an appropriate *figura* for the nocturnal emission. But if a cleric feared that the experience of the nocturnal emission implied a loss of will in his sleeping self, he feared the corruption of will in the waking woman. This differential treatment is reflected in incubus lore. Even female piety could potentially be subverted by seduction, since it was in the imagination that carnal and spiritual impulses met and frequently merged. Thus the thirteenth-century Dominican inquisitor Stephen of Bourbon tells of a female mystic "[who] began at times to think to herself that she was a pure woman and such a one as would be worthy for the Lord to give her visible consolations." One night when she was alone in her room meditating on her own excellence, a marvelous light appeared. From this light, a beautiful king with a glittering entourage emerged, claiming he was Christ and that his attendants were the apostles. The next night, he visited her alone and seduced her, securing her promise not to reveal their relations to anyone. The third night he was less handsome and not as well dressed. After that he appeared as a knight; then a cleric; then a rustic; then a monk; then a goliard. Finally the woman recognized her error and, in a panic, ran to confession.[92]

Like other propositions of this period that implied portentous moral consequences—a list ranging from the commission of sin to contracts like matrimony or vassalage and well beyond—the sexual relationship between the woman and the incubus was represented as consensual, giving rise to a binding agreement not unlike the pact imputed to the sorcerer and the devil.[93] Of course, a potential face-saving strategy would be for the woman to deny having given her consent, as this would remove all possible culpability. Thomas of Cantimpré tells of a nun who was subject to frequent and prolonged sexual abuse by an incubus. Her denial that she had ever consented to this intercourse was met with complete incredulity by Thomas, since he doubted that God would ever visit such a punishment on an unconsenting soul. When Thomas attempted to make her take an oath in support of her position, she, fearing for her soul, was forced to confess the truth. Her physical corruption was, in fact, only subsequent to her mental corruption.[94]

Once a woman had consented to seduction by an incubus, the resulting bond was seemingly as indissoluble and stifling as a bad marriage. Often the matrimonial overtones are very explicit. Thus, in a miracle from the life of Bernard of Clairvaux (d. 1153), the wife of a knight succumbed to a demon.

That lascivious devil appeared to her in the shape of a knight, particularly handsome in appearance, and by secret inward suggestion and outward flattering speech he falsely bent her spirit to his love. And when he obtained the assent of the woman, with his arms stretched out, he placed one of his hands on her feet, and he covered her head with the other hand and with this sign of the contract he betrothed her to himself.[95]

The idiosyncratic but ritualized gesture performed by the incubus is clearly a formal way of plighting troth, intended to mark the solemnity of the occasion.[96]

Caesarius of Heisterbach provides a sophisticated variant on the basic model of demonic seduction, developing a bifurcated emphasis on consensuality, which simultaneously highlights the sufficiency of consent for the commission of sin and for the contracting of a marriage. (The definition of marriage that prevailed by the end of the twelfth century dispensed with physical consummation in favor of consent as the sole requirement for a legally binding union.) A nun, beset by a handsome youth who repeatedly asks for her hand in marriage, resists—insisting on her commitment to Christ. But the youth persists in his overtures. Bewildered by his perseverance, reasoning that there are many women richer and more beautiful than herself, she eventually gets him to admit that he is a demon. She responds: "'Why then do you demand carnal marriage, which is well known to be contrary to your nature?' And he: 'Only consent, all I want from you is your consent to marriage.'"[97]

As with mundane marriage, the union between the incubus and his human partner was only dissoluble through the intervention of appropriate authorities—occasionally through a timely application of the sacrament of confession but more often through the intervention of a saint. Thus the knight's wife, who as a consequence of her infernal union was violated by the incubus nightly while she lay in bed with her husband, was freed by St. Bernard. Thomas of Cantimpré's penitent, held in sexual thrall by her relationship with the demon, was helped by two holy women. When she was unable to take communion on the eve of Pentecost, existing, as she did, in a state of mortal sin, a nun named Christine offered to accept the burden of her sin for one night. Christine was almost killed, however, in her struggle with an invisible grunting adversary. The woman was eventually freed from the incubus through the intervention of Lutgard of Aywières.[98] According to testimony at her process of canonization, Bridget of Sweden (d. 1373) also assisted in freeing a woman from her demonic lover. Apparently Bridget detected a charm hidden in the comb that the woman wore in her hair. This charm, given to her by a priest, was intended to ward off a demon who abused her nightly (purportedly leaving all the usual carnal evidence of the sex act). Bridget ordered her to get rid of the charm and to make her confession. The woman was accordingly cured.[99]

The Demon Seed

Woman's reproductive capacity rendered her additionally ripe for uncanny insemination. Supernatural miscegenation, in fact, permeates the very roots of the Judeo-Christian tradition. Thus the Book of Genesis (6.4) describes how the sons of God begat a race of giants on the daughters of men; Paul refers fleetingly to this tradition when he warns women to keep their heads covered because of the angels.[100]

Tales of demonic offspring, such as the incubus parentage of the wizard Merlin or the Hunnish race, continued to be recycled in the high Middle Ages, despite the fact that the incorporeality of demons would seem to undercut such possibilities. But, in contrast with the marked skepticism of many of their predecessors, thirteenth-century scholastics struggled hard to credit these stories.[101] William of Auvergne, for instance, looks to the reproductive capacity of Portuguese mares—an appropriate choice, since the horse, as mentioned earlier, was the only species among which the sexual appetite of the female could compete with that of a woman. These horses could allegedly be impregnated by a hot wind alone, which had a coagulating effect on the female's seed that paralleled the impact of the male seed. William posits similar "inspirations" by demons but also introduces a more traditional theory of insemination as a fallback position in his analysis. The seed of a man, however, was not needed to impregnate a woman: any seed might do. As evidence, he evinces the example of the wife of a Saxon knight who was abducted and repeatedly raped by a bear. The unfortunate woman gave birth to a number of children, all of whom had a rather ursine slant to their faces and who took the name "Ursini." Thus the women who gave birth to the Huns may well have been expelled by their own people for witchcraft. They satisfied their lusts with their familiar demons, who obligingly impregnated them by whatever means came to hand.[102]

William's solution was a disquieting one, and ultimately rejected. Apart from the issues it raised as to the humanity and the possibility of salvation for such children, it tended to sideline the male altogether in the reproductive process by investing the female seed with an eerie independence. The solution that eventually prevailed, perhaps originating with Aquinas and already alluded to above, was that male seed was collected by the feminine succubus, who is then metamorphosed into a masculine incubus in order to impregnate a woman. Thus the children of such unions were fully human and could be saved.[103] Yet this solution was perhaps even more unnerving, since not only was specific paternity doubtful, but the male—allegedly the "active" party in heterosexual intercourse—was entirely absent. Nor was it at all comforting to masculine potency (which was, as we have seen, notoriously vulnerable to demonic interference) that the incubus could simulate huge floods of semen or make the woman believe that she had experienced sexual intercourse forty or sixty times when in fact they had only performed it once or twice—or so William of Auvergne reports.[104] William's lurid anecdotes about incubi are repeated in Nider's enormously popular *Formicarium*. But the discussion of demonic sex is first prefaced by a denunciation of unmarried women who pollute themselves because they do not wish to sacrifice their liberty to a husband.[105]

These wild projections—amalgamating female sexual appetite, capacity, and depraved predilection for independence in the exercising of these faculties—careened around like proverbial loose cannons with the effect of making more than a few scholars nervous. Lurking palpably at the margins of this discourse was the potential consequence for the Virgin Birth. Doubtless, William of Auvergne's hypotheses about the generative possibilities of wind and other "inspirations" were doomed to fail because of the possible aspersions cast over the miraculous nature of the Virgin's conception. The same protectiveness of the Virgin's miraculous prerogative might even have had something to do with the Dominican preference for the Aristotelian one-seed theory, since the female body was clearly so fecund and so amoral.[106] In fact, Aristotle himself had argued against the existence of a female seed precisely because its existence made parthenogenesis possible.[107] Toward the end of the thirteenth century, Giles of Rome, an ardent Aristotelian, would attack the Galenic two-seed theory of conception, arguing that if a woman had her own seed, she would be able to reproduce by herself.[108] But, like a dog returning to its vomit (to cite a popular medieval adage) or a tongue worrying the place of a missing tooth, scholastics could not leave the problem alone. A quodlibetical question addressed by Aquinas goes to the heart of the matter, asking "whether someone is able to be naturally or miraculously virgin and father"—a phenomenon that he grudgingly allows could happen naturally if a nocturnal pollution somehow reached a woman's womb, whether demonically assisted or not. But the problem of the virginal father raises the specter of a virginal mother, making the Virgin Mary the object of a crude skepticism and an unceremonial scrutiny, albeit unavowed.[109] Thus Aquinas also necessarily discusses how a potential mother can naturally, as opposed to miraculously, be impregnated and still retain her virginity. The disturbing example he provides is of a virgin made to sleep in her father's bed—ostensibly so he could safeguard her chastity—who conceives as a result of her father's nocturnal emission.[110] What is not discussed is the object of demonic ardor, the silent partner to the demonic inseminator: a woman corrupted by an incubus whose virginity nevertheless remains intact. It took a century or so for this suppressed corollary to surface. Peter of Aquila (d. 1361) and Denis the Carthusian (d. 1471) would both posit that Antichrist himself would be born of a pseudo-virgin through demonic insemination.[111] And, adding my own theological reflections to this dark mirror of salvation history: not only does Antichrist's mother ape the Virgin Mary's purity, but she simultaneously evokes the never-realized ideal of prelapsarian sex. As Augustine would have it, in Eden, had Adam and Eve never sinned, heterosexual intercourse would have been effected without any violent penetration so that the hymen would have remained intact.[112]

Finally, I would like briefly to revisit our point of departure: my own puzzlement over the lack of symmetry in treatments of male and female pollutions and what this might tell us about perceived gender differences. The deep logic at work can be reduced to a very basic principle: men, who were strongly self-identified with the powers of reason and the will, feared what became of themselves when they slept. But these same men, who were relatively sanguine, even comforted, by the thought of a sleeping woman (or so fairy tales would have us believe), were extremely nervous about women's waking activities. And so female pollutions, foregrounded as conscious and deliberate, ultimately presage the carnal woman's vulnerability to the incubus. This relationship, in turn, anticipates the witch: the epitome of cold, calculating female carnality and malice.

These interpretative coordinates, the fruits of ecclesiastical culture, are still on occasion subject to reversal, as is the case in Marie de France's lai of *Yonec.*[113] The protagonist is a beautiful *malmariée* in a sterile marriage. She is held in captivity by her aged human husband while bitterly lamenting her solitary lot.[114] In her loneliness, she fantasizes about the perfect lover, whereupon a huge bird flies through her window and promptly transforms itself into a handsome knight (ll. 91–115). When the knight asks for her love, she expresses concern over the nature of his religious faith, and he, in turn, offers to receive the sacrament in her form and then metamorphoses, assuming her likeness, in order to do so (ll. 121–88). The love affair is eventually discovered and the knight is slain, but not before he impregnates his lady with a son who will eventually avenge his death.[115]

Taken altogether, these elements evoke many of the points I have been discussing: a woman fantasizing in her room; a made-to-order man appearing mysteriously, whose expressed sole purpose is to cater to her sexual needs; an unnerving shapeshifting ability, which suggests all the virtuosity of the incubus/succubus team; and a pregnancy that one assumes came about through the knight's seed (but who's to say? and what kind of seed does he have, anyway?). And yet the coordinates are reversed, precisely because the author is aligning herself with this unconventional relationship and demonizing ordinary marriage. The bird-knight is presented not only as a romantic exemplar but as a fecund partner as well. More significantly, the sterile husband, who the heroine complains will "never die— / when he should have been baptized / he was plunged instead in the river of hell" (ll. 86–88), is cast as an explicitly diabolical figure. Marie's story, probably written sometime between 1160 and 1199, represents a kind of transitional stage in perceptions of the supernatural. The lady's initial doubts over her suitor's religious beliefs may even signal that the times were changing and that the bird-knight was, historically, doing his last medieval shapeshift from fairy into demon.[116] Fifty years later, Vincent of Beauvais would doubtless have included this remarkable bird-knight in his list of demon-lovers, where it would take its place alongside celebrities such as the prototype for the swan-drawn knight Lohengrin and the serpent-wife Melusine.[117]

Marie's story is potentially most subversive in its tacit alliance with the tradition that posited women's heightened powers of imagination and susceptibility to the demonic. The church fathers unequivocally construed the powers and susceptibility alike as evidence of female weakness; the qualities could also be perceived as establishing a potential position of strength. In the sixteenth-century witch trials of Lorraine, a woman was approached by a man in black (the devil), who claimed his name was "Pensée de Femme"—literally the thoughts of women.[118] The imaginative powers of Marie's nameless heroine are no less potent, though authorially protected from the negative associations that imbue the later event. Janus-faced in their implications, Marie's interpretative reversals shift back and forth between what they affirm and what they deny. Yet her story must finally be read as a tantalizing confirmation of masculine society's worst fears: that whether or not women were actually capable of reproducing with demons, if they could they would—and happily dispense with men altogether. And this, issuing from a female voice, is very deep subversion indeed.

3

Sex in Holy Places

An Exploration of a Medieval Anxiety

"But those who forget their fear of me and in insane wickedness destroy the temples dedicated in My name, or defile that dedication originated by Jacob by polluting holy places with murderous blood or the impure seed of adultery or fornication . . . O woe to those wretches."

—Hildegard of Bingen[1]

Hildegard's prophetic denunciation of sacrilegious pollution is premised on a set of conventional assumptions. Pollution prohibitions in the Christian tradition were of sufficient antiquity to provide the kind of illusory stability essential to religious belief structures. Yet the expression and meaning of a particular anxiety still remained sensitive to historical contingency. This chapter examines a case in point.

A rather startling story enjoyed popularity across all genres of medieval didactic literature in the high and later Middle Ages. A man and a woman have intercourse in a holy precinct: be it a church, a monastery, a cemetery, or near a saint's shrine. As punishment for this inappropriate act, the couple is miraculously stuck together, only to be discovered in this humiliating predicament by a wondering populace, whose reaction ranges from high hilarity to deep disgust. They are eventually released by the united prayers of the community.

This graphic depiction of what specialists call *penis captivus* or *vaginismus* (depending on which set of genitals is preferred as the locus of the drama) is fabricated from a tissue of anxieties.[2] When construed primarily as an expression of gynephobia with the female genitalia as the singular site of danger, the tale can take its place alongside more celebrated motifs like the *vagina dentata*.[3]

The adhesive climax of this particular narrative has enjoyed a measure of transhistorical and transcultural ubiquity. Medical historians have demonstrated the breadth of its dissemination;[4] when I first heard a version of this story it was making the rounds of preadolescent circles as an urban legend. In this latter context, the tale functioned as a generalized warning against the dangers of sex.[5] Yet the historical longevity of this particular motif ought not to beguile us into regarding it as static in either form or meaning. The characteristic medieval rendering of the story focuses on consecrated soil as the locus of transgression and danger. As such, it is specific and timely with respect to origins, meaning, and application, as are its particular variants.

The earliest versions of this topos seem to have surfaced around 1100. In a miracle in the *acta* of St. Guignerius (d. ca. 450), the offense was perpetrated on the tomb of a bishop who had been a member of the household of the father of the saint. The couple, locked together like dogs (*more canum*), was conveyed to the shrine of the saint, "where by the merit of the witness of Christ and by the intercession of the faithful they were liberated."[6]

When compared with later analogues, proximity to the holy is notably oblique in this narrative. The consecration of a cemetery, the site of the offense, is of lesser occasion than that of a church. In the ceremony that evolved to contend with this and other forms of pollution, the cemetery's solitary defilement does not affect the integrity of the church proper. By way of contrast, if the church is polluted in some way, the cemetery is likewise desecrated.[7] Similarly, the deceased bishop whose tomb is the site of the transgression is only remotely associated with the saint in question. Especially noteworthy is the fact that the author of the *acta* takes no pains to differentiate between actions that are unseemly and those that are ritually polluting. In the marvel immediately preceding our incident, for example, two soldiers are punished for urinating on the rock where Guignerius had once anchored his ship. "Divine vengeance struck each without delay. For both were seized by a demon—one of them chewed his tongue into pieces with his teeth, while all the guts of the other were poured out of his rear. And thus each died a horrible death."[8] But, as lurid as these punishments may be, there is all the difference in the world between urine on a rock (even a rock associated with a saint) and semen on consecrated soil, since the latter requires deliberate and public purification. Thus the boundaries for what constitutes "the sacred" seem somewhat amorphous. The once-removed proximity to a rather inchoate holy is complemented by the dearth of information offered concerning the offenders: "a certain corruptor ventured to defile the private parts of a certain woman."[9] It is not at all clear that the woman was a consenting party; the miracle could possibly serve as warning to potential rapists. In short, the multivalence of this story is purchased at the price of specificity and perhaps even didactic efficiency.

As time progressed, the offense tended to move indoors or, at the very least, nearer to more auspiciously consecrated turf. A spotlight is also turned on the identity of the actors. The fourteenth-century Chevalier de la Tour Landry included no less than two versions of this story in the manual of instruction that his chaplains helped him draft for his daughters, purportedly to teach them "how one ought to conduct oneself in church." The first anecdote concerns a sergeant of the church by the name of Perrot Luart, who had sex with an unidentified woman on the altar during a vigil of the Virgin Mary:

> Thus a miracle occurred whereby they were caught and stuck together like dogs, to such a degree that they were also trapped in this way the entire day, so that those from the church and those from the countryside had enough time to come and see them; for they could not separate from one another; and it was necessary that a procession be made to pray to God for them, and finally around evening they separated. Then it was necessary that the church be rededicated and that for penance [Perrot] go for three Sundays around the church and cemetery, beating himself and recounting his sin.[10]

Interestingly, Perrot's punishment simulates the ritual humiliation that sexual offenders were expected to undergo in the thirteenth and fourteenth centuries — a point to which I shall later return.[11]

The second instance allegedly occurred less than three years before the Chevalier compiled his book. On a Sunday, just after matins and before high Mass, the monk Pigière of Poitou, the prior's nephew, was discovered by his confrères in the church adhering to a nameless woman. He remained frozen in this act until all the monks, including his uncle, had witnessed his embarrassment. His shame was so great that he left the monastery.[12] The Chevalier's later narrative heightens the sense of sacrilege by framing the transgression in a holy place within a holy time. A vigil of the Virgin or a Sunday, especially before Mass, was technically sacrosanct and off-limits for sex.[13] The repetition of the story, though easily dismissed as a prurient self-indulgence, gains momentum from one anecdote to the next by accelerating the potential for transgression. Perrot Luart was simply a layperson in a position of trust in the parish who was guilty of sacrilegious fornication; the monk Pigière, however, was himself consecrated to God and thus possessed a greater capacity for sacrilege regardless of where or when he misconducted himself. The Pigière episode, additionally, raises the emotional stakes by emphasizing the compounded shame of exposure in the face of the avuncular presence—a necessary surrogate for the paternal presence, since a parental relationship in a monastic context might be open to misinterpretation.

Since the Chevalier de la Tour Landry was writing for his daughters, one wonders why he resisted the didactic expedient of transforming the offending monk into a nun. But here we encounter an important common feature that holds true for all of the motif's variants: the narrative is ineffaceably gendered male. If a name is given, it is the man's name; if an individual's prolonged absence is noted and a search ensues, it is the man who is missed and is sought; it is also the man who invariably initiates the sex act. This privileging of the male is multiply determined. Our anecdote probably evolved out of legislation that was chiefly shaped around clerical sexual offenses, as will be seen below. But the intellectual tradition also cast the man as the active party in sex, hence the "natural" aggressor, and this tendency would be complemented by a patriarchal disregard of female initiative.[14] On the positive side, this studied ignorance may periodically have exculpated women. In symbolic terms, Eve's transgression was eclipsed by Adam's in discussions of the fall; in practical terms, we can occasionally detect a tendency to underreport female malefactors.[15]

The Formation of an Exemplum: Its Incubation

Why did this story surface when it did? The shedding of blood or the spilling of seed had already been regarded as polluting for many centuries prior to the anecdote's twelfth-century emergence. Such defilement was traditionally considered to have ramifications that radiated beyond the local community.[16] The parish priest could not remedy it insofar as the church required reconciliation by the bishop.[17] And his intervention was dramatic. Circling the church three times, he cleansed the polluted spot with asperions of holy water mixed with salt, wine, and ashes.[18] His prayers were fraught with the language of defilement and purgation:

We most beloved brothers pray suppliantly to God the indulger of crimes, the cleaner of filth, God who purifies the world congealed with original sin by the splendor of his advent, that against the snares of the raging devil, our powerful defender will help, so that if anything were found stained and corrupted by [the devil's] fetid cunning in that spot by his daily infections, let it be purged by celestial compassion.[19]

This prayer was from the liturgy in the Romano-Germanic Pontifical of the mid-tenth century, which became the standard ritual in the West.[20] Despite the relative antiquity of such rites, however, a glance backward at disciplinary literature and legislation suggests that the early church was not particularly sensitive to all the sexual opportunities that consecrated soil afforded. The earliest penitentials did not envisage purposeful sexual activity in a church, though they did mildly penalize the sleeping cleric who experienced a nocturnal emission therein.[21]

By the late eighth and early ninth centuries, probably under the influence of the Carolingian Reform, a more voluntary kind of sexual activity in a church was envisaged in canonical sources. In *The Second Diocesan Statute* of Theodulf of Orleans (d. 821), the offense is categorized under the general rubric of "Irrational Fornication"—thus coupling it with other perceived aberrations like bestiality, homosexuality, and incest: "If, would that it would never be, someone were to have admitted to such a crime in a holy place, his penance should be doubled."[22]

Significantly, this kind of sexual sacrilege did not receive a detailed analysis until the eleventh century, when the reform of the clergy was underway. It elicited greater attention than any other sexual offense in the so-called third Vallicellian penitential.

Concerning those who would have fornicated or committed adultery within the church. At present, there is nothing more dangerous than to sin lethally, and nothing more damnable than, on account of the heat of the flesh, that one shamefully consents to fondle some whore even within the walls of the holy church. Whosoever is affected in such wise, who committed adultery or fornicated within a church [should receive the following penalty]: if a bishop were to presume this, 10 years over the legal penance; a priest, 7 years; a deacon or monk, 5 years; a subdeacon, 4 years; a cleric [i.e., someone in minor orders] or layperson, 3 years. Nor on account of reverence of God and of holy church should that person abstain less than 200 days from all entry into the church. Those mentioned above in orders or without orders, who committed such things, should be separated from the body and blood of Christ until after penance has been done, by reason of urgent necessity; nor should they participate [in communion], as did Judas who the devil immediately overcame after the morsel taken from the hand of the Lord. And from the ecclesiastical order let him irrevocably fall in every instance. However, in that house, which was contaminated by adultery, exorcised water should be sprinkled and it should be sanctified as formerly. . . . If anyone performed fornication in the church, that person should have penance all the days of his life on bread and water, and should offer compliance to God before the doors of the church, and never should communicate, until the time of death. . . . She likewise should do penance who permitted such a wicked deed, consenting shamefully, however in such a manner as behooves women.[23]

Despite an awkward effort to make this into an equal opportunity offense, the woman is seen as merely giving her consent to a wicked act. But it is a masculine crime that is envisaged, specifically a clerical one. His accomplice is a nameless whore (*quum aliqua scortu*) who is equipped with an almost elemental potential for temptation and defilement, but no true volition. For this offense, moreover, the author is clearly struggling to find sanctions of sufficient gravity, but his very zeal generates confusion. Although offending clerics are unambiguously removed from office, it would seem (at least initially) that even a penitent former bishop could be readmitted into the congregation. But eventually it becomes clear that all fornicators, clerical or lay, are subject to perpetual public penance—ever stigmatized and marginalized at the door of the church and deprived of the sacraments until on their deathbed.[24] The same text is also included, with a few modifications, in the canonical *Collection in Five Books* (between 1014 and 1023).[25]

This hectic interest in sacrilegious sex occurred within the ferment of the eleventh century, which, as a period of upheaval and immense social change, was especially susceptible to pollution fears.[26] Successive and overlapping waves of religious reform gave free vent to these fears. The obsession with sexual purity began with the monastic reformers, stimulating a number of popular heresies. Soon this preoccupation animated the entire Gregorian Reform of the secular clergy, which vigorously strove to outlaw and suppress clerical marriage.[27] Nor did these fears, once called into being, entirely recede after the reformers' goals were achieved. The clergy, who had struggled so hard to attain its new level of ritual purity, continued to be particularly sensitive to external sources of defilement. Clerics now defined themselves and rationalized their superiority to the laity in the distance they maintained from women.[28] Not only were clerical wives firmly set aside, but women were scrupulously kept away from the altar. Gratian's *Decretum* reified earlier efforts in this direction; women could not even touch a chalice or an altar cloth.[29] Parallel pollution concerns spilled over into secular legislation. One of the first official acts of the French king Philip Augustus was to restrict prostitutes from receiving their clients in the cemetery of the Holy Innocents.[30] And so it would seem that this particular sacrilegious sex act reinstated everything that had been virulently and by and large successfully suppressed in the campaign against clerical contamination by women. Two lay fornicators under an altar was the most heinous sacrilege, only surpassed by the anecdote about a monk and a laywoman (which would be a double sacrilege, as the pollution of a holy person was considered more offensive than the pollution of a church).[31]

Of course, this web of nightmares was a fecund source of fearful speculation and fantasy that would eventually leave an impression on many different kinds of discourse.[32] Various forms of sexual incontinence were often intuited retrospectively from what might initially appear to be natural disasters. The ostensibly random activity of lightning was interpreted as an especially portentous symbol of divine wrath. Thus Stephen of Bourbon (d. 1261) correlates the frequency with which churches were struck by lightning with their inferred function in abetting concealed fornication. He buttresses this contention with the revelation of a nun near Puy who, in response to episcopal inquiry, revealed that the local church had been struck in retribution for the offense of an adulterous couple.[33] Monasteries were frequently afflicted for the hidden impurities of their brethren. Stephen recounts how lightning struck the choir of a monastery in his native land of Belleville-sur-Saône:

> burning the pavement and certain areas, it wounded to death, moreover, certain older monks (although the little and innocent ones remained untouched), subtly entering through their clothing, consuming and shaving off their lower hairs, and gravely harming their lower regions.[34]

Stephen does not attempt to name what sorts of sins might elicit this form of vengeance, and his exemplum is doubtless all the more effective for his forbearance. Licentious or violent desecrations abound in Guibert of Nogent's twelfth-century autobiography, as do ensuing reconciliations to assuage God's wrath.[35] When Guibert was still a member of the community at Fly, for example, a disaster paralleling the event later detailed by Stephen of Bourbon befell the monks in the choir. In addition to inflicting numerous casualties and fatalities, lightning served a more focused punitive role, again burning away the pubic hair of some. Guibert likewise leaves the precise nature of the offense unspecified, taking refuge in the cryptic comment: "It is impossible to tell how equitable the judgment of God was in this case."[36]

Various sexual transgressions could also result in an atmosphere figuratively and literally redolent with corruption. Thus, in the thirteenth-century *Prose Lancelot,* the lord of the castle of Escalon committed the pivotal transgression of satisfying his lust in a church during holy week. The illicit couple died on the spot in one another's arms, while the inhabitants of the castle endured seventeen years of captivity, darkness, and the horrible stench of unburied corpses (mysteriously placed to decompose in the church through supernatural means).[37]

But the grace of God was equally capable of neutralizing the capacity for the vile acts that occasioned such flamboyant and miraculous intervention. The infamous *Malleus maleficarum* of the mid-fifteenth century, a work that contributed so much to the rise of the witch craze of the early modern period, considered the question of whether demonic succubi and incubi find certain times or places more conducive to their job of seduction. Holy times are pronounced extremely propitious but holy places are not: "it is proved by the words and actions of witches that they [incubi] are quite unable to commit these abominations in sacred places. And in this can be seen the efficacy of the Guardian Angels, that such places are reverenced." (Note the deep negation at work here. The *Malleus maleficarum* is able to entertain sacrilegious sex as a disturbing possibility only by instantly declaring it to be impossible.)[38]

The timely appearance of this motif within a climate of reform is a bold reminder that transgression cannot exist independently of carefully constructed prohibitions. Its proliferation as an exemplum intended for sermon literature suggests that preachers were now peculiarly zealous in their efforts to avert this source of desecration. Indeed, from a pastoral standpoint, sacrilegious intercourse could be construed as the suppressed climax to what every moralist feared was potentially initiated in church. Preachers railed against the evils of flirtation during divine offices. Bernardino of Siena (d. 1444), for example, fulminates: "There are some women so bold and shameless that they trifle with young men even inside the church and the girl's mother, too, becomes her own daughter's procuress, making her sit on the church benches, while her suitor gapes at her, following every movement she makes."[39] Bernardino's contemporary John Dominici similarly berated individuals who went to church expressly to misbehave.[40] Nor were these celebrated preachers alone in their observations. In a fictive confession, Denis the Carthusian (d. 1471) focuses on the wandering gaze of the hypothetical layperson: "[I sinned] by looking around here and there inconstantly and incautiously, gazing lustfully at men or women (which is a grave sin); and I did this at the time of Mass and of the divine Office, and on holy days and festivals."[41] But in all fairness to the clergy, churchgoing did seem to foster some blameworthy and bizarre courtships. In the notorious adultery cases where both the queen of Navarre and her sister-in-law stood accused, the two offending knights confessed that, in the course of their three-year relationships with the ladies, they had frequently availed themselves of holy places as well as sacred seasons. The preconversion Raymond Lull (d. 1316) was said to have pursued his noble female quarry into church on horseback.[42] It was in the church of St. Margaret that Margery Kempe (d. after 1438) was propositioned; she returned to church to submit to the man's overtures, though it is unclear where the couple was to consummate their illicit union.[43]

To summarize, the quickening interest in sacrilegious sex can be traced to the eleventh century, and the adhering couple motif first surfaces in the twelfth. In all of the earliest versions of this topos, the punishment is visited on illicit sexual partners: people with nowhere to go who may be presumed to have taken advantage of the only building that was truly open to the public. But soon the actors would be metamorphosed in an unanticipated way.

From Fornicators to Consorts

Until the twelfth century, sex in a church had been treated as a kind of theft—fornicators engaged in illicit embraces or holy housebreaking were literally apprehended for their ill-gotten gains.[44] But appearing in the thirteenth century, and thereafter even more popular than this "sex as theft" motif, were instances when the malefactors were husband and wife—a contingency never anticipated by earlier writers. Best known through William of Wadington's *Manuel des Pechiez,* wherein the unfortunate Richer and his wife were thus punished for having intercourse in the monastery in which they had taken shelter from the persecution of enemies, this anecdote was translated into English in Robert of Brunne's *Handlyng Synne* in 1303.[45] From these two fonts, the story made its way into many collections of exempla, thus becoming grist for the sermon mill.[46]

The marital state of the offending parties is a remarkable, but subtle, innovation. When Robert of Brunne concludes his lurid anecdote concerning the wages of marital sin, he adds a sobering moralization not present in his source:

For much worse damnation
will befall fornication
And more still for the adultery
Of priests, or wives' lechery
Since God took the revenge, of which many spoke
For a deed that was done in lawful wedlock.[47]

But since the overwhelming logic of the exemplum genre is committed to teaching by negative example, one must ask why Robert withheld the anticipated worst-case scenario: why, by the mid-thirteenth century, were legitimate couples outstripping their fornicating or adulterous counterparts in this particular act of truant intercourse?

The triumph of this misplaced marital act corresponds to important changes in the theological and canonistic assessments of conjugal sexuality over the course of the twelfth and thirteenth centuries. Two symbolic milestones are of particular significance. In Gratian's *Decretum* he dutifully reiterates all of the traditional penitential periods during which married individuals should sexually abstain (which amount to something in the vicinity of half the year); but then he sweeps them aside in his famous *dictum post causam,* which makes the observance of these periods contingent on the consent of both parties. This canonistic innovation is later corroborated by papal fiat when Alexander III describes the traditional penitential periods as counsels as opposed to precepts.[48]

The disregard of traditional restraints may well coincide with the church's more positive assessment of married sexuality. But this assessment is inseparable from the clerical theorists' desire to contain and legislate, activities inevitably undermined by the theorists' uneasy suspicion that marital sexuality might ultimately be uncontainable and unsusceptible to legislation. These tensions become especially clear in the new casuistic discussions surrounding the marital act, or, as the medievals referred to it, the conjugal debt—a concept adopted from St. Paul.[49] Paul had explicitly described husband and wife as debtors, by which he meant that neither was in full possession of his or her body. As property of the other, each must yield to his or her partner's sexual demands, lest he or she be tempted to fornicate. In the high Middle Ages, the western clergy was finally prepared to take Paul at his word. Canonists, theologians, and, more important for our purposes, the writers of pastoral manuals, texts developed by the late twelfth century for assisting the priest in hearing the confessions of his lay charges, all included detailed analyses of the conjugal debt.[50]

By the late twelfth century, the canonist Huguccio had extended Gratian's initial license from holy times to holy places, envisaging situations in which couples might be forced to seek refuge in a church in times of war. The influential *Glossa ordinaria* on Gratian (ca. 1220) concurred with this position.[51] By the thirteenth century, the writers of pastoral manuals were prepared to back the proposition that an individual must pay the debt on a feast day, if so required. But the question of holy places was considerably more controversial. John of Freiburg's influential *Summa for Confessors* (ca. 1297) gives a bird's-eye view of prevailing canonical and theological thinking on the subject. When asking whether it is permitted to render or even exact the debt in a holy place, John first turns to Peter of Tarentaise (d. 1276), who states that the debt should be rendered at all times but not necessarily in all places, because a place can be polluted and require reconciliation while a time cannot. He also argues that the place is more flexible than the time. Thomas Aquinas (d. 1274) adds the practical consideration that one should not render the debt immediately when in public. But Albert the Great (d. 1280) insists that the debt must be rendered in a holy place, if need be. One is only released from this obligation if another place is available.[52] From the tepid Peter of Tarentaise to the bold Albert the Great, John's argumentative trajectory brought him to a conclusion widely shared at the end of the Middle Ages: that submitting to such a sacrilegious sex act was not only licit but obligatory.[53]

By the thirteenth century, irrational intercourse in a church had become a kind of inscribed figure for the dilemma such conduct posed within the edifice of official theology. The peculiar sanctity of building and page alike suffered parallel depredations from the imagined act. Even so, the havoc it created in the theologians' discursive system was not without its uses. By superimposing the obligation to pay the debt onto sacred soil, theorists engaged in a lurid play through which they could explore the limits of conflicting responsibilities. The problem became a vital terminal that channeled the different currents of contemporary debate over marriage, desire, obligation, and gender.

Another, and related, theological construction was opportunistically added to the evaluative criteria by which the morality of sex in holy places was assessed: the privileging of intention over action in the assessment of sin. As the penitentials of the early church would suggest, prior to the twelfth century sin had generally been determined in terms of an external offense. In the 1130s Peter Abelard created something of a revolution in theological thinking by asserting the moral indifference of external acts; sin, for Abelard, was located in the intentions, which could only be properly weighed by God, the reader of hearts.[54] Though theorists considerably refined Abelard's implicitly antisocial doctrine, his effect in relocating sin to the interior person is undeniable.[55] Moreover, this reassessment of culpability complements the new emphasis on the conjugal debt. Theorists revived, or at any rate reemphasized, Augustine's distinction between the spouse exacting the conjugal debt, who was guilty of a venial sin, and the spouse rendering, who was credited with the good of chastity—a distinction that, like Abelard's, privileged intentions.[56] In fact, the optimistic Albert the Great and a few others actually asserted that the rendering spouse performed a meritorious act.[57] And so, in theory, it is possible for us to identify the guilty party in the event that sex is perpetrated in a church: the one who started it. The individual who *sorrowfully* submitted to his or her partner's importunities could, in theory, be sinless.[58]

This assessment more or less accords with the theorists' casuistic treatment of the issue: the exacting party is at fault. Indeed, John of Freiburg's overview of the subject concludes with Albert the Great, who not only excuses the party who renders but even attempts to exculpate the exacting party. If the individual is truly sorry that he or she cannot do without sex in the church and exacts with lamentation (*cum planctu*), even that person has not sinned mortally.[59]

Albert's forbearance toward the sexual initiator would have been regarded with suspicion by his peers. Indeed, more conservative thinkers even questioned whether the spouse who was compelled to render the debt remained unscathed by sin. But the debate was also internalized: individual authors seemed to manifest their ambivalence toward so injudicious a sex act through self-contradiction. The *Rules of Mandates* of John Gerson (d. 1429), for example, declare that "a holy time or place does not seem to excuse [rendering], rather either spouse is bound to render the debt to the one seeking it." And yet in a vernacular treatise, a venue that was infinitely more accessible than its Latin counterpart, Gerson makes the blanket statement that "there is no doubt that [such an act] is a mortal sin."[60] A similar tension is apparent in Thomas of Chobham's *Summa for Confessors* (ca. 1216) over the related issue of rendering the debt during holy times. Although he likens such compliance to voluntarily supplying a madman with a sword, he ultimately requires it, claiming that there is no sin in such a rendering.[61] But the anomaly of the sinless performance of a sinful act is queried elsewhere. In this second context, Thomas argues that, while an individual may be credited for the good deed that he or she intended but lacked the opportunity to perform, there is a wider divide between intending and committing a good deed versus an evil deed from the perspective of culpability. He returns to the ethics of the nuptial chamber to demonstrate his point:

> We say therefore that the woman sins in that act by permitting the deed to be done to her. For she ought immediately to reproach her husband and remove his depraved wish. She does not, however, sin as much as the man.[62]

Adjudication of blame between exacting and complying parties also invited infinite nuances. The thirteenth-century theologian Alexander of Hales, for example, is inclined to think that the exacting party commits a mortal sin. (He seems unable to envisage a scenario in which another, more appropriate place cannot be found.)[63] Yet, he introduces additional complexities by isolating critical areas of theoretical dissonance. While Gratian's *Decretum* had implied that all seed polluted in an undifferentiated way, as did blood, Alexander points out that the church is not polluted in quite the same way by husband and wife as by their fornicating counterparts—at least according to some authorities. True, a church sullied by conjugal relations might require reconsecration, but it would not require the ceremony of reconciliation necessitated by adultery or fornication.[64]

Alexander's distinction was not a popular one. Indeed, his fifteenth-century Franciscan confrères, Bernardino of Siena and Cherubino of Spoleto, flatly forbade conjugal sex in holy places precisely because the desecrated spot would require reconciliation.[65] At the same time, the restrictions that these same pastoral advisers attempted to place on married sexuality contribute a degree of plausibility to this exemplum — at least the circumstances, if not the outcome. Both Bernardino and Cherubino emphasize the way in which children are corrupted by the sound of their parents' sexual activity and urge that a private and secret place be found. Indeed Cherubino evokes the law of nature, adducing that all animals seek privacy for the sex act, save for one species of bird, which is indiscreet enough to have intercourse within the nest.[66] Considering the limited opportunities for privacy in the medieval household, an empty church might well beckon.

Thus by the high Middle Ages the increased sensitivity to the conjugal debt, the privileging of intentions, and even a misguided sense of discretion could, in theory, precipitate so disorderly a sex act in a church between a husband and wife. Even so, this act would be in direct conflict with the strictures governing sacrilege. Moreover, this competition between codes would inevitably generate considerable confusion and anxiety in an individual.[67] One can see something of this ambivalence at work in the writings of the great Abelard himself. In his *Ethics,* Abelard discusses the utility of punishing outer acts for the sake of the public good, so the community would not be scandalized by a bad example. But the hypothetical instance he evokes is instructive.

> For let us suppose that someone has corrupted a certain woman by having sexual intercourse in a church. When this has been brought to people's ears, they are disturbed not so much by the violation of a woman and a true temple of God as by the infraction of the physical temple, although it is more serious to take advantage of a woman than of a building.[68]

The logic of his argument implies that, if the act and intentions were licit, the place would be of little consequence. And yet there is an autobiographical dimension to the example. Subsequent to his castration at the behest of his wife's uncle and a precipitous entrance into religion, Abelard silences his estranged wife Heloise's passionate reproaches for his present neglect and anguished reminiscences of their sexual past by reminding her of how their passion for one another led to sacrilege:

> *After our marriage,* when you were living in the cloister with the nuns at Argenteuil and I came one day to visit you privately, you know what my uncontrollable desire did with you there, actually in the corner of the refectory, *since we had no where else to*

go. I repeat, you know how shamelessly we behaved on that occasion in so hallowed a place, dedicated to the most holy Virgin. Even if our other shameful behaviour had ended, this alone would deserve far heavier punishment. (Italics added)[69]

In all likelihood, the personal letters were written in the early 1130s, slightly before the *Ethics*.[70] This presumed sequence might imply that the example from the *Ethics* is introduced to challenge the earlier privileging of pollution fears in the personal letters. Instead, the *Ethics* recognizes that the real transgression was "the violation of a woman and a true temple of God." Abelard's letter condemning their rash act had, after all, contained other painful memories of violation: "Even when you were [sexually] unwilling, resisted to the utmost of your power and tried to dissuade me, as yours was the weaker nature I often forced you to consent with threats and blows."[71] This depiction of the male's aggression effects a dramatic assimilation of two orders of violation: woman and holy site. Indeed, this association, though always hovering at the margins of the topos, possibly gains momentum when applied to married transgressors insofar as the husband was the most obvious beneficiary of the sex-on-demand policy advocated by theoreticians of the conjugal debt.[72]

Yet, in the context of Abelard's letter as a whole, the association of woman and church tends to ratify rather than challenge traditional taboos, thus working against the general tenor of the *Ethics*. And so, rather than indicating a progression in Abelard's thinking, the different emphases of his letter to Heloise and the *Ethics* could mean that Abelard was opportunistically, and perhaps even cynically, prepared to deploy whichever position was best suited to his immediate end. His resurrection of their earlier sacrilege was intended to shock the sensitive Heloise into submissively resigning herself to the religious life, to which she was now committed; alternatively, the quasi-autobiographical episode he evokes in the *Ethics* was a stunning and memorable exemplum that would provide a different kind of shock for his audience.

A third possibility, coexisting with and probably even complementing either of the other two, is that Abelard, though undoubtedly better morally and mentally equipped to grapple with this problem than anyone else, was nevertheless divided. He was no more able to do away with the ambivalence created by the notion of sacrilege than were his peers. And so, while he knew that sins against other human beings, made in God's image and his true temples, were far more grievous than offenses against an inanimate building, he felt otherwise.

Scandal: The Symbiosis of Individual and Community

Given Abelard's probable ambivalence toward the ticklish question of sacrilege, it is not surprising that later thinkers, though quick to emphasize intention in the commission and inner contrition in the forgiveness of sins, developed the external bogeyman of scandal as a potential check against the dangers of license inherent in the mitigating concept of intentionality. The verb *scandalizare* was adapted from the Greek and literally means "to cause to stumble."[73] One who scandalizes occasions sin in another, though the sin may occur unbeknownst to the person who was the purported corruptor, and the words or deeds that occasioned the sin may not be innately sinful.[74] In essence, the concept of scandal is a powerful realization of the ramifications of Christian community and a recognition of the price of interdependence. Scandal is an acknowledgment that a person cannot be assessed in isolation from his or her impact on others. Denis the Carthusian provides a telling illustration of this principle in his simulated confession, cited above. His hypothetical layperson is not only guilty of a wandering and lustful gaze but admits: "Also I showed the pride of my heart, the anger, the concupiscence, the vanity, and dissolution frequently through my gaze, *and so I scandalized others by showing my inner vices on the outside*" (italics added).[75]

There is nothing new about scandal: Christ himself vehemently denounces those who dare to scandalize one of his "little ones" (Matt. 18.6–10). But a quickening interest in scandal is apparent in the canonistic and theological casuistry of the high Middle Ages, and this interest is symptomatic of the age. In a period so clearly preoccupied with individuality, an analysis of scandal could be used as a clue for exploring an individual's responsibility to self, to family, to community.[76] As becomes clear in the work of the casuists, this competing set of priorities was fraught with boundary disputes that generally resisted clear resolutions.

A case in point: what if an individual's ascetical practice, such as fasting or sexual continence, had the potential for scandalizing various members of the community? Should one (or *can* one) cultivate the inner self if this impinges on the spiritual well-being of one's neighbor? In answer to this and like predicaments, the authorities generally urged that God's athlete at times defer, conceal, or even relinquish certain pious acts to avert scandal.[77] Such maneuvering was not only permissible but laudable, provided that truth in life, justice, or doctrine was not jeopardized.[78]

But the possibility of forgoing spiritual benefits on behalf of another conjured up still toothier demons. Should a person commit a venial sin if this would save another from committing a mortal sin? This question automatically evokes some of the treacherous shallows of conjugal relations. Aquinas meets this challenge with a fine bit of prestidigitation: "But this implies contraries. If it really must be done, it is not evil nor a sin, since a sin is not to be chosen."[79]

Finally, one of the most vexing problems of all, destined to baffle confessor and penitent alike, is how to assign penance for a sin that has the potential for scandalizing the community. Thomas of Chobham was especially exercised over this contingency, dedicating the last chapter of his lengthy *Summa for Confessors* to it.

> *Concerning penance for scandal.* For the scandalous sin, moreover, it is burdensome and difficult to enjoin fitting penance, because it scarcely happens that someone sins without scandalizing others through that sin. And often the Lord is more offended through the publication of the sin than through the work of sin, as is read in Jeremiah: *they published their sins just as in Sodom; they published their sins and did not hide them.* For whoever sins in secret kills nothing but his own soul, and perhaps does not offend anyone except God alone. Who, moreover, sins in public kills his own soul and through scandal the souls of others, and perhaps offends the entire church. Thus it behooves him who sins publicly to make much more satisfaction and much more penance should be enjoined on him than if he had sinned in private. Whence the Wiseman says: if you cannot be chaste, be careful.[80]

And so a further twist in the sensitive issue of scandal is that, just as surely as scandal inhibits zealous ascetics from demonstrating the full extent of their spiritual prowess, so it restricts sinners from the salvific act of openly confessing their sins. Furthermore, the advice of the nameless and seemingly proverbial "Wiseman" already anticipates a possible contingency arising from this level of discretion: is the Wiseman concealing his sins out of love for his neighbor or is he guilty of a specious altruism that permits him to play the hypocrite with a clear conscience?

Abelard had already drawn attention to the potential problems of scandal as a controlling factor in the economy of salvation in his *Yes and No* when he asks whether it is better to sin openly or conceal a sin hypocritically. In favor of the secret sin, he cites two passages from Isidore of Seville, both of which invoke biblical authority (Isa. 3.9; Eph. 4.31). But three entries by Augustine, Prosper of Aquitaine, and Jerome utterly condemn such duplicity. Jerome's statement is especially to the point: "In comparing the two sins, it is a lighter sin to sin openly than to dissemble and pretend sanctity."[81] Designed as a workbook for his students, the format of *Yes and No* enabled Abelard to leave the matter unresolved. But in an entirely different venue, a rather sententious poem to his son Astrolabe, Abelard comes down in favor of the secret sin when he urges: "If you cannot be chaste, be careful."[82] And so, it could well be that when invoking the proverbial "Wiseman," Thomas really had Abelard in mind—someone with whom Thomas was acquainted by work and reputation and who knew better than anyone the dangers of being caught *in flagrante* in a scandalous act.[83]

The emphasis on scandal, the way in which it harms the community, and the "altruistic" motives for concealing a sin, would tend to push a matter like secret sacrilege further underground, and this would, in turn, create further ambivalence. And so we return to our initial problem: supposing one was required to pay the conjugal debt in a church. Should one make this information public—thus scandalizing the community—so that the ritual of reconciliation can be performed, or should one hypocritically suppress the offense?

The conflict between hidden and manifest, private and public, good intentions and sacrilegious scandal, corresponds with the distinct pastoral discourses through which the laity would receive their sexual education. The clergy was concerned lest frank preaching on sex have potential for scandal. Thus, explicit information regarding the exigencies of the conjugal debt was generally relegated to the confessional—an exceptionally privileged zone.[84] It was here and only here that the church moved beyond the judgment of external infractions and assumed a limited jurisdiction over the realm of conscience, which in the thirteenth century came to be known as the internal forum. The confessional, as window into the internal forum, was the home of the hidden, the private, the intentional.[85] And it was also here that the astonished penitent might learn that he or she was required to submit to a spouse's sexual overtures in a church. In contrast, the predicament of the adhering couple was designed for sermons delivered in the external forum—the home of the manifest, the public, and, often, the scandalous. Even so, we can see that the two forums were not so separate as to have no effect on one another. The fact that the original fornicators of this topos were gradually being supplanted by a husband and wife team betrays the influence of the confessional discourse that had so earnestly engaged the issue of paying the conjugal debt in a church. The widely disseminated exemplum of Richer and his wife is further premised on the couple's forced residence in a monastery due to persecution by enemies—a situation that seems deliberately reminiscent of learned pretexts for such a payment. Moreover, the irony of this version of the exemplum is highly instructive in that it details a public offense that was, potentially, perpetrated in compliance with the best and most progressive private counsel.

Only divine intervention can heal these fissures in the individual that widen out into the community. Nor does God hang fire. Through a miracle, secret sacrilege is made manifest, thus giving rise to scandal. And so, in the event that the married parishioners were prepared to act on any of the new and frightening options offered to them by progressive theorists, the exemplum, operating as an agent of backlash, is a grim reminder that the old rules live on. In the words of Mary Douglas, "a polluting person is always wrong. He has developed some wrong condition or crossed some line which should not have been crossed and this displacement unleashes danger for someone."[86]

The danger unleashed for the couple is obvious. What becomes equally apparent is the couple's symbiotic relationship with the community. And here we encounter an essential element that spans all the different versions of this story—the emphasis on the community's prolonged gaze. All of the narratives explicitly state that the hapless couple was united long enough for everyone to see them. And so, in a period when advances in theology were progressively encouraging individuals to associate God with the intentions and the inner self, this instance offers an important counterexample by associating the communal gaze with the divine gaze. The community is seeing what, under ordinary circumstances, only God sees—the hidden sin. Moreover, it judges and punishes this offense as God does. The spectacular display of the sinners before the communal gaze is a chastisement that is divinely wrought. But this particular punishment also parallels and dignifies communal practice, which ordains public fustigations in undergarments and similar kinds of ritual humiliation. Finally, the community is complicit with the divine will in its role as witness—the sine qua non for every miracle.

The exemplary reassertion of the errant couple's symbiosis with the community does not end with their spectacular punishment. They can only be released through the prayers of the stunned onlookers, since, according to Christian tradition that can be traced at least as far back as the third-century theologian Origen, sexual intercourse suspends the capacity for prayer.[87] The couple's ill-considered act has unleashed danger for the community as well. But now that the other parishioners have been alerted to the desecration of their church, the building can be properly reconciled. And so, having speciously explored the implications of changing sexual mores for the purpose of dramatically rejecting them, the tale is brought to a close. The couple is unstuck, their offense is purged, and everyone can go home.

4

The Priest's Wife

Female Erasure and the Gregorian Reform

Dullard: Not just now, but a little while ago I heard such things against women in sacred scripture, intended as a warning to the virile sex, [that] my spirit was struck with this doubt: why is the fragile sex not more fortified in sacred letters, so that they may beware the treacheries of men, than the male—who is more constant in spirit? . . .
Theologian: Because [men] are nearer to God in nature and on that account, if defiled, are infected worse.

—John Nider

"Now you'll think I mean to say something insulting, but really I've no such intention." We realize that this is a rejection, by projection, of an idea that has just come up. Or: "You ask who this person in the dream can be. It's *not* my mother." We emend this to: "So it *is* his mother."

—Sigmund Freud[1]

IN THE ELEVENTH CENTURY, the western clergy, Europe's intellectual elite, reinvented itself—an imaginative act necessarily accompanied by efforts to eradicate evidence of past identity. Elites are wont to do this, and, since they command the communicative media with representational authority, they generally succeed. Reinvention is a faltering process, and the result is never seamless. There are always discontinuities, fissures, awkward persistences—historical anomalies that mark the difference between the official story and other rejected versions of the past. The eleventh century, particularly the period from midcentury onward known as the Gregorian Reform, is illustrative of this process in that the very boldness of the clergy's imaginative exercises left so palpable a residue of unwanted truths. Moreover, these remnants seem to coalesce around and reanimate arguably the most compelling, but certainly the most poignant, instance of historical detritus from this period: the priest's wife. From the eleventh century onward, she would haunt the church's official story. She is with us still.

In this and the following chapter, I consider the priest's wife, both for her own sake and as a figure and stand-in for all those mundane, particularly sexually active, women who imperil sacerdotal and ritual purity. The very success of the Gregorian Reform makes the ordinary woman suspect in this generalized sense. Even as carnal woman may be construed as representing a rejected option for the clergy, the Virgin Mary is introduced as her purified substitute. Thus in the course of these chapters, the designation of priest's wife (i.e., rejected womanhood), though constantly mutating to include categories like the saint or the witch, is also applied specifically to the clerical concubine. These different avatars are unified by the distinctly female threat they present to sacerdotal ambitions, which in the aftermath of the reform will be most clearly symbolized in the cult around the Eucharist.

The conditions responsible for the spectralization of the priest's wife are well known. The reforming clergy wished to sever itself from and, in so doing, to raise itself above, lay society. The establishment of clerical celibacy as a mark of both difference and superiority was central to this project and part of a larger program to reify binaries such as clerical/lay, celibate/married, male/female.[2] These ends were, in part, achieved by a remarkable spate of pollution-laden rhetoric unequaled in the previous history of the western church and probably never matched in subsequent centuries.[3] The reformers needed every bit of the assistance that a heated polemic might confer: the delegitimization of clerical marriage, and its ultimate outlawing, constituted a formidable task that meant meddling with a long tradition.[4] Even though the church had never been comfortable with such unions, clerical marriage was nevertheless tolerated until the mid-eleventh century. While a priest was officially forbidden to marry after ordination, the marriage was still valid should he do so. Priests who were married at the time of ordination, on the other hand, were theoretically required to abstain sexually from their wives. But some of the most authoritative canons of the church forbade the married priest to separate from his wife, lest she be left destitute.[5]

The measures taken against clerical wives in and after the eleventh century were severe in the extreme: some canons went so far as to suggest enslavement.[6] But considering the number of married clergy and their vigorous resistance to the new order—resistance that is described in detail for cities such as Milan—the success of the program was quite remarkable.[7] This is certainly true for the long term. Studies such as Christopher

Brooke's examination of church disciplinary activities show that clerical marriage was effectively stamped out in such backwaters of reform as England by the end of the twelfth century.[8] But even in the short run, it is uncanny how the wives contemporary with the Gregorian Reform seem to have melted away. Where they went has been the subject of some historical speculation. The little bit we know about the actual women who were repudiated and disinvested is largely guesswork: thus Georges Duby and Jo Ann McNamara speculate that such women became a part of the growing number of rootless poor, while the mysterious "prostitutes" described amid the entourage of itinerant preachers such as Robert of Arbrissel may be a shorthand for rejected clerical wives.[9]

The most frequently avowed reason for suppressing the clerical wife was that her sexual presence polluted the minister of the altar. The frequently withheld reason was that she was a drain on church resources and her children would entail the alienation of church property.[10] Yet her potential for disturbing the symbolic order far transcended ritual or even economic concerns, striking at the heart of the reformers' classificatory system that was so essential to church hierarchy. Aspects of this particular transgression were consciously acknowledged. Thus Peter Damian, for example, wrote to Countess Adelaide of Savoy that God recognizes only three kinds of women: virgins, wives, and widows. Women who do not fit into one of these categories—and he argues that the clerical wife does not—do not arrive in God's presence.[11]

But the clerical wife's potential boundary crossing can clearly be pushed much farther than Damian's familiar triune division of women. As anthropologist Mary Douglas has so deftly demonstrated, the animals perceived as abominations in the Book of Leviticus are precisely those creatures that transgress against apprehended divisions among species: things that live in the sea, but crawl; animals with cloven feet that refuse to chew their cud like the "clean" animals of the flock.[12] The priest's wife is a vivid representation of this kind of anomaly—numerically squared and historically writ large—precisely because her mixed, hybrid, "impossible" status is ambiguous in a way that reveals the seams in classificatory categories. At a time when reformers were insisting on a strict division between clergy and laity,[13] she defies both categories as being neither entirely lay nor fully clerical. From ancient times she was referred to as *presbyteria* or *sacerdotissa*, and according to some rites even received a distinct garb and special blessing at the time of her husband's ordination.[14] She wobbles between heretical and orthodox, depending on the ideology of whoever apprehends her.[15] To the reformers she was the image of overcranked lust;[16] to those opposing the reform she was the mainstay of clerical domestic economy.[17] In the event that she and her husband abstained sexually upon his ordination, in accordance with the disciplinary requirements of the early church, she hovers somewhere between marriage and celibacy. If sexually active, she was perceived as incestuous due to her relationship with her spiritual father—the priestly husband.[18] Though ineffaceably female, she nevertheless challenges prescribed gender separation by her invasion of sacred space, now being rigorously redefined as masculine.[19] Her domination of her husband through money and sex was perceived as threatening to masculine ascendancy.[20] Moreover, as a result of reform measures, she takes a frightening status dive from respectable wife to concubine or whore in a relatively brief period, as do her children, who go from legitimate heirs to disinherited bastards.[21]

In the eleventh century she was already a living artifact attesting to an earlier truth—dangerous detritus ripe for disavowal. Thus she came to epitomize all of the practices that were targeted by the reformers in the course of this ideological struggle. In the reformers' very vehemence in disowning her, however, they frequently overstepped themselves, betraying some of their worst fears about the faith—often through enumerating aspects of the perceived threats she presented in an incomplete or unsuccessful effort to vanquish them. Therefore the priest's wife, as historical remainder or, to use my earlier image, as specter, deserves special notice for her capacity to unsettle the history of the western church. Not only is she a remembrance of what the church would like to forget but she also acts as a mechanism for eliciting threatening subtexts that the reformers would have consciously disowned.

Thus, even if the historical wives of priests have been effectively erased, I would nevertheless argue that their image remains as a kind of shadow text in a badly executed palimpsest, as does the historical problem they present. The clerical wife's downward-shifting social trajectory and the conflicted positions she was forced to assume unleashed anxieties that challenged the very core of Christian doctrine. These anxieties were fought and temporarily abetted by a theological focus on the material presence in the sacrament of the altar and the rise of the cult of the Virgin Mary. And yet the same fears would persist long after the occasion for their appearance had been officially banished. It is by following the trail of negation, disavowal, and doubt that the threatening image of the priest's wife, relegated to an effaced subtext, may be rendered historically visible.

St. Severus and the Reiterative Swerve

Polemical works denouncing clerical marriage in general or clerical wives in particular abound for the eleventh century and are doubtless the most direct route for identifying the kinds of anxieties identified above. But before exploring some of these possibilities I would like to consider sources that do not announce their interest—particularly renarrations of the past. A successful renarration wrought by the reforming camp would aspire to neutralize disavowed truths, discrediting them or delimiting their power to persuade. Alternatively, it would provide an opportunity to stabilize clerical identity by reiterating carefully chosen truths in a way that effaced or overwhelmed alternative possibilities. And yet, such efforts at containment or effacement are bound to fail at their intended purpose. This contemporary truism, so frequently associated with a postmodern sensibility, was already a factor in Freud's analysis. Thus he described how a patient's defense mechanisms can be duped into reinstating repressed symptoms, characterizing this self-defeating response as "a good example of the rule that in time the thing which is meant to be warded off invariably finds its way into the very means which is being used for warding it off." The act of reiteration renders itself complicit with this reappearance, since its inevitable lapses, slips, and dodges open spaces within which the repressed can make a comeback. Controlled repetition is thus an impossible proposition. Foreign or repressed elements are introduced unwittingly, engendering a dangerous swerve from the professed telos.[22]

Around the year 1070, at the very height of reforming ardor, two contemporary authors chose to renarrate the story of the fourth-century St. Severus of Ravenna, who was not simply purported to be a married priest but a married archbishop.[23] From a small but distinguished cohort of saintly married clerics, only Severus attracted authorial interest as a married priest during the period of the Gregorian Reform.[24] His memory is more encumbered with the basic furniture of historicity than is the case with many of his celestial peers. He was present at the Council of Sardica (342) and underwrote its constitutions. He is depicted in Justinian's mosaics in St. Apollinare in Classe. His name also appears in the earliest martyrologies.[25]

The first attempt at any sort of vita for Severus seems to have been Agnellus's *Pontifical Book of the Church of Ravenna,* written between 830 and 832, which was the font for subsequent eleventh-century recastings of Severus's life.[26] The work as a whole is understandable in terms of the author's pride in Ravenna's unique ecclesiastical history, which distinguished it from the other archbishoprics of western Europe. Ravenna had been the headquarters of Byzantine rule in Italy. Although definitely part of the Latin as opposed to the Greek church, for some time it was outside of the Germanic orbit. This changed when Ravenna was invaded by the Lombards in 751, soon to be reconquered by Pepin and given to the pope in about 754—a bequest that was confirmed by Charlemagne. Even so, the archbishops of Ravenna resisted any implication of subservience to Rome, while Agnellus himself exhibited hostility to Rome throughout his history.[27]

At the time that Agnellus wrote, Europe was experiencing an early series of attacks on clerical marriage under the auspices of the Carolingian Reform. Even Ravenna, with its relatively worldly clergy and its tradition of separateness from Rome, must have felt these tremors. Agnellus, though by no means a reformer himself, was seemingly aware of the ways in which the perceived decadence of the Ravennese clergy could further imperil its tenuous independence. He thus pays lip service to reform-inflected rhetoric when he criticizes the decadence of Ravenna's bishops—accusing them of hawking, singing dirty songs, and even driving priests away from their sacramental duties in church.[28] Agnellus is also attuned to the particular sensitivity of the subject of clerical marriage throughout his history, and he does his best to make any instances conform to the most estimable prototypes. In addition to Severus, the first instance Agnellus discusses, he recounts the pontificates of two other bishops who were at some point married: Agnellus (556/557–569/570) and Sergius XL (ordained between 742 and 752). With respect to Bishop Agnellus, his chronicler-namesake is careful to underline that the bishop's wife had died before her husband was ordained deacon.[29] Even so, our chronicler is conscious that the mere mention of a bishop ever having been married still had the capacity to confound. He thus goes on to muse that one naturally wonders how a married man managed to secure such a prestigious position in the church, using this rhetorical occasion to remind his audience of the apostle's ordinance that a bishop may be married once (1 Tim. 3.2). That the matter had not yet been brought to satisfactory closure and continued to rankle is suggested by Agnellus's promise to return to the question of clerical wives — a promise that he does not actually keep.[30]

According to Agnellus's testimony, Bishop Sergius, the other married bishop, had his wife ordained as a deaconess at the time of his elevation. We are even told that she remained in her habit for the rest of her life.[31] Despite this precaution, the account of Sergius's turbulent reign demonstrates Agnellus's awareness of just how irregular it was for a layman to be directly elevated to bishop in the eighth century — even with the vow of chastity implicit in the wife's reception of the veil. Bishop Sergius was, as we learn, imprisoned by the pope, who questioned him closely about his marital status in an attempt to strip him of his title.[32] Agnellus's sensitivity on this score is even more apparent in a telling omission. He suppresses altogether from his narrative a second and failed attempt to elect a layperson as bishop, which occurred immediately after the reign of Sergius.[33]

Thus Agnellus was very much aware of clerical marriage, not simply as an undifferentiated issue in the wider context of clerical corruption, but as a singular problem that in recent history had threatened the independence of the entire Ravennese church. His treatment of Severus's life imbibes these tensions. From a chronological and narrative standpoint, the account anticipates and prepares the way for the discussion of the other married bishops. The very fact that Severus was a married bishop who was actually honored as a saint serves as a tacit exoneration of the later married incumbents, particularly the beleaguered Sergius, whose sudden elevation from layman was exactly parallel to that of Severus.

Yet Agnellus's treatment of Severus, while in a certain sense capitalizing on his sainthood, does not conform to the typical chronological progression of hagiography; instead he prefers an idiosyncratic structure better suited to his purpose of acknowledging yet ultimately assuaging the sense of the wife as threat or problem. The events of Severus's life are related through a series of marvels.[34] These amount to a mere four and are treated in the following order: a mystical ecstasy, which Severus undergoes while performing Mass, during which time he attends the burial of his colleague Bishop Geminiano; a miracle at the funeral of his daughter, Innocentia; his marvelous death;[35] and his heavenly election as bishop. With the exception of the ecstasy, his wife, Vincentia, plays a crucial role in these miracles. In fact, it is no exaggeration to say that she is at the center of his holy repertoire.

At the time of the miracle at the burial of the daughter, the first in Agnellus's triad of conjugal miracles, his wife Vincentia is already dead and buried in the family tomb. When the tomb is opened for the daughter Innocentia's burial, the bystanders advise Severus that there is insufficient room in the grave. Severus tearfully reproaches his wife:

> "O woman, why do you trouble me? Why don't you make a place for your daughter? Acknowledge what you carried, what was taken from your flesh; don't hesitate to receive her. Look, I entrust to you what you gave to me. Don't be stupid: from whence she came, she returned. Make room for her burial. Don't make me sad."[36]

This rather sharp address is not without effect. Vincentia's bones move with such great speed "that living bodies of humans can scarcely move faster," and the funeral proceeds apace.[37]

Severus's abrasive, even hectoring, tone is revealing, as is the source of his exasperation. The wife, even in death, is portrayed as taking up too much space. Her body's awkward over-presence may be understood in the context of external events that were transforming the clerical wife into a spiritual embarrassment. And this is implied in Agnellus's narration. The possible prototypes for this kind of miracle may be used as a gauge to measure the extent of uxorial angst.

First, there is Gregory the Great's story of a monk who is informed he will die and promptly begins digging his grave. When the abbot of the community sickens and bespeaks a place in the monk's grave, the monk at first refuses on the grounds of insufficient room. Although the abbot assures him that they will both fit, when the tomb is opened for the monk's funeral there is not enough space. When one of the monks acting as pallbearer calls out, " 'Father Abbot, what of your promise that the grave would hold both of you?' " the body immediately turns on its side. If this was Agnellus's source, the attending monk's exasperation with the deceased abbot, now magnified in Severus's vita, was transferred to the deceased wife—which is significant in itself.[38] But if Agnellus was familiar with the graveside miracles related by Gregory of Tours, the exasperation expressed is even more at odds with his prototype—which was meant to emphasize the spiritual solidarity of the couple. According to Gregory of Tours, at the funeral of Riticius, a confessor saint, the recently dead husband revives just long enough to remind his long-dead wife of his promise (which he made in response to her tearful entreaties) that they should be buried together, using the most gentle address. Her body immediately moves to accommodate him.[39]

In the account of the death of Severus himself, the third marvel, Agnellus revisits the posthumous site of ambivalent family values, correcting (or at least containing) the saint's fractious tone. The bishop is celebrating Mass and, just after receiving the body and blood of Christ, gives orders for the family sepulcher to be opened. Wearing his pontifical stole, Severus enters the grave, lies between his wife and his daughter, and orders the seal to be replaced. Then, while in prayer, he expires.[40]

The final marvel, chronologically prior to these earlier miracles, is couched in the events surrounding his election to office. Severus, we now learn, was a humble weaver of wool. When it came time to elect a new bishop of Ravenna, he told his wife that he wished to be present in order to witness the predictable miracle that attended the appointment of all archbishops of Ravenna: a dove would descend from heaven and alight on the head of the bishop elect.[41] Vincentia's response is scornful: "'Sit here and work; don't be so lazy. Whether you go or not, the people won't make you bishop. Get back to work.'"[42] When Severus persists, his wife changes the direction of her sarcastic sallies, replying that he is sure to be made bishop as soon as he arrives. Vincentia's words prove an ironic prophecy. Although Severus hides behind the doors to conceal his filthy clothes, the dove alights on his head, not once but three times. "'When she heard what she had recently derided, she then rejoiced over him.'"[43] She had, after all, predicted his unlikely triumph.

By breaking with a normative temporal flow in his arrangement of the miracles, Agnellus has effectively foregrounded the wife as a disturbing surplus. And yet his idiosyncratic chronology also seems to have been governed by a desire to lead with the miracle that incorporates, and therefore anticipates, the other two in his narrative. Thus at the burial of Innocentia, the harsh words of Severus to the troublesome remains of his wife serve as a tacit response to her jibes on the day of his election—though this becomes clear only later. Her body's ready obedience, moreover, suggests that she has learned due conjugal submission. The image of mother and daughter at rest in the collective tomb anticipates the death of Severus himself. Any efforts to reconstruct the reasons behind this ordering of events are necessarily very tentative. But it is doubtless significant that Agnellus begins with the episode that literally and symbolically buries wife and daughter—those two most awkward vestiges of Severus's earlier life, which are causally and, in this instance, spatially linked. Indeed the daughter, the most significant fruit of the fraught union, is only mentioned in this anecdote—seemingly introduced into the narrative for the sole purpose of being buried. In a similar vein, it is extremely appropriate that the wife's body is immediately problematized for its recalcitrance in the first marvel. And yet, there can be little doubt that by putting Severus's acerbic remarks first and Vincentia's shrewish behavior on the day of his election last, by the time we reach the chronologically prior but sequentially later episode, the harsh contours of uxorial reproach are softened considerably. From this perspective, conjugal quarrels on either side of the grave ultimately neutralize each other in this interesting triptych. Similarly, the tensions surrounding the clerical wife as a constituted problem are confronted and then dispelled. What remains at the center and also, in many ways, central to this account is the image of peace when the family is finally reunited in death.

Agnellus does not discuss the necessary transition to chastity that a sudden elevation to bishop would entail. As in the instance of Sergius XL, whose ordination corresponded to his wife's consecration as deaconess, the transition from wife to sister is formulaic and goes without saying.[44] But the Frankish monk Liudolph, writing shortly after 858, who recounts the illicit translation of Severus's relics to Germany at the hands of a thief who specialized in relics, recognizes an affirmative possibility for emphasizing the transition to chastity and seizes upon it. Upon hearing about the election of Severus, both daughter and wife assume veils: the former's signifying virginity, the latter's signifying widowhood. That these symbols of sexual abstinence do not mark the separation of domiciles is evident from Liudolph's account of the death of Severus. In a conflation of the miracle at the daughter's funeral with the events surrounding the bishop's own demise, Liudolph omits Severus's rancorous words to his wife, preferring a gentler address directed to both wife and daughter: "'Give me space for sleeping with you so that those who lived in this world in common may also use a common grave.'"[45] This rerendering also conveys a suppressed truth that was latent in Agnellus's account: that the wife was where she should be—however awkwardly and embarrassingly so—as was her offspring. The husband's place was with them.

Liudolph's account is based on his own inquiries in Italy, where he was at pains to understand the history behind the new relics just acquired. Never doubting that Germany was the beneficiary of not just one, but a conjugal cluster of saints, Liudolph attempted to learn from his informant, a monk at Classis, the actual feast days for the two holy women. The answer was disappointing: due to the various invasions, the precise dates for the deaths of mother and daughter were forgotten, so they were commemorated at the same time as Severus. But at least this confirmed the existence of a modest cult for mother and daughter alike. And the group commemoration underscored clerical marriage as the mechanism of sanctification. In other words, this dubious conjugal unit was still in the ninth century a potential springboard into grace.

The accounts of both Agnellus and Liudolph present a compelling picture of sacerdotal conjugality according to the old school: a carnal union transformed into a spiritual marriage; a familial grave; graveside miracles projecting the continuation of the marriage bond beyond the grave;[46] a bishop completing Mass and descending into the grave to join his family in pontifical garb; a nuclear family achieving sainthood. For the latter part of the eleventh century, this was undoubtedly volatile subject matter in uneasy times and thus required concerted efforts at stabilization and control. In addition to an anonymous life, probably written by a monk of Classis, two sermons were dedicated to Severus by Peter Damian, one of the spearheads of papal reform.[47] Clearly both authors had a particular investment in the saint's patronage. The monastery not only bore the saint's name but still continued to claim his relics.[48] In contrast, Peter Damian was born in Ravenna and took every opportunity to praise his native city, writing sermons to commemorate several of its archbishops.[49] But whatever degree of personal investment can be reconstructed on behalf of these authors, one of the factors encouraging a reconsideration of Severus was doubtless his marital condition. The fact that the spirited wife was something of a thorn in the bishop's flesh was especially apposite in this time of extraneous wives.

The anonymous author rearranges the four marvels at the heart of Severus's life chronologically, but otherwise conforms closely to Agnellus's rendition. Nevertheless, whatever clarity a chronological structure might impart to the narrative is ultimately undercut by the texture of the vita in its entirety. The account of the saint's life is sandwiched between an introductory chapter treating Severus's fatherland, marriage, and work in general terms and two concluding chapters—appropriately rubricated as "digressions." The life as a whole, but especially these three sections framing its particulars, are ideological minefields, riven by the author's diatribes against imaginary foes, thus ultimately creating a troubled and self-interrupting narrative. For instance, the introductory chapter discusses Ravenna's venerable tradition of divine election through the descent of the dove, a sign associated with the city's first twelve pontiffs. But this symbol of grace sets the stage for a gratuitious denunciation of simony and the contemporary traffic in ecclesiastical offices.[50] The later account of Severus's election proper likewise prompts a lively attack on those who criticize monks who preach—the connecting link allegedly being that both Severus and the monks are, in the author's eyes, enabled by the principle of divine election. These two areas of concern—certainly the question of simony but also the defense of uppity monks—would ostensibly mark the author as a supporter of aspects of the reform.[51] And yet a third, and certainly the most obsessive, area for self-interruption concerns the question of Severus's marriage. Here our author seems to break with any distinct reform platform.[52]

The author's tirades on marriage frame, but do not intrude on, the central events of Severus's life. The introductory chapter blends the saint's commendable poverty (deduced by the fact that he ate by the labor of his own hands) with his marriage.

In this spot if any supercilious individual with an enigmatic mind and tasteless objection detracts from the holy man because he was married when he acceded to the archbishopric of Ravenna, let him hear the Apostle responding on that. That all things are pure to the pure [Rom. 14.20]. Therefore just as the eating of foods does not pollute a man unless that schemer (*insidiatrix*) concupiscence precedes, so indeed legal marriage does not pollute the Christian who in no wise binds himself by a vow of virginity or continence, unless earlier that deceptress (*deceptrix*) desire (*libido*) corrupts by the foment of obscene love. But if anyone is bound by a vow, he is compelled to render; in which place it is written, Vow and render [Ps. 75.12].[53]

The vow clearly alludes to the conjugal debt, which is premised on Paul's insistence that husband and wife do not have autonomous control over their own bodies but must submit to the other's sexual demands (1 Cor. 7.4). In other words, the purity of Severus's life is warrant against the potentially dangerous pleasures inherent in eating and sex—two activities that were related in ascetical tradition and in the minds of contemporaries.[54]

The digression immediately following the events of Severus's life proper extends the premise animating the author's exculpation of a married person who accedes to a bishopric on the basis of the inherent purity of the individual. This principle, still guided by the metaphor of ingestion, is applied not only as a commendation of Severus's purity but also as a condemnation of his potential critics — now designated as heretics.

> Indeed no place of remonstrance is left to the heretics who judge Severus, the blessed of the Lord, that to be tied in marriage is to the dishonor of the church. Each one covered in the feces of their own obscenity, they are ignorant of the grace of the Holy Spirit, who do not recognize it in others in any way because they feel [it] so little in themselves. If a person therefore never will have tried the taste of honey, he does not know of its savor in any way. But against those who use wormwood alone, neglecting other herbs, the bitter seems to them excessively sweet and they imagine the other herbs to be equally bitter on account of their inexperience with its taste.[55]

The author goes on to affirm the goodness of marriage when used legitimately. Moreover, he contends that the singular purity of Severus anticipated his selection by the Holy Spirit's descent in the form of the dove and that this event, in turn, confirmed his preexisting purity. His state of innocence is likened to the prelapsarian sexuality of Adam and Eve before shame entered the world — a guarantee against incorrect usage.

> And so blessed Severus with his dove-like eyes looking on all the works of God, also understood marriage to be especially good, if someone used it legitimately; because if it were not good, woman would never have been created as helpmate by God. . . . Indeed the first couple lost these eyes, when completing their prevarication, they were abandoned by God, and the eyes of both were opened. After, moreover, they lost these eyes of doves, they blushed immediately; because death entered through the windows of the carnal eyes.[56]

This evocation of the fall, particularly the traditional association between sex and death, would have been an unmitigated indictment of marriage if Severus was not proof of the reversibility of this gloomy sentence. In his pristine state with his dovelike innocence, Severus is likened to a child who has yet to learn shame: "For he does not blush at his members . . . thinks nothing unchaste; desires no illicit things because the Holy Spirit who inhabits him, who keeps him with an uncorrupted mind, knew nothing of these things."[57]

Thus was the enviable condition of Severus before, during, and presumably after marriage. To be sure, the author ultimately backs away from his potentially daring contention regarding the innocence of correct usage in marriage, which if followed to its logical conclusion would challenge any moral argument for clerical celibacy. Instead, he proceeds to acknowledge that Severus's marriage preceded his election to the bishopric, after which his wife was turned into a sister, as was the case with the apostle Peter.[58] Even so, an argument for the possibility of purity in a sexually active marriage is still implicitly advanced. Thus the final digression again emphasizes that Severus's eventual transition to chastity was anticipated by his high degree of continence in marriage—a claim vindicated by the dove's miraculous election: "That we may confess the truth that the chastity and continence [of Severus] existed before the Episcopacy, the Holy Spirit itself clearly demonstrated through the dove in the election, which flew over many Priests and Deacons and assigned its beloved an inner place within itself."[59] The miracle he performed at his daughter's funeral when he ordered his wife's body to one side is then interpreted as alluding to both his past married life and its chaste terminus:

> The most Holy Pontiff of his church seems secretly [*latenter*] to satisfy his earlier reputation as husband. . . . For it is believed that he remembered his earlier pristine life, when it is read that he was bound in marriage by Christian license. That, moreover, he ordered with so imperious an authority that the body of his dead wife bent itself to the side clearly shows how secure he was from her touch, after he was made Bishop.[60]

The word "secretly," of course, speaks volumes. Even in the case of this near-apologist, an admission of the need for secrecy and discretion (and hence an acknowledgment of difficult external circumstances) slips in. In fact, most of the turbulence of these various renditions results from this fitfully acknowledged aspect of "his earlier reputation as husband."

The monk of Classis displays no absolute political agenda on clerical marriage. Certainly he is supportive of aspects of the contemporary reform movement, as his condemnation of simony would suggest. But his possible resistance to the position that the reformers took with respect to clerical marriage can be gleaned, I would argue, from the rhetorical targeting of his fictive heretics. There had been heretics in the early eleventh century who claimed that all marriage was evil. These groups had, however, long disappeared, their zeal for purity having seemingly been absorbed by the reforming platform.[61] The opponents that the anonymous author is instead addressing are probably the ideologues who permitted (and sometimes even abetted) the riots against married priests and ordered the laity to boycott their masses. Yet the anonymous author's main strategy against his imagined heretics was to exaggerate their position by implying that their rigid standards would necessarily condemn a worthy saint like Severus — a rather confused rearguard action. And so, given that Bishop Ulric of Imola had actually written a treatise demanding the instant legalization of clerical marriage around this time, the monk of Classis's approach seems rather timid.[62]

Consciously or not, the monk of Classis had positioned himself at a couple of junctures to make a meaningful intervention in the debate, if he had so chosen. The application of "all things are pure to the pure" to the married condition resonates with unrealized revolutionary content. Historical hindsight also teaches us what the author's emphasis on election might imply or to what it might have been applied. In addition to his contention that certain monks are elected to preach, the monk of Classis also argues that Severus was divinely elected to the bishopric as a married man, while many (chaste) clerics were passed over. Writing in about 1100, at least several decades after our hagiographer, the Norman Anonymous, certainly the most original and defiant defender of clerical marriage, had insisted that only the Holy Spirit made priests on the basis of divine election — a contention with extreme predestinary overtones. Disciplinary considerations, like chastity, were thus void.[63]

The overall impression that the anonymous life of Severus leaves is one of agitation and confusion. The author's dueling with imagined foes detracts from the image of conjugal sanctity at the center of the earlier narratives. Although the impulse to apologize for Severus's married state is certainly one of the factors that provoked the monk of Classis to write, his defense is, nevertheless, indirect rather than frontal — sacrificing the wife by relegating her to relative obscurity, rather than upholding her position and *fama*. For not only does the anonymous author fail to acknowledge the ancient cults of mother and daughter, but he even suppresses the mother's name altogether.[64] Certainly, it was in keeping with the spirit of the age to downplay female sanctity, since in this period of reform the number of female saints plummeted to an all-time low. And the claims of a clerical wife must, necessarily, have been worse than negligible.[65]

If the position of the anonymous monk of Classis remains elliptical, Peter Damian's is clear. He was one of the major ideologues for the papal reform movement.[66] At papal behest, he undertook a mission to Milan directed against the married and simoniac priests. He was also active against married clergy in other cities, such as Lodi.[67] His virulent criticism of clerical marriage is well attested in his writings.[68] Indeed, the priest's wife seems to have occupied a special place in Damian's psychological development. According to his biographer, John of Lodi, Damian owed his life to the wife of a priest, since his mother, suffering from postpartum depression, initially refused to care for the infant Peter until a neighboring priest's wife intervened and began nursing the baby herself. Lester Little alerts us to the fact that this story could be apocryphal: that the child succored by a priest's wife would live to be the scourge of clerical marriage perhaps smacks of too literary a type of ironic symmetry to be entirely credible. If this be the case, John's invention backfired in certain ways. When characterizing the intervention of Damian's benefactress, he describes her as "the wife of a priest who performed the office of a priest when she softened the maternal disposition to piety." This is a strange slip for the biographer and disciple of a man who denied the legitimacy of such marriages, one that made the editor of Damian's vita in *Patrologia Latina*, the venerable Dom. J.-P. Migne, scramble for cover. Migne hastily attached a footnote to John's overgenerous designation, remarking that elsewhere the priest's wife is referred to as "the sinful little woman" (*peccatrix muliercula*). This is a modest reminder of the *presbyteria*'s capacity to warp the woof of any text. Again we see that, in the act of evoking her in order to contain her, John cannot unsay what he has said: the genie is out of the bottle and impossible to put back.[69]

Of particular interest is Damian's own account of the lasting impression he received from a clerical couple who lived next to him during his student days in Parma. The woman was "of lewd appearance, alluring in her shameless beauty."[70] The priest was a jolly man, well dressed, with a fine singing voice. This attractive couple filled their days with laughter and joking.

> From these passionate and abandoned goings-on, I could not distance myself mentally, because I was so physically near them. What could I do, since as I saw all this happening, I was so tempted by sexual excitement, that even after I came to the hermitage, the memory of this alluring scene often attacked me? I must confess that frequently the devilish enemy flashed these images before my eyes and tried to persuade me that people who live such delightful lives are the most happy and fortunate. But now that I have told of the beginning of this merry affair, let me also report on how it ended. . . . After they had lived together in such wanton pleasure for almost twenty-five years, they were found in the house, dying together in the flames. And thus the heat of passion gained for them a fiery holocaust.[71]

Damian's description of their death constitutes a deliberately inverted hagiography. Whereas the handful of married saints of the early church are frequently perceived as having achieved salvation through a shared martyrdom, anticipated in the common life of their carnal marriage, the united death of the priest and his wife leads only to perpetual damnation — again a projection of their sinful carnal union.[72]

In short, far from becoming the object of gratitude (if we believe the infancy narrative) or sympathy, the priest's wife emerged as a target for Damian's most intense hostility — a hostility exacerbated when the priest's wife rose unbidden to his thoughts as "the devilish enemy flashed these images before [his] eyes." Damian, a man who by his own admission experienced extreme agitation at the sight of a pretty woman even when he was no longer young, compared the way he guarded his eyes from young women with how children are kept from fire[73] — an evocative image considering his memory of the fire in Parma. His monastic conversion occurred around the age of twenty-eight, long after his adolescence in Parma.[74] Since he spent a number of years as a secular cleric, a wife would necessarily represent a rejected alternative in a way that she would not be for someone who had entered a monastery as a child oblate. Damian's own agony over the apparent felicity of the clerical couple attests to this. His commitment to celibacy was seemingly renewed with every vituperative return to the clerical wife in his writings, the only occasion on which he permitted himself consciously to evoke her otherwise banished image.

But, in addition to his interest in Severus and his leading role in the attack on clerical marriage, Damian was possessed of certain personality foibles that fostered inadvertent self-revelation. At one point he claims to write "that I might restrain my wandering and lascivious mind with a leash."[75] Elsewhere he admits that he was especially prone to the vice of scurrility — a proclivity for excessive, buffoonish, and perhaps even prurient talk. Through ascetical practices, such as flagellation, he could temporarily repress (*reprimere*) his scurrility but could never entirely conquer it.[76] Damian's verbal excesses, spurred by the release he found in writing, constitute an imaginary archive of things better left unsaid as well as things just barely left unsaid.

If the reality of the priest's wife of Parma was too appealing, the specter of Severus's sharp-tongued wife would be irresistible to Damian, given his personal polemical needs. Indeed, in the first of his two sermons on Severus, Vincentia receives pride of place, though once again her name is suppressed. Damian begins this sermon with a reminder that Severus's feast day corresponds with the presentation of Christ in the temple—an event recalling that original act of humility, the incarnation, which enabled humanity's subsequent elevation. The theme of the sermon is thus that those who humble themselves shall be exalted (Luke 18.14).[77] Embarking on a terse recapitulation of the events occurring on the day of the election, Damian presents Severus as an exemplar of this salubrious humility. His general poverty, lowly occupation, and squalid clothes all testify to this virtue.[78] But it is particularly the curmudgeonly wife who permits him to exercise his preeminent forbearance.

Severus is described as being contented with the humble, even the womanly job of wool worker (*muliebri contentus officio*). He chose it as an opportunity to cultivate charity between himself and his wife, since by sharing the same work there would be no disparity between them. When she repaid him with biting words, he answered with the mildness of a dove. Nor did he seek to avenge himself, as would be in keeping with the power that he, as husband, rightfully exercised over his wife. Instead, he bore in mind the apostolic injunction to love his wife and not behave harshly to her (Col. 3.19). Moreover, through a peculiar application of Paul's formulation of the conjugal debt (1 Cor. 7.4)—a citation almost invariably reserved for sexual prerogative in marriage—Damian emphasized that Severus did not act as if he possessed autonomy over his person but only departed to witness the election of the new bishop after his wife had given her begrudging permission.[79] In a burst of warm adulation, Damian invites his monastic audience to admire a man who, though able to be stubborn with any man, humbly obeys a subject woman; who, though capable of rendering evil for evil, tolerates his wife's jibes with equanimity; who would avenge himself against those who harmed him, but not against his wife.[80]

Even as the long-suffering and feminized husband is presented as a vessel of grace, so the outspoken and domineering wife is described as an explicit agent of the devil.

> For the ancient enemy—who was not able to provoke him to impatience by poverty, affliction of hard work, nor from the deformity of mean clothing—kindled the mind of the wife to inflicting abusive words and stimulated her tongue to the injury of biting rebukes.[81]

The stellar resistance of Severus is likened to a noble edifice besieged, which a hostile impetus cannot overthrow. Because the devil finds Severus virtually impregnable, he needs steps. Thus the devil uses the woman as a ladder to assail the husband's heart. Again, through a specious use of scripture, Severus is described as rebuffing his wife's jibes by theoretically attending to the prohibition of women teaching (1 Tim. 2.12).[82] And so the devil, who had conquered Adam, loses to this humble woolworker. The devil, moreover, is foiled, since he inadvertently set the wife—the flawed helpmate whom he had kindled to the abuse of bitter rebuke—on the path to learning patience. Moreover, Damian's use of the possessive pronoun in "his own helpmate" (*adiutricem suam*) of itself creates doubt. While one assumes that the wife is Severus's helpmate in keeping with the designation of Eve in Genesis, "his own helpmate" could also be read as the devil's own helpmate. In fact, this latter reading, arguably more correct grammatically, is also vindicated by context.[83] The biblical patriarchs Job and Tobias are then invoked, since they too had successfully withstood the taunts of their evil-minded wives. Yet, in balance, Damian grants that there is a certain ironic justice in this uxorial scourge, since Adam should never have listened to Eve in the first place.[84]

Damian's treatment of Vincentia certainly counteracted the allure of the priest's wife in Parma. But there was a danger in going too far, especially considering that Vincentia was (or had been) honored as a saint in some circles. Thus Damian winds up:

> But we do not say these things so that we may assert that the wife of the holy man perished with her womanly reproaches. For if he knew that she were excluded from the destiny of the elect, by no means would the man filled with the Holy Spirit wish to share a tomb with her. Their common burial indicates that a diversity of merits does not distinguish the souls of the blessed spouses.[85]

This delightfully grudging compromise nevertheless grants what Damian has hitherto only affirmed through negation—a process memorably captured by Freud in the present chapter's epigraph. Damian's suppressed truth is that the wife is not only saved but is as deserving of veneration as the husband. To justify his concession, Damian notes that the wife did penance after the election when she became aware of her error. He also adds that she did, after all, congratulate her husband when he was elected. Still, Damian cannot resist noting in his second sermon on Severus that when the bishop ordered the wife's body to one side, her prompt and necessarily wordless response was a divine judgment against her wordy insubordination in life.[86] The saint's exasperated reproach that provoked the miracle at the daughter's grave is not, however, recorded. Clearly it would be out of keeping with Severus's reputation for humble endurance.

The final marvel, in which Severus learns of his approaching death while saying Mass and enters the tomb in his pontifical stole to be reunited with his family, is, significantly, omitted. The immediate juxtaposition of the sacrament and the family tomb may have unnerved Damian. This omission is ideologically in keeping with the strict clerical/lay divide, which Damian maintained throughout his writings.[87] In any event, he was more interested in presenting a fractious and turbulent family life that was hardly in keeping with any image of eternal rest.

Peter Damian and the Empty Altar

While the monk of Classis had evoked an Adam and Eve of a prelapsarian sexual purity—a purity that Severus enjoyed and managed to retain in marriage—Damian's primordial couple was definitely postlapsarian, bequeathing a legacy of power struggles and petulant paybacks. By exaggerating Severus's forebearance and even distorting traditional biblical exegesis in order to suggest that this level of passivity is divinely mandated, Damian presents an unattractive picture of domineering wife and meek, cowering husband. The institution that would foster such reversals, moreover, is accordingly as comfortless as the relationship itself. The wife as the devil's helpmate radiates with an evil but as yet unrealized potential for even more extensive acts of malice.

Damian's recasting of Severus's vita is still only covertly hostile. The gloves come off in Damian's actual writings directed against the practitioners of clerical marriage. Two themes in particular seem coextensive with his sermons on Severus. The disturbing process of feminization, which Severus undergoes as a kind of spiritual discipline, achieves full visibility (and a more markedly negative valence) in Damian's portrayal of the female-dominated clergy. Similarly, Vincentia's domineering contumaciousness develops into an even more exaggerated alliance with the devil in Damian's polemical writings.

Damian presents contemporary priests' companions (from whom he withholds the title of wives) as unabashedly diabolical, even as their method of domination is explicitly sexual. With characteristic rhetorical panache, Damian gives vent to his scurrility:

> O you the clerics' charmers, devil's choice tidbits, expellers from paradise, virus of minds, sword of souls, wolfbane to drinkers, poison to companions, material of sinning, occasion of death. You, I say: I mean the female chambers of the ancient enemy, of hoopoes, of screech owls, of night owls, of she-wolves, of bloodsuckers. . . . whores, prostitutes, paramours, wallowing pools of greasy hogs, bed chambers of unclean spirits, nymphs, sirens, lamiae, followers of Diana.[88]

In stark contrast to the monk of Classis's reflection on good and bad eating, that all things are pure to the pure, Damian subtly deploys the interconnectedness of gluttony and lust by tracing how these women's sinful relations with Satan implicate them in a diabolical food chain. The devil feeds on clerical concubines: "for on [them] he feasts just as on delicate viands, and is crammed by the exuberance of [their] lust."[89] In the case of the women, however, lust arises directly from their own feeding. They are, for instance, likened to tigresses who drink blood. This image is indebted to the bestiary tradition, a genre in which Damian was clearly an adept, having written a bestiary of his own. He further associates the clerical wives with an assortment of mythological women (such as harpies and sirens) who feed on men.[90] The mythological series is rounded off by a reference to that most treacherous of female animals, the viper. A momentary glance at Damian's own bestiary reveals why the viper was, to his mind, apposite: "This species is also naturally endowed with this manner of intercourse . . . : the male thrusts its head into the mouth of the female. Impatient in her lovemaking, she bites off the head and swallows it."[91] Accordingly, Damian's parallel attack on clerical wives associates them with: "furious vipers who out of ardor of impatient lust decapitate Christ, the head of clerics, in [their] lovers."[92] After an interlude, during which the women in question are accused of "tear[ing] unfaithful men from the ministry of the altar which they enjoyed, so that [the women] suffocate them in the slippery glue of [their] love" and persuading their consorts to worship the Beast (Rev. 14.9–11),[93] Damian returns to the metaphor of eating.

Just as Adam perversely chose the one forbidden fruit over all the licit foods in paradise,

> So from the entire multitude of humankind only those men who are entirely prohibited from every confederation of womanly desire are chosen by [these women]. . . . Meanwhile the ancient enemy pants to invade the summit of ecclesiastical chastity through [these women]. Let me clearly and not undeservedly acknowledge that [such women] are asps or serpents, who thus suck the blood from wretched and reckless men, as [the women] inflate [the priest's] guts with lethal poison.

Barely skipping a beat, Damian moves from the desecration of the chastity of the church's ministers to the very substance of their holiness.

> And by what audacity of mind are [the women] not horrified to touch the hands anointed by holy chrism or oil, or even [those hands] accustomed to [touch] the gospels or apostolic pages? The scripture says concerning the malign enemy that his food is elect [Hab. 1.16]. Through [these women], therefore, the devil devours his elect food, while he tears the very holy members of the church with his teeth just as with two millstones of suggestion and delectation, and when he joins [the priests] to [their sexual partners], he transposes [the priests] into his own guts as it were transferring them.[94]

This diabolical digestive feat, by which the devoured priests are mysteriously decanted into the devil's belly from the bellies of his unholy female accomplices, will in turn introduce a justification of Leo IX's ordinance that the women of priests be enslaved to the Lateran palace. Damian reflects on the aptness of this arrangement: "Namely by the law of equity that those who are convicted of having raped (*rapuisse*) the sacred altars of the servants of God should supply this servile offering of their forfeited rights immediately to the bishop."[95]

The clerical wives' demonically inspired cannibalism anticipates the horrors that would be alleged against witches centuries later—the main difference being that what was advanced at the level of metaphor in the eleventh century was by the fifteenth century being claimed as real. Real witches were believed to eat real people. Even so, Damian's cannibalism was arguably as real for him, albeit in a different register. The women in question are seen as consuming the priesthood by compromising what was "holy" in them according to the Hebrew Bible's sense of the word: what is set apart for God and what must remain whole and complete.[96] To Damian's mind, sexual purity was the sine qua non of sacerdotal holiness. And so the clerical concubine's sexual presence was a kind of rape of the altar in the double meaning of the word *rapire*—a sexual crime against the animate offering to God, the priest; and a theft perpetrated against the Christian community at large. The bifurcated nature of the concubine's offense is also implicit in the cannibalistic imagery. On the one hand, she is devouring the priest by contaminating what has been set apart for God. The act of eating, moreover, stokes her lust, so that she will continue to be an unsated, and hence ongoing, source of contagion. On the other hand, she is devouring what benefits should accrue to the community through the celebration of the Mass, a fact that is subtly suggested by the inverted and diabolical Eucharist that is at the center of the above invective.

The theology implicit in the rape of the altar is not immediately clear, since at no time does Damian consciously assume a Donatist stance, which would be to urge deliberately that sacraments administered by an unworthy priest were invalid. Any such tendency was seemingly put to the test over the question of simony. In a work that Damian himself called *The Most Gratuitous Book* (*Liber gratissimus*), he had vigorously opposed the more radical view articulated by men such as Humbert of Silva Candida, who had argued that clerics purchasing their offices were devoid of any sacerdotal efficacy. Damian explicitly denies that the Eucharist is any less efficacious when performed by wicked priests,[97] extending his demonstration of God's willingness to work through unworthy priests to the example of Rainaldus, the bishop of Fiesole. This married simoniac with numerous concubines and progeny was still permitted to work miracles.[98] Even so, as Damian's *Book of Gomorrah,* an unprecedented attack on homosexual practices among the clergy, would certainly indicate, Damian was obsessed with the question of sexual purity in all forms in a way that his fellow reformers, who had little or no interest in acting against homosexuals, were clearly not.[99] His attachment to purity was not always negatively defined, however, as Damian's pivotal role in the promotion of the cult of the Virgin Mary would suggest.[100] In any event, given Damian's preoccupation with purity, it is natural that the issue of clerical marriage was perceived as more dangerous than simony (which he was moderately concerned about) or lay investiture (which he cared very little about)[101]—the other two planks of the reforming platform.

And so Damian, while consciously opposing Donatism, remained convinced that clerical impurity robbed the faithful by effecting an essential change in the intended effects of the sacrament. At times Damian seems to perceive this change in terms of a distinct reversal of Christ's salvific work. The sacrifice of the altar was intended to be the source of grace. But when offered by a polluted priest, it inspired divine ire and possible punishment. This grim substitution of a curse for a blessing was perhaps linked to Damian's frequent musings on the Pauline censure of those who receive the sacrament unworthily, therefore eating and drinking damnation rather than salvation (1 Cor. 11.29).[102] Hence, in the imaginary indictment of a married bishop, Damian thunders:

> What business have you to handle the body of Christ, when by wallowing in the allurements of the flesh you have become a member of antichrist? . . . Are you unaware that the Son of God was so dedicated to the purity of the flesh that he was not born of conjugal chastity, but rather from the womb of a virgin? And if that were not enough, that only a virgin should be his mother, it is the belief of the Church that his foster father also was a virgin. . . . If he wished to be fondled by hands that were unsullied as he lay in the crib, with what purity does he now wish to surround his body as he reigns on high in the glory of the Father's majesty? . . . If you commit incest with your spiritual daughter, how in good conscience do you dare perform the mystery of the Lord's body?[103]

Here, as elsewhere, aspects of Mariology (as well as a precocious introduction of the cult of St. Joseph) served to reinforce the sense of outrage implicit in so sacrilegious an offering.[104] Damian's reflection that the son of a virgin should be handled by a virgin, in fact, was repeated frequently in his writings.[105]

This citation might imply that the offending bishop was only risking his own safety, and thus his sin was of a personal nature. Elsewhere, for instance, Damian cites God's warning to Moses that those who pollute the temple with uncleanness may die in their own filth (Lev. 15.31).[106] But the implications of a polluted priest performing Mass far exceed personal consequences. To his make-believe bishop, for instance, Damian alleges:

> Since all ecclesiastical orders are accumulated in one awesome structure in you alone, you surely defile all of them as you pollute yourself by associating with prostitutes. And thus you contaminate by your actions the doorkeeper, the lector, the exorcist, and in turn all the sacred orders, for all of which you must give an account before the severe judgment seat of God. As you lay your hand on someone, the Holy Spirit descends upon him; and you use your hand to touch the private parts of harlots.[107]

Moreover, a vitiated priesthood has dire consequences for the entire community, as is evident in his *Book of Gomorrah:* "To what purpose are you so eager to ensnare the people of God in the meshes of your own perdition? Is it not enough that you yourselves are plunging headlong into the depths of sin? Must you also expose others to the danger of your fall?"[108]

The threat of a retributive justice visited on the entire community, in fact, still represents an assurance of God's power manifested through the Eucharist, albeit in reverse. But Damian's rhetoric also nervously skirts a possible absence at the center of the mystery, try as he may to disguise it. What, for example, does he mean when he implies that a bishop implicated in a sin contaminates all of the lesser orders in the church? Is he arguing that the pontiff's power of ordination is in some way impaired? If this be the case, the sacraments administered by one whom he ordained may be worthless. Or, worse still, is he suggesting that a bishop's fall would harm not only those ordained subsequent to his fall but all of his spiritual clients retroactively—the kind of spiritual domino effect that was believed to occur in the later Cathar heresy when a Perfect fell from grace?[109] If, as Damian implies, the besmirched bishop's power to ordain to the priesthood is in some way impaired, how can he simultaneously maintain that the Holy Spirit still descends with the bishop's laying on of hands? On many occasions, Damian upbraids the polluted priests who continue to minister in their contagion when, as he argues, their sacrifices are spurned by God.[110] He also describes the married clergy as an illegitimate, soft, effeminate lot, degenerating from the genuine nobility of the order of priests.[111] At one precarious juncture, he even refers to those who abuse the body of Christ through whatever means—from sexual incontinence to using moldy bread in their celebration of Mass—as pseudopriests who are destroying the work of the apostles.[112]

Damian's rhetoric of sacerdotal illegitimacy and potential inefficacy is best described as an emotional, as opposed to an intellectual, Donatism. His apparent ambivalence concerning the masses of married priests corresponds to aspects of the disciplinary measures mobilized in this period. In particular, the papacy, following the lead of the Milanese Patarene, forbade married priests to say Mass and ordered the laity to boycott the masses of married priests—an interdict that could be construed as a covert recognition of the inefficacy of the sacrament when administered by unworthy hands.[113] Any Donatist tendencies in Damian are, however, muted by the more frequent motif of retributive justice. And yet, once aware of both aspects of Damian's rhetoric, the Donatist strains seem to rise unbidden even through his rather smug anticipations of divine vengeance. Thus in an imaginary appeal to the priests themselves, Damian marvels that priests "do not dread to touch the obscenities and impure contagion of women," since at the moment of consecration:

> The sky is opened, the highest and the lowest things rush together in one, and what sordid individual does not dread to hurl himself audaciously [into holy things]? Angelic powers assist trembling, the divine power descends between the hands of those offering [the Mass], the gift of the Holy Spirit flows, and that pontiff, whom the angels adore, does not recede from the sacrifice [*hostia*] of his body and blood, and yet he [the married priest] does not tremble to be present, whom the fire of hellish lust inflames.[114]

In other words, Christ is present and the married priest should fear to be present. And yet, the rhetoric of retributive justice only barely conceals a worse possibility than a polluted altar, and that is an empty one—empty by virtue of a sacramental inefficaciousness, which Damian's rhetoric simultaneously denies and implies.

Damian's discursive response to the married celebrant—the overt threat of retributive justice versus the covert and ultimately pessimistic fear of sacramental inefficacy—sustain one another in a creative tension. They are contradictory insofar as the sacrament's awesomeness could hardly sit easily with its potential worthlessness. Even so, they are an integral unit. Retributive justice not only presupposes sacramental efficacy but, with its heightened sense of sacrilege, is an implied guarantee of the miraculous nature of the sacrament. It is necessary in order to quiet the numbing fear of sacramental inefficacy that strikes at the heart of the Eucharist: the fear that when the priest says the appropriate words, there is only bread and wine—no change, no grace.

The increasing emphasis on the material presence of Christ in the sacrament of the altar opened up a huge chasm in the symbolic order, the very emphasis on presence conjuring up anxieties over absence. But eleventh-century Christendom was nevertheless provided with an excuse. The priest's wife, now cast in the role of devil's colleague and concubine, has metaphorically raped and plundered the altar and made off with the Host. The majority of the western Christian world concurred with this assessment. The sacramental benefits rightfully belonging to the community were being siphoned off. Somebody was stealing them, and the priest's wife was the most likely suspect. Thus, targeted by the mob through violent demonstrations and pious vandalism, she was exposed to vehement repression.[115]

5

Avatars of the Priest's Wife

The Return of the Repressed

Evil told Good that it would be advantageous for them to have a woman servant, and Good was pleased with the idea. And as soon as they had her, Evil told Good to take her from the waist to the head, and that he, Evil, would take the parts from the waist to the feet. . . . And Good's half of the woman did what was needful around the house, and Evil's part was wed to him and had to sleep with her master. And the woman became pregnant and bore a son, and after he was born, his mother wanted to suckle him.

Now when Good saw this, he said that she could not do so, since the milk came from his part and that he would in no way consent to the suckling.

—Don Juan Manuel[1]

The Host, the Priest, and the Lady

Efforts to consolidate clerical chastity, hence ensuring sacramental efficacy, moved well beyond the rhetorical strategies of eleventh-century polemicists. Devotional beliefs, pious practices, and theological innovations all united in augmenting the awesomeness of the Eucharist against the necessary backdrop of a polluting presence. At the very heart of these interlocking discourses was the preoccupation with the material presence of Christ in the sacrament of the altar. Attendant upon and, in fact, intrinsic to this sacramental focus was the rise of the cult of the Virgin Mary. Clearly, an emphasis on the mother's physicality would sustain the claims for the son's material presence in the sacrament. Moreover, insistence on the symbiosis of purified physicality in mother and son alike would be among the most compelling didactic means of realizing the reformers' vision of a purified clergy. Mary not only existed as a counterfoil to her incompletely canceled opposite, the clerical wife, but in a deeper sense (and one that would strike many modern interpreters as highly ironized) she was offered to the clergy as a kind of purified substitute for their rejected wives and the polluting presence of women, generally. Indeed, the Virgin's enhanced prominence at each moment of clerical reform emerged not only as a mere psychological palliative but also as a precondition of institutional redefinition.

The logic for the concurrence of clerical celibacy, the material presence, and Mariology becomes clearer if we compare the eleventh-century situation with the ninth-century eucharistic controversy, placing the earlier episode within its larger context of the Carolingian Reform.[2] As alluded to in Chapter 4 with reference to the Severus legend, efforts to impose sacerdotal celibacy resulted in a prolonged attack on clerical marriage. The reformers' requirements for ritual purity coincided with and were dramatically vindicated by attention to the miraculous change of the bread and wine into the body and blood of Christ. But this very insistence meant stressing Christ's human and corporeal dimensions. Compatible with this interest was an unprecedented flourishing of devotion to Mary in her maternal function. This emphasis is apparent in Radbertus's *On the Body and Blood of the Lord* (between 831 and 833) — not only the first eucharistic treatise in western history, but one that embraced an uncompromising insistence on Christ's material presence in the Eucharist.[3] Throughout this work, Radbertus accordingly underlined the continuity between Christ (the sacrament of the altar) and the flesh of the maternal womb that produced this offering.[4] The new Carolingian orientation toward the feast of Mary's purification after birth (as opposed to the earlier focus on the concurrent presentation of Christ in the temple) becomes entirely comprehensible in this context but might also be open to misconstruals. Clerical reform was animated by the conviction of the dangers of woman's polluting presence to the ministers of the altar. Yet the focus on Mary's purification must not be understood as implying her *need* for purification, hence returning her to the common lot of women.[5]

It was precisely to delineate Mary's special status that Radbertus, a marked devotee of the Virgin, wrote a companion treatise for his eucharistic polemic entitled *On the Parturition of the Virgin* (after 844).[6] Radbertus's contemporary and confrère at the monastery of Corbie, Ratramnus, had challenged the supernatural prerogatives that had, since the fourth century, been accorded to Mary in the birth of Christ.[7] Thus Radbertus's prime aim was to defend Mary's intact virginity, especially her virginity postpartum. His main argumentative strategy was to emphasize repeatedly that Mary had experienced none of the travails linked with ordinary childbirth. Such tribulations were associated with the curse of Eve, "and on that account the common law of birth is not from nature but from corruption and fault."[8] He is especially adamant about Mary's exemption from any of the bodily impurities associated with childbirth, a point that receives even more attention than her intact hymen. Thus he argues against opponents

> who say that [Christ], as with all the rest [of children being born], opened the doors of [his mother's] belly and womb and drew out after him the impurities of blood and the defilements of afterbirth, since in all [women] the *pains and sorrow are multiplied, the sorrow and tribulations* [cf. Gen. 3.16] are augmented so that no one gives birth to a child without these.[9]

Radbertus also sharply rebukes any effort to adduce Mary's commonality with other women on the basis of the ritual of purification that she underwent. Mary, "[whose] blessed and chaste virginity remained immaculate and uncorrupt,"[10] had submitted to this rite in pious fulfillment of the law. The purgation of ordinary women was one thing: they were purged both for crimes [*delicta*] of the soul and for defects [*vitia*] of the body. But the purgation of Mary was something different altogether because in her, who gave birth to the incarnate purifier of all things, there was nothing to purge.[11] Moreover, Radbertus had already established at an early stage in the treatise that Mary's purity far exceeded that of a normal intact virgin. Although conceived and born from flesh tainted by original sin, she was already purified at the time of the angelic salutation in anticipation of the overshadowing of the Holy Spirit and the conception of Christ.[12] Indeed, warming to his subject, Radbertus even goes so far as to posit that Mary herself enjoyed hitherto unimagined privileges of purity: "Now moreover, because she is venerated by the authority of the entire church, it is agreed that she was immune from all original sin, through whom not only is the curse of mother Eve dissolved, but also a blessing is delivered to all."[13] The context of this statement—arising, as it does, within a discussion of her birth—fosters an extreme ambiguity: is Radbertus simply anticipating her future purification (which would occur at some unspecified time prior to the annunciation) or could he be implying that her immunity from sin actually pertained in utero?[14] This question, left unresolved in Radbertus's age, would reemerge with redoubled insistence in the high Middle Ages.

The Carolingian controversy suggests how in a later period the resurgent subjects of clerical purity and the material presence would again lead to a particular preoccupation with the Virgin Mary. The period of eleventh-century clerical reform corresponded to the reawakening of eucharistic controversy, which had more or less slumbered since the ninth century. Damian was a highly visible and vocal proponent of Christ's material presence in the mystery of the altar — a view complementing the one championed by Lanfranc against Berengar.[15] To this end, Damian gives graphic accounts of the transformation of the bread and wine into the body of Christ. Thus he urges the Eucharist as a safeguard to chastity, since the devil, forced to bear witness to the truth underlying the sacrament, is horrified and repelled by the sight of red blood on an individual's lips.[16] Elsewhere, he relates an incident in which a consecrated Host was stolen by a woman for use as a love potion on her adulterous husband. The misappropriated Host was miraculously changed so that half appeared as flesh and half appeared as bread, a marvel that receives the following explanation: "That she would discern the appearance of true flesh in what before she believed to be pure bread, as it seemed, and thus would condemn the sacrilegious audacity of the wicked deed undertaken by her own judgment."[17] Again, in the dominant realist mode, echoing the position of Radbertus, Damian advanced the symbiotic claims of the material presence and Mariology by stressing the Eucharist's continuity with the maternal body.

> O blessed breasts which, when they pour delicate milk into puerile lips, supply the food of men and angels. . . . The fluid flows from the breasts of the Virgin and is turned into the flesh of Christ. . . . It is indeed that body of Christ which the most blessed Virgin bore, which she cherished in her womb, that [body] I say without any doubt and no other that we now receive from the sacrament of the altar and his blood we drink in the sacrament of our redemption.[18]

Not only did Damian explicitly encourage devotion to the Virgin by promoting her office,[19] but he was also a major innovator and disseminator of Marian miracles.[20] Other highly placed reformers had parallel orientations. Thus in his letter to Mathilda of Tuscany, Gregory VII encourages the countess in her devotions to Mary — advice that is significantly conjoined to his recommendation for frequent communion. Similarly, Anselm of Bec was active in spreading the cult of the Virgin.[21] Marian iconography also achieved unprecedented visibility in this period, particularly in the centers of reform.[22]

The most ambitious proponents of Mariology in the later period picked up the ball where Radbertus had dropped it and ran, focusing on the thorny question of Mary's conception. If Radbertus did flirt with the tantalizing option of Mary's acquittal from the sentence of original sin, his claim was ephemeral and secondary to his main purpose, which was to emphasize the perpetual purity of the Virgin's flesh as indicated by her unparalleled experience of childbirth. The late eleventh century and twelfth century's reengagement with this question moved backward in Marian history in an effort to purify Mary in utero. This preoccupation again corresponds with the dual foci of clerical purity and the material presence—emphases that, giving pride of place to the Virgin's flesh in the incarnation and the Eucharist, had then to attach a higher premium to its purity.

The exact interaction of this nexus of associations is difficult to discern in the earliest evidence concerning the feast of the conception, since its origins are extremely obscure. There is some suggestion that Leo IX had authorized the feast of Mary's conception at the Council of Vercelli (1050) when Berengar's eucharistic position was condemned.[23] But the most reliable evidence points to England for the initial celebration and the later defense of this feast in the West.[24] Apparently, the feast of the conception was observed in pre-Conquest England by several monastic communities. Like the other Marian feasts, the feast of the conception was imported from the Byzantine world. In the East, the feast had focused on the annunciation by the angel to Mary's father concerning the birth of the Virgin, the miraculous fecundity of Mary's hitherto sterile parents, and the projected birth of the savior of humankind.[25] In other words, the celebration made no claims for Mary's miraculous exemption from original sin (which was a western, not an eastern preoccupation in any event). Doubtless, the English monks who initially adopted the feast were likewise modest in their interpretation of its implications. But the feast was suppressed by Lanfranc when he became archbishop of Canterbury. As a trained theologian, he probably recognized that the mere celebration of such a feast would passively encourage the exceptionalist claims about the Virgin's pristine purity—claims that could have endangered Christ's salvific work, dependent, as it was, on the universality of sexually transmitted original sin.[26] As one might predict, this suppression had the effect of making these passive claims active.

The chief protagonist in the early promotion of the feast of the conception of the Virgin was Eadmer, the secretary to Anselm of Bec. Though Eadmer was doubtless influenced by his esteemed master's devotion to the

Virgin, he eventually broke with Anselm's more cautious view that Mary had been conceived in sin.[27] In the treatise *De conceptione sanctae Mariae* (ca. 1125), Eadmer's solution to how Mary, being conceived in the ordinary way, should escape from the legacy of original sin was winning for both its economy and its simplicity. Likening her in utero state to a milk-white chestnut surounded by a spiky coat, he argued that God simply removed the outer layer. One need not inquire any further into this mystery: God clearly was able, he wished to; thus if he wished to, he clearly did it.[28]

While a solution very much like Eadmer's would eventually win acceptance for the feast in certain circles when propounded two centuries later by Duns Scotus (d. 1308),[29] it did not prevail in the current theological climate. Even so, the devotional zeal for the feast was not easily stemmed by mere theological censoriousness. The feast continued to be celebrated defiantly in some communities in England, while the observance soon spread to the continent, where it met with the well-known opposition of Bernard of Clairvaux.[30] Bernard, though so often celebrated for his devotion to the Virgin, also recognized the feast's latent potential. While many scholars focus on Bernard's unease with exempting Mary from original sin, since such an exemption would remove all indebtedness to Christ for her redemption,[31] it is very clear by his reaction that Bernard was equally concerned that the validation of the feast would have the effect of purifying conjugal intercourse, which he plainly perceived as a danger. In a stern letter to the monks of Lyons (ca. 1140), who had apparently adopted the English practice, he scoffs at any implication that sanctity could be engendered amid conjugal embraces.

> Therefore, where is the sanctity of conception? Should it be said that with the sanctity preceding she was conceived already holy, and through this her conception was also holy? In what way is she said to be already sanctified in the uterus, so that a holy birth also follows? . . . Or perhaps sanctity mixed itself among marital embraces to the conception, so that she was sanctified and conceived at the same time?[32]

Bernard's opinion would be upheld by the major theologians of the Middle Ages until Duns Scotus's opposition disturbed all semblance of consensus.[33]

The widespread impetus to purify the Virgin's conception could ultimately be construed as vindication of the reforming platform concerning clerical chastity. It ensured the purest of maternal hostels for the exemplary purity of the Host, which, in turn, was destined for the purest of sacerdotal hands.[34] To this end, the traditional polarization of "Ave" (i.e., the angel's salutation to Mary at the time of the annunciation) and "Eva" invited new separatist disquisitions.[35] Thus the Virgin's role in the reparation of humanity stimulates Eadmer's revisitation of the primal disaster that made such intervention necessary. He, accordingly, lambastes Eve for her transgression, even augmenting her offense by suggesting that perhaps she wanted to be God—a suggestion that automatically likens her to Lucifer. Adam's consent is then construed as an acquiescence to the future divinity of his consort, clearly signaling a depraved reversal in the gender hierarchy. But at least Adam was not seduced into Eve's particular folly, since he understood the serpent to be a liar. Eve does not escape so lightly:

> You however were wretchedly seduced [1 Tim. 2.14], and imbued with semen from the manifold traces of perverse desires, you enticed him [Adam] to consenting to you by enticing eloquence, presaging in this work of yours that it was a true opinion of the man of God, namely that women even make the wise apostasize [Sir. 19.2].[36]

Henceforth, fallen humanity stands in relation to God as sullied menstrual rags (Isa. 64.6). Mary is the clear fountain of David created for the ablution of this menstrual flow (Zech. 13.1).[37]

The pious legends that developed over the course of the twelfth century in order to justify the miraculous origins of the feast also point to a direct psychic link between Mariology and clerical celibacy. In the most widespread version, the Anglo-Saxon abbot Elsinus was saved from a shipwreck through the intervention of the Virgin, who, in return, called for the instigation of the feast of the conception.[38] Yet competing or supplementary explanations also presented themselves. An anonymous twelfth-century sermon on the feast of the conception, for example, begins with the Elsinus legend[39] but then buttresses it with two additional miracles. The first is set in Carolingian times. An ordained deacon who was a special devotee of Mary was being pressured into marriage by his relatives. On his wedding day, after the nuptial blessing and Mass, he stood before the image of Mary saying her office. At the antiphon, "You are beautiful and comely, O daughter of Jerusalem," the image came to life and reproached him, asking why, if she was so beautiful, he was rejecting her for another woman. When he reassured her of his devotion and asked what she advised he do, she told him that if he put aside his carnal wife and celebrated the feast of the conception, he would obtain Mary herself as spouse in heaven. Naturally, he behaved accordingly. The second miracle concerns a canon of Rouen who, having just committed adultery, is precipitately drowned while, luckily, saying the office of the Virgin. In recognition of his devotion to her, Mary resuscitates the priest, rescuing him from a host of eager demons, and urges him to emend his ways and to celebrate the feast of her conception.[40]

The motif of Mary as substitute wife and antidote to clerical incontinence would increase as the Middle Ages progressed, as emphasized by the steady stream of miracles in which Mary intervened to save the priesthood from sexual errancy.[41] Nor was this relationship limited to the rarefied terrain of Marian miracles. The adolescent Edmund Rich (d. 1240), future archbishop of Canterbury, was urged by a certain priest to seal his chaste resolution by a marriage to an image of the Virgin. Edmund took this advice to heart, marrying the statue with a ring engraved with the angelic salutation in token of his commitment. He subsequently appealed to his celestial spouse every time his chastity was imperiled.[42] The purified alternative Mary presented to real wives, epitomized in her freedom from pollution in giving birth to Christ and consolidated in Christendom's cumulative impulse to free her entirely from the sexually transmitted taint of original sin, exacerbated the dichotomy between Mary and mundane women (epitomized in Eve). This polarization is again parallel to the psychoanalytic concept of "splitting," discussed earlier in this work. Splitting designates a less than successful strategy for assuaging anxiety, whereby the neurotic subject divides the world into positive and negative paradigms. The mother's breasts are, significantly, the first items to be subjected to this binary system.[43] The Virgin's radical separation from natural womankind and subsequent idealization could be perceived as analogous to this process.

And yet, even in the context of her singular privilege, the Virgin's own body was still susceptible to partition. The division of the hypothetical woman by Good and Evil, described in the epigraph for this chapter, vividly exemplifies what we might expect from such a division, even as the identity of the proprietors for the different zones imparts an unequivocal meaning to the metaphoric vivisection. Good laid claim to the upper half; Evil to the lower. Likewise in the wake of the reform, the division of Mary was effected horizontally. Although at odds with the vertical division of left from right that marks the initial stages of the psychoanalytic model of splitting, both patterns of division continue to focus attention on the upper half of the body, suggesting a similar preoccupation with the maternal breasts. Sound theological motives underwrote the medieval fascination. As is clear from Peter Damian's earlier emphasis on the relation between Mary's milk and Christ's flesh, a widespread association to which Charles Wood has drawn attention, the devotional emphasis on the lactating Virgin had an important didactic function as well. Since breast milk was considered to be purified blood, Christ's suckling affirmed his full humanity as it did Mary's.[44] The concentration on Mary's breasts, particularly their milk, was also conditioned by the fact that Mary was believed to be bodily assumed into heaven. With no corporeal remains at hand, churches had to settle for vials of breast milk as relics. But Mary's milk would very soon be foregrounded in direct and nurturing ways. In one of the earliest collections of Marian miracles, Mary herself appears and bedews the ulcers around a dying monk's mouth with her milk, thus effecting his cure.[45] The Virgin's miraculous suckling of select favorites would culminate in the famous lactation of Bernard of Clairvaux.[46]

The image of Mary's breasts, the upper half of the body, was so compelling and soothing a substitute for mundane woman that in the twelfth century a whole spirituality evolved around the fecund potentiality of lactation. Indeed, as the work of Caroline Walker Bynum suggests, the image was now so purged of the negative connotations associated with women's polluting capacities that it was ripe for widespread male appropriation. Bynum analyzes the way in which the maternal breast of mercy is used in contrast to the rigidity of paternal discipline. Bernard, in particular, liberally applies this image to men in authority—be they abbots, like himself, or an idealized and feminized projection of Christ.[47]

The lower half of the female body was also negatively available for symbolic appropriation, however. The male clergy would invoke fallen humanity's dripping menstrual rags when referring to their own or humanity's weakness and sinfulness.[48] But they could just as quickly distance themselves. In contrast, women's inability to disassociate themselves from their own nether regions is forcefully brought to mind by *On Contempt for the World,* the extremely influential treatise by Lothario de Segni (the future Innocent III):

But listen by what food the conceived child is nourished in the uterus. Indeed by menstrual blood, which ceases in woman after conception, and from which the conceived child is nourished in the woman. Which is said to be so detestable and unclean, that grains that come in contact with it will not germinate, shrubs will wither, plants will die, trees will lose their fruit, and if dogs then were to eat it, they would run mad. Fetuses conceived [during menstruation] contract the defect of the seed, so that lepers and elephantics are born from this corruption. Thus according to Mosaic law, a menstruating woman is reputed as unclean [Lev. 15.19]; and if anyone were to approach a menstruating woman [sexually], he is ordered to be killed [Lev. 20.18]. And on account of the uncleanness of menstruation it is ordered that if a woman gives birth to a male child, she should not enter the temple for forty days, if a female child, eighty days [Lev. 12.2–5].[49]

Mundane woman had still to contend with the polluted and polluting lower half of the body. And this association necessarily aligned her with that object of contempt, the priest's wife.

Eucharistic Anxieties and the Return of the *Presbyteria*

The eventual triumph of the Eucharist, which began in the late eleventh century, was consolidated over the course of the twelfth. The cult surrounding the reserved Host—a powerful and suggestive "proof" of Christ's material presence in the sacrament—dates from the condemnation of Berengar.[50] The twelfth century continued to witness the continual elevation of the Host, both ritually (since the priest began to raise it for the laity to see ca. 1200) and symbolically.[51] This elevation is epitomized in the opening declaration of faith of the Fourth Lateran Council (1215), which included a brief phrase about the transubstantiation of bread and wine into the body and blood of Christ.[52] The general statement of faith was framed in particular to counteract the dualist faith of the Cathars, who, believing the material world evil, necessarily denied the incarnation. Indeed, there could be no more graphic demonstration of the goodness of the material world as well as the sacrificial telos of the incarnation than in conciliar reassurances of the material presence of Christ in the Eucharist.

The emphasis on the material presence and the incumbent elevation of the Host are also inextricably tied to the augmentation of the priest's role, both socially and ritually.[53] He is, in turn, expected to live a more austere life than the layperson, as evidenced by a now incontrovertible insistence on compulsory celibacy. As of the second Lateran Council in 1139, clerical marriage was outlawed. Members of the clergy (subdeacon and above) who were already married were to be separated from their wives or risk loss of benefice. The explanation was given in terms Damian would have commended: "Since they [the priests] ought to be in fact and in name temples of God, vessels of the Lord and sanctuaries of the Holy Spirit, it is unbecoming that they be enslaved by impure things and bed chambers."[54] Those who contracted marriage subsequent to ordination were condemned with the terse words "we do not deem there to be a marriage" (*matrimonium non esse censemus*).[55] This legislation was buttressed by Lateran IV, which ordained that the sanctions against clerical incontinence be scrupulously observed. If a cleric suspended for his unchastity persisted in celebrating divine services, he should be penalized with the loss of ecclesiastical benefices and perpetual deposition. A special warning was issued against the sons of secular canons lest they accede to their fathers' positions.[56] In other words, the stabilization of sacerdotal purity is the cornerstone of the priest's new role. The priest, pure and set apart, works the miracle of summoning Christ's body before his people at the moment of the consecration—the corollary being that the priest, permitted to work this unparalleled miracle, had better be pure and set apart.

And yet clerical purity would necessarily resist stabilization. Although clerical marriage was invalid according to the letter of the law, concubinage remained rife among the secular clergy.[57] Moreover, while officially thundering anathemas and enacting harsh legislative sanctions, time and again the officials backed away from this uncompromising standard. Many authorities were, for example, prepared to punish only the most flagrant and public infractions of the rule of celibacy.[58] Clerical bastards, though theoretically disinherited and barred from holy orders, frequently found their way into their fathers' benefices.[59] Ecclesiastical dispensations further paved the way for the offspring of such unions to pursue careers in the church.[60] This kind of accommodation inspired derision and disaffection. The lecherous priest became a stock figure in the anticlerical arsenal of secular letters. Moreover, the accusation of clerical incontinence was one of the favored taunts among the growing number of heretics in the high and later Middle Ages.[61]

Thus, while the very success of the Gregorian Reform can be measured by the rise of eucharistic piety and Christendom's internalization of the exacting state of purity commensurate with proper reverence for the sacrament, the distance between the ideal and the actual fostered doubts about the efficacy of the Eucharist. The remainder of this chapter will focus on these doubts, first examining mechanisms for their palliation and containment. I conclude by turning to the residual fears that could not be dispelled and that tended to manifest themselves symptomatically. Thus the images in which these symptoms clothe themselves were borrowed from the register of elements that initially had been repressed, however incompletely, in an effort to constitute the priesthood as pure. This was the context in which the priest's wife would stage a covert return.

The clergy adopted a set of shifting strategies to buttress eucharistic devotion. One method that proved particularly effective for countering Cathar skepticism was to foster and enlist the support of eucharistic piety burgeoning among female mystics—the type of spirituality that has been memorably explicated in Bynum's *Holy Feast and Holy Fast*.[62] James of Vitry was among the first to harness this potential in his vita of Mary of Oignies, written shortly after Lateran IV. The prologue of this work, particularly, stresses the intense eucharistic hunger of these women:

> Some of them ran with such desire after the fragrance of such a great Sacrament that in no way could they endure to be deprived of it; and unless their souls were frequently invigorated by the delights of this meal, they obtained no consolation or rest but utterly wasted away in languor. Let the heretic infidels be ashamed who receive the delights of this food neither in the heart nor with faith.[63]

In general, women's reverence for the sacraments, and the clergy who administered them, made them useful as living exempla for the faithful—if not in their actual devotional acts, which were often excessive, then certainly in the nature of the devotion implicit in the acts.[64]

A more banal strategy for ensuring Christendom's "right thinking" about the Eucharist was through preaching.[65] The exempla or illustrative tales embedded in sermons proved to be a particularly effective means for graphically upholding the material presence of Christ in the mystery of the altar. Mariology again played an important part in the dissemination of this message. For instance, Caesarius of Heisterbach (d. 1240) reports that in a monastery near Groningen, a simple lay brother attending Mass was watching a statue of the Virgin and Child. At the reading of the gospel, Christ got up and took the crown from his mother's head and placed it on his own. He returned the crown to Mary upon the words of the Nicene Creed "and was made man." The mentoring monk of the dialogue interpreted the crown as the glorious flesh of the Virgin, ennobled by her royal ancestors. Christ's assumption of the crown represented the incarnation. By returning the crown to Mary he was in essence saying: "'Mother, as I through you am made partaker of human substance, so you through me are made partaker of divine nature.'"[66]

The link between Mariology and the material presence was also enacted in a more literal and somber form that traditionally enlisted the Jews as the unfortunate witnesses to the theological premise at the center of the sacramental moment. Already in Carolingian times, Radbertus told of a Jewish boy who, naively attending Christian communion, received a consecrated Host that miraculously turned into flesh. When he took it home, his father, enraged by his son's perceived defilement, threw him into a furnace, from the flames of which he was miraculously preserved by the intervention of the Virgin Mary. This story would surface again in the twelfth-century Honorius Augustodunensis's sermon on the purification of the Virgin as well as in various collections of Marian miracles.[67] It has a number of equally grisly analogues, enacted through Jews and impious Christians alike—an exemplifying impetus anticipated in the graphic anecdotes related by Peter Damian. Jews torture a stolen Host and it begins to bleed, much to their confusion. A woman places a consecrated Host in a box, which becomes radiant: upon opening it, she is stunned when the Host is transformed into bleeding flesh. A man afflicted with religious disaffection sees blood pour forth from the chalice. The Host is suddenly metamorphosed into the Christ Child. Even brute animals are depicted as sensitive to the mystery of the altar: thus bees create a shrine around a Host hidden in a tree trunk. Swine similarly prostrate themselves before a Host that thieves left in a field.[68]

The issue of unworthy priests is also met head-on in this genre, since the clergy wisely recognized that there was no evading this issue. Caesarius of Heisterbach, for example, threatens divine reprisals against priests who consecrate unworthily, pointing to the example of the Hebrew priest Oza (2 Kings 6.6), who, when his oxen threatened to upset the ark of the covenant, rashly reached out to stabilize it after a night of conjugal intercourse.

> If a priest going to raise the figurative ark is punished with death for this cause, what punishment do you think the priests deserve if being adulterers and fornicators, they touch the true body of Christ with defiled hands. If John [the Baptist] as said S. Augustine had lived in a hermitage from his youth up, as he was sanctified even in

the womb of his mother did not dare to touch the Head of the host so revered by angels, how should you a polluted sinner presume not only to touch but as it were to shut up and imprison in a part of your defiled body I do not say the head only, but the whole Christ both God and man?[69]

The reason that Caesarius assigns for Oza's punishment is, as it happens, extrabiblical, although extremely effective. But after this flamboyant sally, Caesarius says he will desist from divulging all he knows about the evil of priests, preferring to relay stories that edify. In fact, he has already said plenty about clerical incontinence and will continue to proffer still more details, many of which contradict his contentions about the inevitability of retributive justice. Indeed, rather than being the object of divine wrath, the potentially polluting priest is frequently saved from the perpetration of a sacrilegious act when a miracle intervenes and the Host is spirited away.[70] Sometimes the offenders even seem to be rewarded. Thus in one episode, the concubinous priest Adolphus has doubts about the Eucharist and wistfully asks aloud why God seems to bestow visions on saints who do not need them, as opposed to doubting sinners like himself. Adolphus accordingly receives a vision of the Host transforming itself first into the Virgin and Child, then into a lamb, and then into the crucified Christ.[71]

As inapplicable as these stories might seem to any readily perceivable disciplinary end, they were essential in reestablishing that it was the responsibility of God alone to judge the priesthood—a message that ran counter to the instincts of the post-Gregorian laity. A number of these exempla suggest just what level of resistance this moral encountered. James of Vitry tells of a man who refused the sacrament from an unworthy priest. That night, he dreamed that he was parched with thirst and saw a well where a leper was drawing beautifully clear water from a gorgeous vessel by a golden rope. When he approached for a drink, he was rebuffed with the remark "How is it that you want water from a leprous hand when you scorn to receive sacraments from unworthy priests?"[72] By the same token, Francis of Assisi's unquestioning devotion to priests, however incontinent, was almost immediately absorbed and set in motion by collections of exempla.[73] These tales thus constitute a stunning reversal of the eleventh-century papal policy over the lay boycott of masses.[74]

Potential disaffection is thus evoked and allayed in the same frame. And yet, despite the sacerdotal triumphalism implicit in contemporaneous perceptions of transubstantiation and its attendant proofs, these stories are actually driven by pressures exerted by past practice. Earlier reforming strategies (such as the lay boycott), while initially securing the reformers' victory, are now admitted to the narrative on condition of their refutation. But the price for readmission, even for the purposes of extirpation, is nevertheless acknowledgment on some level. Accordingly, surface reassurances that depredations such as sexual impurity in no way undermine the power of the Mass are constantly undercut by the potent—yet insufficiently vocalized—contentions that they are seeking to refute. These exempla thus emerge as a compelling gauge that measures Christendom's eucharistic ambivalence—an ambivalence registered through an overt refutation of doubt that both conceals and protects a covert admission.

A signal mark of her continuing power to disturb is that, on the rare occasion when the priest's wife is herself readmitted into eucharistic narratives, efforts at keeping doubts at bay can give way to comfortless assertions of sacramental inefficacy.[75] James of Vitry, for instance, relates a story of a different kind of theft of the Host that tends in precisely the opposite direction to a consolidation of eucharistic power.

Truly unfortunate and insane are those [priests] who rather strive to adorn the cadavers of concubines than the altars of Christ. More intricate and more glittering is the mantle of the whore than the altar cloth, and more intricate and precious is the nightgown of the whorish concubine than the surplice of the priest. Indeed they [the priests] spend so much on the clothes of their concubines that they are made paupers and are dressed in vile rags. Whence a certain man was accustomed to say that he knew the best way to recognize which priests have concubines from among other priests, and he looked to those who had torn sleeves a cubit long. In certain regions, moreover, priestesses of this kind [*huiusmodi sacerdotisse*] are so abominated that the [lay parishioners] do not wish to give them the kiss of peace in church nor to receive it from them. For the general opinion of the people is that if they [the lay parishioners] were to receive the kiss of peace from the concubines of priests, they [the recipients of the kiss] would have no share in the mass. Whence it is customary to say to the derision of [these women] in the vernacular, as it were, a certain little charm by which the charmed mice may be kept away from their [the people's] grain with these words:

Je vos convie sorriz et raz,
Que vos n'aies part en ces tas,
Ne plus que n'a part en la messe,
Cil qui prent puis a la presteresse.

That is: "I adjure you mice and rats that you may have no share in this gathering of bundles or in this heap of grains, just as a person who receives the kiss of peace from a priestess [*sacerdotissa*] does not have a share in the mass." And they maintain that the mice afterward do not touch the bundles or the grains.[76]

The formal names *sacerdotissa* or *presbyteria*, once designating an honorific position in society and thus withheld from women during the period of reform, are restored to them now that they have been safely devalued into terms of derision.[77]

The women in question are seen as implicated in a twofold theft, both material and spiritual. Their extravagance beggars the priest and, by implication, the church—an image that is brought home by the analogy between the woman's and the altar's dress, which she plunders. Indeed, the maintenance of the former requires the depletion of the latter. But the material theft is, as it were, just the setting for the more alarming spiritual aggression that robs the sacrament of its power. All of these charges were present in the heated polemic of Peter Damian, who aspired to win support for the suppression of clerical wives. Similarly, James's zeal for clerical chastity and his desire to enlist popular support to this end have overridden pressing theological concerns, which must argue for excluding this interesting bit of regional superstition from his sermons.

The spiritual theft perpetrated by the priest's wife remains true to a traditional view of woman's contaminating sexuality. Its effect is inadvertent rather than purposeful, passively rather than actively destructive. Her presence, automatically negating the virtue of the Host, is comparable to the legion of negative capabilities associated with the menstruating woman, such as souring milk or tarnishing silver.[78] But in an attempt to heighten the offense of the priest's wife, Gregorian reformers, like Damian, had gone far beyond the mere stigmatization of her passive pollution, imputing an active malice to her unwelcome presence. And the negative valence of woman's actively hostile powers of pollution, once set in motion, gathered strength in the singular momentum of the high Middle Ages. Thus women would soon be perceived as aligning themselves with that jealous and sorry group of purported Host-desecrators, the Jews. For instance, every church had a sacristan—a person required to attend to the fabric of the church, particularly to those instruments employed in divine worship. The sacristan was not necessarily in holy orders. He could even be a married layman. Even so, it was a position of considerable trust with quasi-clerical overtones. As Miri Rubin's recent research indicates, in anti-Semitic tales of Host-desecration it is frequently the sacristan's wife who is the weak link in the chain of Christian loyalties, selling the Host to the Jews.[79]

The ancillary role played by the sacristan's wife is essentially a mercenary one. Although greed motivates her complicity with the Jews, now perceived as agents of the devil and archenemies of the Christian community, she has not yet fully separated herself from her own kind. The ultimate female aggression against the Host emerges with the growth of witchcraft beliefs, particularly the fear of the Host-stealing witch.[80] This theme was again anticipated in Damian's tale about a woman who pilfered the Host for a love potion in order to win back her adulterous husband's affection. Damian's anecdote was but an early expression of the insistence on the material presence of Christ's body in the sacrament of the altar. The witch's aggression against the Host similarly extends and ratifies the sacrament's truth quotient. But her conduct also literalizes the concern that women were raping the altars of the Lord. Moreover, if we return to Damian's rhetoric, casting the priest's wife as the devil's concubine, we find a similar reification of what presumably began as a metaphor. According to the witchcraft dogma of the later Middle Ages, witches of all degrees had sex with demons.[81] In other words, all of these earlier anxieties eventually seem to coalesce and manifest themselves externally. It was as if the vituperative words of Peter Damian were made flesh, resulting in an evil incarnation.

The Host-stealing witch is, as Peter Dinzelbacher and others have pointed out, the dark counterpart to the Host-eating saint.[82] But these apparent polarities have a common origin in women's exclusion from the altar and the violent way—both rhetorically and physically—this expulsion was effected. It was this ban that gave rise to the "splitting" into eucharistically inflected positive and negative paradigms of woman. The positive paradigm manifested in the female saint is, as we have seen, consciously readmitted and publicly fostered by the male clergy. This was ultimately a doomed strategy. Despite all the labor expended in defining these symbolic opposites and holding them apart, the image of sanctified woman was subject to recolonization by putatively banished traits. As apparent with the eucharistic exempla, which simultaneously affirm what they ostensibly seek to negate, the saint likewise summons the powers she was called upon to dispel. Thus the presence of a force with an equal and opposite intensity to saintly fervor could issue in the paradoxical discovery of a disturbing affinity. In short, the saint's ardor for the Eucharist could not be conclusively separated from the illicit aspirations of figures like the priest's concubine, the sacristan's wife, and the witch. Both negative and positive models were potential conductors of suspect currents. Certainly some of the most widely admired traits of female spirituality in the high Middle Ages tended to foster suspicion and alarm in church authorities. Bynum has shown how the holy woman's desire for frequent communion met with considerable resistance from the clergy. She has also pointed to the noteworthy correlation between female eucharistic frenzy and the reformers' vigorous efforts to keep women away from the altar.[83] Furthermore, the sharp scrutiny and criticism of the relations between confessor and female penitent were in proportion to the very intensity of the spiritual bonds that developed—bonds that in many ways could be construed as substitutes for marriage.[84]

Occasionally we see the positive and negative halves occupying the same frame, as will become apparent with respect to the life of the Beguine Agnes Blannbekin (d. 1315). From the age of eleven, Agnes began to long for the Host. She rushed to become a Beguine as soon as she was permitted in order to communicate more often.[85] Her life and revelations were all deeply imbued with an intense eucharistic spirituality. For instance, on the day of Christ's circumcision her meditations resulted in the mystical presence of his foreskin in her mouth.[86] Another time, she shuddered with horror when a priest who had just deflowered a virgin dared to say Mass and prayed to God that she, rather than the sinful priest, should receive the celebrant's consecrated Host—a wish that God apparently granted: "the priest, when he ought to receive the body [of Christ], looked here and there on the altar thus, as if he lost something." Meanwhile, Agnes savored that characteristically sweet eucharistic moment in her mouth.[87] God even worked modest miracles appropriate to Agnes's eucharistic intensity. Once, for example, when she feared that she had missed Mass, she was permitted to happen upon a tardy celebrant in her local church.[88]

On a particular occasion, Agnes was in the church alone after compline when a mysterious rustic woman, whose face was covered, told Agnes that a host was lying on the altar and ought to be brought to the attention of a priest. Agnes suspected the woman, wondering if perhaps she was responsible for placing the body of Christ there. Then Agnes approached the altar and, seeing a partial host, was filled with fear and doubt as to whether it was consecrated or not.

> And bending her knees there in front of the altar she immediately felt consolation of the spirit, and her mental conflict left her. And when she rose, again she began to doubt whether it was the body of the Lord or not? And her conflict of mind was very painful. However many times she rose, that temptation invaded her, and when she bent her knees it left her.[89]

When the sacristan arrived, she drew the host to his attention, and he handled it reverently and reserved it until they could ascertain its status. Immediately following this seeming resolution, Agnes was prompted to think about witches. She wondered, for example, whether the body of the Lord, when handled disrespectfully by them, remained the body of the Lord. At this point divine inspiration intervened, informing her that nothing can defile the body of God—not even if one tramples it or casts it in a toilet. It was made impassible through Christ's passion.[90]

This divine reassurance may have achieved some semblance of theological closure, superseding the encroachment of doubts upon the Eucharist. Even so, the episode itself remains extremely puzzling. Rather than vindicating the efficacy of the consecrated Host, this anecdote instead poses the question of whether a host was consecrated or not. There would be nothing novel about this quandary: female mystics frequently demonstrated the ability to discern between a consecrated and an unconsecrated Host. These mystics were cast as benign scourges to priestly negligence or arrogance. A negligent priest might forget to consecrate the Host; an arrogant priest might covertly withhold the consecrated Host to thwart a holy woman's pious impulse to frequent communion.[91] But, if the point of this episode was to tout Agnes's gifts of discernment, it clearly misfired, since she proved incapable of discerning accurately. In fact, at its farthest interpretative horizon, this anecdote calls into question the intentions of the actors. The holy woman, Agnes, is ostensibly protected from reproach by the presence of her dark double, the potentially desecrating witch. As the sequence unfolds, however, these fixed points of contrast entirely elude stabilization. Who was this unknown woman? Why, if she commended the host to Agnes's attention for safekeeping, was she suspect? And, most crucial, what was the exact nature of Agnes's temptation? The tale offers its own overt, but finally unsatisfactory, interpretative structure: the mysterious woman (a witch?), who Agnes thought had in some unspecified way interfered with the Host, and the discussion of witches' abuse of misappropriated Hosts. So what ultimately stands out is the narrative's inability to hold its own positive and negative poles apart. The mysterious woman was, after all, a rustic like Agnes. Moreover, the source of Agnes's temptation remains unresolved. As a result, Agnes is insufficiently insulated or separated from her own bad counterpart.

Agnes's revelations, whether reflecting her own self-doubt and insecurity or, more assuredly, those of her hagiographer, alert us to the dangers of the later Middle Ages when the proven strategy of splitting would no longer work. Boundaries would collapse; positive and negative categories mingle and merge; and female piety would be regarded with escalating suspicion. Eucharistic desecration/piety was at the very center of these developments. But this polarity, and the very intense debates surrounding these central axioms, were initially conditioned by the war on clerical marriage. And this obscured origin introduced a suppressed element into the paradigm of the chaste cleric who performs the ceremony of the altar, attended by his ardent female devotee. This suppressed element is the priest's banished wife, who remains eligible to stage an unsettling return from her exile at any time. Her status is spectral, but subsequent history suggests that, as a specter, she could turn up anywhere. Driven from center stage, the priest's wife continued to cast a long shadow over the female workers in the sacramental field, be they benign or malevolent.

6

On Angelic Disembodiment and the Incredible Purity of Demons

With a man you will not mix in coitus as with a woman because it is an abomination. You will not copulate with any beast: nor will you be defiled with it. A woman will not lie with a draught-animal, nor will she copulate with it: because it is an enormity. Do not pollute yourselves in any of these things with which all the [other] nations were defiled, whom I will cast out before your sight. And by which things the land was polluted: whose enormities I will punish so that [the land] may vomit forth its inhabitants. . . . For all those cursed things the inhabitants of the land who were before you did, and they polluted it. (Lev. 18.22–25, 27)[1]

So spoke the Lord to the people of Israel, articulating a series of injunctions and prohibitions designed to distinguish the Jews, hallowed and set apart by their purity, from the other depraved people of the world. The twelfth-century *Glossa ordinaria* explains just exactly who constitutes these other nations by glossing them as follows:

Demons: who on account of their multitude are called all the nations. Who rejoice in every sin: but especially in fornication and idolatry: because in these sins both the body and the soul are stained and the entire person which is called the land. But God visited the land, that is the human race.[2]

Farther on, the gloss cautions that anyone who dares partake of such abominations after the preaching of the gospel will not enjoy the destiny of humans, but rather share in the fate of the expelled demons.[3]

There is much in the gloss's characterization of demons that accords with what we have already seen: demons, in their capacity as enemies of humanity, acting as effective agents of pollution. In a general sense, this designation pertains throughout the Middle Ages. And yet, the gloss's alignment of demonic activity with the perpetration and encouragement of

Levitican abominations, such as same-sex intercourse or bestiality, has the effect of making the gloss glaringly anachronistic in terms of changing perceptions in the high and later Middle Ages. For over the course of the twelfth and thirteenth centuries, such a reading would lose credibility altogether as demons gradually lost their bodies. This chapter will explore the reasons for demonic disembodiment, particularly the ways in which this change corresponds to the church's new validation of the human body and its response to the threat of heresy. I then consider some of the uses to which these newly reconstituted demons, purged of all bodily taint, could be put, focusing on how they are ironically deployed as gatekeepers of sexual morality even as they emerge as the symbiotic allies of heretics.

The Fall Out of the Body

There is little doubt that both angels and demons had bodies in the first three centuries of the Christian era. In fact their bodies were, in a certain sense, required because the majority of the church fathers construed the fall of the angels in terms of a sexual offense—a conviction sustained by the apocryphal Book of Enoch but also accessible in Genesis 6.2, which recounts how the sons of God (construed as angels) mated with the daughters of men.[4] Even after the western church fathers substituted the sexual lapse for the more will-oriented notion of pride as the quintessential diabolical pitfall, the bodies of good and bad angels remained relatively undisturbed—perhaps as an awkward vestige of the earlier belief. Augustine (d. 430), though often speaking tentatively, tended to credit angels with ethereal bodies and demons with aerial bodies—a distinction that was frequently lost on later generations of scholars. According to Augustine's view, demonic bodies were transformed as a result of the fall, after which they were drawn from the lower and coarser air.[5] We have also seen, moreover, that he was reluctant to discard popular accounts of incubus lovers.[6] Similarly Cassian, though vehemently denying that incubi could generate with human women, nevertheless suggested that they spurned human partners in any event, as they would doubtless prefer to exercise their lasciviousness with their own kind.[7] There was the occasional reversion to the earlier fall narrative. The anonymous author of the fourth-century *On the Singleness of the Clergy,* a work directed against priests who lived in chaste cohabitation with consecrated virgins, fulminated: "Let us be confident in employing the example of the angels. For we who know are now not able to deny that the angels fell with women."[8] Whether the anonymous writer actually believed this or not, the analogy effected between the clergy and angels was probably too hard to resist.[9]

Later authorities, heavily influenced by Augustine, continued to betray misgivings about angelic and demonic corporeality but were still not prepared to jettison the bodies entirely. One of the reasons for this reluctance was a desire to retain the privilege of absolute incorporeality for God alone. Thus Gregory the Great (d. 604), when asking why humanity should eventually be forgiven its transgression while demons never would be, argues that demons were spirits and, unlike humans, did not have to bear the infirmity of flesh and were therefore not vulnerable in the same way as Adam and his heirs—an opinion with consequences that would resurface later.[10] Even so, the incorporeality of good and bad angels alike is merely relative: "Just as those spirits in comparison with our bodies are spirit, in comparison with the highest uncircumscribed spirit they are body."[11] Isidore of Seville (d. 636), recycling most of Gregory's views (who had, in turn, borrowed from Augustine), argued that originally the angelic body was celestial in nature, but that the fall transformed it into air. This view is repeated almost verbatim by Hrabanus Maurus (d. 856), who, however, fumbled the ball when he substituted "ethereal" for "aerial"—thus undercutting the difference between the pre- and postlapsarian angelic state.[12]

But this consensus about the existence of angelic bodies, already fissured and uneasy, began to dissolve in the twelfth century.[13] Nowhere is this uncertainty more in evidence than in the *Sentences* of Peter Lombard (d. 1160), which was destined to become the standard text for theological study throughout the rest of the Middle Ages and beyond. Peter attempts to meet the problem squarely in the question:

> Whether angels are corporeal: that seems [to be the case] to certain people, with whom Augustine seems to agree since he says that all angels before the fall had fine and spiritual bodies, but the bodies of the evil ones were changed for the worse in the course of the fall so that they were able to suffer in them.[14]

He begins by justifying the implied metamorphosis, which "some people imagine—supported by the words of Augustine," by noting that the pristine angelic body (which he again designates as aerial versus Augustine's original ethereal body) was formed by the higher part of the air and was designed with a view for useful activity, not for suffering (*ad faciendum habilia, non ad patiendum*). With the advent of sin, the demonic body was henceforth drawn from the lower, gloomier air—an element that would be susceptible to the higher element of fire.[15] Peter further supports this view with a quotation from Augustine himself, ultimately derived from *On the Literal Meaning of Genesis.* But as Peter's editors note, the immediate source for this passage was the *Glossa ordinaria* on Genesis 1.20, which introduces a mild prevarication: "Demons are called animals of the air." In point of fact, Augustine was less conditional in this instance, simply stating that "demons *are* animals of the air."[16] Yet Peter seizes on this opportunity to point out in the next rubric that "to certain people it seems that Augustine was not expressing his own opinion but the opinion of others."[17] These same people (who remain unidentified) also advanced that many Catholic thinkers (also unidentified) were in agreement and taught that angels are entirely incorporeal, though they may, on occasion, assume a body especially prepared by God for use in their ministry, which they immediately set aside once their mission is fulfilled.[18] Peter then goes on to explore aspects of Augustine's various perplexities. It would certainly seem that God himself appears to mortals in material form.[19] But are these corporeal manifestations a new creation manifesting the Godhead, or do angels appear in his stead? If the latter, do angels cover their spiritual bodies with a more solid form (perhaps taken from the bodily material of lower elements)—a special body that would act as a kind of clothing that can be changed into any kind of bodily shape? Or do their own bodies change shape?[20] Apart from conceding that God does not appear directly, but only via an angelic proxy, the remaining questions are left in limbo.[21] Peter concludes his inquiry by warning the reader that Augustine himself never resolved these problems. And yet "in some of his comments Augustine seems to attest that angels are corporeal, and have their own spiritual bodies."[22] For his part, Peter conceals his own view, made more conditional still by his own recasting of the master.

Not everyone would voluntarily submit to the entrapment of Augustinian ambages and doubt. Independent thinkers, like Hugh of St. Victor (d. 1142), as well as the anonymous author of the *Summa of Sentences* (ca. 1150), were prepared to dismiss past authorities and state unequivocally that the angelic nature was incorporeal.[23] Still others, perhaps slightly in advance of the midcentury malaise over the status of angelic corporeality, risked speculating further on the implications of aerial bodies and the respective attributes of the corporeality common to angels and demons. Thus Rupert of Deutz (d. 1129) argues that angels were not made in heaven but were moved there at some later point, even as Adam was moved to paradise after his creation. No one derives from heaven except God, who alone is uncircumscribed and incorporeal. We call angels spirits, but this is only by comparison to ourselves. When compared to God, however, they are corporeal.[24] All angels were formed from the vapory shadows at the moment when God said, "Let there be light"—a concurrence ultimately derived from Augustine. But angelic sin seems to have corresponded exactly with the moment of their creation. Thus the rebel angels, immediately wanting, never received the light, which was their intended birthright.

> Indeed part of that same creation, subjected through humility to God the light, merited to be made or to remain light through his grace. The devil and his angels, however, because they existed as rebels to the light, fell from that grace and were made dark, and not light.[25]

Angelic bodies were initially derived from air, but the good angels received celestial bodies and the bad angels received dark bodies from that same inferior air that would serve as their prison until the day of judgment.[26] Nor should it be construed as an insult to angelic dignity that they came by their bodies in this fashion; Christ, after all, took his own body from earth.[27]

Certain scholars attempted to have it both ways. Honorius Augustodunensis (d. after 1140), for example, fashions the bold rubric "That God, and souls, and angels do not have bodies, just as justice and wisdom, and that they are seen by the mind alone."[28] Herein, he maintains that while the body has the dimensions of height, width, and depth, which maintain its form, angels, as spirit, have none of these qualities and hence no form. Even so, he goes on to argue that angels have ethereal bodies, demons have airy bodies, and humans have terrestrial bodies. The bodies of angels and demons are subordinated to their marvelous shapeshifting abilities, which are exercised in their dealings with humans. "Just as humans are able to color their bodies, namely to whiten or darken them or cover them with clothes, so demons are able to transfigure their bodies into various forms—either to show splendid [bodies] for deceiving or hideous ones for terrifying."[29] With a similar alignment of form to function: the archangel Michael appeared to Joshua armed; Gabriel was in a crystalline form when he announced the kingdom of Christ to Daniel; Raphael was girded when he freed Sarah from the demon and cured her father Tobias from blindness, and the list goes on.[30]

And yet, Honorius was not entirely impervious to his own implicit inconsistencies. In one of his fictive dialogues, the interlocutor, a disciple, challenges his master's insistence that angels were created from fire, since fire, however pure an element, is still a body and hence inferior to spirit. The master defends his position with vigor:

> Only a crazy person would say that the spirit is created from the body, but the assertion that the body is created from bodies or from the elements is the truth. Angelic spirits, human souls, and unformed matter of the world were created from nothing. . . . But all bodies were formed from the four elements—namely whatsoever body is attributed particularly to that element which most abounds in it. . . . Moreover the bodies of the angelic spirits are fiery, as scripture says: *He that maketh his angels spirits, and his ministers a flame of fire* [Heb. 1.7], which is to say, God made the angelic spirits from nothing; but he created their bodies from fire [Gen. 1.3]. . . . For just as a human is called a rational soul dressed in a body, so an angel is an intellectual spirit dressed in a body. Angels formerly did not appear to men in strange bodies, but in their own bodies, through which they spoke.[31]

Other authoritative writings, which either were or would become standard texts that would be consulted for the duration of the Middle Ages, continued to transmit an unrevised view of demonic corporeality. When commenting on the creation of the world and the distribution of animals in the various elements, the *Glossa ordinaria*—on which the Lombard had depended for at least some of his Augustinian knowledge—placed demons in their aerial bodies under the firmament.[32] Similarly Gratian (fl. 1140), attempting to indicate how the subtlety of their senses permits demons to predict the future, continued to transmit without comment Augustine's views on the aerial bodies of demons.[33]

But the dominion of Augustine's angelic/demonic body was only compellingly rejected altogether by thirteenth-century scholasticism, with the added disciplinary virtue of not just proclaiming incorporeality by fiat but demonstrating more clearly why this should be the case. Bonaventure (d. 1274) states explicitly that the materialism of angels is a vexed area of inquiry where there is no consensus amongst authorities, but he nevertheless attempts to uphold an unalloyed incorporeality for the angelic host.[34] He further exploits whatever tentativeness or loopholes may have existed in past authorities in an effort to push them toward a position affirming incorporeality.[35] Thus, using individuals like Bernard of Clairvaux as representative adversaries, Bonaventure contests the position that every creature needs both body and soul for perfection, instead urging that whatever is nobler is closer to God—a premise that implies angelic incorporeality. From the perspective of the order of creation, given the distinction between spirit and matter, a universe without a purely spiritual being would be an acephalous anomaly. The angel's potential "need" for a body in the course of its ministry should, instead, be recast in terms of humanity's need, which is a function of carnal frailty.[36]

Bonaventure also goes into considerable detail about the nature of the bodies that angels assume when they appear to humans. He contests the view that angels utilize a celestial body in accordance with their superior nature, instead opting for an elemental body.[37] But there remains a wide array of choices. Some argue that the angel's temporary body is a mixture of all the elements, with one predominating—making it somewhat similar to the human body.[38] Still others contend that the angel assumes and discards its body too quickly for it to qualify as a fully mixed body. Nor do these assumed bodies endure the indignity of putrefaction. Rather this second group of scholars favors the pure element of air as the sole ingredient, which is divisible and condensible. The air in question would be in some way solidified, analogous to the way water is crystallized into ice. Different areas of this body would be subject to greater and lesser degrees of solidification, however, in order to simulate muscle, bone, and flesh.[39] But Bonaventure finds this second position complicated and arcane. It also fails to account for the presence of color in angelic bodies—an effect that cannot be achieved without a fuller cooperation of more than one element. Thus he chooses a medial position between the two, maintaining that the angelic body is principally air that has been mixed with all of the vapors of the elements. Angels assume their bodies from the higher air; demons from the lower.[40] The body itself is held together by angelic power for as long as it is needed, at which time it immediately returns to its preexisting matter.[41]

Despite these apparent argumentative advances, Bonaventure still held that angels are composed of matter and form, although we must bear in mind that he maintained a distinction between corporeal and spiritual matter. Angelic composition, of course, was aligned with this second category.[42]

Thomas Aquinas (d. 1274) cut the Gordian knot, severing angelic nature from any vestige of corporeality.[43] He was certainly less conciliatory to past authorities than Bonaventure had been, an undoubted advantage in an area where so many of the giants had faltered.[44] But it was ultimately Thomas's philosophical positioning that saw him through. From his rigorously Aristotelian perspective, matter was solely an attribute of bodies, so the question of spiritual matter was quickly dispatched.

> Now a moment's reflection is enough to show that there cannot be one and the same matter for spirits and bodies, in the sense that one particular division of matter had both a spiritual and a corporeal form; for in that case the same identical thing would be both a spirit and a body. But could we perhaps say that the common matter is divided up so that one part receives a spiritual form and another part a bodily form? But then, how is the division of matter into parts conceivable except in terms of quantity? Take quantity away and substance remains indivisible, as Aristotle says [*Physics* 6.3]. And if this be true, then Avicebron's theory would imply that spiritual beings contained a matter that existed as quantity. But this is impossible; therefore there cannot be a matter common to spirits and bodies.[45]

Angels were thus established as pure form.

Even so, the Thomistic solution is in agreement with Bonaventure on a number of points. Aquinas similarly advances that angels and demons assume bodies of condensed air, which they use out of deference to our needs, not their own.[46] He also argues that a purely spiritual form was necessary for the perfection of the order of creation.[47] And yet, the completion of Thomas's conception of the universe called not simply for incorporeal beings but for beings with a necessarily intellectual essence.[48] Good and bad angels emerge as preeminently austere entities, comprised of pure intellect and will. Their intellectual nature made any permanent union with matter not only otiose but simply impossible.[49]

The emphasis on pure intellectuality, and what this entailed, sealed angels and demons in their respective destinies more securely than ever before.[50] It had been widely acknowledged since patristic times that the good angels were confirmed in their goodness after the fall, while the bad angels were equally wedded to their malice.[51] But Aquinas attempted to make it eminently clear why this should be so. As purely intellectual beings, who chose freely, adherence to their chosen course was unalterable. The demons' will to do evil was unabated, as was their punishment.[52] Their intellectual powers, although deprived of grace, remained essentially undiminished, so they were fully aware of the interminable nature of their plight.[53]

Aquinas also severely circumscribed the nature of any possible pleasure demons might experience by virtue of the sins they inspired. For instance, in *The City of God* (2.4), Augustine had claimed that "demons take pleasure in lewd and carnal sins."[54] Aquinas qualifies this remark by emphasizing that, lacking bodies, demons could derive pleasure in these acts solely from the prospect of humanity's ruin.[55] Indeed, they are impervious to all sinful emotions that rely on the flesh—whether avarice, lust, anger, concupiscence, or sloth. This narrows the field considerably. "So it is clear that the only purely spiritual sins, and so the only ones of which devils are capable, are pride and envy—understanding envy, of course, not as an emotion, but as the wilful repugnance to another's well-being."[56]

Thus demons, pure intellect without body, stood in a strange voyeuristic relation to humanity, deriving perverse and at most deflected and vicarious pleasure from the sins of the embodied. As purely spiritual sinners, not prone to the whims of passion or the alibi of ignorance, their transgression pertained not to the natural order but to the supernatural order. They had chosen their fate, and there was no way back.[57]

Why Demons Lost Their Bodies

The rejection of demonic and angelic corporeality corresponds with the new and potentially positive valuation placed on the human body in the high Middle Ages, a change that can be perceived in twelfth-century angelology. The angelic state was traditionally, by its very nature, reputed to be of considerably greater dignity than was the human condition. Humanity was made in the image of God. But the angel was much closer than a mere image, both in resemblance and in signification: the angel was a *signaculum*—a veritable sign of God.[58] To live a life comparable to that of the angels after the resurrection—a promise proffered by Christ himself (Matt. 22.30)—was nothing less than a staggering elevation. Even so, there was a decided difference between living as angels and living for angels. And many twelfth-century theologians vociferously resisted past assertions that the creation of humankind, which was commonly understood as destined to repair the number of the angels, was in any way contingent on Lucifer's fall.[59]

But the affirmation of humanity's embodiment went much farther than this, raising the human condition to hitherto unparalleled heights. For instance, one of the various perspicacious disciples of Honorius's invention asks why Christ did not assume a fiery body like an angel's, since fire is a purer and worthier element than earth. His master responds that the center is more worthy than the circle. Earth, fixed and stable, is the center of the elements. Fire is a circle of unstable motion. While all elements are equal in dignity, the center has a kind of primacy. Thus God made two rational creatures: the angels, which he glorified from fire in heaven, and humanity, which he deified from earth.[60] Elsewhere, Honorius represents the human body as a microcosm in its harmonious combination of the four elements.[61] In his later work, Honorius would throw caution to the wind, unabashedly proclaiming that humanity is worthier than the angels by virtue of the incarnation.[62] Likewise, Rupert of Deutz would posit a double paradise for the resurrected human body, compared to the single delight of the angels: "There beatified in the body by the eternal resurrection one may eat, moreover, if one likes from every beautiful and most delightful tree, not out of necessity but from great and ineffable desire."[63]

The many other concurrent symptoms of a revised estimation of physicality are so familiar to modern scholars as scarcely to require rehearsing. Anselm's landmark work *Why God Became Man* (1098);[64] the rise of eucharistic piety; the physicality of medieval spirituality, with respect to both the rise of a vigorous penitential culture and the flourishing of a somatic mysticism—all these converging phenomena attest to a new optimism about the physical body as the way back to God.[65]

The Fourth Lateran Council (1215) is once again the zone in which many of these factors received official notice. The form this notice predominantly took was through a kind of rearguard action. First, the council aimed at offsetting the threat of heresy, particularly Catharism—a dualist faith that repudiated the corporeal optimism of orthodoxy. Lateran IV also sought to channel Christendom's buoyant new religious fervor, a zeal that presented clear challenges from a pastoral standpoint but that must nevertheless be read as a resounding affirmative in favor of an embodied faith. The restriction of the number of religious orders and the institution of auricular confession can undoubtedly be interpreted in these contexts: screening for heterodoxy and containing orthodoxy.[66] In addition to such disciplinary measures, certain theological innovations were also in evidence in the general statement of faith, which was particularly framed with the

Cathar threat in mind. Most spectacular, of course, was the famous articulation of the transubstantiation of the bread and wine at the moment of consecration in the Mass. But along with transubstantiation, we also find in the council's general declaration of faith, which was a subtle elaboration of the Nicene Creed, a statement that God is

> One principle of all things, creator of all things invisible and visible, spiritual and corporeal; who by his almighty power at the beginning of time created from nothing *both spiritual and corporeal creatures, that is to say angelic and earthly,* and then created human beings composed as it were of both spirit and body in common. The devil and other demons were created by God naturally good, but they became evil by their own doing.[67] (italics added)

Even as thirteenth-century theologians were left to wonder what transubstantiation meant well after it was first articulated, they were similarly fated to ponder the official promulgation of angelic incorporeality. But the two dogmas, in fact, constitute a united program: if transubstantiation represents the headiest reaches of corporeal potential, demonic incorporeality should be construed as the most poignant representation of the repercussions of bodily absence. By lending coherence to the official position of human corporeality versus angelic incorporeality, the scholastic theologians may be perceived as retrospectively confirming the body's salvific potential (already dramatically demonstrated in contemporary spiritual life), as well as jealously protecting this potential as a uniquely human prerogative.

Reconciliation with God depends on a body; a demon does not have a body; ergo a demon cannot be saved. I hasten to add that any theologian deserving of the name would never have subscribed to so crude a syllogism. And yet there had always been sufficient undertow in medieval angelology that might lend credence to a slightly more nuanced claim: namely, reconciliation with God depends on an *incarnate* body; a demon lacks *this kind* of body; ergo a demon cannot be saved. For instance, both Gregory the Great (as we have seen) and Isidore of Seville, echoing Gregory, had argued that God was moved to pardon humanity for its offense precisely because of the body's carnal frailty. The apostate angels, according to the same logic, were inexcusable by virtue of the absence of any such infirmity.[68] Although humanity longs to join the angels in heaven, we should always remember that we are flesh and must first wipe off the stain of our dust (a reference to the body's elemental origin) with the hand of penance.[69] This line of thinking undoubtedly contributed to Rupert of Deutz's assertion that angels enjoyed only one source of grace, while humanity partook of two. Both creatures shared in the original division of God's grace. But humanity also enjoyed grace through the remission of sins—a source unavailable to the apostate angels and inconsequential to the loyal ones, now confirmed in their beatitude.[70]

Even human reproduction (the ultimate pollutant insofar as original sin was still considered to be seminally transmitted)[71] and death (yet another legacy of the fall) were enlisted to argue in favor of humanity's ultimate celestial franchise versus diabolical disenfranchisement. Anselm of Canterbury maintained that humanity could be saved only by the God Man, prepared to die on humankind's behalf. Similarly, the devil would have to be reconciled by a God Angel who would die in his stead—an impossibility, given angelic immortality. But even if such a hypothetical sacrifice were to occur, diabolical reconciliation would still be an oxymoron, since angels were not created by reproduction. Although a God Angel might participate in the angelic nature, there was not (nor could there be) such a thing as a common angelic race (*genus*), the latter category being premised on reproduction. Not all angels are derived from one angel in the same way that all humans are derived from one human. And so, the devil could never be reconciled.[72] Honorius Augustodunensis would venture a comparable argument.[73]

In the thirteenth century, certain popular forums would pursue similar problems in perhaps a more whimsical but no less sophisticated fashion. Caesarius of Heisterbach (d. 1240), a Cistercian monk, was particularly fascinated by the demons' plight and showed more than a passing interest in the possibility of their rehabilitation. One of his demons actually goes to confession, having observed the immense comfort that humans seemed to draw from the sacrament. (As one might predict, however, the demon proves constitutionally incapable of seeking God's forgiveness, which was the sole penance assigned to him.)[74] Caesarius also argues that certain demons only passively consented to the fall, and that these ones are not as evil as the others. Thus when a seemingly loyal servant revealed his diabolical identity to his master, who, in turn, marveled that a demon would serve a human master so faithfully, the demon answered simply: "'It is my greatest consolation to be with the sons of men.'"[75]

But of particular interest is Caesarius's account of a conversation between two demons, effected through the medium of two female demoniacs who met up in a church in Cologne. The demons immediately begin arguing and insulting each other until one of them says: "'Miserable that we are, why by consenting to Lucifer did we fall for ever from eternal glory?'"—a question that significantly remains unanswered. Instead, the other demon asks why the first demon consented to Lucifer. But this question is also ignored. Rather, the first demon goes on to describe its remorse in terms that "almost sounded like repentance." At this point its colleague breaks in peremptorily to chide: "'Be silent, this repentance comes far too late; never can you go back.'"[76] A demon in the exemplum immediately preceding this one had openly scorned the hypothetical prospect of a return to heaven, alleging that it would much prefer to take a single human soul to hell than once again to enjoy celestial glory—a sentiment that well accords with the official view of a demon's obdurate malice.[77] But, as Caesarius himself notes, the maudlin demon who putatively repented its offense responded very differently when bystanders put the same question to him:

"If . . . there were a column of burning iron set up from earth to heaven, and if it were furnished with the sharpest razors and blades of steel, and if I were given flesh capable of suffering, most gladly would I drag myself up it from now till the Day of Judgment, now climbing up a little and now slipping down again, if once I might at the last win home to the glory in which once I dwelt."[78]

The French inquisitor Stephen of Bourbon (d. 1261) has a similar tale to tell. In the early days of the Dominican order, when the ardent friars manifested their zeal through dangerous degrees of sleep deprivation and abstinence from food, the devil, taking advantage of their beleaguered state, further afflicted them corporeally. In retaliation, the brothers decided to call on the good angels at matins by singing *Te sanctum Dominum*. The devil, in turn, took his revenge through the body of a possessed friar, who declared:

"O wretched ones! You don't know what you sing. You don't know how sublime they [the angels] are but I know—I who fell from the company of them. And since I do not have flesh in which I can do penance, I am not able to climb there anymore; but certainly, if I had as much flesh as is in the human thumb, I would do so much penance in it that I would yet rise to a higher place."[79]

Thus both Caesarius and Stephen imagine scenarios in which the spirit is willing but the flesh is worse than weak: it is absent.

Both stories were produced within and proselytize on behalf of a vigorous penitential culture. This is even more apparent when buttressed by seeming disavowals. Thus while Stephen's anecdote is ostensibly antipenitential, told with a view to curtailing the ill effects of excessive bodily asceticism, the devil's temptation foregrounds the conviction on which this asceticism is premised: the amazing potential of corporeal penance.

It is probable that neither author had yet imbibed the new dogma of demonic incorporeality. Although Stephen does not commit himself, this is certainly true of Caesarius, who treats the demonic body explicitly in a section entitled "How demons are in men." Caesarius correctly maintains that demons are incapable of entering the higher reaches of the soul (*mens*), but his reasoning is linked to an increasingly obsolete view: "to pass into the soul is only possible for the Creator, because His substance is incorporeal by nature, and so is adapted to enter His own creation." The devil, alternatively, can enter the body "because he is able to pass into its empty cavities such as the bowels."[80] Other tantalizing and often bizarre details present themselves, further illuminating what may have been a rather idiosyncratic view of demonic physiology. On the authority of a learned but unnamed man, Caesarius opines that demons made visible and tangible bodies for themselves from wasted human seed—a point already touched on in Chapter 1. This less than perfect route to embodiment may in some wise be linked to the surprising revelation that demons are reluctant to turn around. As one incubus responded when questioned as to why it always exited a room by walking backward: "'We are allowed to take human form, but nevertheless we have no backs.'" Caesarius also posits that, at least according to one observer, demonic feet do not touch the ground, as they are powers of the air.[81]

In the context of Caesarius's corporeal (but admittedly nonincarnate) demons, it is worth reposing the remorseful demon's unanswered question: "'*Why* by consenting to Lucifer did we fall *for ever* from eternal glory?'" The silence suggests that the question is unanswerable because the judgment is inexplicable. Even so, the moral thrust of the tale, constructed within the context of penitential enthusiasm, goes farther than past theological feints in voicing the unthinkable: that the right kind of body might have the effect of reversing this judgment.

The wide interpretative berth we must allow for any moral to be adduced from such tales of repentant demons becomes wider still if we consider the great potential for slippage between "flesh" and "body"—a distinction that both our authors, commendably, managed to keep intact (although, interestingly, Caesarius's modern translator did not). Whether a lay audience would be aware of such niceties is an open question. But the laity was doubtless aware that demons suffered the fires of hell—a dogmatic belief that even scholastic theologians had to respect, as mysterious as this punishment becomes in the face of demonic incorporeality.[82] The discarded Augustinian perspective, that the angelic body was changed from ether into air precisely so that it could suffer in the corporeal fires of hell, had the merit of lending more coherence to the demons' infernal punishment. And yet the uncomfortable question persists: why, if a demon truly repents its sins and especially since it feels these flames, was it never given the opportunity of reconciliation that was extended to humanity—especially in a period when "the birth of purgatory" managed to prolong humanity's window of opportunity for atonement beyond death?[83]

In fact, as we will see, certain heretics did dare to ask this question. But, from an ecclesiastical perspective, such speculations were better left to theologians equipped with tools designed for opening up (and, more important, closing down) discussion in an orderly fashion. It was much safer to get rid of the demonic body altogether. Then if, perchance, some layperson came to believe the less nuanced syllogism (i.e., reconciliation with God depends on a body; a demon does not have a body; ergo a demon cannot be saved), at least this position did not grant the devil or his followers any spiritual upward mobility. In its drastically reductive logic, this syllogism undoubtedly articulates a theological absurdity; but this absurdity had the merit of being metaphysically "true."

The kind of anecdotage discussed above was probably being disseminated in sermons (for both Stephen and Caesarius were significant contributors to the medieval store of exempla) at the time when the scholastic discussion over demonic bodies was reaching a crescendo. But it hardly constitutes evidence that theologians such as Aquinas were aware of any lay foibles encouraged by daring pastoral praxis, or that they would have cared. Even so, in excising the demonic body, they fell into line with Lateran IV, simultaneously affirming humanity's corporeal privilege and the irrevocable nature of divine judgment by putting the devil in his place.[84] The decision was in every way timely, as both the putative privilege of human corporeality and the efficacy of divine judgment—particularly with regard to the implacable sentence of the angels—were under sharp attack. The orthodox position corroborated God's decision by essentially limiting the effects of his mercy to human versus angelic malefactors. Disembodiment was the symbolic cherubim with a flaming sword that barred the fallen angels' return to the beloved homeland, ensuring that there was no way back.

"Demons Our Brothers": An Alternative Cosmology

The disembodiment of demons had the effect of drawing firmer lines between the natural and supernatural worlds, driving an important wedge between God's two rational creations: the human race and its angelic counterpart. But only in light of Cathar cosmology is the orthodox separation between corporeal and incorporeal beings fully comprehensible.[85]

The works of two anti-Cathar polemicists, Alan of Lille (d. 1203) and the Waldensian theologian Durand of Huesca (d. after 1207), each writing at the end of the twelfth century, cast the threat of Cathar metaphysical assertions into sharp relief.[86] Both authors are addressing a radical dualist contingent, who maintain the existence of two coeternal and coextensive creators—one good and one evil. The good God is responsible for the creation of the invisible spiritual world; the evil one is the creator of the material world.[87] The fallen angels, the creation of the good God, were not only the most immediate but also the most significant casualties in the ongoing hostilities between these rival deities. From the moment of the fall, angelic destiny becomes inseparable from human salvation history.

According to Alan, the heretics argue that human souls were not new souls, infused into bodies on the same day as these bodies were created. Instead, these heretics allege that "the apostate angels alone, who fell from heaven, are infused into human bodies by God's permission, to the end that they may do penance therein."[88] The spirits of the fallen angels are given the opportunity of inhabiting eight successive bodies in order to achieve their reconciliation with God. There is no such thing as a human "soul" per se, only a fallen angel in the place of a soul.[89] Support for this theory is adduced from biblical texts. Christ's comment that he was sent for the sheep of the house of Israel that perished (Matt. 15.24) is read as a direct reference to the fallen angels. The angelic essence of humanity is further corroborated by a citation of John 3.13: "No man hath ascended into heaven, but he that descended from heaven, the Son of man, who is in heaven"—a text that, as becomes clear in Alan's later refutation, is seen to imply that only the spiritual (angelic) nature of humanity will be saved, not the physical, bodily nature.[90] The rationale for the angels' peculiar punishment is explained as follows: "because the angels sinned in a spiritual nature, God wished to punish them in a corporeal substance, and [have them] do penance there; for free will was not taken away from them, as they say, nor the power of doing penance; otherwise, they would have been unjustly treated."[91]

Durand of Huesca's adversaries allegedly held similar views on the celestial origin of human souls: "they say that souls in the beginning of the world sinned and [fell] from the heavens to the earth and merited bodies and diverse chains, avowing that the world was made for this reason."[92] He also cites the same biblical loci that the heretics used in support of their claims.[93] But in contrast to Alan's reticence about the machinations of the evil God, which led to the corruption of the angels and their ensuing expulsion from heaven, Durand is more forthcoming:

> they say that [the evil God] entered the court of the celestial Father in order to deceive the angels, and they believe that he caused certain [angels] to fornicate. And for this reason they say that the Father rose up against him [the evil God] and expelled him and the angels that he had seduced from the celestial homeland.[94]

Durand is also more explicit about what is arguably his primary purpose in countering heretical angelology: he wishes to demonstrate that no spirit that fell from heaven can ever return.[95]

Despite the limitations and occasional purposeful distortions of orthodox polemics, the relative fidelity of these two twelfth-century authors to the basic premises of Cathar doctrine is corroborated many times over by both orthodox sources and the fragmentary heretical texts that remain. One of the greatest areas of elaboration is, predictably, the precise relation between human sexuality and the fall—a preoccupation that is reminiscent of early Christian debates on the subject.[96] A number of sources, for instance, claim that an angel, entrapped in the body of Adam, was forced to have sex with Eve. Some of the same authorities also allege that Eve was first seduced by the serpent, which corrupted her with its tail, and subsequently gave birth to the demonic race of Cain.[97] But most important for our purposes is that, in addition to the ubiquitous view among heretics that it was angels that were responsible for animating human bodies, we also find other lucid statements that these bodies were intended for an explicitly penitential function, facilitating a given angel's return to heaven.[98]

The church may well have expostulated in the face of such heretical contentions, but many orthodox exponents either unconsciously refracted, or were even passively complict in, the Cathar program by the very nature of their inquiries. There is an undeniably antiphonal quality to the way in which orthodoxy asked and heterodoxy answered. The exemplum tradition posited some plausibly contrite demons who were incapable of doing penance without adequate bodies. Heretics were prepared to give demons the requisite bodies so they could serve their term. It was widely held in orthodox circles that some demons were less culpable than others: though never actually consenting to Lucifer's suasions, they failed to put up suitable resistance. From a heretical perspective, it was precisely these passive victims of celestial revolution who were the beneficiaries of the upward mobility implicit in the penitential body.[99]

But while these orthodox queries necessarily skirted the unfathomable abyss of divine judgment, the heretical answers vigorously attemped to reconceive God within a comprehensible ethical program. In order to give proper consideration to the creativity of heretical thinking, and to comprehend fully the degree to which such speculations disturbed orthodox perceptions of both divine and human justice through the vehicle of angelic embodiment, it is necessary to turn to the testimony of people who lived by and with these ideas. The inquisitional proceedings of Jacques Fournier, bishop of Pamiers, undertaken between 1318 and 1326, are unparalleled among heretical records for the sheer range of subjects broached and the meticulous detail with which witnesses' answers were redacted.[100] As a matter of course, the kinds of questions raised in this chapter would be at the very heart of the inquisitor's own probings.

The favored version of the fall among this particular community of Cathar sympathizers touched on a number of the themes evoked above.[101] It was generally communicated through the sermons of the Perfect—the Cathar elite.[102] In the beginning, the celestial father made all the spirits and souls in heaven (or in some depositions, just souls or just angels), where they lived in great bliss. The devil stood at the gates of heaven for many years (most accounts specify thirty-two; one claims a thousand) without gaining access. When he was finally admitted, he told the denizens of heaven that their life was not as good as it seemed. In heaven, they were subjected to the celestial father, but the devil could offer them fields, vines, gold and silver, wives, and mastery over others in his own country. (Or, according to some accounts, the angels possessed only repose and peace, while the devil could give them material goods; or they possessed only good, while the devil could give them both good and evil.) Many of the spirits and souls followed the devil, who had made a hole in the heavens for their exit. (Though, according to a more aggressive reading, God himself made the hole and pushed out the recalcitrant spirits.) Through this gap in the heavens, spirits and souls poured out onto earth like the most minute raindrops for nine days and nights. Eventually, the father noticed that heaven was being depleted of its inhabitants. (Though, according to some, he was only alerted to the crisis by a faithful spirit.) The father rose from his throne and placed his foot over the hole.

The sexual nature of the fall is foregrounded in certain renditions. Thus the devil managed to smuggle a woman into heaven, promising each of the spirits (or souls) that they would have a woman of their own. (Though, according to Arnaldus Baiuli, the devil took more direct action by himself appearing as a woman. The besotted angels eagerly followed the devil to earth.) Because woman was thus instrumental in the fall, the heavenly father accordingly decreed that no woman could enter the kingdom of heaven but must first be transformed into a man.[103]

Once on earth, the spirits instantly realized they had been tricked.

> Repenting that they left the heavenly Father, they began to sing the Songs from the songs of Syon, as they customarily sang when they were with the celestial Father. Hearing this, Satan said to them: "And do you still remember the songs of Syon?" And they answered, yes. And then Satan said to them: "I will place you in the land of forgetting in which you will forget those things which you said and had in Syon!" And then he made them tunics, that is the bodies of the land of forgetting.[104]

So effective were these "inverted tunics of forgetfulness" that the enclosed spirits were invariably bent on a doomed cycle of incarnations, though the allotted number of bodies varied from witness to witness.[105] This repetition was based on a misrecognition of the first order. As soon as a body died, a given soul or spirit was so terrified that it would instantly enter another body—even if the body in question belonged to an animal.[106] Demons were believed to "cook" the naked soul, torturing it until it sought the comfort of another incarnation.[107] Souls were thus destined to move from tunic to tunic until they entered their last body, where they finally received reconciliation with God by means of the Cathar ritual of *consolamentum*.[108] The fallen souls and spirits were reminded of their true origin and ultimate end (and instructed in the salvific ritual of *consolamentum*) only when the celestial father sent one of his good spirits down from the sky with a celestial text of remembrance. This spirit, whom God adopted as his son, did not inhabit a real body, only a simulated one.[109] His phantasmic body was "shadowed forth" from Mary.[110]

In a period where orthodox eucharistic devotion had elevated the body to the ultimate mnemonic device, representing the apex of humanity's union with God, the Cathar body as an unmitigated instrument of forgetting seems like a shocking denial.[111] Similarly, while orthodoxy teleologically yearned for the resurrection of the body and its reunification with the soul as the final reward, the Cathars, perceiving the body as the ultimate pollutant, anticipated a blissful release from the body.[112]

Yet orthodox theologians were doubtless aware of uncomfortable resonances.[113] For instance, in the twelfth century, theologians such as Honorius Augustodunensis and Peter Lombard (following Augustine) had used the image of dress to describe the body assumed by an angelic/demonic spirit.[114] Not surprisingly, in light of dualism's baleful tunics, this image loses its appeal for thirteenth-century scholastics. Similarly, orthodox descriptions of the birth of Christ—in an effort to separate his birth from the pain and pollution of the usual process—have much in common with the Cathar perception of Mary "shadowing forth" Christ's simulated body.[115] A suspicious variety of dualism permeates the writings of many an orthodox theologian. Thus for William of Auvergne (d. 1249), the mechanism of mystical rapture—a state of being "in spirit"—is the polar opposite of being "in body." Unlike most theologians, who perceive rapture as an unnatural state, William construes it as entirely natural, at least for the soul. The body weighs the soul down with its noxious molestations: rapture, in contrast, reminds individuals that they have two lives and two habitations.[116]

But what most forcefully aligns and simultaneously drives the two systems apart is the pivotal role that the body occupies from a penitential standpoint. The orthodox body, though transmitter of original sin and frequent instigator of sin, was nevertheless a privileged zone in which the penalty for sin could be alleviated prior to death. In Catharism, the body itself was not understood to be the source of any *significant* sin.[117] This is not to say that the Cathars had no notion of right or wrong or that an incarnate soul could not act sinfully. But for participants in a greater cosmic drama, these behavioral epiphenomena were peripheral to central concerns. Rather than excessively stigmatizing isolated bodily acts, the mere existence of the body is understood as a symptom of past sin. The spirit's subsequent term of embodiment is both perceived and repeatedly described as penance in and of itself, albeit to compensate for a celestial offense not committed in the body but occurring outside of time.[118] The extreme asceticism and ritualized purity of a perfected Cathar, who was believed to have achieved this state only at the end of a long series of incarnations, should thus be read as an anticipation and a projection into a blessed future that (in his or her instance) was close at hand.[119]

And thus, eschatologically speaking, the Cathar body might seem totally despised because it was ultimately disposed of and not glorified. Yet, from a penitential standpoint, it was equally as enabling as the orthodox body—in fact more so, since it was part of a penitential process that could not fail: "the devil can take nothing away from God, but he can cause delay."[120] Earthly sin could slow down the return of God's beloved souls, but it could not detain them forever. It was through human embodiment that the hole in the sky would be repaired, when the celestial souls and spirits returned to their pristine glory.[121]

Final judgment and the end of the world would coincide with the return of the last reconciled soul. But it is difficult to assess how the reaches of divine mercy should be measured in the Fournier register. Were all souls and spirits beloved by God, or did some belong to Satan? Would every celestial being ultimately be reintegrated into the heavenly kingdom? If not, who exactly was condemned and why? Although there was no consensus on these most crucial issues, a number of witnesses seem to have subscribed to a graduated fall—a tendency we have already observed as common to both orthodox and heretical thinkers. According to Arnaldus Textoris, when the skirmish broke out in heaven, certain spirits approached the hole in the sky and fell out by mistake. These souls (not entirely innocent, since they should have fled at the first sign of trouble) will eventually return to the sky.[122] Others similarly testified that those who explicitly consented to Satan's propositions became demons, who could not return.[123]

But there were also more clement readings of the same events. According to Sybilia Petri, for example, God said to the fallen spirits, "'You may go for a time and for now,'" which meant that all the souls would eventually return to the sky. Even so, bishops and great clerics, who had formerly acted as evil counselors in this celestial calamity, could return only with the greatest difficulty.[124]

Although sin in the strictest sense was widely understood to have occurred in another sphere prior to the fall into bodies, certain offenses nevertheless achieved cosmic significance—what Petrus Maurini (possibly adapting Mark 3.29) referred to as sins against the Holy Spirit. These heinous transgressions were especially associated with the denunciation of heretics. Cathars subsequently converting to orthodoxy, who are described as possessed by demons, are especially culpable, as they were privy to the understanding that a mere orthodox denouncer lacked.[125] In a similar vein, Johannes Maurini alleges that Judas, Pontius Pilate, and those denouncing heretics had committed ostensibly unforgivable offenses. Whether or not they could be saved was one of God's secrets.[126]

"One of God's secrets": this compassionate escape clause was twice resorted to by Johannes when he was on the brink of circumscribing the extent of God's unfathomable mercy, which according to this witness's understanding was especially capacious. Indeed, in Johannes's view, the one unforgivable sin an individual could commit was to despair of God's mercy.[127] This generous principle was corroborated by a sermon that he recounts: that though Christ freed everyone except Judas from hell, Judas will himself be freed when he seeks God's mercy.[128] Johannes also prevaricates when asked if all the souls would return to heaven, or only some.

> He answered that he heard from Guillemus Belibasta the heretic that not one of the spirits who expressly consented and believed the devil, because they became demons, should ever revert to heaven—or [not return] until the day of judgment. But if on the day of judgment they were to return to heaven or not, all or some of them, nobody knows, because this is one of the secrets of God, and they will rely on the mercy and the will of God over this [question].[129]

In a similar vein, Johannes also observes that he had heard that if a criminal were captured by a temporal lord, the lord ought to pardon the culprit when he sought mercy. If the lord went ahead and executed the offender, he would have committed a sin: "because a person ought to have as much mercy for another person as he wished that God would have for him." Although Johannes has some doubts as to whether or not murderers and traitors should receive automatic pardon, he is certain that it would be a great sin to kill a heretic.[130]

The reach of God's mercy is considerably extended by the confusion throughout the register of soul versus spirit—a distinction that tends to lose its meaning when all of the fallen creatures are of celestial origin. In this context, the destiny of Satan and his cohorts necessarily comes to the fore. What was their status and their trajectory for the future? Petrus Maurini was interrogated on precisely these points. Although the witness admitted that he had never heard the experts say explicitly that Satan, his demons, and the spirits of evil men were not created by God the father, he did not believe that they were part of God's creation. But Petrus had heard that after every creature of God had returned to heaven, Satan and his accomplices would be submerged in a lake—a zone understood to be coterminous with the hell that is this world. Therein they would be perpetually damned. Even so, Petrus was not entirely satisfied with this explanation.

> And so they [the heretics] seemed to say that Satan, the demons and the spirits of evil men, those [beings] who did not descend from heaven, were not creatures of God the father.
>
> Sometimes nevertheless they seemed to say that no work of the devil endured, but ceased to exist, and thus if the demons and the evil spirits were made by the evil god, it was fitting that they would cease to be and not last perpetually, and thus they would not be able to live and exist perpetually in hell. But [the witness] testifying did not hear [the heretic] explain or solve this contradiction.[131]

Others, however, perhaps less daunted by the metaphysical nuances of the problem, did pronounce more definitely. In response to Arnaldus Cicredi's questioning, a heretical preacher replied that no one went to hell after the death of the body, since there was no hell except the material world in which spirits did their penance in bodies. Johannes Rocas similarly would declare that there were no demons, only wicked men and women. Hell was where they were.[132] The full import of the elimination (or rather the assimilation) of demons was not lost on Hato de Las Lenas. Testifying against Arnaldus Textoris, Hato relates his conversation with Arnaldus in which the latter offered his own rendition of the fall. Hato then remarks:

> "If it is just as you say, it is not necessary for us to be afraid of demons, since they are our brothers!" And then the said Arnaldus replied: "Behold, now he has grasped the matter."[133]

Demonic (human) embodiment was thus a direct path back to God. This Cathar conviction not only reversed the orthodox perceptions of divine judgment, which had been for the first time exercised at the dawn of creation through the condemnation of Lucifer and his angels, but it simultaneously struck at the roots of secular tribunals. The Cathar critique of orthodox judgment was, moreover, entirely consistent with their comprehension and approval of the dietary regime of their elite. For the Perfect's abstinence from meat was not merely (or perhaps not even primarily) a ritualized and personal form of purity; it also represented an absolute interdict on killing a rational being, no matter in what kind of body this being may temporarily have found shelter.[134] Killing a heretic was interfering with his or her penance and ultimately hampering God's salvific plan for humanity—one of the few offenses for which, according to some, there was no pardon. Thus by removing all traces of the demonic body, orthodoxy was not only negating the possibility of a return to God by demons in Cathar bodies; it was simultaneously affirming the church's right to judge, condemn, and execute heretics, even as God had condemned Satan. The metaphysical shift away from demonic embodiment was thus a symbolic insurance that the inquisitors' judgment would be upheld not only in this world but also in the next. The damned must remain damned. There was no way back.

On the Uses of Disembodiment

I will conclude this discussion of demonic embodiment by suggesting some of the ways in which the reconceptualization of demons was opportunistically deployed by orthodoxy. Not only did demonic incorporeality become something of a marker of the boundaries between the natural and the supernatural world, the demons themselves were enlisted to patrol those boundaries.

Many scholars have remarked on the new elevation and idealization of nature that occurred in the twelfth century. *The Plaint of Nature* by Alan of Lille epitomizes this tendency. In this poem, the Goddess Nature stridently declaims against the subversion of her procreative plan for humanity by same-sex intercourse. Her quasi-humorous plaint (couched as it is in examples of unsightly linguistic joinings) is retrospectively a grim anticipation of what is yet to come.[135] In the thirteenth century, with the help of Aristotelian philosophy, the stigmatization of sexual acts deemed "unnatural" was well underway. Abstract intellectual formulations were accompanied by secular legislation against same-sex intercourse.[136] From the mid-thirteenth century in cities such as Bologna, which had a significant heretical presence including Cathars, the persecution of sodomites and heretics went hand in hand, as did secular and religious persecution.[137]

Demons play a modest, but interesting, role in securing "normative" sexual categories through their revulsion from "unnatural" sex—a response distinctly at odds with previous tradition. From a patristic perspective, demons were eager to exploit every avenue of sexual temptation: in his life of St. Anthony, Athanasius (d. 373) cast the spirit of fornication in the form of a seductive Ethiopian boy; Lactantius (d. ca. 320) also perceived the devil as the motor behind same-sex intercourse; Cassian seemed to link the sin of masturbation with demonic inspiration; while John Climacus (d. 649) thought demonic temptation could culminate in bestiality.[138] The twelfth-century *Glossa ordinaria,* cited at the beginning of this chapter, would continue to align demons with the sexual "abominations" outlined in the Book of Leviticus. According to the testimony of the French abbot Guibert of Nogent (d. 1125), moreover, a pact with the devil was secured by a masturbatory libation of semen.[139]

Yet as demons gradually shed their bodies, they acquired a new and highly idiosyncratic modesty, which, though seemingly undercutting their implacable will to do evil and their unabated efforts at polluting humanity, was clearly believed to be more in accordance with their newly established incorporeal nature.[140] In a chapter with the rubric proclaiming "Demons blush over the vice against nature," Thomas of Cantimpré (d. ca. 1270–72) asserts that in all the places in which one reads about incubi and their seductive activities, he has never seen it alleged that they have ever been implicated in unnatural sexual acts.[141] Through a series of exempla, he proceeds to demonstrate that demons not only are repelled by, but even attempt to curtail, masturbatory practices.[142] This rarefied demonic censure is corroborated by a skillful conflation of natural law and salvation history. The authority of Aristotle is invoked to demonstrate that "no animal ejects semen outside [of heterosexual intercourse] except for man and in this he is more contrary to the regulation of nature than a beast." In the same chapter immediately following the citation of Aristotle, moreover, Thomas further alleges via Jerome that sins against nature were sufficiently heinous for the incarnation to be deferred until nature's enemies (designated as sodomites) could first be eliminated.[143] Vivid anecdotes depict how individuals given to same-sex intercourse are at odds with nature: the very land dries up where they walk; even the morning dew withholds itself from the spots where such acts have occurred.[144] Thomas also reintroduces the Christological motif with reference to the purportedly widespread belief that no one who engages in such practices can live past the age of thirty-three. This stern interdict, interestingly poised on the boundaries of the natural and the supernatural, does admit of some exceptions (and Thomas himself is forced to acknowledge that he knows of several). But such exceptions can only exist through a special dispensation of the Redeemer. The age thirty-three, Christ's age at the time of his death, is significant in two ways for Thomas. The first reason is that during the lifetime of Christ—"the friend of nature" (*amicus naturae*)—there were no such unnatural acts. Second, if an individual were to continue in this offense past the stipulated age, it would be virtually impossible for him to stop.[145] This last point is poignantly vindicated by an episode from Thomas's own past in which a relapsed penitent was smitten by God's vengeance and died in grief and horror.[146]

Thomas is in essence arguing that nothing is more unnatural than the sodomitical potential of humanity's already blighted sexual appetite. All of creation unites in censuring human perversity, and this includes even demons. A similar shift in perceptions of demonic sensibility is apparent in the writings of William of Auvergne, an author who posited demonic incorporeality, albeit in a conflicted and unsystematic way.[147] As discussed in an earlier chapter, William argued vociferously against the notion that demons derived any sexual pleasure from their efforts to pollute humanity. The strongest evidence contradicting William's position is, of course, the many instances of alleged demonic interbreeding with humanity—a necessary expedient, since (according to the rationale of William's hypothetical contenders) the demonic species lacks females. In countering these assertions, William points to the hetero-normal activity of incubi and succubi, always appearing in the sex opposite to the human object of their polluting designs. Therefore, demons were definitely capable of simulating phantasmic gendered opposites in demon form, should they so wish to vent their passions on their own kind. He further adduces:

If they were so unrestrained with such great ardor of lust, how is it that they would be immune from the sodomitic lust, since neither in our men nor in their own male [shapes] were they [so] unrestrained in lust. But the blessed almighty [Lord] thus preserved the virile quality in men from their [the demons'] outrages until today, so that no man has as yet been heard to have been polluted by that nefarious lust. Nor ought it to be omitted that neither are they [the demons] said to practice this abomination among themselves, namely sodomy, or ever to have practiced it. On which account the infamy of the sodomites is greatly confounded, since the evil spirits, who are vigilant in their efforts to defile human nature and work with all their power, restrain themselves from those things.[148]

Thus we find certain sexual activities designated as so debased and unnatural that even demons fear to tread. The human perpetrators are, by implication, automatically cast as something worse than merely demonic, since their enormities actually exceed the ambit of natural and supernatural orders. John Nider (d. 1438), who drew extensively on both Thomas of Cantimpré and William of Auvergne, similarly would argue that demons are most certainly restrained from inciting individuals to commit acts of sodomy, owing to the residual angelic nobility in which they were created. Indeed, John goes much farther than his predecessors, alleging that demons are even repelled by the simple act of fornication: "nor do they approach a man when he has fornicated—especially for the first or second day due to the freshness of the sin."[149]

The trend to naturalize and even purify demonic sexuality became sufficiently insistent that it eventually went to work on the incubus/succubus relation, albeit retrospectively. As discussed earlier, the favored scholastic solution to the riddle of demonic insemination was that a demon succubus procured the seed from a man and then changed into an incubus in order to impregnate a woman. Both Thomas Aquinas and Bonaventure had believed that this kind of insemination was the work of one demon, who obliged by playing both roles.[150] Later interpreters differed. Although it was impossible to do away entirely with the disturbingly performative aspect of gender in this model, it could perhaps be somewhat normalized by dividing the task between two demons. This is exactly what the authors of *Malleus maleficarum* did.

It may happen that another devil may take the place of the Succubus, receive the seed from him, and become an Incubus in the place of the other devil. . . . Perhaps because one devil, allotted to a woman, should receive semen from another devil, allotted to a man, that in this way each of them should be commissioned by the prince of devils to work some witchcraft; since to each one is allotted his own angel, even from among the evil ones; or because of the filthiness of the deed, which one devil would abhor to commit. For in many inquiries it is certainly shown that certain devils, out of some nobility in their natures, would shrink from a filthy action.[151]

To be sure, these efforts at hetero-normalization are ultimately defeated by the fact that the demons themselves have no fixed gender. Even so, the division of labor between two demons eschews any bisexual role for either entity.

I have already argued that the decision to deprive demons of bodies had the effect of ensuring that human and demonic destinies would be irretrievably severed, at least from the perspective of their discrete salvific potential. Even so, demonic disembodiment also served to unite humanity and the diabolical world in a new and different way. It was as if demons, lacking bodies, needed human agents to enact their revolt against God on earth. Accordingly, particular groups—especially heretics and Jews (the latter people's faith now often being recast as a kind of heresy)—were more insistently marked as the devil's people.[152] Moreover, the ways in which humanity was now being defiled extended far beyond the mere physical pollution of errant sexual impulses. Heresy was perceived as highly contagious, infecting the soul directly. The mere threat of heresy, with its heightened powers of contamination, carried a lethal spiritual taint which outstripped that of simple sexual pollution—though admittedly this spiritual taint was perceived as resulting in every kind of sexual depravity. Thus, heretics were routinely accused of every sexual enormity imaginable.[153] As a result of this growing perception of the increased ambit of demonic activity, the individual body was no longer the singular zone of demonic besiegement; a new solicitude emerged for the integrity of the corporate structure of the church. In this context, one of the traditional terms for signifying heresy—*fornicatio spiritualis*—resurfaces, pregnant with new meanings and new applications.[154]

The direct link between demonic disembodiment and the new relationship of demons and heretical humanity may seem rather inferential for the thirteenth century. There was, as yet, no explicit acknowledgment that their rapport is quickened by the embodiment of the one or the disembodiment of the other. But this very correspondence would receive retrospective corroboration by the subsequent understanding that developed concerning the relation between demon and witch. Kramer and Sprenger, the authors of the mid-fifteenth century *Malleus maleficarum*, would go to great lengths to demonstrate the mutual reliance of the devil and the witch. The devil's spiritual nature demands the cooperation of an embodied accomplice. Each can work much more harm when acting in concert.

> For every act which has an effect upon another some kind of contact must be established, and because the devil, who is a spirit, can have no such actual contact with a human body, since there is nothing common of this kind between them, therefore he uses some human instruments, and upon these he bestows the power of hurting by bodily touch.[155]

So anxious were these authors to gain their point that they even dared to cast doubt on a woman's natural polluting powers as epitomized in her lethal gaze. Many authorities, including Aquinas (who followed Aristotle in this), had believed that a woman (by virtue of the poisonous fumes of menstruation) could inflict physical harm through a mere glance—an effect likened to the gaze of a basilisk.[156] The authors of *Malleus maleficarum* explicitly contested this belief, arguing that a woman's purported power of malevolent fascination was really contingent on the fear instilled in the victim's imagination. In other words, the recipient, not the bestower, of the baleful look was ultimately responsible for its deleterious effect. This refutation of a woman's innate power to harm was purposefully formulated in order to consolidate the witch's pivotal reliance on the devil.[157] Dependent on her dark lord, she was now incapable of perpetrating evil by natural propensity alone.

The *Malleus maleficarum* is an interesting transitional text. To be sure, its evolution from a distinctly medieval fight against heresy is unmistakable. And yet the work would help to inaugurate a new period in demonology as the anxiety over witchcraft escalated—one area of shared solicitude for both Catholic and Protestant segments of the otherwise riven Christian world.[158] In this later context, demons were stripped of all anomalous vestiges of angelic modesty.[159] Some thinkers, particularly demonologists, were even prepared to reinvest the devil with corporeality—a tendency that was doubtless corroborated by the increased emphasis on the witch's ritual intercourse with the devil as the salient part of her demonic pact.[160] So while the earlier emphasis on demonic disembodiment advanced the mutual dependence between the devil and the witch, the later move toward reembodiment could be construed as both reifying and multiplying the possibilities for illicit and shameful congress. These shifts certainly suggest that the stakes had changed, perhaps signaling the success of the earlier campaign against sexual deviance in which demons had but served as humble foot soldiers. Clearly, sins "against nature" were so successfully stigmatized that demonic modesty could be dispensed with altogether. By the same token, if some rogue scholars were prepared to break with scholastic tradition by restoring the demonic body, this could now be done with relative impunity. The Cathars were dead. And even if any cognizance of the rehabilitative potential they had claimed for the demonic body remained, few would argue that Lucifer and his servants (human or demonic) could ever successfully sue for mercy. Nor were many prepared to challenge the tribunals, divine and human, that sentenced the witches, heretics, and their diabolical master alike. The purity of Christian society dictated that the sentences meted out be absolute and irrevocable. Even the possession of—or (in the case of demons) the reinvestment with—a potentially penitential body would offer no way back.

Afterword

Priest: Did you approach a menstruating woman, a pregnant woman or a woman not yet purified?
Penitent: Often. . . .
Priest: Have you sinned with a man?
Penitent: With many.
Priest: Did you introduce any innocent party to this?
Penitent: Three scholars and one subdeacon.
Priest: Tell how many you abused and how often and your rank and their rank. . . .
Penitent: I am a subdeacon and [I did it with] three subdeacons for half a year; and a married man once. . . .
Priest: Have you had nocturnal pollutions?
Penitent: Frequently. . . .
Priest: Did you ever sin in a holy place?
Penitent: No. . . .
Priest: After those enormities did you ever approach the altar for celebrating unconfessed?
Penitent: Never.

Anonymous[1]

THIS RAMBUNCTIOUS DIALOGUE is taken from a formulary attached to Robert of Flamborough's early thirteenth-century *Penitential Book*—an appendix to the main body of the work that was perhaps written by Robert himself. A formulary is basically a medieval "how to" manual. The one in question attempts to furnish some guidelines for a priest hearing confession. Bent on maximum efficiency, the author has compressed as many sins of the flesh as possible into his model interrogatory. In keeping with the efficiency paradigm, the status of the fictional penitent shifts to suit the sin in question. Thus when asked about incestuous relations with his relatives by marriage—a section omitted in the above excerpt—the respondent is appropriately married. For the last part of the sequence cited, however, he is designated a subdeacon—the grievousness of his offenses thus being compounded by clerical rank. Nor has the author neglected to signal the ways in which the sinner's various forms of personal pollution could impinge upon communal worship, summoning the specter of a sacrilegious sex act into sacred precincts.

Even in the context of an energetic simulation of sexual licentiousness and excess, the author places firm limits on the nature and implications of the offenses denoted. In so doing, he attempts to impose interpretative restraints on the dialogue's intended audience. Thus the question of whether the penitent enacted any of his acknowledged sexual offenses in holy places, once raised, promptly meets with a firm rebuttal. In a similar vein, when asked if he ever participated in celebrating the sacrament of the altar under the opprobrium of unconfessed carnal sins, the penitent again answers no.

The wider ramifications of admitted offenses are additionally mitigated by the penitent's relatively modest position in the clerical hierarchy. For several centuries, the subdeacon's exact status was one of supreme ambivalence. Although initially perceived as belonging to minor orders, there had been sporadic efforts to extend the ban on marriage to the subdiaconate, particularly over the course of the eleventh and twelfth centuries. This impetus engendered considerable confusion since compulsory celibacy was generally associated with major orders. The question was officially settled in 1207 when Innocent III instated the subdeacon as the lowest of the major orders. Robert of Flamborough (writing sometime between 1208 and 1215) was clearly aware of these changes, not only classifying the subdeacon in accordance with recent papal pronouncements but also repeating the interdict on marriage. The anonymous formulary, appended to various manuscripts of his work, however, may have been composed as early as 1198, when the situation was still in need of clarification.[2] But whatever the exact chronology of manual and formulary, the formalization of this subdeacon's status was very recent at best, his past still alarmingly present. In other words, the scandalous edge on the sins of our hypothetical penitent was blunted both by virtue of his precarious tenure in major orders and by tacit comparison with a cleric in a more elevated office. Even had the profligate subdeacon approached the altar unconfessed for the celebration of the Mass, the potential for scandal was again limited, since his role would necessarily have been an ancillary one, merely assisting the presiding priest-celebrant by preparing the bread and wine and the various eucharistic vessels. He did not have, nor had he ever, the power to consecrate the bread and wine.

Even so, despite the author's energetic gestures toward damage control, a number of ways remain in which this imaginary exchange moves dangerously off-course from its professed goal. From a textual standpoint, the battle against sacrilegious pollution was in a certain sense lost as soon as the subdeacon's transgressions were admitted as possibilities and accorded a place in the discursive register. The fictional penitent's stalwart denial of such acts may be read psychoanalytically as a reluctant affirmation disguised by negation. Yet, however much this text concedes in the way of transgressive possibilities, it is animated by a subtle but coherent pastoral policy. For the writers of such manuals attempted to stave off the subversion of textual intent effected by various kinds of sexual arousal. To this end, sexually explicit subject matter was presented as inexplicitly as possible. For example, the formulary's treatment of lust begins with the commonplace: "Let the priest beware when inquiring that he not inquire about something unknown to the person confessing, lest from the mention of that sin the penitent should seize the occasion of sinning—which occurs frequently."[3] This perception is seconded by the manual proper with regard to sins against nature: if the priest's inquiries are met with questions about just what exactly such acts would entail, he must not answer.[4] But it was not only the priest who could act as an instrument of inadvertent corruption. A detailed confession, especially on behalf of a reluctant penitent who required coaxing, placed the confessor at considerable risk of unsolicited and inopportune erotic stimulation through a vicarious identification with the sins detailed. This pastoral trepidation also applied to written directives for extracting a confession, since the written word could serve as a dangerous stimulant. Robert of Flamborough accordingly counsels the priest to use extreme caution in uncovering "sins against nature" while simultaneously insisting that these wily strategies not be committed to writing.[5]

Thus, as apparent in Chapter 1, confession, ostensibly the salvific bulwark raised against pollution, operates in a situation of lessened vigilance as a possible abettor of pollution. Medieval authorities located the source of this seeming anomaly in the real traitor to the program of sacramental grace, the imagination—that sensually charged spiritual faculty weighed down and infected by the fallen body and, in turn, interpenetrated by demons. With a keen awareness of this lethal nexus of polluting forces, medieval thinkers partially (albeit incompletely) anticipated the postmodern perception of the dangers implicit in naming any censured activity, thereby according it a discursive home.

In periods of rapid social redefinition, certain figures become sites of heightened semiotic importance for the expression of social tensions and anomalies. The subdeacon is one such site; the priest's wife is, of course, another. Both reside temporarily in the disputed discursive terrain that was created in the course of the Gregorian Reform. But, while the subdeacon's position was eventually resecured by the ascendant reforming party, the priest's wife was cut loose entirely in terms so strident and excessive that they eventually took on a life of their own. In closing, I would like to revisit this striking instance of textual insurrection: the representation of the priest's wife as the zone of the proscribed, condemned, but viscerally imagined and richly articulated. In this particular context, textual insurrection resides in the literal realization of the derisive terms wrought for the purposes of her annihilation. The advent of the witch provided unprecedented and unintended corroboration for the images that spawned her.

The eleventh-century evocation of the priest wife's by Peter Damian was temporally conditioned by what he perceived as a life-and-death struggle for the purity of the clergy. No imagistic holds were barred. Particularly noteworthy was the lurid construction of the priest's wife as devil's mistress, whose cannibalistic rape of her clerical lover was represented as a black and diabolical Eucharist in the service of her true master. As noted earlier, Damian's imaginative "acts" have an eerie prescience: his words seem to make things happen. By the fifteenth century, such verbal execrations were no longer metaphoric but were accepted as representations of reality. With the rise of witchcraft charges, actual women were now perceived as concubines of the devil and willing participants in his unholy black mass.

How are we to understand this change? In what mysterious circumstances do heated polemic—generated for the purposes of persecution, yet sufficiently replete with exaggerated rhetorical flourishes that would seem to ensure that such images never be mistaken for reality—nevertheless come to be accepted at face value? How do words become "real"? The Judeo-Christian tradition is hardly at a loss to produce any number of instances in which words are possessed of material results. The God of Genesis created the heavens, the earth, and all that was within them through the medium of words; the Gospel according to St. John casts Christ's incarnation in terms of the Word assuming flesh; and with the words "this is my body" a hitherto unconsecrated host becomes the flesh of Christ. In its own way, the history of sorcery attests to the belief in the power of certain speech acts to produce physical consequences. But the charged phrases considered in these examples were, in essence, performative utterances: the words and the effects were simultaneous and inseparable.[6] This is not the case with Damian's words, which seem to have been destined for a slower embodiment over the course of the high Middle Ages until these (and parallel flourishes by others) were transformed into the conviction that these women, who were so perversely allied with the devil, actually existed.

The gradual progression from imagistic metaphor to its fleshly materialization occupies an entirely different register than the self-enacting utterances discussed above. In contrast to these other instances, this change emerges as a historical process, one that occurs over time. A similar process has been memorably evoked by Nietzsche when he describes "truth" as: "A mobile army of metaphors, metonymies, anthropomorphisms, in short a sum of human relations, which have been enhanced poetically and rhetorically, transmitted, embellished, and which after long usage appear firm, canonical and compulsory for a people."[7] Among other things, my own work sheds light on how images of pollution, sexuality, and demonology—subject to repetition in shifting contexts—made the materialization of the witch "canonical and compulsory for a people." Belief in witches, moreover, did not remain simply a matter of dogma but was the motor behind deliberate collective actions that resulted in widespread persecution and murder.

The witch's eventual embodiment was the work of centuries—a development that we, as historians, might glimpse, but that medieval authorities (positioned *in medias res*) probably could not. Indeed, on the frequent occasions when they were obliged to recognize their own experience as discontinuous with that of their forebears, this perception neither challenged nor undermined the belief in witches. The explanatory ingenuity of most scholastic theologians was directed at defending the emergent orthodoxy by combating the incredulity or downright skepticism of past writers over the existence of witchcraft. This tendency reached a crescendo when *Malleus maleficarum* associated such doubts with heresy. The *Malleus* further assessed the dramatic rise in the apparent number of witches in terms of the increasing perversity of the women themselves who, once resisting, now welcomed the incubus lover.[8] The reification of the embodied witch was, moreover, consonant with medieval perceptions of the devil's intimate relationship with the human imagination. Medieval thinkers would doubtless have been dismayed, but not surprised, by Satan's ability to choose the very material of horrific fantasy as his chief mechanism for wreaking havoc. In short, Satan might have elected to model his future relations with witches along the contours of precisely those human fears that were so memorably expressed by Peter Damian.

Although probably unaware of this movement from verbal image to purported embodiment, medieval intellectuals were nevertheless conversant with a model for an analogous transformation — one that may, in turn, provide modern historians with an intriguing figure for pondering the relation between hate literature and the construction of the Other. The great patristic theologian Origen (d. ca. 254) denied that the fall of the angels was occasioned by any specific sin, instead positing a gradual and inevitable fall of spiritual substances into matter — a perception that would later seem so akin to the perspective of the Cathars that many medieval theologians, such as Aquinas, frequently referred to the Cathars as Origenists.[9]

I propose that we consider the "fall" from the abstract to the literal as comparable to Origen's vision of an inevitable devolution from spirit to matter. For our purposes, however, an important caveat must be sounded: the inevitability of the Origenist descent needs to be recast in terms of a distinct but not necessary momentum, one that is always contingent on the right historical circumstances. For the high Middle Ages, certain developments discussed in the course of this study — whether of a disciplinary, intellectual, devotional, or doctrinal nature — provide the gravitational pull toward the materialization of the witch. Particularly pertinent in this regard are the impetus to clerical purity during the Gregorian Reform, the rise of the cult of the Virgin Mary, and the development of the doctrine of transubstantiation — factors that, I have argued, are more closely related than is frequently acknowledged and that were all in different ways bound up with the ambiguities and ambivalences surrounding pollution fears. The growing importance of scholastic Aristotelianism, both for its construction of the female body and for its increasing fascination with the demonic world, was also integral to this process. Finally, the multiply determined emphasis on embodiment must be considered. The focus on the material presence of Christ in the sacrament of the altar and the incumbent physicality of late medieval spirituality are inseparable from the same scrutinizing impulse that eventually severed demons from their bodies once and for all. Nor should the ultimate disembodiment of demons be divorced from the eventual embodiment of witches. To the authors of *Malleus maleficarum,* the immateriality of the one required the materialization of the other. These factors were generated within a matrix of material circumstances not discussed in this work: conditions such as women's new (but costly) demographic prominence, the accompanying rise of the celibate female, and the growing competition between the sexes in the marketplace were crucial to this mix. Taken together, these different contingencies made the materialization of the witch—that most compelling and dire of the many negative images of women—virtually irresistible.

Notes

Introduction

1. See, for example, Howard Eilberg-Schwartz, *The Savage in Judaism: An Anthropology of Israelite Religion and Ancient Judaism* (Bloomington: Indiana University Press, 1990), pp. 200–205.

2. Mary Douglas, *Purity and Danger: An Analysis of the Concept of Pollution and Taboo* (London: Routledge and Kegan Paul; Ark Paperbacks, 1966; rprt. 1988), p. 60; for a discussion of Jewish dietary rules, see Chap. 3, "The Abominations of Leviticus," pp. 41–57; also see pp. 60–61.

3. Peter Brown, *The Body and Society: Men, Women, and Sexual Renunciation in Early Christianity* (New York: Columbia University Press, 1988); Dale B. Martin, *The Corinthian Body* (New Haven, Conn.: Yale University Press, 1996); Elaine Pagels, *Adam, Eve, and the Serpent* (New York: Random House, 1988); Aline Rousselle, *Porneia: On Desire and the Body in Antiquity,* trans. Felicia Pheasant (Oxford: Blackwell, 1988). Also see Michel Foucault's *The Care of the Self,* which stresses that many of the same developments associated with Christian influence were concurrently afoot in pagan culture (vol. 3 of *The History of Sexuality,* trans. Robert Hurley [New York: Vintage, 1986]).

4. Numerous rationales for chastity were present in scripture. See Brown, *Body and Society,* pp. 41–57; and Dyan Elliott, *Spiritual Marriage: Sexual Abstinence in Medieval Wedlock* (Princeton, N.J.: Princeton University Press, 1993), pp. 16–23.

5. See Brown, *Body and Society,* pp. 357–58.

6. Douglas describes the fissures between action and intention as pollutions in their own right, which she likens to witchcraft (*Purity and Danger,* p. 136; cf. p. 102).

7. See Pliny's discussion of the menstrual fluid's destructive powers (*Natural History* 7.64, ed. and trans. H. Rackham et al., Loeb Classical Library [Cambridge, Mass.: Harvard University Press; London: William Heinemann, 1942], 2: 546–49; cf. 28.23, ed. W. H. S. Jones, 8: 54–58). Such classical views were popularized in the medieval West by Isidore of Seville (*Etymologiae* 11.1.140–42, *PL* 82, col. 414). As with many poisons, however, menstrual blood was seen as capable of effecting amazing cures (see Pliny, *Natural History* 28.23, 8: 58–63). On the theoretical underpinnings of this kind of reversal, see Heinrich von Staden, "Women and Dirt," *Helios* 19 (1992): 7–30, esp. 13–20. The twelfth-century Hildegard of Bingen would likewise maintain the curative potential of menstrual blood (Joan Cadden, *The Meanings of Sex Difference in the Middle Ages: Medicine, Science, and Culture* [Cambridge: Cambridge University Press, 1993], p. 72). Also see Clarissa Atkinson, *The Oldest Vocation: Christian Motherhood in the Middle Ages* (Ithaca, N.Y.: Cornell Uni-

versity Press, 1991), pp. 39–40, and Chap. 5, pp. 115–16, 122. For a general and cross-cultural overview, see Janice Delaney, Mary Jane Lupton, and Emily Toth, *The Curse: A Cultural History of Menstruation,* rev. ed. (Urbana: University of Illinois Press, 1988), esp. pp. 37–53.

8. See Douglas, *Purity and Danger,* where she also summarizes the views of some of her predecessors (pp. 7–10). This relationship between the unclean and the holy is clearly demonstrated by the fact that certain ritual sacrifices render the officiating priest who performs them unclean, thus in need of purification. See, for example, the sacrifice of the red heifer, in which the officiating priest becomes unclean, as do the attendants required to gather up its ashes (Num. 19.2–10).

9. See Eilberg-Schwartz's discussion of menstruation in Judaic scripture, in which he observes that only certain types of blood are polluting. Menstruation is, while the blood of circumcision is not. The implicit distinction is that blood shed voluntarily (male blood) is not polluting, while involuntary issues of blood (female blood) do pollute—a set of associations that aligns men with control and women with lack of control. Eilberg-Schwartz notes, however, that the man with an involuntary nonseminal discharge from his penis is treated almost identically to the female menstruant (*Savage in Judaism,* pp. 180–81, 187–89). Cf. Chap. 1, esp. nn. 71 and 74, below. On the progressive demonization of menstruation in Judaic culture, a trend that accelerated in the Middle Ages, see Daniel Boyarin, *Carnal Israel: Reading Sex in Talmudic Culture* (Berkeley: University of California Press, 1993), pp. 96, 105.

10. Eilberg-Schwartz, *Savage in Judaism,* p. 202.

11. Mark 7.15, 21 (unless otherwise stated, all translations are from the Douay-Rheims version of the Vulgate). Eilberg-Schwartz analyzes the movement away from objective, external pollution toward an emphasis on intention and voluntary action in terms of a shift from hereditary, ascribed status (as would be the case with the priestly Levites) toward achieved status. Although the Christian community went farthest in this respect, this new focus is also apparent in the community of ascetics at the Dead Sea as well as in the early Rabbinic movement (*Savage in Judaism,* pp. 195–215). Note, however, that the prophetic tradition had already stressed sin as the real source of pollution. See Ezech. 36.17–26.

12. With regard to food, for example, Paul argues that nothing is unclean in and of itself, but if the eating of certain kinds of food gives scandal to the weak, a person should abstain out of charity (Rom. 14.15; 1 Cor. 8.4–13). Dale Martin, however, makes the compelling argument that Paul was deeply concerned with pollution in a different sense: the way in which the permeable body of the individual Christian would pollute the purity of the corporate body of the church (*Corinthian Body,* pp. 168–76). This preoccupation likewise colors Paul's views on the consumption of meat formerly sacrificed to idols. The "weak" could become demonically polluted, and this would, in turn, pollute the church (p. 182).

13. The *Didascalia* attempts to ridicule this argument by pushing it one stage farther: since the Holy Spirit was absent from these women, they would therefore be filled with demons. See Shaye J. D. Cohen, "Menstruants and the Sacred in Judaism and Christianity," in *Women's History and Ancient History,* ed. Sarah B. Pomeroy (Chapel Hill: University of North Carolina Press, 1991), pp. 289–90.

From a teleological standpoint, this remark could be considered prescient in view of the contours of demonology in the later Middle Ages.

14. This letter, preserved in Bede's *Ecclesiastical History,* is not included in the official papal registry for Gregory, which survives for these years. Hence, its authorship is in doubt.

15. Bede, *Ecclesiastical History of the English People* 1.27, ed. and trans. Bertram Colgrave and R. A. B. Mynors (Oxford: Clarendon Press, 1969), pp. 92–93.

16. Ibid., pp. 90–91. In a similar vein, the twelfth-century biblical *Glossa ordinaria* would allege that women were denied circumcision, a prefiguration of the resurrection, and forced to remain in their uncleanness because of Eve's original disobedience—which was responsible for the uncleanness and filth in us (marginal gloss for Lev. 12.3, ad v. *die octauo*, in *Textus Biblie cum glosa ordinaria, Nicholai de Lyra postilla, moralitatibus eiusdem* [Basel: Johannes Petri et Johannes Frobenium, 1506], vol. 1, fol. 235v).

17. Cf. Atkinson, *Oldest Vocation,* pp. 79–80. Even the positive association of woman and Christ's humanity, described in Caroline Walker Bynum's *Holy Feast and Holy Fast: The Religious Significance of Food to Medieval Women* (Berkeley: University of California Press, 1987), is ultimately premised on this alignment.

18. See the late seventh-century penitential attributed to Theodore of Tarsus, archbishop of Canterbury, and written down by his disciple (ed. J. H. Schmitz, *Die Bussbücher und die Bussdisciplin der Kirche nach handschriftlichen Quellen dargestellt* [Mainz: Franz Kirchheim, 1883], 1.14.17, 1:536; trans. John T. McNeill and Helena M. Gamer, *Medieval Handbooks of Penance: A Translation of the Principal "Libri poenitentiales"* [New York: Columbia University Press, 1938; rprt. 1990], p. 197). Pierre Payer notes that a number of the prohibitions in this text duplicate precisely the concerns that "Gregory" 's letter to Augustine seeks to refute (*Sex and the Penitentials: The Development of a Sexual Code, 550–1150* [Toronto: University of Toronto Press, 1984], p. 36). Prohibitions surrounding menstruation would remain in circulation. See, for example, *Poenitentiale Vindobonense* c. 86, ed. H. J. Schmitz, *Die Bussbücher und das kanonische Bussverfahren nach handschriftlichen Quellen dargestellt* (Düsseldorf: L. Schwann, 1898), 2:356. This work would go on to bar all women from touching the chalice or altar cloth or from entering the chancel or sanctuary (c. 89, 2:356; see Chap. 1, n. 92, below; and Chap. 3, n. 29, below). The *Poenitentiale Vindobonense* was written in the second half of the ninth century.

19. This is again true of the penitential attributed to Theodore of Canterbury (ed. Schmitz, *Die Bussbücher und die Bussdisciplin der Kirche,* 1.14.18, 1: 536; trans. McNeill and Gamer, *Medieval Handbooks of Penance,* p. 197). The same prohibition is present in the eleventh-century penitential of Burchard of Worms (*Decretum* 19.5, *PL* 140, col. 959).

20. This particular eleventh-century *ordo* was edited by Adolph Franz in his *Die kirchlichen Benediktionen im Mittelalter* (Freiburg im Breisgau: Herder, 1909), 2:224; for other texts, ranging from the eleventh to the fourteenth centuries, see 2:224–29. Also see the *ordines* edited by E. Martène in *De Antiquis Ecclesiae Ritibus,* rev. ed. (Venice: Redmondini, 1788), 1:134–37. The emergence of a coherent ritual of purification in the eleventh century, versus the less formal blessing spoken of by "Gregory," corresponds with the Gregorian Reform's preoccupation with the pol-

luting presence of women (see Chap. 4, below). Some of these rituals make explicit reference to the polluting effect of afterbirth: thus one twelfth-century formula asks God "to cleanse this your servant from every pollution of the flesh" ("hanc famulam tuam ob omni inquinamento carnis emundare," Franz, *Die kirchlichen Benediktionen im Mittelalter,* 2:227). Gratian's treatment of this subject, however, consists entirely of extracts from "Gregory" 's letter to Augustine (D. 5 c. 1–4). Traditionally, this rite has been recognized as a purification rather than just a simple blessing (see Franz, *Die kirchlichen Benediktionen im Mittelalter,* 2:213 ff.; and Walter von Arx, "La Bénédiction de la mère après la naissance: histoire et signification," *Concilium* 132 [1978]: 81–92, esp. 82–90). This is not to privilege this interpretation as the only or even the main meaning that would be attached to this ritual by its participants. Several recent articles point to the fact that in the later Middle Ages, the post-Reformation period, and beyond, women actively embraced this rite. See Gail McMurray Gibson, "Blessing from Sun and Moon: Church as Women's Theater," in *Bodies and Disciplines: Intersections of Literature and History in Fifteenth-Century England,* ed. Barbara Hanawalt and David Wallace (Minneapolis: University of Minnesota Press, 1996), pp. 139–54; and David Cressy, "Purification, Thanksgiving, and the Churching of Women in Post-Reformation England," *Past and Present* 14 (1993): 106–46.

21. "In sanctam et singularem custodiam commendo tibi animam[as] et corpus[pora] famule[larum] tue[arum] et omnes cogitationes et actus eius [earum], ut eam [eas] a malignis spiritibus defendas, ut nunquam transeat[ant] in eorum potestatem neque hic neque in futuro," Franz, *Die kirchlichen Benediktionen im Mittelalter,* 2:211–12. When not otherwise indicated, translations are mine.

22. See Charles Wood, "The Doctors' Dilemma: Sin, Salvation, and the Menstrual Cycle," *Speculum* 56 (1981): 710–27, esp. 721 ff. Also see the section entitled "The Host, the Priest, and the Lady" in Chap. 5, below.

23. Thomas Aquinas, *Summa theologiae* 3a, q. 31, art. 5, resp. ad 3, ed. and trans. Fathers of the English Dominican Province (London: Blackfriars, 1972), 52: 26–29.

24. William of Auvergne, *De legibus* c. 6, in *Opera omnia* (Paris: A. Pralard, 1674; rprt. Frankfurt am Main: Minerva, 1963), 1:36–37. See Chap. 6, n. 156, below. The impact of new and more widely disseminated medical writings is also apparent in the explanations for women's need of purification after birth in the high Middle Ages. Thus the biblical *Glossa ordinaria* explains that a woman who gives birth to a girl child is impure for 80 days (versus the 40 days assigned to the birth of a boy child) because girls take twice as long to be formed in the uterus (marginal gloss for Lev. 12.4, ad v. *triginta tribus diebus etc.,* in *Textus Biblie,* vol. 1, fol. 235v). Nicholas of Lyre goes into still more detail. Because sufficient heat is absent in the conception of a female child, the unclean matter is processed and purified more slowly (*Postilla,* Lev. 12.5, ad v. *Sin autem feminam perperit etc.,* in *Textus Biblie,* vol. 1, fol. 235v).

25. See Ezech. 36.17–18, which aligns the sinner with the menstruating woman and the idolator. For similar use of menstrual imagery in the Hebrew Bible, see Eilberg-Schwartz, *Savage in Judaism,* pp. 180–81; and David Biale, *Eros and the Jews: From Biblical Israel to Contemporary America* (New York: Basic Books, 1992), pp. 30–31. The biblical *Glossa ordinaria* thus construes the menstruating woman as an individual who corrupts herself with depraved thoughts—even if these thoughts

are not enacted in deed. Her filth signifies the corruption of idolatry (marginal gloss for Lev. 15.19 ad v. *mulier quae etc.,* vol. 1, fol. 241r). Like the menstruant, whose contagion is communicated to others, so ought the idolator to be shunned (marginal gloss for Lev. 15.22, ad v. *qui tetigerit vestimentum eius,* in *Textus Biblie,* vol. 1, fol. 241r; note that the standard version of the Vulgate has the words *qui tetigerit lectum eius*). Cf. the interpretation of the woman who suffered from a spontaneous flux of blood for many days (marginal gloss for Lev. 15.25, ad v. *mulier quae etc.,* vol. 1, fol. 241v; marginal gloss for Lev. 15.29, ad v. *offeret pro se sacerdoti,* vol. 1, fol. 241v; and the interlinear gloss, passim).

26. William of Auvergne, *De legibus* c. 6, in *Opera omnia,* 1:36. Jeremiah censures women who make cakes to offer to the moon—there described as the queen of heaven (7.18). The association of menstrual blood with sorcery, especially love potions, was seemingly widespread throughout the Middle Ages, but the practice was regarded with ever-increasing censoriousness. Thus the eleventh-century Burchard of Worms assigns five years of penance to a woman who mixes menstrual blood in her husband's food to increase his love—although only two years for a woman who kills a fish in her afterbirth and then cooks and feeds it to him (*Decretum* 19.5, *PL* 140, col. 974). By the fourteenth century, parallel practices were matters for the inquisition. Thus one of the charges pursued against Beatrix de Ecclesia by Jacques Fournier was that she saved the blood from her daughter's first period in order to feed it to her future bridegroom (ed. Jean Duvernoy, *Le Registre d'inquisition de Jacques Fournier, évêque de Pamiers (1318–1325)* [Toulouse: Edouard Privat, 1965], 1:247–48).

27. Nicholas of Lyre, *Moraliter,* for Lev. 15.25, ad v. *mulier quae patitur multis diebus etc.,* in *Textus Biblie,* vol. 1, fol. 241v.

28. Caesarius of Heisterbach, *Dialogus miraculorum* 1.23, ed. Joseph Strange (Cologne: J. M. Heberle, 1851), 1:92; trans. H. Von E. Scott and C. C. Swinton Bland, *The Dialogue on Miracles* (London: Routledge, 1929), 1:102.

29. For the early church and the theoretical underpinnings for Paul's differential treatment of women, see Martin, *Corinthian Body,* pp. 219–47. Also see Elizabeth A. Clark, "Sane Insanity: Women and Asceticism in Late Ancient Christianity," *Medieval Encounters* 3 (1997): 211–13.

30. According to Freud, the unconscious is largely constituted by what is repressed by the conscious mind. See *Repression,* in *The Standard Edition of the Complete Psychological Works of Sigmund Freud,* ed. James Strachey (London: Hogarth Press, 1957), 14:147–48; cf. *The Unconscious,* 14:173. All citations to Freud are from *The Standard Edition.*

31. See Freud, *Repression,* 14:147; cf. *On Narcissism: An Introduction,* 14:93.

32. Freud, *Repression,* 14:148.

33. Ibid., 149.

34. Ibid., 149–50, 151; cf. *The Unconscious,* 14:182.

35. The potential fecundity of these unions was especially threatening to church proprietary rights. This is discussed in Chap. 4, pp. 83, 84, 214 n.10, and Chap. 5, pp. 117, 234 n.59, below.

36. Note, however, that repression is only one of several strategies for coping with unwanted sexual impulses. In another context, Freud identifies three other responses: reversal into its opposite (e.g., love turned into hatred), turning upon

the subject's own self (e.g., sadism replaced by masochism), and sublimation (see *Instincts and Their Vicissitudes,* 14: 126–28). As we will see in Chap. 1, certain clerical circles consciously attempted sublimation as a solution to the requirements of clerical celibacy. But we also find parallels to the other strategies as well. In the context of clerical antifeminism, love transformed into hate seems especially pertinent. In addition, the image of the predatory demon-woman stalking the passive cleric—an image that will recur periodically in the present work—accords with Freud's description of the reversal of an instinct so it redounds upon the subject.

37. From a psychoanalytical perspective, one might say that their repressive strategies were failures, thwarted in their primary aim—the avoidance of unpleasure (see Freud, *Repression,* 14: 155, 157).

38. The concept of the double is foundational in Freud's definition of "the uncanny" (Freud, *The Uncanny,* 17: 234–35). The experience of the uncanny, both hauntingly familiar and yet disconcertingly strange, is described as replete with "all the unfulfilled but possible futures to which we still like to cling in phantasy, all the strivings of the ego which adverse external circumstances have crushed, and all our suppressed acts of volition which nourish in us the illusion of Free Will" (17:236; also see 17:241).

39. See Chap. 6, below—particularly the section, "Why Demons Lost Their Bodies."

40. Nicholas of Lyre, *Moraliter,* Gen. 6.2, ad v. *videntes filii dei; filias hominum; acceperunt uxores sibi,* in *Textus Biblie,* vol. 1, fol. 50r). On this passage, see Chap. 3 nn. 85 and 100, below and the section entitled "The Fall Out of the Body" in Chap. 6, below.

41. Geoffrey Chaucer, *The Riverside Chaucer,* ed. Larry D. Benson, 3d ed. (Boston: Houghton Mifflin, 1987), ll. 878–80, p. 117.

42. Thus Ginzburg isolates "the importance of the anomalies, the cracks that occasionally (albeit very rarely) appear in the documentation, undermining its coherence," *Ecstasies: Deciphering the Witches' Sabbath,* trans. R. Rosenthal (New York: Pantheon, 1991), p. 10; cf. idem, *The Cheese and the Worms: The Cosmos of a Sixteenth-Century Miller,* trans. J. Tedeschi and A. Tedeschi (Harmondsworth: Penguin, 1980), p. xix. Many literary scholars would undoubtedly be critical of such claims. See, for example, Ruth Morse's incisive article, "Telling the Truth with Authority: From Richard II to *Richard II,*" *Common Knowledge* 4 (1995): 111–28.

43. For this use of the exemplum, see Jacques Le Goff, "Ecclesiastical Culture and Folklore in the Middle Ages: Saint Marcellus of Paris and the Dragon," in *Time, Work, and Culture in the Middle Ages,* trans. A. Goldhammer (Chicago: University of Chicago Press, 1980), pp. 159–88; and Jean-Claude Schmitt, *The Holy Greyhound: Guinefort, Healer of Children Since the Thirteenth Century,* trans. M. Thom (Cambridge: Cambridge University Press; Paris: Editions de la Maison des Sciences de l'Homme, 1983). This division between ecclesiastical and popular culture is also sustained in Aron Gurevich, *Medieval Popular Culture: Problems of Belief and Perception,* trans. J. M. Bak and P. A. Hollingsworth (Cambridge: Cambridge University Press; Paris: Editions de la Maison des Sciences de l'Homme, 1988). See his discussion on p. xvii. Also see Gábor Klaniczay's definition of popular versus elite in *The Uses of Supernatural Power,* trans. S. Singerman (Princeton, N.J.: Princeton University Press, 1990), p. 3.

44. See Roger Chartier's impressive articulation of some of these difficulties in *Cultural History: Between Practices and Representations,* trans. Lydia Cochrane (Oxford: Polity Press, 1988), pp. 37–39.

45. My perspective may have something in common with the Althusserian revision of a decentered totality, possessed of multiple rhythms and lacking any unifying or causal ideology. See Robert Young's discussion of this position in *White Mythologies: Writing History and the West* (London: Routledge, 1990), pp. 57–62.

46. John Van Engen, "The Christian Middle Ages as an Historiographical Problem," *American Historical Review* 91 (1986): 519–52. Van Engen's essay was written in reaction to works by the exponents of popular religion, who frequently focused on marginal groups in medieval culture—a focus that, in his opinion, stressed the outlandish. He thus argues that "the examination of 'popular religion' now threatens to eclipse work on popes, theologians, and bishops" (p. 535). More recently, Eamon Duffy's *The Stripping of the Altars: Traditional Religion in England* intends a religious history of a majority that, as he describes it, has been marginalized by current historiography (New Haven, Conn.: Yale University Press, 1992). As the title indicates, Duffy rejects the term "popular religion" in favor of "traditional," arguing that "no substantial gulf existed between the religion of the clergy and the educated elite on the one hand and that of the people at large on the other" (p. 2). The first part of the book, dealing with the Middle Ages, tends to efface conflict, intentionally avoiding any discussion of heresy.

1. Pollution, Illusion, and Masculine Disarray

An earlier version of this chapter was presented at the conference "Constructing Medieval Sexualities," sponsored by the Newberry Library's Center for Renaissance Studies in Chicago, 4–5 March 1994. I would like to thank Peter Brown for several valuable suggestions about sources. I am also grateful to David Brakke for allowing me to read his paper on nocturnal emissions in the early church prior to its publication.

1. "Capsa plena vestibus si dimissa fuerit longo tempore, putrefient in ea vestes: Ita et cogitationes nostrae si non fecerimus eas corporaliter," cited by Vincent of Beauvais, *Speculum historiale* 15.100, in *Speculum quadruplex; sive Speculum maius* (Douai: B. Belleri, 1624), 4: 617.

2. "Quid per animam nisi mentis intentio; quid per ossa nisi carnis fortitudo designatur? Omne autem quod suspenditur procul dubio ab imis eleuatur. Anima ergo suspendium eligit ut ossa moriantur, quia dum mentis intentio ad alta se subleuat omnem in se fortitudinem uitae exterioris necat," Gregory the Great, *Moralia in Iob* 8.25.44, ed. Marcus Adriaen, *CCSL,* vol. 143 (Turnhout: Brepols, 1979), p. 415. Cf. Freud's definition of sublimation: "[the process of sublimation] enables excessively strong excitations arising from particular sources of sexuality to find outlet and use in other fields, so that a not inconsiderable increase in psychical efficiency results from a disposition which in itself is perilous," *Three Essays on Sexuality,* in *The Standard Edition of the Complete Psychological Works of Sigmund Freud,* ed. James Strachey (London: Hogarth Press, 1953), 7: 238.

3. The effort to realign female sexuality in accordance with the male "norm"

accords with the unisex model of the body discussed by Thomas Laqueur in *Making Sex: Body and Gender from the Greeks to Freud* (Cambridge, Mass.: Harvard University Press, 1990), pp. 25–62. Despite these attempts at realignment, however, authorities like Albert the Great had to concede that women were less prone to nocturnal emissions than men. See *Animalium libri XXVI* 9.1.1, in *Opera omnia,* ed. A. Borgnet (Paris: Vivès, 1891), 11: 498.

4. Eve Kosofsky Sedgwick, "Jane Austen and the Masturbating Girl," in *Tendencies* (Durham, N.C.: Duke University Press, 1993), p. 111.

5. See David Brakke's discussion in "The Problematization of Nocturnal Emissions in Early Christian Syria, Egypt, and Gaul," *Journal of Early Christian Studies* 3 (1995): 419–60.

6. John Cassian, *Conférences* 12.7, ed. and trans. E. Pichery, *SC,* no. 54 (Paris: Editions du Cerf, 1958), 2: 131–33. For Serenus's spiritual mutilation, see *Conférences* 7.2, *SC,* no. 42, 1: 245. Alardus Gazaeus notes the analogues to Serenus's castration in Gregory the Great's account of Equitius (*Dialogues* 1.4) and in the life of Thomas Aquinas (see Gazaeus's commentary on Cassian's *Collationes* 7.2, *PL* 49, cols. 669–70, note c). Also see Michel Foucault's discussion of Cassian, "The Battle for Chastity," in *Western Sexuality: Practice and Precept in Past and Present Times,* ed. P. Ariès and A. Béjin, trans. A. Forster (Oxford: Blackwell, 1985), pp. 14–25.

7. Cassian, *Conférences* 12.11, *SC,* no. 54, 2: 139; 2.23, *SC,* no. 42, 1: 134.

8. Cassian, *Institutions cénobitiques* 6.7.2, ed. and trans. Jean-Claude Guy, *SC,* no. 109 (Paris: Editions du Cerf, 1965), pp. 270–72.

9. Cassian, *Conférences* 22.3, *SC,* no. 64, 3: 118.

10. Cassian, *Institutions* 2.13.1–2, *SC,* no. 109, p. 82; cf. his discouragement of sleep after matins (3.5.1, p. 106).

11. John Climacus, *Scala paradisi* 15, *PG* 88, cols. 881–82, 891–92; trans. Colm Luibheid and Norman Russell, *The Ladder of Divine Ascent* (New York: Paulist Press, 1982), pp. 172, 178.

12. See Athanasius, Ep. 48, To Amun, *PG* 26, cols. 1169–76; trans. A. Robertson, in *St. Athanasius: Select Works and Letters,* ed. P. Schaff and Henry Wace, *LNPNFC,* 2d ser., vol. 4 (Grand Rapids, Mich.: Eerdmans, rprt. 1987), pp. 556–57. Also see Brakke's discussion of Athanasius ("Problematization of Nocturnal Emissions," pp. 442–44).

13. For an overview of early Christian attitudes toward dreams, see Jacques Le Goff, "Christianity and Dreams (Second to Seventh Century)," in *The Medieval Imagination,* trans. Arthur Goldhammer (Chicago: University of Chicago Press, 1988), pp. 193–231; and Steven F. Kruger, *Dreaming in the Middle Ages* (Cambridge: Cambridge University Press, 1992), pp. 35–56.

14. Augustine, *Confessionum libri XIII* 10.8.12 ff., ed. Lucas Verheijen, *CCSL,* 27 (Turnhout: Brepols, 1981), pp. 161 ff.; trans. R. S. Pine-Coffin, *Confessions* (Harmondsworth: Penguin, 1961; rprt. 1979), pp. 214 ff. Regarding the nature of the memorial phantasm and the twofold process of storage and recollection, see Mary Carruthers, *The Book of Memory: A Study of Memory in Medieval Culture* (Cambridge: Cambridge University Press, 1990), pp. 46–71.

15. See Eve Kosofsky Sedgwick's citation of Francis Broucek, in "Queer Performativity: Henry James's *The Art of the Novel,*" *GLQ* 1,1 (1993): 5.

16. Augustine, *Confessionum libri XIII* 10.30.41, ed. Verheijen, *CCSL*, 27, pp. 176–77; trans. Pine-Coffin, pp. 233–34. See Peter Brown, *The Body and Society: Men, Women, and Sexual Renunciation in Early Christianity* (New York: Columbia University Press, 1988), pp. 404–8.

17. Slavoj Žižek, *Looking Awry: An Introduction to Jacques Lacan through Popular Culture* (Cambridge, Mass.: MIT Press, 1991), p. 16.

18. On Augustine's progressive mistrust of dreams, see Le Goff, *Medieval Imagination*, pp. 216–18.

19. See Michel Foucault's analysis of Artemidorus in *The Care of the Self*, vol. 3 of *The History of Sexuality*, trans. Robert Hurley (New York: Vintage, 1986), pp. 3–36.

20. Augustine, *De civitate dei* 14.15, 14.17, ed. Bernardus Dombart and Alphonsus Kalb, *CCSL*, 48 (Turnhout: Brepols, 1955), pp. 437–38, 439; trans. Gerald G. Walsh et al., *City of God*, *FC*, vol. 14 (New York: Fathers of the Church, 1952), pp. 386, 389. See Brown, *Body and Society*, pp. 416–18; and Dyan Elliott, *Spiritual Marriage: Sexual Abstinence in Medieval Wedlock* (Princeton, N.J.: Princeton University Press, 1993), pp. 46–50.

21. Augustine, *De Genesi ad litteram libri duodecim* 12.15, ed. Joseph Zycha, *CSEL*, 28, 1 (Vienna: F. Tempsky; Leipzig: G. Freytag, 1894), p. 400; trans. John Hammond Taylor, *The Literal Meaning of Genesis*, *ACW*, no. 42 (New York: Newman Press, 1982), 2: 198. Also see Kruger, *Dreaming in the Middle Ages*, pp. 43–45.

22. See the translation from the Greek by Pelagius and John, especially the section entitled "De fornicatione," bk. 5 of *Verba seniorum*, *PL* 73, cols. 873–88. Cassian's *Collationes* were allegedly based on conversations with such desert ascetics.

23. Augustine, *De diversis quaestionibus octoginta tribus* c. 12, ed. Almut Mutzenbecher, *CCSL*, 44a (Turnhout: Brepols, 1975), p. 19; trans. David L. Mosher, *Eighty-Three Different Questions*, *FC*, vol. 7 (Washington, D.C.: Catholic University Press, 1982), p. 43; *De diuinatione daemonum* 5.9, ed. Joseph Zycha, *CSEL*, 41 (Vienna: F. Tempsky; Leipzig: G. Freytag, 1900), p. 607; trans. R. W. Brown, *The Divination of Demons*, in *Saint Augustine: Treatises on Marriage and Other Subjects*, *FC*, vol. 27 (New York: Fathers of the Church, 1955), p. 430. Also see Cassian's similar view, attributed to the monk Serenus (*Conférences* 7.10–15, *SC*, no. 42, 1: 255–59).

24. See Augustine, *De Genesi ad litteram libri duodecim* 12.17, ed. Zycha, *CSEL*, 28, 1, p. 403; trans. Taylor, *The Literal Meaning of Genesis*, *ACW*, no. 42, 2: 201; also see 2: 309, n. 81. The conception of a quasi-omniscient devil, who could read human hearts as God does, was altogether too threatening a notion and was accordingly dropped. Thus Aquinas argues that angels and demons are only capable of reading the mental images of an individual's intellect; they cannot know precisely how these images will be utilized in thought (*De malo* q. 16, art. 8, resp. ad obj. 3–5, in *Opera omnia* [Parma: Petrus Fiaccadori, 1856; rprt. New York: Musurgia, 1949], 8: 415–16; trans. Jean Oesterle, *On Evil* [Notre Dame, Ind.: University of Notre Dame Press, 1995], p. 513). Cf. *Summa theologiae* 1a, q. 57, art. 4, resp. ed. and trans. Fathers of the English Dominician Province (London: Blackfriars, 1968), 9: 137.

25. Eight centuries later, when Aquinas would allege that demons can change the cognitive part of the soul, it was Augustine's graphic description from *Eighty-Three Different Questions*, cited in the text, to which he turned (*De malo* q. 16, art. 11,

sed contra, in *Opera omnia,* Parma edition, 8: 420; trans. Oesterle, *On Evil,* p. 256). Also see the thirteenth-century encyclopedist Vincent of Beauvais's parallel use of the same passage (*Speculum naturale* 2.115, vol. 1 of *Speculum quadruplex,* col. 151).

26. My view of Augustine's reliance on demonic interpolation differs from that of Le Goff, who argues that Augustine placed little emphasis on demons as originators of dreams, viewing dreams as an essentially "psychological phenomenon" (*Medieval Imagination,* pp. 217–18). This difference may be owing to my focus on Augustine's view of erotic dreams. Note, however, that even in *On Care to Be Had for the Dead,* wherein Augustine expresses his most profound skepticism regarding dreams (likening some to the waking ravings of the mad), he still thinks that the truth quotient of dreams is a result of angelic intervention—the flip side of the demonic (*De cura pro mortuis gerenda* 10.12–15.18, ed. Zycha, *CSEL,* 41, pp. 639–52; trans. H. Browne, in *St. Augustin: On the Holy Trinity, Doctrinal Treatises, Moral Treatises, LNPNFC,* 1st ser., vol. 3 [Grand Rapids, Mich.: Eerdmans, rprt. 1978], pp. 544–48).

27. Bede, *Ecclesiastical History of the English People* 1.27, ed. Bertram Colgrave and R. A. B. Mynors (Oxford: Clarendon Press, 1969), p. 101; cf. Cassian, *Conférences* 22.3, *SC,* no. 64, 3: 116–18.

28. Gregory the Great, *Dialogues* 4.50, ed. Adalbert de Vogüé, trans. Paul Antin, *SC,* no. 265 (Paris: Editions du Cerf, 1980), 3: 172–74; idem, *Moralia* 8.24.43, p. 414. Also see the letter in Bede attributed to Gregory the Great, *Ecclesiastical History* 1.27, p. 100. Cassian was probably responsible for this set of associations, as the entry for *illusio* in the *Thesaurus linguae latinae* seems to suggest ([Leipzig: B. G. Teubner, 1934–64], vol. 7, i, col. 393). Note especially the rubric "De nocturnis inlusionibus" (*Conférences* 22, *SC,* no. 64, 3: 113). Also see *Institutions* 2.13.1 (*SC,* no. 109, p. 82), where he addresses the jealous enemy's contamination of a monk's purity through the illusion of a dream (*somni inlusione*).

29. Le Goff, *Medieval Imagination,* p. 228.

30. See Aquinas's citation in *Summa theologiae* 2a 2ae, q. 154, art. 5, resp., 43: 224. Also see Le Goff, *Medieval Imagination,* p. 225, and Alardus Gazaeus's Commentary on Cassian's *Collationes* 22.3, *PL* 49, cols. 1219–20, note e.

31. *Preces nocturnae,* in Alcuin's *Carmina, PL* 101, col. 726.

32. See Alardus Gazaeus's Commentary on Cassian's *Collationes* 7.2, *PL* 49, cols. 669–70, note c.

33. "Aufer a nobis, domine, quaesumus, omnes iniquitates nostras, ut ad loca tuo nomini purificanda puris mereamur mentibus accedere"; "quid aut neglegentia polluit, aut ira committit, aut stimulat ebrietas, aut libido subvertit"; "extinguatur antiqui serpentis invidia," *Reconciliatio violatae aecclesiae,* Cyrille Vogel and Reinhard Elze, eds., *Le Pontifical romano-germanique du dixième siècle,* Studi e Testi, 226 (Vatican City: Biblioteca Apostolica Vaticana, 1963), 1: 182, 183–84, 184. See Chap. 3, pp. 64–65, below.

34. Pierre J. Payer, *Sex and the Penitentials: The Development of a Sexual Code, 550–1150* (Toronto: University of Toronto Press, 1984), p. 50. For a general discussion of nocturnal pollutions in the penitentials, see pp. 49–52.

35. Rudolph of Bourges, *Capitula* c. 45, *PL* 119, col. 726. The greater part of his discussion is drawn from the letter to Augustine of Canterbury, attributed to Gregory the Great.

36. Slavoj Žižek, *The Sublime Object of Ideology* (London: Verso, 1989), pp. 55–56. Cf. Ned Lukacher's discussion of Freud's primal scene, which is to be found not in the past but in the future, "in the projective repetition of the origin as it is elaborated through transference" (*The Primal Scenes: Literature, Philosophy, and Psychoanalysis* [Ithaca, N.Y.: Cornell University Press, 1986], p. 42).

37. See Elliott, *Spiritual Marriage,* pp. 98–104.

38. See Matthew of Cracow's confessor's manual, *De modo confitendi et de puritate conscientie* c. 14 (Paris: Guy Marchant for Denis Roce [?], before 1501); cf. John Gerson's *De praeparatione ad missam,* in *Oeuvres complètes,* ed. Palémon Glorieux (Paris: Desclée, 1973), 9: 42. (All subsequent citations to Gerson are from *Oeuvres complètes.*) Also note that Thomas Aquinas referred to Cassian's monk, who was cured of his precommunion pollutions by receiving the sacrament (*Summa theologiae* 2a 2ae, q. 154, art. 5, resp., 43: 224–26). John of Freiburg also tells this story, citing Aquinas's invocation (*Summa confessorum* bk. 3, tit. 24, q. 73 [Rome: s.n., 1518], fol. 123v).

39. For the official pronouncement, see Lateran IV, const. 1, in Norman P. Tanner et al., ed. and trans., *Decrees of the Ecumenical Councils,* original text established by G. Alberigo et al. (London: Sheed and Ward; Washington, D.C.: Georgetown University Press, 1990), 1: 230. For pre-Lateran IV discussions bearing on this doctrine, see Gary Macy, *Theologies of the Eucharist in the Early Scholastic Period: A Study of the Salvific Function of the Sacrament According to Theologians c. 1080–c. 1200* (Oxford: Clarendon Press, 1984). For the first usage of this term, see Joseph Goering, "The Invention of Transubstantiation," *Traditio* 46 (1991): 147–70. Regarding the lack of consensus over what transubstantiation actually implied, see Gary Macy, "The Dogma of Transubstantiation in the Middle Ages," *Journal of Ecclesiastical History* 45 (1994): 11–41. On the rise in clerical prestige incumbent on the doctrine, see Caroline Walker Bynum, *Holy Feast and Holy Fast: The Religious Significance of Food to Medieval Women* (Berkeley: University of California Press, 1987), pp. 56–60; and Miri Rubin, *Corpus Christi: The Eucharist in Late Medieval Culture* (Cambridge: Cambridge University Press, 1991), pp. 49 ff. Cf. Peter Brown's discussion of transubstantiation in "Society and the Supernatural: A Medieval Change," in *Society and the Holy in Late Antiquity* (London: Faber and Faber, 1982), pp. 326–27.

40. His reason is that emissions were always linked with a dishonest cause ("huiusmodi enim pollutio habet causam semper inhonestam"), be it imagination, gluttony, or the corruption of nature (Vincent of Beauvais, *Speculum historiale,* pp. 284–85). As will be clear from the ensuing discussion, Vincent's view was somewhat more stringent than what would become the prevailing opinion among his fellow Dominicans. For a discussion of Paul's original meaning in the context of contemporary medical understanding, see Dale B. Martin, *The Corinthian Body* (New Haven, Conn.: Yale University Press, 1996), pp. 190–97. For Peter Damian's usage of 1 Cor. 11.29, see Chap. 4, pp. 103–4, below.

41. See Lateran IV, const. 21, in Tanner, ed. and trans., *Decrees of the Ecumenical Councils,* 1: 245. Also see Michel Foucault's stimulating discussion of the impact that this legislated compulsion to confess had on western conceptions of sexuality in *The History of Sexuality,* vol. 1, *An Introduction,* trans. Robert Hurley (New York: Vintage, 1978), pp. 58–67. Cf. Nicole Bériou, "La Confession dans les écrits théologiques et pastoraux du XIIIe siècle: médication de l'âme ou démarche judiciaire?" in

L'Aveu: antiquité et moyen-âge, Actes de la table ronde organisée par l'Ecole Française de Rome avec le concours du CNRS et l'Université de Trieste, Rome, 28–30 March 1984; Collection de l'Ecole Française de Rome, 88 (Rome: Ecole Française de Rome, Palais Farnèse, 1986), pp. 261–82. For the laity's initiation into heightened concerns over pollution, see Chap. 3, below.

42. Robert of Flamborough, *Liber poenitentialis* 4.340, ed. J. J. Francis Firth (Toronto: Pontifical Institute of Mediaeval Studies, 1971), p. 268.

43. Thomas of Chobham, *Summa confessorum* 7.2.1.1.1, Analecta Mediaevalia Namurcensia, 25, ed. F. Broomfield (Louvain: Nauwelaerts, 1968), pp. 330–33.

44. John of Freiburg, *Summa confessorum* bk. 3, tit. 24, q. 73, fol. 123r; cf. Thomas Aquinas, *Summa theologiae* 2a 2ae, q. 154, art. 5, resp., 43: 223, and 1a, q. 84, art. 8, resp., 12: 44–47.

45. John Nider, *De morali lepra* c. 4 (Louvain: Johann von Paderborn, 1481), fols. 21v–22r.

46. "Scripsi pridem aliqua super praeparatione ad missam sub decem considerationibus, occasione sumpta principaliter ex materia pollutionis nocturnae. Nuper autem de pollutione quae videtur accidere vigilando quaesita sunt a me aliqua quae solent timoratas conscientias plurimum exturbare sicut frequenter ex diversis personis utriusque sexus tam in confessione quam extra potui perpendere," Gerson, *De cognitione castitatis,* 9: 50; cf. Matthew of Cracow, *De modo confitiendo et de puritate conscientiae* c. 16.

47. " . . . quia si peccator vult mentiri ac fugere, saepe deprehenditur per talia quae naturaliter accident omnibus, aut rarissime reperitur oppositum; qualia si statim neget, constat eum timere dicere grandiora," Gerson, *De arte audiendi confessiones,* 8: 13–14.

48. "Amice, recordaris quod umquam in pueritia tua, circa decem aut duodecim annos, tua virga vel membrum pudendum fuerit erecta? Si dicit quod non, statim convincitur mendacii et quod vult fugere et timet capi. . . . Si fateatur quod ita, dicat iterum confessor, si ille sit juvenis praecipue: amice, numquid erat illud indecens? Quid ergo faciebas ut non erigeretur? . . . Si nolit respondere, plane petatur consequenter: amice, numquid tu palpabas aut fricabas virgam tuam, quemadmodum pueri solent?" Gerson, *De confessione mollitei,* 8: 71.

49. Gerson, *De confessione mollitei,* 8: 72–73.

50. Gerson, *De cognitione castitatis,* 9: 63; also see p. 61. Cf. Aquinas's recognition that a person could experience a nocturnal emission as a result of pondering these matters in an exclusively theoretical manner (*Summa theologiae* 2a 2ae, q. 154, art. 5, resp., 43: 224).

51. Gerson, *Poetimini: Contre la luxure,* 7, ii: 827; cf. *De cognitione castitatis,* 9: 61. See Caesarius of Heisterbach's anecdote about a noblewoman who told her aged confessor that she was burning with love for him. The confessor managed to dissuade her from her folly. But his immediate action was to cross himself—a gesture that was traditionally held to be effective against diabolical illusion. Caesarius may have been implying that the priest's first response was to regard her as a demonic succubus (*Dialogus miraculorum* 3.43, ed. Joseph Strange [Cologne: Heberle, 1851], 1: 161–62; trans. H. Von E. Scott and C. C. Swinton Bland, *The Dialogue on Miracles* 3.43 [London: Routledge, 1929], 1: 182–83). On the efficacy

of the sign of the cross against demons, see Athanasius, *Vita S. Antonii* c. 23, 35, *PG* 26, cols. 877–78, 893–94; trans. Mary Emily Keenan, *The Life of St. Anthony,* in *Early Christian Biographies, FC,* vol. 18 (New York: Fathers of the Church, 1952), pp. 156, 167; Thomas of Cantimpré, *Bonum universale de apibus* 2.57.33–34 (Douai: B. Bell-eri, 1627), pp. 562–63 (hereafter cited as *De apibus*).

52. Robert of Flamborough, *Liber poenitentialis* 4.224, p. 197. Robert is also representative of the more traditional school of circumspection, arguing that confessors should be careful not to put ideas in their penitents' heads (p. 196).

53. This is apparent not only in the revival of the genre of dream vision (e.g., Alan of Lille's *Plaint of Nature,* or the *Romance of the Rose*), but particularly in the intense interest in classical authors like Macrobius. See, for example, Chaucer's *Parliament of Fowls.*

54. Hildegard of Bingen, *Causae et curae,* ed. Paul Kaiser (Leipzig: B. G. Teubner, 1903), p. 83. Cf. Caesarius of Heisterbach's acknowledgment that one could sin or deserve merit in sleep since dreams were informed by thoughts from our waking hours. He arrives at this atypical position in the course of his explanation of the anecdote concerning how the Virgin denied her blessing to an unruly sleeper — an incident discussed later in this chapter (*Dialogus miraculorum* 7.14, ed. Strange, 2: 17; trans. Scott and Bland, 1: 472).

55. Vincent of Beauvais, *Speculum naturale* 26.1, 26.79, cols. 1841–42, 1887–88). For a discussion of consent and sin in the later Middle Ages, see Thomas N. Tentler, *Sin and Confession on the Eve of the Reformation* (Princeton, N.J.: Princeton University Press, 1977), pp. 148–56.

56. John of Freiburg, *Summa confessorum* bk. 3, tit. 24, q. 73–74, fols. 123r–v.

57. " . . . prout est in somniis sordidis et impuris quando non peccatum est sed similitudo peccati," Gerson, *De praeparatione ad missam,* 9: 44. Also see his short treatise, *De primis motibus et consensu,* 9: 167.

58. "Nichil de somnio est dicendum. quia nulla culpa est ibi," Matthew of Cracow, *De modo confitendi et de puritate conscientie* c. 13. Also see Chap. 2, n. 5, below.

59. According to Macrobius's fivefold classification, the *visio* is one of the most reliable types of dreams with respect to its basic quotient of truth. See his *Commentary on the Dream of Scipio* 1.3, trans. William Harris Stahl (New York: Columbia University Press, 1952), pp. 87–92. Gregory the Great's classification seems to treat the world *visio* more loosely (see *Dialogues* 4.50, *SC,* no. 265, 3: 172–76).

60. Gerson, *Poetimini: Contre la luxure,* 7,ii: 832.

61. For Celestine's various sexual temptations, which culminate in the dream, see *AA SS,* May, 4: 423–24. Celestine's candor generated considerable work for his hagiographer, Peter d'Ailly. After a learned exposition of the dream-parable, differentiating between the rational and the irrational soul, Peter warns that the average person has not achieved Celestine's perfection and thus must interrogate the character of his / her pollution closely before participating in communion. He then offers an excursus on the various kinds of pollution and their attendant degrees of culpability (see *AA SS,* May, 4: 488–89). According to the Bollandists, Peter d'Ailly's vita was written between 1378 and 1408, while Glorieux situates Gerson's treatise in either 1408 or 1412. As the two clerics were close friends, Gerson may have been directed to this anecdote by d'Ailly.

62. Gerson, *De praeparatione ad missam,* 9: 46, 50. Celestine's description of defilement is somewhat more graphic, however. He struggles to convey his disgust by alluding to the wet texture of the excrement ("Ille malus asellus coepit turpiter eijecere de corpore stercus, quasi manducasset herbas teneras," *AA SS,* May, 4: 424). Gerson, on the other hand, euphemistically relates that the ass paid the tribute of its belly ("Hic asinus tributum ventris per viam solvit").

63. Gerson, *De praeparatione ad missam,* 9: 35–36.

64. Note that earlier in the treatise, under the fifth consideration, Gerson compares nocturnal emissions to urination (*De praeparatione ad missam,* 9: 41).

65. Thomas of Chobham, *Summa confessorum* 7.2.1.1.1, p. 331; Gerson, *De praeparatione ad missam,* 9: 44.

66. Gerson, *De cognitione castitatis,* 9: 62.

67. Gerson, *De praeparatione ad missam,* 9: 43.

68. Cassian, *Conférences* 12.8, *SC,* no. 54, 2:135; cf. 2.23, *SC,* no. 42, 1: 134.

69. Vincent of Beauvais, however, does include Cassian's challenging description of the passionless sixth stage in his encyclopedic *Speculum naturale* (31.19, col. 2307). The twelfth-century Nicholas of St. Albans's assertion that Joachim, father of the Virgin Mary, was only aware that he experienced a nocturnal emission upon waking is akin to Cassian's sixth state, albeit in its less threatening guise. See Chap. 5, n. 34, below.

70. For Gerson's appeals to medical expertise, see *De praeparatione ad missam,* 9: 42, 43; and *De cognitione castitatis,* 9: 51.

71. Soranus, *Gynecology* 3.12.45, trans. Owsi Temkin (Baltimore: Johns Hopkins University Press, 1956; rprt. 1991), pp. 168–69. According to Soranus, the lead plate was to be placed under the loins, while Cassian recommended placement above. For discussions of gonorrhea, see Joan Cadden, *The Meanings of Sex Difference in the Middle Ages: Medicine, Science, and Culture* (Cambridge: Cambridge University Press, 1993), pp. 26–27; and Danielle Jacquart and Claude Thomasset, *Sexuality and Medicine in the Middle Ages,* trans. Matthew Adamson (Princeton, N.J.: Princeton University Press, 1988), pp. 147–51. On the association between menstruation and gonorrhea in Talmudic culture, see n. 74, below.

72. Constantine the African, *De coitu,* trans. Paul Delany, *Chaucer Review* 4 (1970): 58. Also see Cadden, *Meanings of Sex Difference,* p. 65 and n. 25.

73. Drawing inspiration from Zechariah 13.1, Gregory points to the fountain open to the house of David and the inhabitants of Jerusalem for the washing of both sinners and unclean women (*menstruatae*). Sinners as diverse as King David, Mary Magdalene, Peter (in his denial of Christ), and the repentant thief at the crucifixion can all be understood to have washed in this fountain. But in Gregory's hands, the unclean woman is a still more subtle imagistic tool than is an active sinner, since she need not be guilty of explicit deeds; she is equally implicated by evil thoughts (*in prava cogitatione*). Thus she pollutes her own flesh and the flesh of all she comes in contact with. Again with respect to the lines "all that seek her shall not fail; in her monthly filth (*menstruis*) they shall find her" (Jer. 2.24), Gregory associates the beasts stalking a female in heat with evil spirits stalking the polluted soul (*Homiliae in Hiezechihelem prophetam* bk. 2, hom. 8, c. 19–20, ed. Marcus Adriaen, *CCSL,* vol. 142 [Turnhout: Brepols, 1971], pp. 350–52). The deployment of this imagery in ancient Israel is discussed above in the Introduction.

74. Note that by eliding men's nonseminal discharge and menstruation with semen, however, Gerson is eliminating an important distinction from the standpoint of Levitican tradition because semen was considered only temporarily polluting (see Eilberg-Schwartz, *Savage in Judaism,* pp. 186–87; also see Introduction, n. 9, above). There is evidence that Talmudic culture continued to preserve this distinction, although the valence of the pollution changed for the purposes of reading scripture. Thus the Tosefta (redacted third century) states that "gonnorheics, menstruants and parturients are permitted to read the Torah, to study Mishna, midrash, religious law and aggada, but men who have had a seminal emission may not" (as cited by Daniel Boyarin, *Carnal Israel: Reading Sex in Talmudic Culture* [Berkeley: University of California Press, 1993], p. 180).

75. "Fluxum pateris nec sanari potes a medicis, tuis scilicet exercitiis, tange plena fide cum hemorrhoissa, Martha secundum Ambrosium, fimbriam vestimenti Jesu, sacrosanctam videlicet hostiam ut purgeris," Gerson, *De praeparatione ad missam,* 9: 48.

76. Gerson, *De praeparatione ad missam,* 9: 49. Note that Gerson is atypical in alleging that there was any afterbirth involved in Christ's birth, since theology generally attempted to spare both mother and child this indignity (see the section entitled "The Host, the Priest, and the Lady" in Chap. 5, below). Regarding the polluting aspects of afterbirth, see Thomas of Chobham, *Summa confessorum* 7.2.2.3, pp. 338–39. One of the women of Montaillou, examined in Jacques Fournier's inquisition, had a crisis in faith inducing her to doubt the doctrine of transubstantiation precisely because the thought that Christ may have been implicated in the filth of afterbirth presented itself to her. See Peter Dronke's discussion of this incident in *Women Writers of the Middle Ages: A Critical Study of Texts from Perpetua (d. 203) to Marguerite of Porete (d. 1310)* (Cambridge: Cambridge University Press, 1984), pp. 213–14. The legend of Pope Joan, who went into labor while in pontifical procession and died giving birth, also turns on a heightened sense of pollution. For a history of the legend, see Cesare d'Onofrio, *La Papassa Giovanna: Roma e papato tra storia e leggenda* (Rome: Romana Società Editrice, 1979).

77. "Patet in mulieribus puerperis quibus siccantur mammae dum non elicitur lac, alioquin semper fluere paratum est," Gerson, *De cognitione castitatis,* 9: 63. On the essential sameness of blood, semen, and breast milk, see Charles T. Wood, "The Doctor's Dilemma: Sin, Salvation, and the Menstrual Cycle in Medieval Thought," *Speculum* 56 (1981): 710–27.

78. "Si me invitam corruperis, mihi castitatis duplicabitur ad coronam," Gerson, *De cognitione castitatis,* 9: 63; cf. Aquinas, *Commentum in quatuor libros sententiarum* bk. 4, dist. 33, q. 3, art. 1, solutio, in *Opera omnia,* Parma edition, 7,2: 976. For more on emissions and merit, see *De praeparatione ad missam,* 9: 44–45. Also see Gerson's analogy between Augustine's exculpation of a consecrated virgin raped against her will (*De civitate dei* 1.25) and a sleeping cleric who experiences a pollution (9: 41). This assimilation was already latent in Augustine, who argued that a violated virgin is no more responsible for the pleasure inadvertently enjoyed in the course of an assault than is a sleeper (see the section entitled "From Masturbation to Mental Defloration" in Chap. 2, below).

79. Regarding the healthy incredulity of previous centuries (extending to major figures, such as Gratian in the twelfth century), see Jeffrey Burton Russell,

Witchcraft in the Middle Ages (Ithaca, N.Y.: Cornell University Press, 1972), pp. 75–80. The Carolingian *Canon episcopi* is the most important document for the official statement of skepticism; see Russell's appendix for the text of *Canon episcopi* and its variations (pp. 291–93). For the importance of scholasticism in validating many folkloric beliefs, see Russell, *Witchcraft in the Middle Ages,* pp. 115–20, 142–47; and Nicolas Kiessling, *The Incubus in English Literature: Provenance and Progeny* (Pullman: Washington State University Press, 1977), pp. 21–23. For widespread belief in demon lovers, see H. C. Lea, *Materials Toward a History of Witchcraft,* ed. Arthur C. Howland (Philadelphia: University of Pennsylvania Press, 1939), 1: 145–62. On the literary tradition, see Peter D. Grudin, *The Demon-Lover: The Theme of Demoniality in English and Continental Fiction of the Late Eighteenth and Early Nineteenth Centuries* (New York: Garland, 1987); and Kiessling, *Incubus in English Literature,* pp. 43ff. For various efforts to refine the doctrine of transubstantiation, see n. 39, above.

80. "Credidisti quod quidam credere solent, quod sint agrestes feminae, quas sylvaticas vocant, quas dicunt esse corporeas, et quando voluerint ostendant se suis amatoribus, et cum eis dicunt se oblectasse, et item quando voluerint, abscondant se et evanescant? Si credidisti, decem dies in pane et aqua," Burchard of Worms, *Decretum* 19.5, *PL* 140, col. 971.

81. This subject was immensely complicated by the fact that, as of the thirteenth century, angels and demons were believed to be entirely incorporeal—a subject I explore in depth in Chap. 6, below.

82. Caesarius of Heisterbach, *Dialogus miraculorum* 3.10, ed. Strange, 1: 122–23; trans. Scott and Bland, 1: 137. For other instances of demon lovers, see 3.6–9, 11, 13, ed. Strange, 1: 116–22, 123–24, 125–27; trans. Scott and Bland, 1: 130–37, 138–39, 140–42. Cf. the profuse treatment by a more scholastically oriented contemporary of Caesarius—theologian and bishop of Paris, William of Auvergne (d. 1249), in *De universo* 3a 2ae, c. 25, *Opera omnia* (Paris: A. Pralard, 1674; rprt. Frankfurt am Main: Minerva, 1963), 1: 1070–73.

83. Caesarius of Heisterbach, *Dialogus miraculorum* 3.4, ed. Strange, 1: 114; trans. Scott and Bland, 1: 128. Other authors imagine much more public and awkward ramifications. The eleventh-century Peter Damian describes how a demon, speaking through a demoniac, triumphs over a monk whose susceptibility to temptation eventuates in a nocturnal emission (Ep. 102, To Abbot Desiderius and the Monks of Monte Cassino, *Die Briefe des Petrus Damiani,* ed. Kurt Reindel, *MGH, Die Briefe der deutschen Kaiserzeit,* 4 [Munich: *MGH,* 1989], 3: 131–32). Cf. Thomas of Cantimpré's similar anecdote about a monk who was publicly humiliated when his unconfessed erotic dream was exposed by a demoniac (*De apibus* 2.57.6, p. 541). This later emphasis on confession shifts the moral of the tale away from purity per se, which was so important in the period of the Gregorian Reform, to focus on the power of sacramental confession. At present, Owen J. Blum's translation of Damian's letters in the *Fathers of the Church* series stops at Ep. 90 of the original 180. Citations for translations are given wherever possible, however.

84. Caesarius of Heisterbach, *Dialogus miraculorum* 5.33, ed. Strange, 1: 316; trans. Scott and Bland, 1: 363. Note that the novice who plays the stooge in the dialogue was shocked that such a heavy punishment would be exacted over an

incident occurring in one's sleep, since "'God is exceeding merciful, and a sleeping man differs but little from one who is dead.'" The older monk suggests that the lay brother may have been negligent with regard to seemly demeanor (hence his exposed state), or was purposefully lingering over erotic thoughts while awake, or had overindulged in alcohol (ed. Strange, 1: 317; trans. Scott and Bland, 1: 363). The fact that this incident occurred at midday is clearly meant to evoke the Noonday demon of Psalm 90.6—a figure associated with sloth (see Penelope B. R. Doob, *Nebuchadnezzar's Children: Conventions of Madness in Middle English Literature* [New Haven, Conn.: Yale University Press, 1974], pp. 29–30, 178–79, 197). Thomas of Cantimpré relates a similar tale about a relative of his who was lying in the dormitory before prime when the demon in the shape of a beautiful woman lay down beside him. But when he began to shout and kick, she disappeared (*De apibus* 2.57.37, pp. 564–65). The fear of women implicit in these tales is self-evident. Cf. the more visceral misogyny of William of Auvergne: a man dreamed he was having sex with a beautiful woman only to awake in the midst of a carcass of a rotting cow (*De universo* 3a 2ae, c. 23, in *Opera omnia,* 1: 1065).

85. Caesarius of Heisterbach, *Dialogus miraculorum* 7.14, ed. Strange, 2: 16–17; trans. Scott and Bland, 1: 470–71; cf. 7.13, ed. Strange, 2: 16; trans. Scott and Bland, 1: 470–71.

86. *Benedicta Regula* c. 22, ed. Rudolph Hanslik, rev. ed., *CSEL,* 75 (Vienna: Hoelder, Pichler, Tempsky, 1977), pp. 84–85; trans. Anthony Meisel and M. C. del Mastro, *The Rule of St. Benedict* (New York: Doubleday, 1975), p. 70. Peter Damian, Ep. 102, To Abbot Desiderius and the Monks of Monte Cassino, *Die Briefe,* 3:130–31). It was the same demoniac who exposed the monk's companion for a nocturnal emission (see n. 83, above). Parallel concerns also present themselves with respect to female religious. Thus in Clare of Montefalco's process of canonization it was reported that, after the youthful Clare had been reprimanded by the abbess for sleeping in such a way that her naked shin was exposed, Clare became accustomed to tying her nightdress to her ankles. See Sisters Marina and Thomassa's responses to article 1 (ed. Enrico Menestò, *Il processo di canonizzazione di Chiara da Montefalco* [Regione dell'Umbria: La Nuova Italia, 1984], pp. 67–68, 98–99). Sister Francesca additionally notes that Clare placed rags between her legs and feet when she slept so that her naked flesh would not rub together (regarding art. 1, p. 330).

87. The concept of "splitting" derives from the work of Melanie Klein, a pioneering psychoanalyst specializing in psychotic disorders in children. See her "Notes on Some Schizoid Mechanisms," in *The Selected Melanie Klein,* ed. Juliet Mitchell (New York: Free Press, 1987), pp. 176–200; also see "The Psychogenesis of Manic-Depressive States," p. 143. Cf. Freud's discussion of the good and bad father in Hoffman's tale *The Sandman* (*The Uncanny,* in *The Standard Edition,* 17: 232, n. 1). Michael Carroll uses the concept of splitting in his analysis of harmful and nurturing images of Mary herself, which is a stricter adherence to Klein's formulations than is my own usage. See *Madonnas That Maim: Popular Catholicism in Italy Since the Fifteenth Century* (Baltimore: Johns Hopkins University Press, 1992), esp. pp. 145–50.

88. Caesarius of Heisterbach, *Dialogus miraculorum* 3.12, ed. Strange, 1: 124; trans. Scott and Bland, 1: 139–40.

89. Thomas Aquinas, *De potentia* q. 6, art. 3, resp., in *Opera omnia,* Parma edition, 8: 129; trans. English Dominican Fathers, *On the Power of God* (Westminster, Md.: Newman Press, 1952), 2: 174–75; *De malo* q. 16, art. 9, resp. ad obj. 10, in *Opera omnia,* Parma edition, 8: 418; trans. Oesterle, *On Evil,* p. 520. Aquinas advances the diabolical appropriation of hidden seeds (an Augustinian concept) to explain the way demons work what appear to be miracles—as was the case with Pharaoh's magicians and their marvelous production of serpents on demand. But he also draws analogies between these effects and the demonic simulation of reproduction, discussed in the following note.

90. Henry Kramer and James Sprenger, *Malleus maleficarum 1487,* photographic facsimile of the first edition (Hildesheim: Georg Olms, 1992), pt. 1, q. 3; pt. 2, q. 1, c. 4, fols. 11r–13v, 55r–55v; trans. Montague Summers (London: John Rodker, 1928; rprt. New York: Dover, 1971), pp. 21–28, 112–13; Aquinas, *De potentia* q. 6, art. 8, obj. 5–7, and resp. ad obj. 5–7, in *Opera omnia,* Parma edition, 8: 140–42; trans. English Dominican Fathers, *On the Power of God,* 2: 209, 211–12; cf. *Summa theologiae* 1a, q. 51, art. 3, resp. ad obj. 6, 9: 43. Cf. Thomas of Cantimpré's account, in which he gives Bede as his source (*De apibus* 2.57.16, p. 548). Also see Lea, *Materials Toward a History of Witchcraft,* 1: 153–57. Note that Aquinas had earlier addressed the possibility of an incubus stealing the semen from a nocturnal emission in a quodlibetical question asking if a man can be both virgin and father, as discussed in Chapter 2. His treatment was fleeting and oblique, however. He did not comment on the probability of so disturbing a paternity (quodlib. 6, q. 10, art. 18, in *Opera omnia,* Parma edition, 9: 550–51). But the Jewish apocryphal tradition maintained that Adam's first wife, the demon Lilith, provoked men to nocturnal emissions and masturbation in order to produce her demon brood (Boyarin, *Carnal Israel,* pp. 95–96).

91. John Nider, *Formicarium* 5.10 (Douai: B. Belleri, 1602), p. 401; idem, *De morali lepra* c. 16, fol. 80r.

92. I am here distinguishing between the practical protocols required by ritual and the fluid use of female imagery in devotional tradition, as discussed by Caroline Walker Bynum. See *Jesus as Mother: Studies in the Spirituality of the High Middle Ages* (Berkeley: University of California Press, 1982). Canon law continued to discuss castration as a possible impediment to the ministry of the altar (see Gratian's D. 55 c. 4; also see X.1.20.4. Cf. John of Freiburg's discussion of castration as an impediment to the ministry of the altar and promotion in orders, *Summa confessorum* bk. 2, tit. 1, q. 6, fols. 52v–53r). Gratian also cites canons forbidding women to approach the altar, implying that their presence is polluting (see D. 23 c. 25; D. 23 c. 34 dpc; cf. X.3.2.1). These prohibitions would eventually be taken up by the scholastic tradition when addressing woman's ineligibility for ordination. See Francine Cardman, "The Medieval Question of Women and Orders," *The Thomist* 42 (1978): 582–99, esp. pp. 591, 593, 597. Also see Aquinas's peremptory discussion, "Whether the female sex impedes the reception of ordination," wherein he argues that a male is necessitated both according to the requirement of the sacrament and according to precept (*Commentum in quatuor libros sententiarum* bk. 4, dist. 25, q. 2, art. 1, in *Opera omnia,* Parma edition, 7,2: 907–8; cf. Cardman, "Medieval Question of Women and Orders," pp. 586–88).

2. *From Sexual Fantasy to Demonic Defloration*

1. See, for example, Augustine, *De civitate dei* 14.17, ed. Bernardus Dombart and Alphonsus Kalb, *CCSL,* 48 (Turnhout: Brepols, 1955), p. 439; trans. Gerald G. Walsh et al., *City of God, FC,* 14 (New York: Fathers of the Church, 1952), p. 389. Also see Peter Brown, *The Body and Society: Men, Women, and Sexual Renunciation in Early Christianity* (New York: Columbia University Press, 1988), pp. 406–7; and Elaine Pagels, *Adam, Eve, and the Serpent* (New York: Random House, 1988), pp. 110–12.

2. One of the factors at work here was doubtlessly the "hidden from history" phenomenon—wherein women's absence from the historical record could work as a mixed blessing, as it does in the history of lesbianism. On this silence, which became more fortunate as the Middle Ages progressed and gay culture came to be actively persecuted, see the introduction to Judith Brown's *Immodest Acts: The Life of a Lesbian Nun in Renaissance Italy* (New York: Oxford University Press, 1986), pp. 3–20. On the hostile climate toward gay culture in the later Middle Ages, see John Boswell, *Christianity, Social Tolerance, and Homosexuality: Gay People in Western Europe from the Beginning of the Christian Era to the Fourteenth Century* (Chicago: University of Chicago Press, 1980), pp. 269–332.

3. See, for example, John Cassian's *Conférences* 22.3, ed. and trans. E. Pichery, *SC,* no. 64 (Paris: Editions du Cerf, 1959), 3: 116–17; cf. the letter attributed to Gregory the Great in response to Augustine of Canterbury's queries, cited in Bede's *Ecclesiastical History of the English People* 1.27, ed. and trans. Bertram Colgrave and R. A. B. Mynors (Oxford: Clarendon Press, 1969), p. 101. Vincent of Beauvais has an extensive discussion of nocturnal emissions, which summarizes many of the important patristic and medical authorities, in *Speculum naturale* 31.14–23, vol. 1 of *Speculum quadruplex; sive Speculum maius* (Douai: B. Belleri, 1624), cols. 2302–11.

4. Even so, a nocturnal emission was considered culpable if arising from "evil waking thoughts," as stated in the letter attributed to Gregory the Great (Bede, *Ecclesiastical History* 1.27, p. 101). There was also an awareness that consent to a sinful dream could occur after the fact. See, for example, John Nider's pastoral manual *De morali lepra* (Louvain: Johann von Paderborn, 1481), fol. 21v.

5. See Augustine, *De Genesi ad litteram libri duodecim* 12.15, ed. Joseph Zycha, *CSEL,* 28, 1 (Vienna: F. Tempsky; Leipzig: G. Freytag, 1894), pp. 400–401; trans. John Hammond Taylor, *The Literal Meaning of Genesis, ACW,* no. 42 (New York: Newman Press, 1982), 2: 198–99. Thomas Aquinas, when asking whether a nocturnal pollution is a sin, resolves the question in the negative in *Summa theologiae* 2a 2ae, q. 154, art. 5, resp., ed. and trans. Fathers of the English Dominican Province (London: Blackfriars, 1967), 43: 223–27. Cf. Vincent of Beauvais, *Speculum naturale* 31.21, col. 2308, which has the rubric "Cur pollutio nocturna secundum se culpabilis non sit" ("why nocturnal pollution is not culpable, according to himself [i.e., Vincent's own view]") and summarizes many authorities on this point; Albert the Great, *De bono* tract. 3, q. 3, art. 6, ad 5, ed. Heinrich Kühle et al., in *Opera omnia,* ed. Bernhard Geyer (Aschendorff: Monasterium Westfalorum, 1951), 28:164; and John Gerson, *De cognitione castitatis,* in *Oeuvres complètes,* ed. Palémon Glorieux (Paris: Desclée, 1973), 9: 54. Also see Thomas N. Tentler, *Sin and Con-*

fession on the Eve of the Reformation (Princeton, N.J.: Princeton University Press, 1977), pp. 148–56.

6. Vincent of Beauvais, *Speculum naturale* 26.79, cols. 1887–88.

7. See Bede, *Ecclesiastical History* 1.27, pp. 92–93.

8. Albert the Great, Thomas of Cantimpré, Thomas Aquinas, and Vincent of Beauvais were all Dominicans (as was the fifteenth-century John Nider). William of Auvergne, a French theologian and bishop of Paris, was a secular cleric. But through his often unsuccessful attempts to combine Plato and Aristotle, he paved the way for the later Dominican adoption of Aristotle. For the Dominican dissemination of Aristotelianism and its impact on perceptions of gender, see Prudence Allen, *The Concept of Woman: The Aristotelian Revolution, 750 BC–AD 1250* (Montreal: Eden Press, 1985), pp. 362ff.

9. See, for example, Helen Rodnite Lemay's discussion of the relation between a thirteenth-century Aristotelianized treatise on women's bodies and the inquisitional *Malleus maleficarum*—both of which were generated within Dominican circles—included in *Women's Secrets: A Translation of Pseudo-Albertus Magnus's "De secretis mulierum" with Commentaries* (Albany: State University of New York Press, 1992), introduction, pp. 49–58.

10. For an introduction to the author and his work, see Serge Lusignan, *Préface au "Speculum maius" de Vincent de Beauvais: réfraction et diffraction,* Institut d'Etudes Médiévales, Université de Montréal, Cahiers d'Etudes Médiévales, 5 (Montreal: Bellarmin; Paris: Vrin, 1979), esp. chap. 1, pp. 15–27.

11. Vincent of Beauvais, *Speculum naturale* 22.24, 22.30, cols. 1622, 1625–26; cf. Albert the Great for his discussion of mares, which, like women, will occasionally permit coitus after pregnancy, in *Animalium lib. XXVI* 9.1.5, in *Opera omnia,* ed. A. Borgnet (Paris: Vivès, 1891), 11: 510. Also see Joan Cadden, *The Meanings of Sex Difference in the Middle Ages: Medicine, Science, and Culture* (Cambridge: Cambridge University Press, 1993), pp. 148–49; and John Baldwin, *The Language of Sex: Five Voices from Northern France Around 1200* (Chicago: University of Chicago Press, 1994), pp. 135–37. For the classical discourse surrounding female insatiability, see Lesley Dean-Jones, "The Politics of Pleasure: Female Sexual Appetite in the Hippocratic Tradition," *Helios* 19 (1992): 72–91, esp. 76–83. Note, however, that according to this analysis, female appetite in the Hippocratic tradition was entirely physiological—divorced from pleasure and even the need for the stimulus of a love object. As will be seen below, the medieval continuators of this tradition were prepared to grant considerably more psychological and emotional agency to the female appetite.

12. The belief in a female seed, albeit of a lesser kind when compared to its masculine counterpart, is associated with Galen and is in contrast to Aristotle's view of a singular male seed. See Ann Ellis Hanson, "Conception, Gestation, and the Origin of Female Nature in the *Corpus Hippocraticum,*" *Helios* 19 (1992): 41–42; and Anthony Preus, "Galen's Criticism of Aristotle's Conception Theory," *Journal of the History of Biology* 10 (1977): 78–84.

13. Thomas Laqueur, *Making Sex: Body and Gender from the Greeks to Freud* (Cambridge, Mass.: Harvard University Press, 1990), esp. chap. 2, pp. 25–62.

14. Vincent of Beauvais, *Speculum naturale* 32.26, col. 2313. On the expulsion of seed and pleasure in rape, see Cadden, *Meanings of Sex Difference,* pp. 94–97, 117–

30; Danielle Jacquart and Claude Thomasset, *Sexuality and Medicine in the Middle Ages*, trans. Matthew Adamson (Princeton, N.J.: Princeton University Press, 1988), pp. 61–70, esp. pp. 63–64; and Thomasset, "La Représentation de la sexualité et la génération dans la pensée scientifique médiévale," in *Love and Marriage in the Twelfth Century*, ed. Willy Van Hoecke and Andries Welkenhuysen (Louvain: Louvain University Press, 1981), p. 11. This nexus of beliefs, potentially so prejudicial to women, concurs with the etymological slippage between sexual violence and pleasure discussed by Kathryn Gravdal in *Ravishing Maidens: Writing Rape in Medieval French Literature and Law* (Philadelphia: University of Pennsylvania Press, 1991), pp. 3–11. William of Conches's position would, of course, undermine the already weak position of the plaintiff in a rape trial, since conception was perceived as hidden complicity (cf. Laqueur, *Making Sex*, pp. 161–62 and p. 284, n. 36). Such prejudices accord well with the practice of medieval secular courts in rape trials. Convictions were extremely low, and the courts tended to dismiss cases where the plaintiff was not a virgin and/or of sufficiently high status. See Barbara A. Hanawalt, *Crime and Conflict in English Communities, 1300–1348* (Cambridge, Mass.: Harvard University Press, 1979), pp. 104–10; and John Marshall Carter, *Rape in Medieval England: An Historical and Sociological Study* (Lanham, Md.: University Press of America, 1985). Also see the discussion below regarding the rape of a consecrated virgin. Generally the Galenic two-seed theory has been perceived as according women more agency than the Aristotelian one-seed theory insofar as it seems to acknowledge the female orgasm. But see Dean-Jones's forceful rehabilitation of Aristotle's reputation in this respect, partially based on the grounds that he acknowledged that women could become pregnant without any enjoyment ("Politics of Pleasure," p. 85).

15. "Cum autem mulier naturaliter frigida sit et humida, vnde potest accidere quod viro feruentior est in libidine? Respondeo, ignis difficilius in humidis lignis accenditur, in eis tamen accensus diutius et fortius ardet. Calor ergo luxuriae in muliere quae naturaliter est humida accensus fortius et diutius ardet," as cited by Vincent of Beauvais, *Speculum naturale* 31.5, col. 2294.

16. Ibid. Elsewhere Vincent presents a series of anecdotes from lives of the various desert fathers in which memory is excoriated as the real enemy of chastity (*Speculum historiale* 15.97; in *Speculum quadruplex*, 4: 615–16).

17. Vincent of Beauvais, *Speculum naturale* 31.5, cols. 2294–95. Many books circulated under the name *Liber de anatomia:* Vincent may have been referring to the one by Ricardus Anglicus, otherwise known as Richard of Wendover (d. 1252). On his life, see the entry by C. L. Kingsford, in *Dictionary of National Biography* (Oxford: Oxford University Press, 1917), 16:1087–88. Women refusing to nurse their own children were perceived as a general evil throughout the Middle Ages. On this theme, see Ole Jørgen Benedictow, "On the Origin and Spread of the Notion That Breast-Feeding Women Should Abstain from Sexual Intercourse," *Scandinavian Journal of History* 27, 1 (1992): 65–76. Despite the condemnation of moralists, wet nursing was widely practiced throughout the Middle Ages. See Christiane Klapisch-Zuber, "Blood Parents and Milk Parents: Wet Nursing in Florence, 1300–1530," in *Women, Family, and Ritual in Renaissance Italy*, trans. Lydia Cochrane (Chicago: University of Chicago Press, 1985), pp. 132–64.

18. Vincent of Beauvais, *Speculum naturale* 26.75, col. 1885. Vincent's discus-

sion of vision is heavily indebted to Augustine's threefold schema. Only the two lower sorts of vision—corporeal and spiritual—rely on the images created by physical objects. The highest, intellectual vision, apprehends abstract concepts independently of images and cannot err (see *De Genesi ad litteram libri duodecim* 12.25, ed. Zycha, *CSEL,* 27, 1, pp. 417–18; trans. Taylor, *The Literal Meaning of Genesis,* 2: 215–16).

19. Vincent of Beauvais, *Speculum naturale* 25.82, col. 1827.

20. Ibid., 31.40, col. 2322; cf. 22.36, col. 1629. The story of Jacob's rods is also alluded to in 22.43, col. 1634. One of the commentators on the Pseudo-Albert's *Women's Secrets* also discusses this process, citing Galen (see commentator B, trans. Lemay, p.116). Cf. the instance in which a woman is freed from suspicions of adultery when it is determined that the child resembled the bedspread (*An Alphabet of Tales: An English 15th Century Translation of the "Alphabetum narrationum" of Etienne de Besançon,* ed. M. M. Banks, *EETS,* o.s., nos. 126–27 [London: Kegan Paul, Trench, Trübner, 1904 and 1905; rprt. Millwood, N.Y.: Kraus, 1987], no. 741, pp. 494–95. This collection is now believed to be the work of the fourteenth-century Arnold of Liège). The Dominican Rudolf von Schlettstadt relates a disturbing anecdote with the same implicit principle at work. A man is frustrated by the fact that his wife only gives birth to daughters, and says angrily that he would prefer a goat or a dog. This comes to pass the following year when the wife brings forth both animals. A local Dominican recommends that the frightened midwives bury the monstrous offspring alive, which they proceed to do (*Historiae memorabiles: zur Dominikanerliteratur und Kulturgeschichte des 13. Jahrhunderts,* ed. Erich Kleinschmidt [Cologne: Böhlau, 1974], p. 114). On this motif, see Frederic C. Tubach, *Index Exemplorum: A Handbook of Medieval Religious Tales,* Folklore Fellows Communications, no. 204 (Helsinki: Suomalainen Tiedeakatemia, 1969), no. 5288. Such beliefs were a commonplace in antiquity. See, for example, Pliny, *Natural History* 7.12, ed. and trans. H. Rackham et al., Loeb Classical Library (Cambridge, Mass.: Harvard University Press; London: William Heinemann, 1942), 2:540–45.

21. " . . . ex affectu cupientis et conspicientis trahere in se colores et imagines rerum conspectarum in feruore voluptatis extremae" (Vincent of Beauvais, *Speculum naturale* 21.40, col. 2322).

22. Augustine, *De trinitate* 11.2, as cited by Vincent, *Speculum naturale* 22.36, col. 1629.

23. Vincent of Beauvais, *Speculum naturale* 31.40, cols. 2322–23.

24. "Et primo quidem intendit generare sibi simile, si potest virtus propria vincere; sin autem alia virtus quae vincit assimilabit sibi quod gignitur," ibid., col. 2323.

25. "Spermata masculi et femine diversarum intentionum sunt, ut dicit Galienus. Intentio enim spermatis masculi est informare ad similitudinem eius a quo separatum est, nisi aliud prohibeat. Intentio spermatis mulieris est incipere formam secundum similitudinem eius, a quo separatum est," Thomas of Cantimpré, *Liber de natura rerum* 1.71, ed. H. Boese (Berlin: Walter de Gruyter, 1973), 1:72. He abruptly dismisses Aristotelian one-seed theorists: "Hence certain individuals say that only the virile seed suffices for conception and that the female seed is not necessary. Clearly those who say this lie" ("Proinde dicunt quidam solum virile

semen sufficere ad conceptum nec necessarium semen femineum. Mentiuntur plane qui hoc dicunt," 1.72, 1: 72). Note, however, that in the Galenic two-seed context, we were never dealing with a level playing field. The weaker and colder female contribution could only dominate when there was some deficiency in the usually stronger and hotter male presence. See, for example, the eleventh-century Constantine the African's treatment, translated by Paul Delany, "Constantinus Africanus' *De coitu:* A translation," *Chaucer Review* 4 (1969): 57–59. On Vincent's incorporation of Thomas of Cantimpré's work in later versions of the *Speculum naturale,* see Bruno Roy, "La Trente-sixième main: Vincent de Beauvais et Thomas de Cantimpré," in *Vincent de Beauvais: Intentions et réceptions d'une oeuvre encyclopédique au Moyen-Age,* Actes du XIVe Colloque de l'Institut d'Etudes Médiévales, organisé conjointement par l'Atelier Vincent de Beauvais (A.R.Te.M., Université de Nancy II) et l'Institut d'Etudes Médiévales (Université de Montréal), 27–30 April 1988, ed. Monique Paulmier-Foucart, Serge Lusignan, and Alain Nadeau; Cahiers d'Etudes Médiévales, Cahier spécial 4 (Montreal: Bellarmin; Paris: Vrin, 1990), pp. 241–51.

26. On the one-seed versus the two-seed theory, see n. 12, above. For the view of conception as warfare between rival seeds, see Hanson, "Origin of Female Nature," pp. 43–44. Note that Aristotle continued to be influenced by this tradition, envisaging male semen and female mense as possessed of "powers" struggling for mastery. The conflict is somewhat muted in comparison to the Galenic view insofar as it is defined in terms of how much of the semen's activity the mense accepts or rejects (Preus, "Galen's Criticism," p. 79). This struggle is apparent on a microcosmic level in Vincent's work itself. Compare, for example, William of Conches's defense of the two-seed theory with Aristotle's minimizing discussion of menstrual blood (Vincent of Beauvais, *Speculum naturale* 31.26, col. 2313, 22.53, col. 1639; 31.24, col. 2312). The belief in the imagination's impact on conception was extremely long-lived. See Ian Maclean, *The Renaissance Notion of Woman: A Study in the Fortunes of Scholasticism and Medical Science in European Intellectual Life* (Cambridge: Cambridge University Press, 1980), p. 41.

27. Vincent of Beauvais, *Speculum naturale* 25.84, col. 1828. Though Vincent attributes the *Liber de anima et spiritu* to Hugh of St. Victor, it was probably written by the twelfth-century Alcher of Clairvaux. The treatise is printed in *PL* 40, cols. 779–832.

28. The following Latin passage is paraphrased in the text: "*Hvgo ubi supra.* Quaedam autem ignea vis aere temperata a corde ad cerebrum ascendit, ibique colata, et purificata per instrumenta sensuum egrediens ex contactu interiori formata quinque sensus facit. Porro ipsa vis ignea, quae exterius formata sensus dicitur, eadem formata per ipsa sensuum instrumenta per quae ingreditur, et in quibus formatur natura operante introrsum ad cellam phantasticam vsque retrahitur, et reducitur atque imaginatio efficitur, postea eadem imaginatio ab interiori parte capitis ad medium transiens, ipsam animae rationalis substantiam contingit, et excitat discretionem intantum iam purificata, et subtilis effecta, vt immediate spiritui coniungatur, veraciter tamen naturam corporis retinens." Vincent of Beauvais, *Speculum naturale* 25.97, col. 1835.

29. "Est itaque imaginatio similitudo corporis, per sensus quidem corporis ex

corporum contactu concepta. atque per eosdem sensus introrsus ad partem puriorem corporei spiritus reducta eique impressa. In summo scilicet corporalis spiritus, et in imo rationalis corporalem informans, et rationalem contingens," ibid. Thomas of Cantimpré also cites this passage verbatim but does not acknowledge his indebtedness (*Liber de natura rerum* 2.15, 1: 95–96). Cf. the account of sense reception from Aristotle's *De somno et vigilia,* also cited by Vincent. A sensible object creates a *passio* in the senses and, when this object recedes, a *phantasma* or a *simulchrum* is created and deposited on the inside — the source of the various *phantasiae* that we experience in our inner senses when asleep (*Speculum naturale* 22.16, col. 1617). Also see Vincent's citation of Avicenna's account of the five powers of apprehension, the second of which is imaginative (25.86, col. 1829).

30. Vincent of Beauvais, *Speculum naturale* 26.75, 78, 96, cols. 1885, 1887, 1903. Vincent is again citing Augustine's *De Genesi ad litteram libri duodecim* 12.6–12.

31. Vincent of Beauvais, citing Aristotle's *De anima,* in *Speculum naturale* 24.98, col. 1835.

32. Ibid., 25.84, col. 1828.

33. Ibid., 31.26, col. 2313. See Cadden, *Meanings of Sex Difference,* p. 93; and Jacquart and Thomasset, *Sexuality and Medicine,* pp. 34–35, 203, n. 63. This bizarre doctrine, which owed more to speculations concerning animals (particularly pigs) than humans, has been traced back by Fridolf Kudlien to late antiquity, in "The Seven Cells of the Uterus: The Doctrine and Its Roots," *Bulletin of the History of Medicine* 39 (1965): 415–23.

34. Albert the Great, *Animalium lib. XXVI* 9.1.5, in *Opera omnia,* ed. Borgnet, 11:510.

35. See Geneviève Hasenohr's discussion of spiritual rules for laywomen, "La Vie quotidienne de la femme vue par l'église: l'enseignement des 'journées chrétiennes' de la fin du moyen-âge," *Frau und spätmittelalterlicher Alltag,* Internationaler Kongress krems an der Donau 2. bis 5. Oktober 1984, Veröffentlichungen des Instituts für mittelalterliche Realienkunde Österreichs, no. 9 (Vienna: Österreichischen Akademie der Wissenschaften, 1986), esp. pp. 41–50, 66–67; and Chiara Frugoni, "Female Mystics, Visions, and Iconography," in *Women and Religion in Medieval and Renaissance Italy,* ed. Daniel Bornstein and Roberto Rusconi, trans. Margery J. Schneider (Chicago: University of Chicago Press, 1996), pp. 130–32.

36. Thomas of Cantimpré, *Bonum universale de apibus* 1.25.5–8 (Douai: B. Belleri, 1627), pp. 102–6 (hereafter cited as *De apibus*).

37. See Caroline Walker Bynum, *Holy Feast and Holy Fast: The Religious Significance of Food to Medieval Women* (Berkeley: University of California Press, 1987), esp. chaps. 8–9; eadem, "The Female Body and Religious Practice in the Later Middle Ages," in *Fragmentation and Redemption: Essays on Gender and the Human Body in Medieval Religion* (New York: Zone Books, 1991), pp. 181–238, 365–93.

38. Bynum, *Holy Feast and Holy Fast,* pp. 200–201. See, for example, the instance of the thirteenth-century Elisabeth of Spalbeek, whose stigmata are described by Abbot Philip of Clairvaux. The Franciscans, however, anxious to protect the privilege of Francis, attempted to deny the efficacy of her wounds (W. Simons and J. E. Ziegler, "Phenomenal Religion in the Thirteenth Century and Its Image: Elisabeth of Spalbeek and the Passion Cult," in *Women in the Church,* ed. W. J. Sheils

and Diana Wood, Studies in Church History 27 [Oxford: Blackwell, 1990], pp. 117–26, esp. pp. 117, 123).

39. These miraculous markings and the events leading up to their exposure are discussed extensively in Clare's process of canonization. See articles 159–76 as well as Abbess Johanna's deposition on these articles in Enrico Menestò, ed., *Il processo di canonizzazione di Chiara da Montefalco* (Regione dell'Umbria: La Nuova Italia, 1984), pp. 26–29, 85–95. Also see Katherine Park's description of these events within the context of contemporary dissection practices in "The Criminal and the Saintly Body: Autopsy and Dissection in Renaissance Italy," *Renaissance Quarterly* 47 (1994): 1–33.

40. Gerson, *De mystica theologia practica* c. 2, in *Oeuvres complètes,* 8:22.

41. Peter Pomponazzi, *De naturalium effectuum admirandorum causis sive de Incantationibus,* in *Opera* (Basel: Henricpetrina, 1567), c. 5, pp. 67–68, 81–84; also see c. 3, p. 32. Cf. Gabriella Zarri, *Le sante vive: cultura e religiosità femminile nella prima età moderna* (Turin: Rosenberg and Sellier, 1990), p. 59; and Dyan Elliott, "The Physiology of Rapture and Female Spirituality," in *Medieval Theology and the Natural Body,* ed. Peter Biller and A. J. Minnis (Woodbridge, Suffolk: York Medieval Press in association with Boydell and Brewer, 1997), pp. 158–61. On Pomponazzi, see Martin L. Pine, *Pietro Pomponazzi: Radical Philosopher of the Renaissance* (Padua: Editrice Antenore, 1986).

42. On this kind of subterfuge, see Gabriella Zarri's edited collection, *Finzione e santità: tra medioevo ed età moderna* (Turin: Rosenberg and Sellier, 1991). These studies are for the most part postmedieval. John Nider has many accounts of feigned instances of sanctity. See, for example, *Formicarium* 3.1, 8, 11 (Douai: B. Belleri, 1602), pp. 184–86, 230–32, 247–50. For an analysis of one of Nider's most striking instances of fraudulent rapture, see Elliott, "Physiology of Rapture," pp. 169–71.

43. " . . . quod ea que vidit vel alias apprehendebat per sensus corporales, reflectebat et aplicabat ad compassionem et conformitatem et ymaginationem passionis Christi," Menestò, *Il processo,* p. 7.

44. Caroline Walker Bynum cites Hugh of St. Victor to make this point when discussing the importance of models to medieval spirituality in her "Did the Twelfth Century Discover the Individual?" in *Jesus as Mother: Studies in the Spirituality of the High Middle Ages* (Berkeley: University of California Press, 1982), pp. 97–98.

45. William of Auvergne, *De universo* 3a 2ae, c. 24, in *Opera omnia* (Paris: A. Pralard, 1674; rprt. Frankfurt: Minerva, 1963), 1:1066; cf. Vincent's account of women who claim they ride with Diana and Herodotus (*Speculum naturale* 2.111, col. 149). On this phenomenon, see Jeffrey Burton Russell, *Witchcraft in the Middle Ages* (Ithaca, N.Y.: Cornell University Press, 1972), pp. 75–81, 175–76, 210–11; and Norman Cohn, *Europe's Inner Demons: An Enquiry Inspired by the Great Witch-Hunt* (New York: Basic Books, 1975), pp. 212–14.

46. "Qualiter autem hoc possunt, si non est eis accessus ad animas eorum, et si non est eis facultas pingendi cogitatum hujusmodi in imaginationibus eorum, et forsitan virtute intellectiva ipsorum?" William of Auvergne, *De universo* 3a 2ae, c. 23, in *Opera omnia,* 1:1061.

47. "Sicut speculum si admoueatur speculo, forma impressa in vno resultat in alio, licet anima credat eas tantummodo in seipsa formari, propter vehementem applicationem maligni spiritus ad eam," Vincent of Beauvais, *Speculum naturale*

2.119, col. 153; for the way the devil applies himself to the body's humors, see 2.118, col. 152; cf. 26.66, col. 1879.

48. "... furnario diabolus comparatur, quia corpori se immiscens, incendit animam in suggestione sua quasi clibanum, nec tamen intrat, sed foris stat sicut furnarius," Vincent of Beauvais, *Speculum naturale* 26.69, col. 1881.

49. Hanson, "Origin of Female Nature," pp. 53–54; Lesley Dean-Jones, "The Cultural Construct of the Female Body in Classical Greek Science," in *Women's History and Ancient History*, ed. Sarah B. Pomeroy (Chapel Hill: University of North Carolina Press, 1991), p. 119.

50. Henry Kramer and James Sprenger, *Malleus maleficarum 1487*, photographic facsimile of the first edition (Hildesheim: Georg Olms, 1992), pt. 1, q. 2, fol. 9r; trans. Montague Summers (London: John Rodker, 1928; rprt. New York: Dover, 1971), p. 17. Even though the *Malleus* cites luminaries like Aristotle, Avicenna, and Aquinas for their endorsement of this view, it ultimately modifies it, preferring to emphasize the child's sensitivity to the angry gaze. The reasons for this demurral are discussed in Chap. 6, pp. 154–55, below, where the menstruant's lethal glance is further treated. Also see the discussion of menstruation above in the Introduction.

51. For instance, the late seventh-century penitential of Theodore, archbishop of Canterbury, mentions male masturbation four times and female masturbation only once. See 1.1.9, 1.8.4, 1.8.9, 1.8.11, 1.1.13, in H. J. Schmitz, ed., *Die Bussbücher und die Bussdisciplin der Kirche nach handschriftlichen Quellen dargestellt* (Mainz: Franz Kirchheim, 1883), 1: 526, 531, 532 bis, 526; trans. John T. McNeill and Helena M. Gamer, *Medieval Handbooks of Penance: A Translation of the Principal "Libri poenitentiales"* (New York: Columbia University Press, 1938; rprt. 1990), pp. 185, 191, 192 bis, 185. On masturbation in penitential literature, see Pierre J. Payer, *Sex and the Penitentials: The Development of a Sexual Code, 550–1150* (Toronto: University of Toronto Press, 1984), pp. 46–47.

52. See Burchard of Worms, *Decretum* 19.5, *PL* 140, col. 968 (on men), and cols. 971–72 (on women).

53. Peter Damian, Ep. 168, To Archbishop Alfanus of Salerno, in *Die Briefe des Petrus Damiani*, ed. Kurt Reindel, *MGH, Die Briefe der deutschen Kaiserzeit*, 4 (Munich: *MGH*, 1993), 4: 242. It is also possible that this story alludes to lesbian activity, however. Damian also included an admonitory story to Countess Blanche (who had left the world to become a nun) regarding a monk corrupted by another monk through mutual masturbation (Ep. 66, *Die Briefe*, ed. Reindel, 2: 267–68; trans. Owen J. Blum, *Letters, FC*, Mediaeval Continuation, 3 [Washington, D.C.: Catholic University of America, 1992], 3: 58).

54. "Incipit etiam tunc puella desiderare coitum, sed in desiderio non emittit: et quanto plus coit, aut etiam manu se confricat, tanto plus appetit, eo quod per talem confricationem humor attrahitur, sed non emittitur, et cum humore attrahitur calor: et cum muliebre corpus sit frigidum, et clausuram patiens pororum, non cito emittit semen coitus: et haec est causa, quod quaedam puellae circa annum quartumdecimum non possunt de coitu satiari: et si tunc non habent virum, tamen mente pertractant coitum virilem, et saepe imaginantur veretrum virorum, et forte saepe confricant digitis vel aliis instrumentis quousque laxatis viis per calorem con-

fricationis et coitus exit humor spermaticus, cum quo exit calor: et tunc temperantur ipsarum inguina, et tunc efficiuntur castiores.

Tunc etiam accidit fluxus menstrui, et multiplicantur pollutiones tam in somnis quam in vigilia: et tunc se comprimunt crura plicando unum crus super alterum, et sic una partium vulvae scalpat aliam: quia ex hoc oritur delectatio et pollutio," Albert the Great, *Animalium lib. XXVI* 9.1.1., in *Opera omnia,* ed. Borgnet, 11: 497; also see Cadden, *Meanings of Sex Difference,* pp. 147–48; and Jacquart and Thomasset, *Sexuality and Medicine,* pp. 152–53.

55. " . . . ex calore confricationis extenduntur viae, et efficiuntur ampliae, et implentur humore: et etiam rememoratio coitus excitat tunc appetitum," Albert the Great, *Animalium lib. XXVI* 9.1.1, in *Opera omnia,* ed. Borgnet, 11: 498.

56. " . . . in se habebat tantam clausuram virginitatis quod non poterat facere vel emictere ea que mulieres communiter faciunt et emictunt, etiam sine opere alicuius creature," Witness 47, Brother Francis, formerly of the Franciscan house of Damiano in Montefalco, presently a guardian of Todi (i.e., a Franciscan official), in Menestò, *Il processo,* regarding art. 1, p. 266. The witness may even be implying that Clare had ceased to menstruate—a highly esteemed attribute in the profile of female sanctity (see Bynum, *Holy Feast and Holy Fast,* pp. 138, 148, 211, 214).

57. "Quibusdam tamen accidit numquam pollui in somnis vel emittere sperma coitus propter dispositionem aliquam complexionis, sicut diximus jam ante: et hoc accidit plus mulieribus quam viris, eo quod earum corpora sunt minus porosa, et non ingreditur ex eis semen coitus, nisi per longam confricationem," Albert the Great, *Animalium lib. XXVI* 9.1.1, in *Opera omnia,* ed. Borgnet, 11: 498. In addition to the help such a woman would receive from her complexion, Albert notes the possible importance of her diet (see p. 497). This is in contrast to the Hippocratic corpus, which maintains, at least at one juncture, that women do not masturbate—an assertion in keeping with the repression of female pleasure (Dean-Jones, "Politics of Pleasure," p. 80).

58. Thomas of Cantimpré, *De apibus* 2.30.2–5, pp. 320–22.

59. In this instance, a cleric reached down to touch himself, only to discover that his penis had turned into a serpent (Thomas of Cantimpré, *De apibus* 2.30.6, p. 322). Alternatively, Thomas presents men as more inclined to sodomy, offering no examples of same-sex relations between women. On the condemnation of "unnatural sex" by Thomas of Cantimpré and others, see the section entitled "On the Uses of Disembodiment" in Chap. 6, below.

60. "There is no doubt concerning such women, who so unnaturally and violently corrupt themselves, that they are indeed corrupted" ("Non est dubium de talibus, quae se sic innaturaliter et violenter corrumpunt, quin sint corruptae"), Albert the Great, *De bono* tract. 3, q. 3, art. 6, ad 3, in *Opera omnia,* ed. Geyer, 28:164.

61. See Barbara Newman, "Flaws in the Golden Bowl: Gender and Spiritual Formation in the Twelfth Century," in *From Virile Woman to WomanChrist: Studies in Medieval Religion and Literature* (Philadelphia: University of Pennsylvania Press, 1995), pp. 28–29; cf. her introduction, p. 5; also see Clarissa Atkinson, "'Precious Balsam in a Fragile Glass': The Ideology of Virginity in the Later Middle Ages," *Journal of Family History* 8 (1983): 137–38.

62. "Incorruptio praecipue est in eo quod maxime corrumpi potest," Albert the

Great, *De bono* tract. 3, q. 3, art. 4, ad 6, in *Opera omnia,* ed. Geyer, 28:159; and ad 12, p. 160.

63. See particularly *Peter Abelard's "Ethics",* ed. and trans. D. E. Luscombe (Oxford: Clarendon Press, 1971). For Abelard's influence in the twelfth century, see Odon Lottin, *Psychologie et morale aux XIIe et XIIIe siècles,* 2d ed. (Louvain: Abbaye du Mont César; Gembloux: J. Duclot, 1954), 4, 1: 310–21. Also see Colin Morris, *The Discovery of the Individual, 1050–1200* (New York: Harper and Row, 1972), pp. 64–79; and M.-D. Chenu, *L'Eveil de la conscience dans la civilisation médiévale* (Montreal: Institut d'Etudes Médiévales; Paris: Vrin, 1969), esp. pp. 17–32.

64. On the relation between forced marriage and the female vocation, see Donald Weinstein and Rudolph M. Bell, *Saints and Society: The Two Worlds of Western Christendom, 1000–1700* (Chicago: University of Chicago Press, 1982), pp. 88–97; and Dyan Elliott, *Spiritual Marriage: Sexual Abstinence in Medieval Wedlock* (Princeton, N.J.: Princeton University Press, 1993), esp. chap. 5. Concerning a grisly hagiographical motif premised on the extreme vulnerability of consecrated virgins, see Jane Tibbetts Schulenburg, "The Heroics of Virginity: Brides of Christ and Sacrificial Mutilation," in *Women in the Middle Ages and Renaissance: Literary and Historical Perspectives,* ed. Mary Beth Rose (Syracuse, N.Y.: Syracuse University Press, 1986), pp. 29–72.

65. Jerome, *Adversus Jovinianum* 1.43–46, *PL* 23, cols. 286–87; trans. W. H. Fremantle, *St. Jerome: Letters and Select Works, LNPNFC,* 2d ser., vol. 6 (Grand Rapids, Mich.: Eerdmans; rprt. 1979), pp. 381–83. For Augustine's explicit condemnation of suicide in such circumstances, which even takes the Roman matron Lucretia to task, see *De civitate dei* 1.19–27, ed. Dombart and Kalb, *CCSL,* 47, pp. 20–28; trans. Walsh, *City of God, FC,* vol. 8, pp. 49–62.

66. Ep. 111, to Victorianus, *Epistolae,* ed. A. Goldbacher, *CSEL,* 34, 1 (Vienna: F. Tempsky; Leipzig: G. Freytag, 1895), pp. 656–57; trans. Wilfrid Parsons, *Saint Augustine: Letters, FC,* vol. 18 (New York: Fathers of the Church, 1953), pp. 253–54.

67. Augustine, *De civitate dei* 1.16, ed. Dombart and Kalb, *CCSL,* 47, p. 18; trans. Walsh, *City of God, FC,* vol. 8, p. 46. Later, however, he hints that perhaps such a horrible fate was visited on the women in question for an overweening pride in their virginity (*De civitate dei* 1.28, ed. Dombart and Kalb, *CCSL,* 47, pp. 28–29; trans. Walsh, *City of God, FC,* vol. 8, p. 63). This tendency to blame the victim would, of course, continue. Thus in a chapter entitled *De virginibus lapsis* (*On Fallen Virgins*), Vincent of Beauvais lumps together victims of rape with those who were responsible for the loss of their virginity. For instance, he cites Augustine's discussion of the rape of consecrated virgins in *City of God* and the letter to Victorianus, but follows with harsh condemnations of fallen virtue. To this end, he enlists the support of the *Liber de lapsu Susannae virginis consecratae* (*The Book Concerning the Fall of the Consecrated Virgin Susanna*), which denounces the allegedly fallen Susanna as "virgin of God [who] has become a corruption of Satan, from the bride of Christ to an inexorable whore" ("de Dei virgine facta es corruptio sathanae, de sponsa Christi scortum execrabile," *Speculum naturale* 30.49, col. 2249). The anonymous *Liber de lapsu,* which Vincent attributes to Jerome, but is also sometimes attributed to Ambrose, was written to incite repentance in its addressee. It is printed in *PL* 16, cols. 383–400.

68. Augustine, *De civitate dei* 1.25, ed. Dombart and Kalb, *CCSL,* 47, p. 26;

trans. Walsh, *City of God, FC,* vol. 8, p. 59. Augustine's views are used by John Gerson with reference to nocturnal emissions in *De cognitione castitatis,* in *Oeuvres complètes,* 9:58. See Chap. 1, n. 78, above.

69. "Quia valde est difficile quod in tali delectatione aliquis placentiae motus non insurgat, ideo Ecclesia quae de interioribus judicare not potest, cum exterius corrupta sit, eam inter virgines non velat," Aquinas, *Commentum in quatuor libros sententiarum* bk. 4, dist. 38, q. 1, art. 5 ad 4, in *Opera omnia* (Parma: Petrus Fiaccadori, 1858; rprt., New York: Musurgia, 1948), 7, 2: 1013. Although Gratian, heavily reliant on passages from Augustine, argues that a virgin does not lose her chastity through rape, she can no longer dare to accompany the virgins in the procession following the Lamb—a place of privilege allotted to virgins in the afterlife, according to the Book of Revelations (C. 32 q. 5 c. 13 dpc; cf. c. 14 and dpc). He also prefaces his entry on forcibly violated virgins with the riposte of St. Lucy to her would-be rapist: if he violated her against her will, she would be double-crowned (C. 32 q. 5 dac 1)—an anecdote in the spirit of the Augustinian tendency to liken such violation to the wounds of martyrdom. This analogy was widely used, though it did not affect the general consensus that violated virgins could not be veiled: see, for example, Aquinas, *Commentum in quatuor libros sententiarum* bk. 4, dist. 33, q. 3, art. 1, resp., in *Opera omnia,* Parma edition, 7,2: 976; and Albert the Great, *De bono* tract. 3, q. 3, art. 4, ad 11, in *Opera omnia,* ed. Geyer, 28: 160. Note that Albert first uses Lucy's remarks to affirm that forcibly violated women do not lose the reward of virginity, but then argues in terms similar to Aquinas that the almost inevitable pleasure involved in such a rape means that these women cannot be considered true virgins. Also see John Nider's use of Lucy's retort, which at least has the merit of pointing out the clash between the Augustinian perspective and the ecclesiastical refusal to veil such violated women (*Formicarium* 2.10, pp. 162–63).

70. Thomas reasons that there are two points at issue in this delicate problem. The first is the integrity of the virgin's mind and body, which God can repair—reintegrating the mind through grace and consolidating the body by a miracle. But the reason for the virgin's integrity, namely that she was not known by a man, cannot be repaired. God is incapable of intending anything so contradictory as a complete reparation. Note that Thomas uses Jerome's remarks about God's incapacity in this regard (as cited by Gratian C. 32 q. 5 c. 11) as the pivot for his response (quodlib. 5, q. 2, art. 3, resp., in *Opera omnia,* Parma edition, 9: 529). For Jerome, see n. 74, below.

71. Newman, "Flaws in the Golden Bowl," in *From Virile Woman,* pp. 19–45, 252–62.

72. See Atkinson's deft demonstration of this in "'Precious Balsam in a Fragile Glass,'" pp. 139ff. Also see Newman, "Gnostics, Free Spirits, and 'Meister Eckhart's Daughter,'" in *From Virile Woman,* pp. 176–77.

73. Margery Kempe, *The Book of Margery Kempe,* ed. Sanford Meech Brown and Hope Emily Allen, *EETS,* o.s., no. 212 (London: Oxford University Press, 1940; rprt. 1960), 1.21, pp. 48–49.

74. "See to it that God say not some day to you: 'The virgin of Israel is fallen and there is none to raise her up' (Am. 5.2). . . . Though God can do all things, He cannot raise up a virgin when once she has fallen. He may indeed relieve one of her sin, but He will not give her a crown. . . . Virginity may be lost even by a thought.

Such are evil virgins, virgins in flesh, not in spirit," Jerome, Ep. 22, To Eustochium, c. 5, in *Epistulae,* ed. Isidore Hilberg, *CSEL,* 54, rev. ed. (Vienna: Verlag der österreichischen Akademie der Wissenschaften, 1996), p. 150; trans. Fremantle, *St. Jerome: Letters and Select Works, LNPNFC,* 2d ser., vol. 6, p. 24; cf. "A virgin in flesh and not in mind (*in mente*) will have no reward in the promised time," Isidore of Seville, *Sententiae* 2.40.7, *PL* 83, col. 644. Both authors are cited by Vincent of Beauvais in his chapter on fallen virgins (*Speculum naturale* 30.49, col. 2249; note that this edition erroneously gives book 1 for Isidore).

75. "Sed et absque alienae carnis consortio uirginitas plerumque corrumpitur, castitas uiolatur, si uehementior aestus carnem concutiens, uoluntatem sibi subdiderit, et rapuerit membra," Aelred of Rievaulx, *De institutione inclusarum* c. 15, ed. C. H. Talbot, in *Opera omnia,* ed. A. Hoste and C. H. Talbot, *CCCM,* 1 (Brepols: Turnhout, 1971), p. 651; for the devil's activities, see c. 16, p. 652. Cf. the anonymous thirteenth-century English rule, which describes virginity as more fragile than glass: "For glass does not break unless something touches it, and it, as regards loss of virginity, can lose its wholeness through a stinking desire—so far can that proceed and last so long. But this kind of break can be mended afterwards, made altogether as completely whole as it ever was, through the medicine of confession and repentance," *Ancrene Wisse: A Guide for Anchoresses,* trans. Hugh White (Harmondsworth: Penguin, 1993), p. 81. On the treatment of virginity in this genre, see Newman, "Flaws in the Golden Bowl," in *From Virile Woman,* pp. 28–34. For parallel concerns about male chastity, see Matthew of Cracow's thirteenth-century confessor's manual, which describes how certain men can become polluted through the mere presence or speech of their beloved, through a light touch, or their own obsessive imaginings (*De modo confitendi et de puritate conscientiae* c. 16 [Paris: Guy Marchant for Denis Roce [?], before 1501], unpaginated). According to Thomas of Chobham, many men are so lascivious that they get erections from the most casual friction—whether riding or walking—and ejaculate immediately through the impatience of their desire. Moreover, they sin mortally unless all possible precautions are taken to reduce friction in their genital region and liberal use is made of nettles and cold water (*Summa confessorum* 7.2.1.1, ed. F. Broomfield, Analecta Mediaevalia Namurcensia, 25 [Louvain: Nauwelaerts, 1968], p. 331).

76. Aquinas, *Commentum in quatuor libros sententiarum* bk. 4, dist. 33, q. 3, art. 1, resp., in *Opera omnia,* Parma edition, 7,2: 976; cf. resp. ad obj. 4, p. 977; and quodlib. 6, q. 10, art. 18, resp., in ibid, 9: 551.

77. "Et dico 'ex voluntate,' quia quandoque fit cogitatus de coitu et membris pudibundis et aliis ad concupiscentiam facientibus cum intentione et studio concitandi aestum concupiscentiae et delectandi in illo, et talem cogitationem sequitur corruptio ad distillationem foedi humoris et perfectam coitus delectationem. Et dico talem amittere virginitatem per illam completam delectationem corpus corrumpentem," Albert the Great, *De bono* tract. 3, q. 3, art. 6, solutio, in *Opera omnia,* ed. Geyer, 28: 163; cf. tract. 3, q. 3, art. 4, ad 1, p. 159. Also see Jacquart and Thomasset, *Sexuality and Medicine,* p. 150. Albert's violent example of a sword piercing a hymen is still in the spirit of Augustine, who uses the analogy of a clumsy midwife who, in the course of an internal examination, breaks a virgin's hymen—arguing that the victim of such a misfortune should still be reckoned a virgin (*De*

civitate dei 1.18, ed. Dombart and Kalb, *CCSL,* 47, p. 19; trans. Walsh, *City of God, FC,* vol. 8, p. 48). See Aquinas's use of this text in quodlib. 6, q. 10, art. 18, resp., in *Opera omnia,* Parma edition, 9: 551.

78. " . . . extenduntur spiritus ad membra genitalia in actum delectationis et incipit delectari complete et pollui ad imaginationem sicut ad rem," Albert the Great, *De bono* tract. 3, q. 3, art. 6, ad 2, in *Opera omnia,* ed. Geyer, 28: 164.

79. Albert the Great, *De bono* tract. 3, q. 3, art. 6, ad 2, in *Opera omnia,* ed. Geyer, 28: 164. Albert does allow, however, that a virgin who considered marriage could regain her position after penance (tract. 3, q. 3, art. 4, ad 8, p. 159).

80. Albert the Great, *De bono* tract. 3, q. 3, art. 7, solutio, in *Opera omnia,* ed. Geyer, 28: 166.

81. "Nullo scilicet modo debere virginem reputari, quam sopita sensuum ratione in carnali delectatione fluxus concupiscentiae polluisset, etiamsi pudoris sigillum intactum, incorruptum, et integrum conseruetur," Thomas of Cantimpré, *De apibus,* 2.29.35, p. 315; for Thomas's own endorsement of a more benign position, perhaps influenced by his considerations of male virginity, which he acknowledges has no outer markers, see 2.29.35–36, p. 315. Cf. Aquinas's views in *Commentum in quatuor libros sententiarum* bk. 4, dist. 33, q. 3, art. 1, resp. ad obj. 4, in *Opera omnia,* Parma edition, 7, 2: 977. Note that even the deeply conservative *Ancrene Wisse* seems to see penance as an antidote for mental defloration (see n. 75, above).

82. Gerson, *Poetimini: Contre la luxure,* in *Oeuvres complètes,* 7, ii: 828.

83. Gerson, *De cognitione castitatis,* in *Oeuvres complètes,* 9: 51–52. Gerson bases his exoneration on the fact that there is little or no pleasure in such emissions, since they have little food concentrated in them, unlike seminal fluid. He does, however, grant that this is sometimes linked with the presence of any beloved person—whether beautiful or ugly, young or old. For a discussion of various kinds of seminal and nonseminal fluids, see Cadden, *Meanings of Sex Difference,* pp. 141–42.

84. "Quod si per complementum delectationis ex talibus absque omni seminatione corrumpatur vere ipsa virginitas, juxta sententiam quorumdam magistrorum, heu proh dolor, quam in paucis maneret virginitas cogitare stupor est, nisi forsitan in pueris et puellis hanc excuset defectus sufficiens judicii rationis," Gerson, *De cognitione castitatis,* in *Oeuvres complètes,* 9: 52, 58–59. Albert the Great discounts prepubescent sexual activity on the basis of the child's deficiencies in both the deliberative process and the heat that produces pleasure (*De bono* tract. 3, q. 3, art. 6, ad 3, in *Opera omnia,* ed. Geyer, 28: 164).

85. Augustine, *De civitate dei* 15.23, ed. Dombart and Kalb, *CCSL,* 48, p. 489; trans. Walsh, *City of God, FC,* vol. 14, p. 471; also see *De civitate dei* 3.5, ed. Dombart and Kalb, *CCSL,* 47, p. 68; trans. Walsh, *City of God, FC,* vol. 8, p. 134. Elsewhere, Augustine again treats the problem of angels allegedly sleeping with human women and resolves that, since angels do not have flesh, they could not have committed this offense. He does, however, leave the door open for demons coupling with women and, in turn, seems to acknowledge that this caveat undermines his resolution about angels: "Thus it is more believable that it was just men, either called angels or sons of God, that fell from concupiscence [and] sinned with women since angels, not possessing flesh, would not be able to descend to that sin; although so many things are said by many individuals about certain demons who behave unworthily with women that it is not easy to give a definitive opinion about this matter," ("Vnde

credibilius est homines iustos appellatos uel angelos uel filios dei concupiscentia lapsos peccasse cum feminis quam angelos carnem non habentes usque ad illud peccatum descendere potuisse; quamuis de quibusdam daemonibus, qui sint inprobi mulieribus, a multis tam multa dicantur, ut non facile sit de hac re definienda sententia," *Quaestionum in Heptateuchum libri VII* bk. 1, q. 3, ed. I. Fraipont, *CCSL,* 33 [Turnhout: Brepols, 1958], p. 3). Cf. his discussion of demonic bodies in *De Genesi ad litteram libri duodecim* 3.10, ed. Zycha, *CSEL,* 28, 1, pp. 73–74; trans. Taylor, *The Literal Meaning of Genesis,* 1:83–84 (note Taylor's remarks in 1: 243–44, n. 32). Also see E. Mangenot, "Démon d'après les pères," *DTC* 4,1, cols. 339–84, esp. 370–72.

86. See Aquinas, *Summa theologiae* 1a, q. 51, art. 1–3, 9: 31–43; *Commentum in quatuor libros sententiarum* bk. 2, dist. 8, q. 1, art. 1–3, in *Opera omnia,* Parma edition, 6: 455–56; and Vincent of Beauvais, *Speculum naturale* 2.125, col. 154.

87. William of Auvergne, *De universo* 3a 2ae, c. 2, in *Opera omnia,* 1: 1017–18; 3a 2ae, c. 25, 1: 1070, 1072.

88. Caesarius of Heisterbach, *Dialogus miraculorum* 3.9, ed. Joseph Strange (Cologne: J. M. Heberle, 1851), 1: 122–23; trans. H. Von E. Scott and C. C. Swinton Bland, *The Dialogue on Miracles* (London: Routledge, 1929), 1: 137. For a general overview of the medieval incubus and its classical antecedents, see Nicolas Kiessling, *The Incubus in English Literature: Provenance and Progeny* (Pullman: Washington State University Press, 1977), pp. 1–30.

89. William of Auvergne, *De universo* 3a 2ae, c. 24, in *Opera omnia,* 1: 1066. On women's related susceptibility to demonic possession, see Barbara Newman's "Possessed by the Spirit: Devout Women, Demoniacs, and the Apostolic Life in the Thirteenth Century," *Speculum* 73, 3 (July 1998). I am grateful to the author for sharing her findings with me prior to publication.

90. John Nider, *Formicarium* 5.10, pp. 403–7. As an example of a woman who wrongly believed that she was vexed by an incubus, John cites an occurrence borrowed from William of Auvergne in which a woman thought she was known from within by a demon, thereby feeling scarcely credible things (see William, *De universo* 3a 2ae, c. 13, in *Opera omnia,* 1: 1040). Anxiety around male potency would eventually reach epidemic proportions, if Kramer and Sprenger's inquisitional manual *Malleus maleficarum* is any indicator. Here we discover the witch's fabulous, but illusory, penis tree in which stolen phalluses are harvested and kept in a nest (see pt. 2, q. 1, c. 7, 1487 edition, fols. 59r–59v; trans. Summers, p. 121; cf. pt. 1, q. 9, 1487 edition, fols. 28r–30r; trans. Summers, pp. 58–61). Note that scholastics such as Aquinas anticipated this development. For instance, Aquinas argues that *maleficia,* rather than making one impotent with all, works on the imagination of one man by creating an aversion to one woman. The terms he uses to describe the phenomenon clearly indicate that it is the man who is most inclined to suffer in this respect ("Nam maleficium consistit in imaginatione viri respectu unius mulieris; inquantum scilicet operatione daemonis fit illi abominationi alicujus mulieris, quam propter horrorem refugit et respuit," quodlib. 11, q. 9, art. 11, resp., in *Opera omnia,* Parma edition, 9: 618).

91. Athanasius, *Vita S. Antonii* c. 5, *PG* 26, cols. 847–48; trans. Mary Emily Keenan, *The Life of St. Anthony,* in *Early Christian Biographies, FC,* vol. 15 (New York: Fathers of the Church, 1952), pp. 138–39.

92. "Incepit ipsa aliquando apud se cogitare quod esset munda mulier, et talis que esset digna quod Dominus daret ei visibiles consolaciones," A. Lecoy de la Marche, ed., *Anecdotes historiques, légendes et apologues tirés du recueil inédit d'Etienne de Bourbon* (Paris: Renouard, 1877), pp. 198–99.

93. The consensual nature of sin is discussed above. For the increased emphasis on consent in the formation of marriage, see John T. Noonan, "Power to Choose," *Viator* 4 (1973): 419–34. On the pact between the sorcerer and the devil, which, according to Aquinas, could be expressed or tacit, see Russell, *Witchcraft in the Middle Ages,* pp. 144, 147. In their zeal to emphasize that women had become more depraved over the centuries, the authors of *Malleus maleficarum* tended to efface the role that consent played in these earlier accounts. See the Afterword, below.

94. Thomas of Cantimpré, *De apibus* 2.57.14, p. 546.

95. "[Apparuit autem ei lascivus ille diabolus in specie militis, valde pulchri aspectu, et in amorem suum intus suggestione latenti, extra locutione blandienti animum ejus fallaciter inclinavit. Cumque mulieris assensum obtinuisset, expansis brachiis, pedes ejus super una manuum suarum posuit: altera vero manu caput ejus operuit, sibique eam foederis hujus signo dotavit]," Ernaldus, Abbot of Bona-Vallis, *S. Bernardi vita et res gestae* 2.6.34, *PL* 185, col. 287 (Ernaldus is only responsible for book 2 of this multiauthored contemporary life). Note that this entire passage in square brackets is from a different codex (see the editor's note, cols. 223–24). Caesarius of Heisterbach makes reference to this episode in *Dialogus miraculorum* 3.7, ed. Strange, 1: 120; trans. Scott and Bland, 1: 134.

96. For instance, the younger kinsman in *Ruodlieb* proffered the betrothal ring to his bride on the tip of his sword, warning that if she was unfaithful to her troth, she would lose her head (*Ruodlieb: The Earliest Courtly Novel [After 1050],* ed. and trans. Edwin H. Zeydel, University of North Carolina Studies in the Germanic Languages and Literatures, no. 23 [Chapel Hill: University of North Carolina Press, 1959], c. 14, ll. 63–68, p. 124). Over the course of the high Middle Ages the bride's ritualized reception of three gifts would become the dominant rite: the ring (following the mutual exchange of consent), the arrhes (generally coins or jewelry), and the dowry. Occasionally, the bride would mark her reception of these gifts by a full prostration before the groom (see Jean-Baptiste Molin and Protais Mutembe, *Le Rituel du mariage en France du XIIe au XVIe siècle,* Théologie Historique, 26 [Paris: Beauchesne, 1974], pp. 161–62). Note that in the twelfth century, the distinction between betrothal (a promise to marry) and marriage (the actual contract) had begun to disappear.

97. Caesarius of Heisterbach, *Dialogus miraculorum* 3.6, ed. Strange, 1: 116; trans. Scott and Bland, 1: 130. Elsewhere, Caesarius says explicitly that the devil cannot induce one to sin unless a person consents in his or her heart (5.51, ed. Strange, 1: 336; trans. Scott and Bland, 1: 386). Also see his discussion of the respective roles of reason and will when succumbing to sin (8.44, ed. Strange, 2: 115–16; trans. Scott and Bland, 2: 43). Cf. the tale of the priest's daughter besieged by an incubus. When her father sent her away in an attempt to preserve her imperiled sanity, the demon accused him of stealing his wife (3.8, ed. Strange, 1: 121; trans. Scott and Bland, 1: 135–36). On the secondary nature of consummation in the formation of a marriage in the twelfth century and beyond, see Charles Donahue, "The Policy of Alexander III's Consent Theory of Marriage," in *Proceedings of the Fourth Interna-*

tional Congress of Medieval Canon Law, Toronto, 21–25 August 1972, ed. Stephan Kuttner, Monumenta Iuris Canonici, Series C: Subsidia, vol. 5 (Vatican City: Biblioteca Apostolica Vaticana, 1976), pp. 251–58; James Brundage, *Law, Sex, and Christian Society in Medieval Europe* (Chicago: University of Chicago Press, 1987), pp. 264–65, 268–69, 351–55; and Elliott, *Spiritual Marriage,* pp. 137–39.

98. Thomas of Cantimpré, *De apibus* 2.57.15, pp. 547–48; also see idem, *Vita S. Lutgardis* 2.11, in *AA SS,* June, 4: 198; trans. Margot King, *The Life of Lutgard of Aywières* (Saskatoon, Sask.: Peregrina Publishing, 1987), pp. 39–40.

99. Isak Collijn, ed., *Acta et processus canonizacionis Beate Birgitte* (Uppsala: Almqvist and Wiksells, 1924–31), pp. 538–39.

100. 1 Cor. 11.2–15. On this earlier, but eventually suppressed, version of the fall of humanity, see Norman Powell Williams, *The Ideas of the Fall and of Original Sin: A Historical and Critical Study* (London: Longmans, Green, 1927), pp. 19–29; also see Cohn, *Europe's Inner Demons,* pp. 62–63. Augustine was quick to humanize the sons of God, instead viewing them as erstwhile holy men who had succumbed to carnal lust (*De civitate dei* 15.22, ed. Dombart and Kalb, *CCSL,* 48, pp. 487–88; trans. Walsh, *City of God, FC,* vol. 14, pp. 468–70). Cf. n. 85, above.

101. See, for example, William of Auvergne, *De universo* 3a 2ae, c. 25, in *Opera omnia,* 1: 1070; and Caesarius of Heisterbach, *Dialogus miraculorum* 3.12, ed. Strange, 1: 124; trans. Scott and Bland, 1: 139–40. As will be seen below, Vincent of Beauvais also incorporates a number of seemingly "good" supernatural lovers from folklore into the incubus tradition. On the skepticism of the early Middle Ages, see Kiessling, *Incubus in English Literature,* pp. 21–22; and Russell, *Witchcraft in the Middle Ages,* pp. 75–80, 115–20, 142–47.

102. William of Auvergne, *De universo,* 3a 2ae, c. 25, in *Opera omnia,* 1: 1071.

103. Aquinas, *De potentia* q. 6, art. 8, resp. ad obj. 7, in *Opera omnia*, Parma edition, 8: 141–42; trans. English Dominican Fathers, *On the Power of God* (Westminster, Md.: Newman Press, 1952), 2:212, and *Summa theologiae* 1a, q. 51, art. 3, resp. ad obj. 6, 9: 43; *Commentum in quatuor libros sententiarum* bk. 2, dist. 8, art. 4, quaestinuncula 2, in *Opera omnia,* Parma edition, 6: 456.

104. William of Auvergne, *De universo* 3a 2ae, c. 25, in *Opera omnia,* 1: 1072.

105. Nider, *Formicarium* 5.10, pp. 398–401.

106. Cf. Jacquart and Thomasset, *Sexuality and Medicine,* p. 67.

107. Dean-Jones, "Politics of Pleasure," p. 85; Hanson, "Origins of Female Nature," p. 43.

108. Jacquart and Thomasset, *Sexuality and Medicine,* p. 65; also see M. A. Hewson, *Giles of Rome and the Medieval Theory of Conception* (London: Athlone Press, 1975), pp. 67–94, esp. 71, 88–89. Though a member of the Order of Augustinian Hermits, Giles could be considered an honorary Dominican in that he studied in Paris under Aquinas and defended his master's views when they were attacked in the wake of Bishop Tempier's censure of Aristotelian-inflected writers in 1277 (see pp. 6–9).

109. Potential skepticism is especially apparent in certain less formal forums. For example, Caesarius of Heisterbach has a tale about a cleric who, having impregnated an unmarried Jewish woman, cynically counsels her to tell her parents that she was still a virgin and was about to give birth to the messiah. Unfortunately for the young woman (and the child she bore), the infant was a girl (Caesarius of Heister-

bach, *Dialogus miraculorum* 2.24, ed. Strange, 1: 94–95; trans. Scott and Bland, 1: 105–6). When exploring the possibility of a virginal maternity, John Nider recounts how a young and pious woman was impregnated in her sleep (*Formicarium* 5.10, pp. 402–3). Cf. the *fabliau* "The Snow Baby," in which an adulterous wife claims to have conceived by swallowing a snowflake (*Fabliaux: Ribald Tales from the Old French,* trans. Robert Hellman and Richard O'Gorman [New York: Crowell, 1965], pp. 17–20). Cf. Giles of Rome's discussion of a woman becoming pregnant from bathing in water containing male seed—an instance taken from Avicenna (Hewson, *Giles of Rome,* p. 87).

110. Aquinas, quodlib. 6, q. 10, art. 18, resp., in *Opera omnia,* Parma edition, 9: 551. He ultimately resolves that the role of a miraculous virginal parent was better suited to the female than the male. The reasons given are twofold. First, the manner in which the male releases seed involves an unbecoming level of passion that does not agree with the operation of the Holy Spirit. Second, both man and the Godhead are destined to play active as opposed to passive roles. Thomas again conveys the theological ambivalence surrounding the release of the male seed, in *Commentum in quatuor libros sententiarum* bk. 2, dist. 20, q. 1, art. 2 ad 4, in ibid., 6: 563; also see Pierre J. Payer, *The Bridling of Desire: Ideas of Sex in the Later Middle Ages* (Toronto: University of Toronto Press, 1993), pp. 28–30.

111. See H. C. Lea, *Materials Toward a History of Witchcraft,* ed. Arthur C. Howland (Philadelphia: University of Pennsylvania Press, 1939), 1: 156–57; and Kiessling, *Incubus in English Literature,* p. 27. For variations on this theme, see Richard Kenneth Emmerson, *Antichrist in the Middle Ages: A Study of Medieval Apocalypticism, Art, and Literature* (Seattle: University of Washington Press, 1981), pp. 81–82. On Antichrist's birth, see Renate Blumenfeld-Kosinski, *Not of Woman Born: Representations of Caesarean Birth in Medieval and Renaissance Culture* (Ithaca, N.Y.: Cornell University Press, 1990), pp. 125–42.

112. Augustine, *De civitate dei* 14.26, ed. Dombart and Kalb, *CCSL,* 48, p. 449; trans. Walsh, *City of God, FC,* vol. 14, pp. 406–7. Augustine is speaking in a doubly hypothetical sense, since Adam and Eve fell and were expelled from Eden before they had an opportunity to consummate their relationship.

113. Marie also provides an analogue indicative of male fantasies in the lai of *Lanval.* Here a noble but financially unremunerated knight receives the favors of a fairy woman who provides him with love and cash. Interestingly, however, Lanval, although feeling shunned by his lord, was in no way soliciting love from any quarter, as in the case of the lady in *Yonec.* Both nameless women, human and supernatural, take the sexual initiative. The fairy mistress in *Lanval,* like the bird-lover in *Yonec,* imposes the conventional taboo of secrecy and will appear when summoned. She does not exhibit any shapeshifting abilities, however.

114. Line references in the text refer to *Yonec,* in *The Lais of Marie de France,* trans. Robert Hanning and Joan Ferrante (Durham, N.C.: Labyrinth, 1982), pp. 137–52.

115. The jealous husband places sharp blades in the window, which pierce the bird-lover. Cf. the very similar strategy resorted to by a female recluse who wished to discern the inspiration of the angel that visited her. On the advice of a local monk, she placed a cross of blessed wax on her window ledge. When this proved an impediment to the angel's entrance, she knew it was a demon (Caesarius of Heister-

bach, *Dialogus miraculorum* 5.47, ed. Strange, 1: 332; trans. Scott and Bland, 1: 381–82). For an interesting reading of the lai of *Yonec,* drawing upon *fin amor* and Beguine spirituality, see Newman's "*La Mystique courtoise*: Thirteenth-Century Beguines and the Art of Love," in *From Virile Woman,* pp. 166–67.

116. For dating, see Hanning and Ferrante's introduction in *The Lais of Marie de France,* pp. 5–8.

117. Vincent of Beauvais, *Speculum naturale* 2.126–27, col. 157.

118. See Robin Briggs, *Witches and Neighbors: The Social and Cultural Context of European Witchcraft* (New York: Viking, 1996), p. 27.

3. Sex in Holy Places

A shorter version of this chapter was delivered as a lecture, sponsored by the Frenzel Chair, at the Center for Medieval Studies, University of Minnesota, on 6 March 1992. I am especially indebted to the audience for the stimulating discussion.

1. Hildegard of Bingen, *Scivias* 3.5.25, ed. Adelgundis Führkötter and Angela Carlevaris, *CCCM,* 43a (Turnhout: Brepols, 1978), 2:426; trans. Columba Hart (New York: Paulist Press, 1990), p. 381.

2. The medieval descriptions of this condition have attracted the attention of medical authorities. See J. D. Rolleston, "Penis Captivus: A Historical Note," *Janus* 39 (1936): 196–202; and C. Grant Loomis, "Three Cases of Vaginism," *Bulletin of the History of Medicine* 7 (1939): 97–98. Both articles are reprinted in Joyce E. Salisbury's *Sex in the Middle Ages: A Book of Essays* (New York: Garland, 1991). Also see Danielle Jacquart and Claude Thomasset, *Sexuality and Medicine in the Middle Ages,* trans. Matthew Adamson (Princeton, N.J.: Princeton University Press, 1988), p. 162. For the prevalence of the motif, see Frederic C. Tubach's *Index Exemplorum: A Handbook of Medieval Religious Tales,* Folklore Fellows Communications, no. 204 (Helsinki: Suomalainen Tiedeakatemia, 1969), no. 5276; cf. no. 1056. Saxo Grammaticus reports a non-Christian analogue, allegedly visited on the people of Karentina for their sexual excesses (*Danorum regum heroumque historia: The Text of the First Edition with Translation and Commentary* 14.39, trans. Eric Christiansen [Oxford: B. A. R., 1981], 2: 509).

3. Jacquart and Thomasset make this association, and their interpretation of this motif follows accordingly (see *Sexuality and Medicine,* p. 227, n. 71). For the *vagina dentata* motif, see Stith Thompson, *Motif-Index of Folk-Literature,* rev. ed. (Bloomington: Indiana University Press, 1966), A1313.3.1, F547.1.1. Also see H. R. Hays's popular, but salient, discussion in *The Dangerous Sex: The Myth of Feminine Evil* (New York: Putnam, 1964), esp. chap. 5, "The Perils of Love," pp. 49–62.

4. See Rolleston, "Penis Captivus," pp. 199–201. My colleague Paul Strohm has drawn my attention to an incident reported in a volume that attained wide circulation among adolescent males in the 1950s—purportedly written to allay sexual anxieties. See Eustace Chesser, *Love Without Fear: How to Achieve Sex Happiness in Marriage* (New York: Roy, 1947), p. 213.

5. Modern analyses of rumor reveal its indebtedness to fear and anxiety. Continued circulation of a rumor indicates that many people share a certain fear and find

a particular configuration of it compelling and believable. See Daniel Goleman's "Anatomy of a Rumor: Fear Feeds It," *New York Times*, 4 June 1991, B1, B7. Goleman draws, in part, on Ralph L. Rosnow's "Inside Rumor: A Personal Journey," *American Psychologist* 46 (1991), see esp. 485–88. Edgar Morin's marvelous study of a modern rumor (regarding Jewish merchants who were allegedly selling women into the white slave trade) reveals the way in which a completely fictitious story can disrupt an entire city. See *Rumour in Orleans*, trans. Peter Green (London: Blond, 1971).

6. " . . . ubi merito testis Christi et intercessione fidelium liberantur," *AA SS*, March, 3:457. The author of the *acta* was a certain Anselm. Nothing he says identifies him with the famous Anselm of Canterbury (d. 1110), though he has been so identified by others. This incident is cited by Loomis in "Three Cases of Vaginism," pp. 97–98. The phrase *more canum* (in the manner of dogs) seems to refer to the way in which dogs become inextricably linked in the act of intercourse.

7. This is stated expressly in Durandus's *Pontifical* (late thirteenth century), which reveals more of the rationales behind the different liturgical practices than do its predecessors. See M. Andrieu, ed., *Le Pontifical de Guillaume Durand*, vol. 3 of *Le Pontifical romain au moyen-âge*, Studi e Testi, 88 (Vatican City: Biblioteca Apostolica Vaticana, 1940), p. 511; for the reconciliation of the graveyard alone, see pp. 517–18.

8. "Utrumque confestim divina ultio percussit. Ambo enim arrepti a daemone, alter eorum linguam frustatim concisam dentibus masticavit, alterius viscera per postrema diffusa sunt omnia, et sic uterque exitu expiravit horrendo," *AA SS*, March, 3: 457.

9. "Corruptor quidam gremia cujusdam mulieris incestare praesumpsit," ibid.

10. "Si advint un miracle qu'ilz s'entreprindrent et s'entrebessonnèrent comme chiens, tellement qu'ilz furent aussy pris de toute le jour à journée, si que ceulx de l'esglise et ceulx du païx eurent assez loisir de lez venir veoir; car ils ne se povoient departir, et convint que l'on venist à procession à prier Dieu pour eulx, et au fort sur le soir ilz se departirent. Dont il convint que l'esglise feust puis dediée, et convint par penitence qu'il alast par troix dimenches environ l'esglise et le cymetière, soy batant et recordant son peché," Anatole de Montaiglon, ed., *Le Livre du Chevalier de la Tour Landry* c. 35 (Paris: P. Jannet, 1854), p. 80. I would like to thank Robert Clark for his advice on this translation. Cf. William Caxton's fifteenth-century English translation, which follows the French original quite closely—except that Caxton discreetly positions the couple *under* the altar (*The Book of the Knight of the Tower* c. 35, ed. M. Y. Offord, *EETS*, supp., no. 2 [Oxford: Oxford University Press, 1971], p. 59).

11. At the bishop's consistory court in Rochester, for example, the standard punishment for fornicators was that they be beaten three times around the church (*fustigetur ter circa ecclesiam*). Adulterers, however, often received the additional humiliation of three times around the marketplace (*ter circa ecclesiam et ter circa mercatum*). See, for example, Charles Johnson, ed., *Registrum Hamonis Hetthe Diocesis Roffensis, A.D. 1319–1352*, Canterbury and York Society, vol. 49 (Oxford: Oxford University Press, 1948), 2: 925, 933, 948, 950, 957, 998–99. Also see R. H. Helmholz, *Marriage Litigation in Medieval England* (Cambridge: Cambridge University Press, 1974), pp. 182–83.

12. Montaiglon, *Le Livre du Chevalier* c. 36, p. 81. In Caxton's version, the protagonist is the nephew of the abbot (*Book of the Knight* c. 36, pp. 59–60).

13. On the periods of sexual abstinence that date back to the early church, see Pierre J. Payer, *Sex and the Penitentials: The Development of a Sexual Code, 550–1150* (Toronto: University of Toronto Press, 1984), pp. 23–28; also see James Brundage, "'Better to Marry Than to Burn?' The Case of the Vanishing Dichotomy," in *Views of Women's Lives in Western Tradition: Frontiers of the Past and the Future,* ed. F. R. Keller, Women's Studies, vol. 5 (Lewiston: Edwin Mellen, 1990), pp. 195–216.

14. See, for example, Thomas Aquinas's discussion of whether husband and wife are equal in the marriage act in *Commentum in quatuor libros sententiarum* bk. 4, dist. 32, q. 1, art. 3, in *Opera omnia* (Parma: Petrus Fiaccadori, 1858; rprt. New York: Musurgia, 1949), 7, 2: 962–63.

15. For evidence of this tendency in secular law, see Barbara Hanawalt, "The Female Felon in Fourteenth-Century England," in *Women in Medieval Society,* ed. Susan Mosher Stuard (Philadelphia: University of Pennsylvania Press, 1976), pp. 125–40. This prejudice occasionally held true for ecclesiastical courts as well. In the bishop's consistory court of Rochester, for example, the vast majority of sexual offenders named as defendants seem to have been men. Hugo Maundewyle was charged with adultery with three different married women, but only one of these women was ever charged. Nicholas de Ston' was also cited for adultery with three women, two of whom were married. The women themselves, though named, were seemingly neither summoned nor punished (see Johnson, *Registrum Hamonis,* 2: 950, 957, 948). In the London courts, on the other hand, the sex ratio of individuals charged was roughly equivalent. See Richard M. Wunderli, *London Church Courts and Society on the Eve of the Reformation* (Cambridge, Mass.: Medieval Academy of America, 1981), p. 86.

16. See Lev. 7.26, 15.2, 17.11–13, 22.4; cf. Deut. 23.10. The purification of a leper's house also proved influential in the evolution of the rite (Lev. 14.51). The key texts regarding the reconciliation of churches were assembled by Gratian in his *Decretum* (ca. 1140). The church must be carefully purged and consecrated anew if violated by murder or adultery (*De cons.* D. 1 c. 19). This particular canon, attributed to Pope Eugenius I (654–657), was cited in the earlier collections of Burchard of Worms (d. 1025, *Decretum* 3.12, *PL* 140, col. 675) and Anselm of Lucca (d. 1086, *Collectio canonum una cum collectione minore* 5.13, ed. F. Thaner [Innsbruck: Libraria Academicae Wagnerianae, 1906–15], p. 236). The ultimate source of this canon is probably the *Excerptiones Ecberti Eborcensi archiepiscopi* c. 139, in G. D. Mansi, ed., *Sacrorum conciliorum nova et amplissima collectio* (Paris: H. Welter, 1901), vol. 12, col. 426. The canons in Gratian's *De cons.* D. 1. c. 20, and D. 68 c. 3 require reconsecration in the event of pollution by blood, seed, or fire. Also see S. Many, *De locis sacris,* Praelectiones juris canonici (Paris: Letouzey and Ané, 1904), "De pollutione ecclesiarum et earum reconciliatione," c. 6, pp. 70–86.

17. The *Decretales* of Gregory IX (d. 1241) state explicitly that a simple priest is not equal to the occasion, even if the bishop has blessed the water (X.3.40.9). Note that even an unconsecrated church requires reconciliation (X.3.40.10).

18. These elements were also used in the consecration of a new church. See Cyrille Vogel and Reinhard Elze, eds., *Le Pontifical romano-germanique du dixième siècle,* Studi e Testi, 226 (Vatican City: Biblioteca Apostolica Vaticana, 1963), no. 40, "Ordo ad benedicendam ecclesiam," 1: 137–42. On the symbolism of the ceremony, see Hugh of St. Victor, *De sacramentis Christianae fidei* 2.5, *PL* 176, cols. 439–442;

trans. Roy J. Deferrari, *On the Sacraments of the Christian Faith* (Cambridge, Mass.: Medieval Academy of America, 1951), pp. 279–82; Lee Bowen, "The Tropology of Mediaeval Dedication Rites," *Speculum* 16 (1941): 469–79; and Jules Baudot, *La Dédicace des églises* (Paris: Librairie Bloud, 1909), pp. 5–15. There are many parallels between the rites of consecration and reconciliation.

19. "Deum indultorem criminum, Deum sordium mundatorem, Deum qui concretum peccatis originalibus mundum adventus sui nitore purificavit, fratres karissimi, suppliciter deprecemur, ut contra diaboli furentis insidias fortis nobis propugnator assistat, ut si quid eius virosa calliditate cotidianis infectationibus maculatum in isto loco invenitur atque corruptum, efficiatur caelesti miseratione purgatum," Vogel and Elze, *Le Pontifical romano-germanique* no. 50, "Reconciliatio violatae aecclesiae," 1: 183. The Roman Pontifical adopted this liturgy with virtually no changes in the twelfth century. See M. Andrieu, ed., *Le Pontifical romain du XIIe siècle,* vol. 1 of *Le Pontifical romain au moyen-âge,* Studi e Testi, 86 (Vatican City: Biblioteca Apostolica Vaticana, 1938), no. 18, "Reconciliatio violatae ecclesiae," p. 196. Durandus likewise expands on these earlier versions (see Andrieu, *Le Pontifical de Guillaume Durand* 2.6, pp. 510–17).

20. There were earlier rites, however. See, for example, Grimald of St. Gall (ca. 872), *Liber sacramentorum,* "In dedicatione violatae ecclesiae," *PL* 121, cols. 882–83.

21. For an introduction to this genre, see Payer, *Sex and the Penitentials,* and James Brundage, *Law, Sex, and Christian Society in Medieval Europe* (Chicago: University of Chicago Press, 1987), pp. 152–68. The earliest reference to seminal emissions in a church is in the "Penitential of Cummean" (before 662): "Whoever were to pour forth his semen in the church while sleeping should fast for III days" ("Qui semen in ecclesia dormiens fuderit, III dies jejunet)," in *Die Bussordnungen der aberländischen Kirche,* ed. F. W. Wasserschleben (Halle: Graeger, 1851), 2.21, p. 470. It is repeated in the seventh-century penitential of Theodore (H. J. Schmitz, ed., *Die Bussbücher und die Bussdisciplin der Kirche nach handschriftlichen Quellen dargestellt* [Mainz: Franz Kirchheim, 1883], 1.8.8, 1: 532); and, with some modifications, in the "Merseburg Penitential" (ibid., c. 142, p. 367), and the "Penitential of Egbert" (ibid., 9.11–12, p. 241). This latter work distinguishes between a sleeper who inadvertently ejaculates and one who deliberately stimulates his libido with evil thoughts ("mala cogitatione"). See Payer, *Sex and the Penitentials,* pp. 49–54. A number of these works have been translated by John T. McNeill and Helena M. Gamer in *Medieval Handbooks of Penance: A Translation of the Principal "Libri poenitentiales"* (New York: Columbia University Press, 1938; rprt. 1990).

22. "Si, quod absit, in locis sanctis tale crimen admiserit aliquis, duplicetur illi poenitentia," Theodulf of Orleans, *The Second Diocesan Statute, PL* 105, col. 215; see Payer, *Sex and the Penitentials,* p. 57. Cf. the "Paris Penitential," which imposes lifelong penance, seemingly in service of the church, for this offense: "Qui facit furnicationem in ecclesia, poenitentia est, omnibus diebus vitae suae praebeat obsequium domui Dei" (in H. J. Schmitz, ed., *Die Bussbücher und das kanonische Bussverfahren nach handschriftlichen Quellen dargestellt* [Düsseldorf: L. Schwann, 1898], c. 46, 2: 330; see Payer, *Sex and the Penitentials,* p. 39). Also see the entry in the *Capitula iudicorum,* which is included in a section on clerical discipline (Schmitz, *Die Bussbücher und das kanonische Bussverfahren* c. 41, 2: 229). The *Collection in Nine Books* (ca. 920) has the rubric "De his qui in ecclesia fornicantur" and gives a synodal

judgment as its source (see *Canonum prisca collectio* c. 44, *PL* 138, col. 438; and Payer, *Sex and the Penitentials*, pp. 80–81, 97).

23. "*De his, qui infra ecclesia fornicaverit vel adulteraverit.* In praesentiarum nihil periculosius, quam peccare laetaliter, nihilque dampnabilius, quam propter ardorem carnis, ut, quum aliqua scortu etiam infra parietis sanctae ecclesiae, minime recusat tam turpiter adtractare. Quicumque igitur affectus taliter intra ecclesiam adulteraverit vel fornicatus fuerit, si episcopus hoc praesumpserit, super legitimam poenit. X ann. poenit., presb. VII, diaconus et monachus V, subdiaconus IV, clericus et laicus III. Nec non propter Dei sanctaeque ecclesiae reverentiam non minus, quam CC diebus abstineat se ab omni ecclesiae ingressu. Hii supradicti gradus vel sine gradu, qui talia commiserint, a Christi corpore sanguineque usque post actam poenitentiam prorsum sint remoti, propter ad instanti necessitate, nec ut Judas participent, quem continuo post bucellam de manu Domini percepta diabolus pervasit, et ab ecclesiastico ordine inrecuperabiliter decidat usquequaque. Illi vero domus, quae ab adulteris contaminata fuerit, aqua exorcizata aspergatur et fiat, ut antea, sanctificata. . . . Si quis fecerit fornicationem in aecclesia, poenitentiam habeat omnibus diebus vitae suae i. p. e. a. [in pane et aqua], et ante fores ecclesiae praebeat obsequium Deo, et numquam communicet, nisi ad exitum mortis. . . . Similiter illa poeniteat, quae tale amiserit facinus turpiter consentiens, sic tamen, ut decet mulieres," Wasserschleben, *Die Bussordnungen* c. 7, p. 685; for dating, see p. 91.

24. Public penance could generally only be assigned once in a lifetime for an especially heinous offense. On the origins of public penance, see A. Teetaert, *La Confession aux laïques dans l'église latine* (Wetteren: J. de Meester; Bruges: Ch. Beyaert; and Paris: J. Gabalda, 1926), pp. 1–13. On the liturgy that evolved for the reconciliation of penitents, see L. Duchesne, *Christian Worship: Its Origin and Evolution,* trans. M. L. McClure, 5th ed. (London: Society for Promoting Christian Knowledge, 1931), pp. 435–45.

25. M. Fornasari, ed., *Collectio canonum in V libris* 2.78.1, *CCCM,* 6 (Turnhout: Brepols, 1970), pp. 225–26. The author removes much of the ambiguity from this text by entering the section about the offender's perpetual penitence as a separate canon, attributed to Gregory the Great (2.78.3, p. 227; 2.78.2 is also on this subject).

26. R. I. Moore makes this point in "Family, Community, and Cult on the Eve of the Gregorian Reform," *Transactions of the Royal Historical Society* 5th ser., 30 (1980): 67–68. Also see Janet Nelson, "Society, Theodicy, and the Origins of Heresy: Towards an Assessment of the Medieval Evidence," in *Schism, Heresy, and Religious Protest,* ed. Derek Baker, Studies in Church History, 9 (Cambridge: Cambridge University Press, 1972), pp. 65–77.

27. For the relationship between monastic spirituality and heresy, see H. Taviani, "Naissance d'une hérésie en Italie du Nord au XIe siècle," *Annales ESC* 29, no. 5 (1974): 1224–52; and R. I. Moore, *The Origins of European Dissent* (New York: St. Martin's Press, 1977), pp. 40–41. The reformers' struggles against clerical marriage is discussed in Chap. 4, below.

28. See, in particular, Anselm of Lucca's important *Collectio canonum,* which clearly articulates the papal reform party's ambitions and expectations for the clergy. Bks. 7 and 8 concern clerical discipline.

29. Efforts to restrict women's access to holy objects and places can be found as

early as the sixth century. See Suzanne F. Wemple, *Women in Frankish Society: Marriage and the Cloister, 500 to 900* (Philadelphia: University of Pennsylvania Press, 1985), p. 141. But the Carolingian period, when the first coherent efforts were made on behalf of sacerdotal celibacy, was particularly significant in this respect. See, for example, Regino of Prüm's *De ecclesiasticis disciplinis et religione Christiana* 1.198–99, *PL* 132, cols. 227–28; also see Wemple, *Women in Frankish Society,* pp. 143–48. Note that Regino's collection is sufficiently contradictory that it still contains a canon requiring priests to instruct women on the proper way of preparing linens for the altar (1.60, *PL* 132, col. 203). Not surprisingly, this canon was not picked up in later collections, such as that of Burchard of Worms. Gratian uses a false decretal attributed to the second-century Pope Soter (D. 23 c. 25; also see Gratian's own comments in D. 23 c. 34 dpc). Cf. X.3.2.1, drawn from a late ninth-century council that bars women from approaching the altar during Mass or from acting as server. See René Metz, "Le Statut de la femme en droit canonique médiéval," *Recueils de Société Jean Bodin pour l'histoire comparative des institutions* 12 (1962): 107–8.

30. R. I. Moore, *The Formation of a Persecuting Society: Power and Deviance in Western Europe, 950–1250* (Oxford: Blackwell, 1987), p. 96. Also note that in many jurisdictions where prostitution was legal, brothels were nonetheless closed on holy days. See Ruth Mazo Karras, "The Regulation of Brothels in Later Medieval England," *Signs* 14 (1989): 404 and appendix, 427 (Ordinance A3); Leah Lydia Otis, *Prostitution in Medieval Society: The History of an Urban Institution* (Chicago: University of Chicago Press, 1985), pp. 85–88; and eadem, "Prostitution and Repentance in Medieval Perpignan," in *Women of the Medieval World: Essays in Honor of John H. Mundy,* ed. Julius Kirshner and Suzanne F. Wemple (Oxford: Blackwell, 1985), pp. 148–49.

31. See Thomas Aquinas, *Summa theologiae* 2a 2ae, q. 99, art. 3, ed. and trans. Fathers of the English Dominican Province (London: Blackfriars, 1968), 40: 118–23. According to Guido Ruggiero's analysis, the Venetian secular authorities' concern over this kind of sacrilege escalated over the course of the fourteenth and fifteenth centuries. See *The Boundaries of Eros: Sex Crime and Sexuality in Renaissance Venice* (New York: Oxford University Press, 1985), pp. 72–76.

32. It is the fantasy and the historicity of the fantasy that is the focus of this study. This is not to deny that individuals like the priest Petrus Clergus actually committed this offense. See Jean Duvernoy, ed., *Le Registre d'inquisition de Jacques Fournier, évêque de Pamiers (1318–1325)* (Toulouse: Edouard Privat, 1965), 1: 243. This episode is described in Emmanuel Le Roy Ladurie's *Montaillou, village occitan de 1294 à 1324* (Paris: Gallimard, 1975), p. 236; cf. a parallel but isolated offense mentioned by Ruggiero, in *Boundaries of Eros,* pp. 71, 85. But to trace such occurrences would entail a different kind of study.

33. Stephen of Bourbon, *Anecdotes historiques, légendes et apologues tirés du recueil inédit d'Etienne de Bourbon,* ed. A. Lecoy de la Marche (Paris: Librairie Renouard, 1877), no. 320, pp. 269–70.

34. " . . . comburens pavimentum et quedam loca, quosdam autem majores monachos, parvis innocentibus intactis remanentibus, vulneravit ad mortem, per sinum eorum subtiliter intrans, et pilos inferiores radens et urens, et loca illa inferiora, graviter ledens," Stephen of Bourbon, *Anecdotes historiques,* no. 321, p. 270.

35. For instance, desecration and reconsecration of the cathedral play a pivotal

role in Guibert's account of the famous uprising of the commune of Laon (Guibert of Nogent, *Autobiographie* 3.5, 3.10, ed. Edmond-René Labande [Paris: Société d'Edition "Les Belles Lettres," 1981], pp. 300, 302, 358, 360; trans. Paul J. Archambault, *A Monk's Confession: The Memoirs of Guibert of Nogent* [University Park: Pennsylvania State University Press, 1996], pp. 138–39, 164). Guibert gives a lively rendition of the sermon he preached at the reconciliation of the cathedral after the murder of Gérard de Quierzy (3.6, ed. Labande, pp. 306, 308, 310; trans. Archambault, pp. 139–42). As a sign of the extreme and unprecedented turbulence of the times, he also notes with shock that one priest actually ordered his servants to shoot another priest in the midst of performing Mass, thus being guilty of both willful homicide and desecration (3.11, ed. Labande, pp. 374, 376; trans. Archambault, p. 172).

36. Guibert of Nogent, *Autobiographie* 1.23, ed. Labande, pp. 181, 182; trans. Archambault, *A Monk's Confession,* pp. 79–80.

37. I am grateful to Samuel Rosenberg for bringing this episode to my attention. See his recent translation in *Lancelot-Grail: The Old French Arthurian Vulgate and Post-Vulgate in Translation,* ed. Norris J. Lacey (New York: Garland, 1993), c. 87, 2: 291–96; c. 91, 2: 300–303.

38. Henry Kramer and James Sprenger, *Malleus maleficarum 1487,* photographic facsimile of the first edition (Hildesheim: Georg Olms, 1992), pt. 2, q. 1, c. 4, fol. 55v; trans. Montague Summers (London: John Rodker, 1928; rprt. New York: Dover, 1971), p. 113. Cf. the formulary for interrogations attached to Robert of Flamborough's manual (before 1215), which simulates a mock confession for the instruction of confessors. The hypothetical penitent—while admitting to a vast array of sins, including adultery, incest, and homosexuality—responds with a terse "no" to the question of holy places. See the epigraph to the Afterword, below.

39. As cited by Iris Origo, *The World of San Bernardino* (New York: Harcourt, Brace, and World, 1962), p. 46.

40. Alfredo Galletti, "Una raccolta di prediche volgari inedite del Cardinale Giovanni Dominici," in *Miscellanea di Studi Critici pubblicati in onore di Guido Mazzoni dai suoi Discepoli,* ed. A. Della Torre and P. L. Rambaldi (Florence: Tipografia Galileiana, 1907), 1: 269.

41. "[Peccavi] hinc inde vage et incaute circumspiciendo, viros aut feminas libidinose intuendo (quod est grave peccatum); et tempore Missae ac divini Officii ista feci, diebusque sacris et festivis," Denis the Carthusian, "De laudabili vita conjugatorum" art. 36, ed. the Monks of the Sacred Order of the Carthusians in *Opera minora,* vol. 6 (= vol. 38 of *Opera omnia* [Tournai: Typis Cartusiae S. M. de Pratis, 1909], p. 102). Later in the same article, the imagined layperson confesses to having had sex on a feast day and participating in communion before having done penance. He or she also returns to gazing libidinously at members of the opposite sex during divine office (p. 105).

42. William de Nangis, *Continuatio chronici* ann. 1314, in *Recueil des historiens des Gaules et de la France,* ed. Danou and Naudet (Paris: Imprimerie Royale, 1840), 20: 609; see Allison Peers, *Ramon Lull: A Biography* (London: Society for Promoting Christian Knowledge, 1929), pp. 17–18. Lull's contemporary biography makes no mention of this incident, though it does note that Lull was writing songs for a certain lady when he had his first vision of Christ ("Vita Beati Raimundi Lulli" c. 1–2, ed. B. de Gaiffier, *AB* 48 [1930]: 146–47).

43. Sanford Brown Meech and Hope Emily Allen, eds., *The Book of Margery Kempe* 1.4, *EETS,* o.s., no. 212 (London: Oxford University Press, 1940; rprt. 1960), pp. 14–15. Also see n. 32, above.

44. George L. Kittredge includes our motif as an example of spells and rites that "bind thieves" so that they are paralyzed, unable to escape with their booty; see *Witchcraft in Old and New England* (New York: Russell and Russell, 1956), pp. 200–201 and n. 101. The theft element is more apparent in some versions of the motif than others. For example, one miracle of the Virgin stresses that a man locked in adultery was incapable of returning to his own wife ("miraculum de quadam muliere quae viro conjugato adhaesit et eum non sinebat ad uxorem propriam remeare"). The wife then is portrayed as the wronged party in this strange property suit (Cod. sign. n. 212 [al. 178 2/c], in "Catalogus codicum hagiographicorum bibliothecae civitatis Carnotensis," *AB* 8 [1889]: 88; Joyce Salisbury, *Medieval Sexuality: A Research Guide* [New York: Garland, 1990], no. 193). In a miracle in the life of St. Clitaucus, the punishment does not result from the desecration of a holy place (though, admittedly, the man and his wife were en route to Mass and relatively near the church) but from the unjust seizure of a field (*Nova Legenda Anglie,* ed. Carl Horstman [Oxford: Clarendon Press, 1901], 1: 190; cf. Loomis, "Three Cases," p. 97; and Salisbury, *Medieval Sexuality,* no. 203). This particular collection is a sixteenth-century rearrangement of John of Tynemouth's *Sanctilogium Anglie* of the second quarter of the fourteenth century.

45. Robert of Brunne, *Handlyng Synne* ll. 8937–82, ed. Frederick J. Furnivall, *EETS,* o.s., nos. 119 and 123 (London: Kegan Paul, Trench, and Trübner, 1901; rprt. Millwood, N.Y.: Kraus, 1975), p. 282. This edition gives the Old French *Manuel des Pechiez* in the opposite column as well. The subject of sex in holy places is also introduced much earlier in the course of a discussion of the sixth commandment (on adultery). Sex in a church or churchyard is pronounced a mortal sin (ll. 2016–20, p. 72).

46. The *Liber exemplorum ad usum praedicantium* (ed. A. G. Little [Aberdeen: Typis Academicis, 1908]), for example, retains the protagonist's name (Richerius) and makes explicit reference to the *Manuel des Pechiez* (no. 119, p. 70). This compilation was made by an English friar before 1271.

47. Robert of Brunne, *Handlyng Synne* ll. 8977–82, 282. I have modernized the English of the original passage.

48. See Gratian, C. 33 q. 4 c. 1–11 and dpc 11; and Brundage, *Law, Sex, and Christian Society,* p. 242. For Alexander's intervention, see André Vauchez, *La Spiritualité du moyen âge occidental, VIIIe–XIIe siècles,* Collection Sup., L'historien, 19 (Rome: Presses Universitaires de France, 1975), p. 128.

49. 1 Cor. 7.4. For an introduction to the way in which the conjugal debt was understood in the high Middle Ages, see Brundage, *Law, Sex, and Christian Society,* pp. 241–42, 278–85; Dyan Elliott, *Spiritual Marriage: Sexual Abstinence in Medieval Wedlock* (Princeton, N.J.: Princeton University Press, 1993), pp. 142–55; Elizabeth M. Makowski, "The Conjugal Debt and Medieval Canon Law," *Journal of Medieval History* 3 (1977): 99–114; and Payer, *Bridling of Desire,* pp. 94–97.

50. For the development of pastoral manuals, see Pierre Michaud-Quantin, "A propos des premières *Summae confessorum,*" *Recherches de théologie ancienne et médiévale* 26 (1959): 264–306; and Leonard Boyle, "*Summae Confessorum,*" in *Les Genres*

littéraires dans les sources théologiques et philosophiques médiévales: définition, critique, et exploitation, Actes du Colloque International de Louvain-la-Neuve, 25–27 May 1981, Université Catholique de Louvain, Publications de l'Institut d'Etudes Médiévales, 2d ser., Textes, Etudes, Congrès, vol. 5 (Louvain-la-Neuve: Institut d'Etudes Médiévales, 1982), pp. 227–37.

51. See Payer, *Bridling of Desire,* pp. 101–2.

52. "Utrum liceat debitum reddere vel etiam exigere in loco sacro. Respondeo secundum Petrum dicendum quod liceat debitum reddendum sit omni tempore. non tamen simile est de loco quia locus pollui potest ita vt indigeat reconciliatione non autem tempus. Item locus facilius mutari quam tempus. Thomas etiam dicit quod debitum reddendum sit omni tempore et omni hora salua tamen debita honestate que in talibus exigitur quia non oportet quod statim in publico debitum reddat. Idem dicit Albertus et addit quod si alius locus haberi potest non tenetur reddere in loco sacro. Si non potest alius locus haberi. tunc reddat cum dolore cordis. Et etiam si exigat cum planctu quod sine vsu matrimonii esse non potest. non credo quod peccet mortaliter," John of Freiburg, *Summa confessorum* 4.2.43 (Rome: s.n., 1518), fol. 220v.

53. See William of Rennes, glossator of Raymond de Peñafort, writing in the mid-thirteenth century, in *Summa sancti Raymundi Peniafort de poenitentia, et matrimonio* 4.2.10, gloss k ad v. *abstinendum* (Rome: Sumptibus Joanni Tallini, 1603), p. 516; Hostiensis (d. 1271), *Summa* (Lyons: Iacobus Giunta, 1537; rprt. Aalen: Scientia, 1962), fol. 196v; and John Gerson (d. 1429), *Regulae mandatorum* c. 154, no. 434, in *Oeuvres complètes,* ed. Palémon Glorieux (Paris: Desclée, 1973), 9: 132.

54. See *Peter Abelard's "Ethics",* ed. and trans. D. E. Luscombe (Oxford: Clarendon Press, 1971), esp. pp. 12–15, 22–23, 40–47. On Abelard's view of sin and intention, see Robert Blomme, *La Doctrine du péché dans les écoles théologiques de la première moitié du XIIe siècle* (Louvain: Universitaires de Louvain; Gembloux: J. Duculot, 1958), pp. 128–64.

55. For Abelard's impact on twelfth-century thought, see Odon Lottin, *Psychologie et morale aux XIIe et XIIIe siècles,* 2d ed. (Louvain: Abbaye du Mont Cesar; Gembloux: J. Duculot, 1954), 4, 1: 310–21; and D. E. Luscombe, *The School of Peter Abelard: The Influence of Abelard's Thought in the Early Scholastic Period* (Cambridge: Cambridge University Press, 1969), esp. pp. 194–96, 217–22, 276–79.

56. For Augustine and intentionality, see especially *De bono conjugali* 6.6–7.6, ed. Joseph Zycha, *CSEL,* 41 (Vienna: F. Tempsky; Leipzig: G. Freytag, 1900), pp. 195–96; trans. Charles T. Wilcox, *The Good of Marriage,* in *Saint Augustine: Treatises on Marriage and Other Subjects, FC,* vol. 27 (New York: Fathers of the Church, 1955), p. 17; and Ep. 262, To Ecdicia, c. 2, *Epistulae,* ed. A. Goldbacher, *CSEL,* 47 (Vienna: F. Tempsky; Leipzig: G. Freytag, 1911), p. 623; trans. Wilfrid Parsons, *Letters, FC,* vol. 32 (New York: Fathers of the Church, 1956), pp. 262–63. Cf. Gratian, C. 33 q. 5 c. 5; and Peter Lombard, *Sententiae in IV libris distinctae* bk. 4, dist. 32, c. 2, 2, ed. Fathers of the College of St. Bonaventure ad Claras Aquas, 3d ed. (Rome: College of St. Bonaventure, 1981), 2: 453.

57. See Brundage, *Law, Sex, and Christian Society,* p. 448. Albert's relatively positive assessment is characteristic of the Aristotelianism of the Dominican school. See Fabian Parmisano, "Love and Marriage in the Middle Ages," *New Blackfriars* 50 (1969): 599–608, 649–60.

58. Cf. Raymond de Peñafort, *Summa* 4.2.10, p. 516; Thomas Aquinas, *Commentum in quatuor libros sententiarum* bk. 4, dist. 32, q. 1, art. 5, quaestiuncula 3, in *Opera omnia,* Parma edition, 7, 2: 964; and Bernardino of Siena, *Opera omnia,* ed. Fathers of the College of St. Bonaventure ad Claras Aquas (Florence: College of St. Bonaventure, 1950), serm. 18, 1: 224. They all assert that a sorrowful rendering in holy times is sinless.

59. See n. 52, above.

60. "Tempus et locus sacer non videntur excusare quin alter conjugum teneatur alteri petenti debitum reddere," Gerson, *Regulae mandatorum* c. 154, *Oeuvres complètes,* 9: 132; "Sacrilege est es personnes religieuses ou qui ont ordre sainte, ou quant se fait en lieu d'esglise cunsacree; il n'est point doubte que c'est pechie mortel moult grant," *Poenitemini: contre la luxure,* serm. 369, ibid., 7, ii: 820.

61. Thomas of Chobham, *Summa confessorum* 7.2.2.3, ed. F. Broomfield, Analecta Mediaevalia Namurcensia, 25 (Louvain: Nauwelaerts, 1968), p. 336.

62. "Dicimus ergo quod peccat mulier in illo facto sustinendo fieri in se illud peccatum. Deberet enim statim virum suum corripere et auferre ei pravam voluntatem. Non tamen tantum peccat quantum vir," Thomas of Chobham, *Summa confessorum* 7.2.9.2, pp. 360–61.

63. See Alexander of Hales, *Summa theologica* inq. 3, tract. 5, sect. 2, q. 1, tit. 3, c. 2, resp. ad obj. 6, ed. Fathers of the College of St. Bonaventure ad Claras Aquas (Florence: College of St. Bonaventure, 1930), 3: 635; also see c. 3, resp. ad obj. 5, 3: 637.

64. "It should be said that, strictly speaking, it is called pollution by the manner in which it is polluted through adultery or fornication, not however when it is polluted through coitus with a wife. On account of which there should be a reconsecration, as some say. According to others, however, in certain cases it ought to be consecrated a second time; but if it were adultery, a reconciliation [is required]" (" . . . dicendum quod proprie dicitur pollutio illo modo quo polluitur per adulterium vel fornicationem, non autem cum polluitur per coitum cum uxore, propter quam debeat fieri reconsecratio, sicut dicunt quidam; secundum alios autem in quibusdam casibus debet fieri iterata consecratio; si vero fuerit adulterium, reconciliatio") Alexander of Hales, *Summa theologica* inq. 3, tract. 5, sect. 2, q. 1, tit. 3, c. 2, resp. ad obj. 7, 3: 634.) The editor cites the canonist Huguccio as an authority who argues against marital sex as polluting (see 3: 634, n. 9, and cf. Huguccio's view on the exigencies of a couple taking refuge in wartime, mentioned above). Although the Dominicans were generally more liberal in matters of sexuality, note that when John Nider (d. 1438) raises the question of rendering the conjugal debt in a holy place in his confessor's manual, he cites Peter of Palude (d. 1342), who maintains that a church or cemetery is polluted by marital intercourse (John Nider, *De morali lepra* [Louvain: Johann von Paderborn, 1481], fol. 79v.

For the distinction between the reconsecration and the reconciliation of a church, see Innocent III's response to the archbishop of Compostella (X.3.40.4). Note that earlier sources did not maintain so clear a distinction: see nn. 16 and 18, above.

65. This was something of an obsession for Bernardino. See *Opera omnia,* serm. 18, 1: 223; serm. 17, 1: 211; L. Banchi, ed., *Le Prediche volgari di San Bernardino da Siena, dette nella Piazza del Campo l'anno MCCCCXXVII* (Siena: Edit.

all'inseg. di S. Bernardino, 1884), serm. 21, 2: 172; C. Cannarozzi, ed., *San Bernardino da Siena: le prediche volgari* (Pistoia: Alberto Pacinotti, 1934), serm. 24, 1: 399; and Cherubino of Spoleto, *Regole della vita matrimoniale,* ed. Francesco Zambrini and Carlo Negroni, Scelta di curiosita letterarie inedite o rare del secolo XIII al XVII, Dispensa 128 (Bologna: Romagnoli-dall'Acqua, 1888), pp. 43, 76.

66. For Bernardino, see *Opera omnia,* serm. 18, 1: 224; and Banchi, *Le prediche volgari,* serm. 21, 2: 167; for Cherubino, see *Regole della vita matrimoniale,* pp. 76–77.

67. On the independence of pollution codes from moral codes and the potential for conflict, see Mary Douglas, *Purity and Danger: An Analysis of Pollution and Taboo* (London: Routledge and Kegan Paul; Ark Paperbacks, 1966; rprt. 1988), pp. 128–30. William Bouwsma, applying a number of Douglas's insights, argues that medieval culture's stability was to a large extent premised on clear boundaries that had the effect of holding anxiety at bay; its demise came when these boundaries were no longer appropriate to the increasing complexities of the late medieval world. See "Anxiety and the Formation of Early Modern Culture," in *After the Reformation: Essays in Honor of J. H. Hexter,* ed. Barbara C. Malament (Philadelphia: University of Pennsylvania Press, 1980), esp. pp. 228–30; cf. Douglas, *Purity and Danger,* p. 122. The question of sex in holy places may be a graphic example of this kind of breakdown.

68. Abelard, *Ethics,* p. 43.

69. Abelard, Ep. 4, ed. J. T. Muckle, "The Personal Letters Between Abelard and Heloise," *Mediaeval Studies* 15 (1953): 88; trans. Betty Radice, *The Letters of Abelard and Heloise* (Harmondsworth: Penguin, 1974), p. 146. Abelard also reminds Heloise of their sacrilegious conduct during Holy Week (ed. Muckle, p. 89; trans. Raddice, p. 147). Cf. Augustine's similar admission in *Confessionum libri XIII* 3.3, ed. Lucas Verheijen, *CCSL,* 27 (Turnhout: Brepols, 1981), p. 29; trans. R. S. Pine-Coffin, *Confessions* (Harmondsworth: Penguin, 1961), p. 57. I would like to thank my colleague Rosemarie McGerr for pointing out this parallel.

70. The personal letters were probably written after 1132, the year by which Abelard's autobiography is believed to have been in circulation. The *Ethics* was written sometime between 1135 and early 1138. See Luscombe's introduction, *Ethics,* p. XXX; and idem, "The *Ethics* of Peter Abelard: Some Further Considerations," in *Peter Abelard,* Proceedings of the International Conference, Louvain, 10–12 May 1971, ed. E. M. Buytaert (Louvain: Louvain University Press; The Hague: Martinus Nijhoff, 1974), pp. 73–76. Peter Dronke also assumes the priority of the personal letters. See *Women Writers of the Middle Ages: A Critical Study of Texts from Perpetua (d. 203) to Marguerite Porete (d. 1310)* (Cambridge: Cambridge University Press, 1984), pp. 107, 118. I am indebted to Rita Copeland's penetrating questioning, which led me to recognize the potential significance of the chronological order of these works.

71. Abelard, Ep. 4, "Personal Letters," ed. Muckle, p. 89; trans. Radice, *Letters of Abelard,* p. 147.

72. Note, however, that the other way in which the passive female is construed in this topos is as the nameless temptress, discussed above. This polarity is but another manifestation of the division of woman into positive and negative paradigms, treated more extensively in Chap. 1, pp. 30–31, above, and Chap. 5, pp. 123–

25, below. I also discuss the way in which the conjugal debt benefits the husband at greater length in "Bernardino of Siena versus the Marriage Debt," in *Desire and Discipline: Sex and Sexuality in Premodern Europe,* ed. Jacqueline Murray and Konrad Eisenbichler (Toronto: University of Toronto Press, 1996), pp. 168–200.

73. See Thomas of Chobham's discussion of the etymology (*Summa confessorum* 7.7.13.1, p. 566).

74. Distinctions were developed between active and passive scandal or direct and indirect scandal in an effort to discern varying degrees of intention and, hence, culpability. See Aquinas, *Summa theologiae* 2a 2ae, q. 43, art. 1, 35: 108–15; cf. Thomas of Chobham, *Summa confessorum* 7.7.13.1, p. 566.

75. "Cordis quoque superbiam, iram, concupiscentiam, vanitatem et dissolutionem frequenter ostendi per visum, et sic alios scandalizavi, interiora vitia mea foris monstrando," Denis the Carthusian, "De laudabili vita conjugatorum" art. 36, in *Opera minora,* p. 102.

76. Colin Morris makes this claim for the high Middle Ages. See *The Discovery of the Individual, 1050–1200* (New York: Harper and Row, 1972); also see Caroline Walker Bynum's important examination of the way in which individuality was understood in the context of identification with groups—especially in religious life ("Did the Twelfth Century Discover the Individual?" in *Jesus as Mother: Studies in the Spirituality of the High Middle Ages* [Berkeley University of California Press, 1982], pp. 82–109).

77. For the biblical precedent, see Rom. 14.15–23. See Peter the Chanter's section, which has the rubric "That for avoiding scandal we ought to abstain from the licit things which are able to be omitted" ("Quod ad uitandum scandalum abstinere debemus a licitis que possunt omitti," in *Summa de sacramentis et animae consiliis* c. 318, ed. Jean-Albert Dugauquier, Analecta Mediaevalia Namurcensia, 16 [Louvain: Nauwelaerts; Lille: Librairie Giard, 1963], 3, 2a: 375–76). Cf. idem, c. 224, 3, 2a: 203; Raymond of Peñafort, *Summa de poenitentia* 3.30.1–5, pp. 353–56.

78. This threefold criterion is ubiquitous. See, for example, Peter the Chanter, *Summa de sacramentis* c. 319, 3, 2a: 276; Peter of Poitiers, *Summa de confessione: Compilatio praesens* c. 44, ed. Jean Longère, *CCCM,* 51 (Turnhout: Brepols, 1980), p. 55; and Aquinas, *Summa theologiae* 2a 2ae, q. 43, art. 7, resp. ad obj. 4, 35: 132.

79. Aquinas, *Summa theologiae* 2a 2ae, q. 43, art. 7, resp. ad obj. 5, 35: 132–33.

80. "*De penitentia pro scandalo.* Pro peccato autem scandali grave est et difficile condignam iniungere penitentiam, quia vix contingit quod aliquis peccet aliquo peccato quin scandalizet alios per illud peccatum. Et sepe magis offenditur dominus per publicationem peccati quam per ipsum peccati opus, ut in Ieremia legitur: *publicaverunt peccata sua sicut Sodoma; publicaverunt et non absconderunt.* Qui enim peccat in occulto non occidit nisi suam animam propriam, et forte non offendit nisi solum deum. Qui autem peccat in publico occidit animam suam et per scandalum animas aliorum, et forte totam offendit ecclesiam. Unde multo magis eum oportet satisfacere qui peccat publice et multo maior est penitentia iniungenda quam si peccasset in privato. Unde dicit Sapiens: si non caste tamen caute," *Summa confessorum* 7.13.4, pp. 570–71. Broomfield, the editor, notes that the passage attributed to Jeremiah is really Isaiah 3.9 (p. 570, n. 1). He cannot identify the so-called Sapiens, however (p. 571, n. 2).

81. "In comparatione duorum peccatorum levius peccatum est aperte peccare quam simulare et fingere sanctitatem," *Sic et non* c. 149, ed. Blanche B. Boyer and Richard McKeon (Chicago: University of Chicago Press, 1976–77), p. 509.

82. "'Si nequeas caste, ne spernas vivere caute,'" from *Carmen ad Astralabium filium,* as cited by Peter Dronke, in *Poetic Individuality in the Middle Ages: New Departures in Poetry, 1000–1500* (Oxford: Clarendon Press, 1970), p. 149. Amidst this collection of proverbial sayings, however, Abelard still manages to insinuate his theory of intentionality: "A man can sin only through contempt for God— / only contempt can here make culpable" (as translated and quoted in Dronke, *Abelard and Heloise in Medieval Testimonies,* University of Glasgow, W. P. Ker lecture, no. 26 [Glasgow: University of Glasgow Press, 1976], p. 15).

83. As a student studying in Paris in the milieu of Peter, Thomas was especially likely to be familiar with Abelard's work. Note, however, that due to the various condemnations of Abelard's theological writings, he was rarely cited by name. Anecdotes concerning his uncompromising nature did circulate, however. See John W. Baldwin, *Masters, Princes, and Merchants: The Social Views of Peter the Chanter and His Circle* (Princeton, N.J.: Princeton University Press, 1970), 1: 34–36, 2: 25–27, for Thomas's career; 1: 55, 2: 107–8, for Abelard's legend.

84. See A. Lecoy de la Marche, *La Chaire française au moyen âge,* 2d ed. (Paris: H. Laurens, 1886), p. 434. James of Vitry also expressly recommends that such information be reserved for the confessional. See D. L. d'Avray and M. Tausche, "Marriage Sermons in *ad status* Collections of the Central Middle Ages," *Archives d'histoire doctrinale et littéraire du moyen âge* 47 (1980): 97–98.

85. On the internal forum, see P. Capobianco, "De notione fori interni in iure canonico," *Apollinaris* 9 (1936): 364–74; and idem, "De ambitu fori interni in iure ante Codicem," *Apollinaris* 8 (1935): 591–605.

86. Douglas, *Purity and Danger,* p. 113; also see the discussion of the way in which pollution rules can reduce confusion when moral principles clash (p. 136).

87. See Henri Crouzel, *Virginité et mariage selon Origène,* Museum Lessianum, section théologique, no. 58 (Paris: Desclée de Brouwer, 1963), pp. 60–62, 82. This view is also held by Aquinas: "Although the marriage act is without fault, nevertheless because it oppresses the reason on account of carnal pleasure, it renders a person unfit for spiritual things" ("quod actus matrimonialis quamvis culpa careat, tamen, quia rationem deprimit propter carnalem delectationem, hominem reddit ineptum ad spiritualia"), *Commentum in quatuor libros sententiarum* bk. 4, dist. 32, art. 5, q. 1, solutio, in *Opera omnia,* Parma edition, 7, 2: 964. This line of thinking can be traced back to St. Paul's ambiguous directives that couples separate for prayer (1 Cor. 7.5).

4. The Priest's Wife

1. "*Piger:* Non nouiter, sed dudum cum in sacra scriptura talia contra feminas praeuisando virilem sexum audiui, animum meum tale pulsauit dubium: Cur non plus sexus fragilis muniatur in sacris literis, vt sibi a virorum dolis caueant, quam masculinuis, quem tamen constat animo esse constantiorem? . . . *Theologus:* Quia Deo natura sunt propinquiores, ideo foedati turpius inficiuntur," *Formicarium* 3.4,

pp. 205–6; *Negation,* in *The Standard Edition of the Complete Psychological Works of Sigmund Freud,* ed. James Strachey (London: Hogarth Press, 1961), 19: 235.

2. On this initiative, which Jo Ann McNamara sees as part of a much wider crisis in masculine identity, see her groundbreaking "The *Herrenfrage:* The Restructuring of the Gender System, 1050–1150," in *Medieval Masculinities: Regarding Men in the Middle Ages,* ed. Clare Lees (Minneapolis: University of Minnesota Press, 1994), pp. 3–29, esp. pp. 5–12. Cf. Enrico Cattaneo's discussion of the reforming clergy's efforts to distance themselves from the laity both through creating a heightened aura around the priest and his liturgical function and, on a more concrete level, through proposed architectural change in the church—separating the clergy, laymen, and laywomen ("La liturgia nella riforma gregoriana," in *Chiesa e riforma nella spiritualità del sec. XI,* Convegni del Centro di studi sulla spiritualità medievale, 6 [Todi: Presso l'Accademia Tudertina, 1968], pp. 184–86; also see G. G. Meersseman, "Chiesa e 'Ordo laicorum' nel sec. XI," in *Chiesa e riforma,* pp. 40–42, 68–74; and Dyan Elliott, *Spiritual Marriage: Sexual Abstinence in Medieval Wedlock* (Princeton, N.J.: Princeton University Press, 1993), pp. 94–95, 98–104.

3. On tenth-century anticipation of this pollution-laden rhetoric, see Jo Ann McNamara, "Canossa and the Ungendering of the Public Man," in *Render unto Caesar: The Religious Sphere in the World of Politics,* ed. Sabrina Petra Ramet and Donald W. Treadgold (Washington, D.C.: American University Press, 1995), pp. 136–38.

4. See M. Dortel-Claudot, "Le Prêtre et le mariage: évolution de la législation canonique des origines au XIIe siècle," *L'Année canonique* 17 (1973): 319–44; and Anne Llewellyn Barstow, *Married Priests and the Reforming Papacy: The Eleventh-Century Debates,* Texts and Studies in Religion, vol. 12 (New York: Edwin Mellen, 1982), pp. 19–45. Also see Jo Ann McNamara, "Chaste Marriage and Clerical Celibacy," in *Sexual Practices and the Medieval Church,* ed. Vern Bullough and James Brundage (Buffalo, N.Y.: Prometheus, 1982), pp. 22–33, 231–35. A married priesthood was, and still is, the practice of the eastern church.

5. Dortel-Claudot, "Le Prêtre et le mariage," pp. 336, 340.

6. This was enacted at a Roman council that took place in either 1049 or 1050 under Leo IX. Peter Damian alludes to this legislation with approval, as will be seen below. For an analysis of canonistic antecedents, particularly the Council of Pavia in 1022, see J. Joseph Ryan, *Saint Peter Damiani and His Canonical Sources: A Preliminary Study in the Antecedents of the Gregorian Reform,* Studies and Texts, 2 (Toronto: Pontifical Institute of Mediaeval Studies, 1956), no. 197, pp. 101–2.

7. On the Milanese reform led by the so-called Patarene movement, see H. E. J. Cowdrey, "The Papacy, the Patarenes, and the Church of Milan," *Transactions of the Royal Historical Society* ser. 5, 18 (1986): 25–48. See particularly the impassioned account of Landulf the Senior, himself a married priest, in book 3 of his *Mediolanensis historiae libri quatuor,* ed. Alessandro Cutulo, *Rerum Italicarum Scriptores,* rev. ed. (Bologna: Nicola Zanichelli, 1942), 4, 2: 81–128. One of the leaders of the reform, the deacon Ariald, was eventually murdered by his enemies. His body, described as creating a terrible stench that threatened to reveal where it was hidden, was handed over to his enemies—appropriately castrated (3.30, pp. 121–22). On Peter Damian's mission to Milan, see n. 67, below. It is possible that the married

clergy attempted to buttress their practice by conciliar action. There is, however, no mention of any such efforts in Michael Stoller's study of antireform councils. See his "Eight Anti-Gregorian Councils," *Annuarium Historiae Conciliorum* 17, 2 (1985): 252–321. But considering that Stoller was forced to reconstruct these legislative endeavors from fragments, and that very little of the *acta* remain, it is possible that there were such organized efforts. On a possible council of Trebur, see n. 67, below. For the literary defense of clerical marriage, see Barstow, *Married Priests,* pp. 105–73, and Augustin Fliche, *La Réforme grégorienne,* Spicilegium Sacrum Lovaniense, fasc. 16 (Louvain: Spicilegium Sacrum Lovaniense, 1937), 3: 1–48.

8. Christopher Brooke, "Gregorian Reform in Action: Clerical Marriage in England, 1050–1200," *Cambridge Historical Journal* 12, 1 (1956): 1–21; app. in 12, 2 (1956): 187–88.

9. Georges Duby, "Les pauvres des campagnes dans l'occident médiéval jusqu'au XIIIe siècle," *Revue d'histoire de l'église de France* 52 (1966): 28; McNamara, "The *Herrenfrage,*" p. 12. Jacques Dalarun also assesses the early members of the monastic foundation of Fontevrault as casualties of the eleventh-century marriage crisis. See "Robert d'Arbrissel et les femmes," *Annales ESC* 39 (1984): 1140–60. As Ruth Mazo Karras demonstrates for a later period, it became routine to describe clerical concubines as prostitutes (*Common Women: Prostitution and Sexuality in Medieval England* [New York: Oxford University Press, 1996], pp. 86–138).

10. The question of pollution will be taken up below. With regard to clerical marriage as a drain on church resources, see Gregory VII's very pointed complaint to William the Conqueror against a bishop who used church property to dower his intended (ed. P. Jaffé, *Epistolae Collectae,* Ep. 16, in *Monumenta Gregoriana, Bibliotheca Rerum Germanicarum* [Berlin, 1865; rprt. Aalen: Scientia, 1964], 2: 541–42). But usually property interests are rhetorically subordinated to other concerns. Peter Damian, for example, demonstrates considerable consternation over the depletion of church property when treating other subjects. See Ep. 35, To the Clergy and Laity of the Diocese of Osimo, ghostwritten on behalf of Leo IX, *Die Briefe des Petrus Damiani,* ed. Kurt Reindel, *MGH, Die Briefe der deutschen Kaiserzeit,* 4 (Munich: *MGH,* 1983), 1: 336–39; trans. Owen J. Blum, *Letters, FC,* Mediaeval Continuation, 2 (Washington, D.C.: Catholic University of America, 1990), 2: 61–63; and Ep. 74, To an Anonymous Bishop, *Die Briefe,* ed. Reindel, 2: 369–75; trans. Blum, *Letters,* 3: 151–56. This issue is tactically suppressed in his attacks on clerical marriage, however, except perhaps by innuendo. Thus he argues that the married priests are a bastard line who, like the illegitimate offspring of the patriarchs, will be separated from the true heirs. He also responds to the married priests' claims that they need wives because they cannot afford servants by reasoning that this was, in fact, an argument *against* marriage so as to avoid the additional drain of child-support (Ep. 162, To Archpriest Peter, *Die Briefe,* ed. Reindel, 4: 154–55). The economic considerations are reflected in the hard line taken against the sons of priests, who were theoretically pronounced illegitimate and barred from the priesthood. See n. 21, below, and Chap. 5, nn. 59 and 60, below.

11. "Tres quippe tantummodo feminas Deus novit, quae his plures sunt, in eius adhuc notitiam non venerunt," Ep. 114, To Adelaide of Savoy, *Die Briefe,* ed. Reindel, 3: 299. Damian returns to the question of categories toward the end of his letter

when he somewhat tactlessly reassures Adelaide that "multivirae"—women who have been married many times, as had Adelaide—can be saved. He adds, however, that he does not mention this in order to inspire her to further nuptial escapades (p. 304). Adelaide had been married three times but was a widow when Damian wrote to her in 1064. See F. Cognasso's entry in *Dizionario biografico degli italiani* (Rome: Società Grafica Romana, 1960), 1: 249–51. Gregory VII wholeheartedly adopted Damian's sentiments and, indeed, his rhetoric in this matter (Fliche, *La Réforme grégorienne,* 2: 156).

12. Mary Douglas, *Purity and Danger: An Analysis of the Concepts of Pollution and Taboo* (London: Routledge and Kegan Paul; Ark Paperbacks, 1966; rprt. 1988), chap. 3, pp. 41–57. R. I. Moore first applied aspects of Douglas's analytical framework to this period of reform in his "Family, Community, and Cult on the Eve of the Gregorian Reform," *Transactions of the Royal Historical Society* 5th ser., 30 (1984): 49–69, esp. 66–69; cf. idem, *The Formation of a Persecuting Society: Power and Deviance in Western Europe, 950–1250* (Oxford: Blackwell, 1987), esp. pp. 100–101.

13. Thus Damian argues that contact with the laity corrupts the secular priesthood: "There is something else that displeases me regarding secular priests, namely, that since they associate with laymen by living amid the citizens of a region, many of them are no different from their neighbors in their way of life and irregular morals. They normally involve themselves in secular affairs, and show no restraint in taking part in idle and senseless conversation," Ep. 47, To an Unidentified Bishop, *Die Briefe,* ed. Reindel, 1: 45; trans. Blum, *Letters,* 2: 254–55. Note that Humbert of Silva Candida's insistence on a similar separation between clergy and laity is one of the cornerstones of his arguments against lay investiture. See *Libri III adversus simoniacos* 3.9, ed. F. Thaner, *MGH, Libelli de lite,* 1 (Hanover: Impensis Biblipolii Hahniani, 1891), p. 208. He is especially exercised over the fact that not only laymen but also laywomen control church property in this way (3.12, p. 212).

14. Suzanne F. Wemple, *Women in Frankish Society: Marriage and the Cloister, 500 to 900* (Philadelphia: University of Pennsylvania Press, 1985), pp. 131–32; and Elliott, *Spiritual Marriage,* p. 87. Also see the entries for *presbyteria* in Dom. du Cange, *Glossarium Mediae et Infimae Latinatatis,* rev. ed. (Paris: Librairie des sciences et des arts, 1938), 6: 488–89; and *sacerdotissa,* 7: 255. On the possible quasi-sacerdotal functions of clerical wives, see McNamara, "Canossa and the Ungendering of the Public Man," pp. 133–34.

15. Damian argues that once the married priests attempt to defend their error, they become heretics (Ep. 112, To Bishop Cunibert of Turin, *Die Briefe,* ed. Reindel, 3: 286). The married "heretics" were called Nicolaites, after the heretics described in Rev. 2.6 and 14–15. According to Barstow, Cardinal Humbert of Silva Candida set a precedent for labeling the married clergy and their defenders heretics (*Married Priests,* p. 54).

16. See the section below entitled "Peter Damian and the Empty Altar."

17. See n. 10, above.

18. Peter Damian, Ep. 31, To Leo IX, *Die Briefe,* ed. Reindel, 1:299; trans. Blum, *Letters,* 1: 19. Ep. 61, To Nicholas II, *Die Briefe,* ed. Reindel, 2: 214–15; trans. Blum, *Letters,* 3: 10. Ep. 162, To Archpriest Peter, *Die Briefe,* ed. Reindel, 4: 152.

19. See Ariald's dramatic rebuilding of a church with a high wall separating the

choir (where the clergy was) from the laity—the laity's area being additionally divided between men and women (Andrew of Strumi, *Vita sancti Arialdi* c. 12, ed. F. Baethgen, *MGH, Scrip.* 30,2 [Leipzig: Karl W. Hiersemann, 1934], p. 1058).

20. Cf. Peter Damian's hyperbolic comments to married priests: "I convene you, o uxorious enticers, and enslaved by the riches of dominating women" ("Convenio vos, o prolectarii, uxorii, ac mulierum dominantium ditionibus inserviti," Ep. 162, To Archpriest Peter, *Die Briefe,* ed, Reindel 4: 147).

21. Clerical marriage was condemned, as was the ordination of priests' sons, at Bourges in 1031 (see Fliche, *La Réforme grégorienne,* 1: 99). But this stricture only really began to be enforced for the entire church in the 1070s under Gregory VII. See Barstow, *Married Priests,* pp. 65–77; and James Brundage, *Law, Sex, and Christian Society in Medieval Europe* (Chicago: University of Chicago Press, 1987), pp. 216–19. Note, however, that the classificatory confusion generated over the clergy's sexual partners persisted into the later Middle Ages. Ruth Karras points to the difficulty in determining whether the women who were sexually linked with the clergy were prostitutes who had a clerical clientele or concubines (*Common Women,* p. 30).

22. Freud, *Notes upon a Case of Obsessional Neurosis* (i.e., "Rat Man"), in *The Standard Edition,* 10: 225. Aspects of the foreign particles introduced are indistinguishable from the disavowed material that returns, creating something like the "doubling" effect, which, according to Homi Bhabha's analysis of colonial discourse, invokes disavowed knowledges that return and destabilize authority. See "Signs Taken for Wonders: Questions of Ambivalence and Authority under a Tree Outside Delhi, May 1817," *Critical Inquiry* 12 (1985): 161. I am also influenced here by Jacques Derrida's concept of iterability in *Limited Inc,* trans. Samuel Weber (Evanston, Ill.: Northwestern University Press, 1988), app., pp. 127–29. Cf. Judith Butler's comments on the occasional discontinuities in the repeated acts that constitute gender (*Gender Trouble: Feminism and the Subversion of Identity* [New York: Routledge, 1990], p. 141).

23. By the sixth century there is little mention of married bishops except in Gaul, where such unions are the source of considerable ambivalence. See Brian Brennan, "'Episcopae': Bishops' Wives Viewed in Sixth-Century Gaul," *Church History* 54 (1985): 311–23.

24. Peter Damian did write a sermon commemorating the translation of the relics of Bishop Hilary of Poitiers—a saint who was married and purportedly had a daughter as well (Serm. 2, *Sermones,* ed. Giovanni Lucchesi, *CCCM,* 57 [Turnhout: Brepols, 1983], pp. 3–7). No mention, however, is made of this fact. This sermon, based on a secondhand account by a monk who had read Hilary's life by St. Fredolinus (*BHL* 3170), was probably an occasional piece written during Damian's mission to Gaul in 1063 (see Damian, Serm. 2, c. 3, *Sermones,* p. 4, and Lucchesi's introductory remarks on p. 2).

25. *AA SS,* previous commentary, February, 1: 78–79; Giovanni Lucchesi, *BS,* vol. 11, cols. 997–98.

26. On Agnellus, see P. Lamma's entry in *Dizionario biografico degli italiani,* 1: 429–30; and Thomas Hodgkin, *Italy and Her Invaders,* 2d ed. (Oxford: Clarendon Press, 1892), 1, 2: 900–916. For Agnellus's account of Severus's life, I have used Alessandro Testi Rasponi's edition of the *Liber pontificalis,* in *Raccolta degli Storici*

Italiani, 2, 3, ed. L. A. Muratori (Bologna: Nicola Zanichelli, 1924). My citations are from the later but more prolix Codex Estense. Rasponi's superior but incomplete edition leaves off at chap. 103 of the 175 chapters. For later chapters, I have used O. Holder-Egger's edition in *MGH, Scriptores Rerum Langobardicarum et Italicarum, saec. VI–IX* (Hanover: Impensis Bibliopolii Hahniani, 1878), pp. 265–391.

27. See Hodgkin, *Italy and Her Invaders,* 7: 163, 197–200, 328–41.

28. On the worldliness of the church of Ravenna, see Agnellus, *Liber pontificalis* c. 104, ed. Holder-Egger, p. 345. Also see T. S. Brown, *Gentlemen and Officers: Imperial Administration and Aristocratic Power in Byzantine Italy, A.D. 554–800* (Hertford: Printed by Stephen Austin and Sons for the British School at Rome, 1984), pp. 188–89. Brown overstates his case for worldliness, however, by arguing that many of the minor clergy were married—hardly irregular for this period. Nor for that matter would the marriage of minor clerics be outlawed even after the eleventh-century reform. Brown also notes that some of the archbishops of Ravenna treated by Agnellus were married without qualifying this observation. This is rather misleading, as it implies that they continued to enjoy conjugal rights after ordination, which, as is clear from the following discussion, they were emphatically portrayed as relinquishing.

29. Agnellus, *Liber pontificalis* c. 84, ed. Holder-Egger, p. 333.

30. Holder-Egger, the editor of the volume, also remarks that Agnellus does not, in fact, return to this problem unless one takes chap. 97 into account (Agnellus, *Liber pontificalis* c. 84, p. 334, n. 2). Chapter 97 is an indictment of men who are dominated by their wives, but it certainly does not seem to be addressed to a clerical audience, though Brown clearly reads it this way—possibly because at one point in Agnellus's narration he addresses his audience as "fratres" (c. 97, p. 341; see Brown, *Gentlemen and Officers,* p. 188, n. 23; note that since Agnellus was a monk, "fratres" could signify an even more scandalous but different kind of laxness). In any event, since the author made it clear that the wife died prior to Bishop Agnellus's elevation, his skittishness on this subject suggests that for bishops to be married at any point in their careers was hardly routine.

31. "Iste laicus fuit et sponsam habuit. Quam, post regimen ecclesiae suscepit, eam Eufimiam sponsam suam diaconissam cunsecravit, et in eodem habitu permansit," *Liber pontificalis* c. 154, ed. Holder-Egger, p. 377.

32. Ibid., c. 157, p. 379.

33. Hodgkin, *Italy and Her Invaders,* 7: 339–40.

34. These are, however, prefaced by some preliminary remarks, which include a discussion of the mystical meaning of Severus, an allusion to his miraculous election to office, and a terse mention of his presence at Sardica (Agnellus, *Liber pontificalis* c. 11, ed. Rasponi, pp. 42–44).

35. This incident is followed by one miracle at Severus's grave (ibid., c. 16, pp. 50–51).

36. "'O mulier, cur michi molesta es? Quare non prebes locum filie tue? Suscipe quod portasti, ex tua sumpta est carne, ne dubites recipere. Ece [sic] tibi trado, quod michi dedisti, ne torpeas, unde fuit, reversa est. Locum tribue sepeliendi, nolli me contristare,'" ibid., c. 15, pp. 47–48. Cf. Severus's slightly exasperated tone when the surrounding clergy rouse him from his ecstasy: "'O what did you do? Why do you disturb me?'" ("'O quit [sic] fecistis? Quare inquietastis me?'" c. 14, p. 45).

37. " . . . quanta vix ea animata corpora hominum sic cicius moveri potuissent," ibid., c. 15, p. 48.

38. Gregory the Great, *Dialogues* 3.23, ed. Adalbert de Vogüé, *SC,* no. 260 (Paris: Editions du Cerf, 1979), 2: 360; trans. Odo John Zimmerman, *Dialogues, FC,* vol. 39 (Washington, D.C.: Catholic University of America Press, 1959), p. 156.

39. See Elliott, *Spiritual Marriage,* pp. 70–71.

40. Agnellus, *Liber pontificalis* c. 15, ed. Rasponi, pp. 48–49.

41. Giovanni Lucchesi thinks the fact that all the bishops of Ravenna were allegedly elected this way is suppressed in Agnellus but is more developed in Peter Damian's rendering: the latter refers to the dove's election as "the accustomed way" (*solito more*). See "Il Sermonario di S. Pier Damiani," in *Studi Gregoriani per la storia della "Libertas Ecclesiae",* ed. Alfonso M. Stickler et al. (Rome: Libreria Ateneo Salesiano, 1975), p. 54. But since, in Agnellus's characterization, Severus says ahead of time that he wants to see the miraculous descent of the dove, the tradition strikes me as implicit—compressed as opposed to suppressed.

42. " 'Sede hic, labora, noli ociosus esse. Sive ieris, sive non ieris, te pontificem popullus [sic] non ordinauit; revertere ad opus,' " Agnellus, *Liber pontificalis* c. 17, ed. Rasponi, p. 51.

43. "Quo audito, coniunx eius, quod nuper deriserat, postea super eum gratulabatur," ibid., pp. 51–52.

44. What is implied is, of course, the ecclesiastically endorsed ideal. On the difficulties surrounding a clerical transition to chastity, see Elliott, *Spiritual Marriage,* pp. 83–91.

45. " 'Date mihi locum vobiscum dormiendi: ut qui in hoc seculo communiter viximus, etiam communi sepultura utamur,' " *AA SS,* February, 1: 89.

46. See Elliott, *Spiritual Marriage,* pp. 69–70.

47. This dating is only approximate. With regard to the anonymous life, the Bollandists were only prepared to specify the tenth or eleventh century (*AA SS,* February, 1: 79, editor's introduction). But the rhetoric of reform clearly places it in the later eleventh century. Giovanni Lucchesi, an expert on both Peter Damian and the bishops of Ravenna, tentatively dates Damian's sermons on Severus as 1069 or 1070 (Lucchesi, "Il Sermonario di S. Pier Damiani," pp. 55–56). He posits that the anonymous vita of Severus was written between 1050 and 1070 (*BS,* vol. 11, col. 1000).

48. Severus's relics, along with those of his wife and daughter, were taken to Germany by Otgar, archbishop of Mainz. The translation occurred ca. 857 and is described in the contemporary account by the monk Liudolf (printed in *AA SS,* February, 1: 90–91). This kind of theft was a common phenomenon. See Patrick Geary, *Furta Sacra: Thefts of Relics in the Central Middle Ages* (Princeton, N.J.: Princeton University Press, 1978), generally; on Severus, see p. 58. Seemingly undaunted by the widespread knowledge of this celebrated theft, however, the anonymous monk of Classis claims that the relics are in a marble sarcophagus in the basilica at Classis and alleges that they still work miracles. It does not inspire confidence, however, that his example of a contemporary miracle is lifted from Agnellus (*AA SS,* February, 1: 85; cf. Agnellus, *Liber pontificalis* c. 16, ed. Rasponi, p. 50). Damian, however, does report contemporary miracles in the basilica, particularly water with healing powers emanating from the altar (Serm. 5, c. 9–10, *Sermones,* ed. Lucchesi, *CCCM,*

57, pp. 30–31). Damian, cagily, does not specify which basilica—the one in Italy or Germany, although Lucchesi suggests that the miracles were part of the oral tradition, perhaps reported to him by pilgrims from Germany ("Il Sermonario di S. Pier Damiani," pp. 55–56). Elsewhere Damian reports that the monastery possessed Severus's body but not his heart. See Damian's *Vita beati Romualdi* c. 12, ed. Giovanni Tabacco, Instituto Storico Italiano per il medio evo (Rome: nella Sede dell'Instituto, Palazzo Borromini, 1957), p. 33. This may have been how the monastery finessed the embarrassing absence of its patron. Lucchesi gives 1042 as the date for Damian's vita of Romuald ("Clavis S. Petri Damiani," *Studi su S. Pier Damiano in onore del Cardinale Amleto Giovanni Cicognani,* Biblioteca Cardinale Gaetano Cicognani, 5 [Faenza: Seminario Vescovile Pio XII, 1970], p. 60).

49. Damian also wrote one sermon for Archbishop Eleucadius and three for Apollinarus, archbishop and martyr (Serm. 6 and 30–32, *Sermones,* ed. Lucchesi, *CCCM,* 57, pp. 34–43, 172–203). His antisimoniacal work *Liber gratissimus,* moreover, is dedicated to Henry—archbishop of Ravenna. In the conclusion, Damian alludes to Ravenna's series of saintly bishops as a kind of apostolic senate (Damian, Ep. 40, To Archbishop Henry of Ravenna, *Die Briefe,* ed. Reindel, 1: 507; trans. Blum, *Letters,* 2: 212). On Damian's affection for Ravenna, see Jean Leclerq, *Saint Pierre Damien: ermite et homme d'église,* Uomini e dottrine, 8 (Rome: Edizione di storia et letteratura, 1960), pp. 19, 161.

50. 1.4–5, *AA SS,* February, 1: 82–83.

51. On the reformers' initiative against simony, see Fliche, *La Réforme grégorienne,* 1: 337–40; 2: 136–41. On monks preaching reform, see Barstow, *Married Priests,* pp. 49–50.

52. Note that vita *BHL* 7864, a reworking of the anonymous life, omits the digressions on marriage discussed below, instead adding its own digression on Arianism—a more apposite concern for the fourth century. See the description of codex signatus XXXIX, G. S. III, 12, fols. 152r–177, in the catalogue of hagiographical codices for the Bibliotheca Ambrosiana in Milan, "Catalogus codicum hagiographicorum bibliothecae Ambrosianae Mediolanensis," *AB* 11 (1892): 335–36. The manuscript in question is an eighteenth-century transcription.

53. "In hoc loco si quis superciliosus aenigmatica mente et insulsa objectione beato viro detrahat, quod uxoratus ad archisterium Ravennae accesserit, audiat Apostolum pro illo respondentem. Quia omnia munda mundis. Sicut ergo ciborum edulio non polluitur homo, nisi insidiatrix concupiscentia praecedat; sic quippe legali connubio non inquinatur Christianus, qui se nullatenus vel virginitatis vel continentiae voto alligavit; nisi illum prius corrumpat obscoeni amoris fomento ipsa deceptrix libido. Ceterum si quis voto constringitur, reddere cogatur; qua scriptum est, Vovete et reddite," 1.3, *AA SS,* February, 1: 82.

54. Cassian discusses how excess food results in nocturnal pollutions in *Collatio* 22.3 (*Conférences,* ed. E. Pichery, *SC,* no. 64 [Paris: Editions du Cerf, 1959], 3: 116–17). Also see the interesting pairing of these two forms of indulgence by Honorius Augustodunensis. He poses the question of "Whether it is a sin to marry or to eat meat ("Utrum sit peccatum nubere vel carnes comedere"), which he resolves in the negative. But he then asserts, "It is good not to touch a woman, and good not to eat meat" ("Bonum est mulierem non tangere, et bonum est carnes non comedere"), *Libellus Honorii Augustodunensis presbyteri et scholastici,* ed. J. Dieterich, in *MGH,*

Libelli de lite imperatorum et pontificum, saec. XI et XII, 3 (Hanover: Impensis Bibliopolii Hahniani, 1897), pp. 34–35. (I am deliberately leaving Honorius's name in its Latin form in response to the query raised by Valerie Flint's "Heinricus of Augsburg and Honorius Augustodunensis: Are They the Same Person?" *Revue Bénédictine* 92 [1982]: 148–58; reprinted in *Ideas in the Medieval West: Texts and Their Contexts* [London: Variorum, 1988]). Also see Damian's indictment of married clerics for their presumed gluttony, Ep. 162, To Archpriest Peter, *Die Briefe,* ed. Reindel, 4: 160.

55. "Nullus quippe haereticis relinquitur locus objurgationis, qui Sanctum Domini Severum ad dedecus Ecclesiae putant esse conjugio ligatum, quique suae obscoenitatis faecibus obvoluti, ignari sunt gratiae Spiritus sancti, qui quod in semetipsis minime sentiunt, in aliis nullo modo recognoscunt. Si quis igitur mellis gustum numquam probaverit, cujus saporis sit omnimode nescit. At contra qui solo absinthio, ceteris herbis neglectis, utuntur, his nimirum dulce amarum videtur, et ceteras herbas ejusdem putant esse amaritudinis propter inexperientiam ejusdem saporis," 5.17, *AA SS,* February, 1: 85.

56. "Beatus itaque Severus columbinis oculis omnia inspiciens Domini opera, etiam intellexit conjugium valde esse bonum, si quis eo legitime utatur; quia si bonum non esset, nequaquam mulier in adjutorium a Deo creata fuisset. . . . Hos quidem oculos protoplasti perdiderunt, quando exigente praevaricatione a Deo sunt derelicti, et aperti sunt amborum oculi. Postquam autem oculos columbarum perdiderunt, confestim erubescebant; quia intravit mors per fenestras carnalium oculorum," 5.18, *AA SS,* February, 1: 85–86.

57. "Non enim membra sua erubescit . . . nihil impudicum cogitat, nulla illicita concupiscit, quia inhabitator Spiritus sanctus, qui illum incorrupta mente custodit, nihil eorum novit," 5.18, *AA SS,* February, 1: 86.

58. 5.18–19, *AA SS,* February, 1: 85–86.

59. "Ut enim verum fateamur, cujus castitatis et continentiae ante Episcopatum extiterit, ipse evidenter Spiritus sanctus per columbam in electione monstravit, quae tot Prebyteros et Levitas super volitavit, et dilectum sibi penetral assignavit," 5.24, *AA SS,* February, 1: 87.

60. "Videtur sacratissimus Pontifex Ecclesiae suae latenter satisfacere pro dudum conjugis opinione. . . . Recordari prius eum vitae pristinae creditur, quando Christiana licentia conjugio vinctus legitur. Quod autem tam imperiosa auctoritate jussit, ut defunctum conjugis corpus se declinaret in latus, patenter ostendit, quam securus esset a tactu illius, postquam effectus est Episcopus," 5.24, *AA SS,* February, 1: 87.

61. For an overview of some of these early heresies, all of which stressed sexual purity, see Malcolm Lambert, *Medieval Heresy: Popular Movements from the Gregorian Reform to the Reformation,* 2d ed. (Oxford: Blackwell, 1977; 2d ed., 1992), pp. 9–32. On the connection between the cessation of heresy and the commencement of the reform movement, see R. I. Moore, "The Origins of Medieval Heresy," *History* 55 (1970): 33–34.

62. See Barstow, *Married Priests,* pp. 107–16. Ulric's defense was written in 1060, in response to Nicholas II's reissuing of the ban on clerical marriage. This is the first of a series of eleventh-century defenses. The last efforts had been in the fourth century.

63. Ibid., pp. 157–73.

64. The daughter's name, in contrast, emerges at her funeral as follows: "Erat autem eadem Virgo Innocentiae insignita vocabulo," 4.12, *AA SS*, February, 1: 84.

65. Jane Tibbetts Schulenburg demonstrates that the total number of female saints took a nosedive in the eleventh century and continued to plummet throughout the twelfth ("Sexism and the Celestial Gynaeceum—from 500–1200," *Journal of Medieval History* 4 [1978]: 124–26).

66. See Fliche, *La Réforme grégorienne*, 1: 256; 2: 109–11, 140–41, 156, 240; and Jean Leclercq, *Saint Pierre Damien*, pp. 111–17.

67. Peter Damian describes his successful mission of 1059 against the married and simoniac clergy of Milan in Ep. 65, To Archdeacon Hildebrand (the future Gregory VII), *Die Briefe*, ed. Reindel, 2: 228–47; trans. Blum, *Letters*, 3: 24–39. The oath pronounced by Guido, archbishop of Milan, which renounced the "heresies" of simony and nicolaitism (i.e., clerical marriage), was recorded by the reformer Ariald (*Die Briefe*, ed. Reindel, 2: 244–45; trans. Blum, *Letters*, 3: 37–38). On Damian's mission to Milan, see H. C. Lea, *A History of Sacerdotal Celibacy*, 2d ed. (Boston: Houghton Mifflin, 1884), pp. 213–14; and Constanzo Somigli, "San Pier Damiano e la Pataria," in *San Pier Damiano nel IX centenario della morte (1072–1972)* (Cesena: Centro studi e richerche sulla antica provincia ecclesiastica Ravennate, 1972), 3: 193–206. On the documents and chronology for this mission, see Giovanni Lucchesi, "Per una Vita di San Pier Damiani," in *San Pier Damiano*, 1: 141–45. Elsewhere, Damian describes a campaign in Lodi where he reports that the married priests threatened his life. They justified their married status by claiming its authorization at the Council of Trebur (Ep. 112, To Bishop Cunibert of Turin, *Die Briefe*, ed. Reindel, 3: 266–67). Damian claims he had never heard of this council, and modern scholars are likewise baffled. Ryan suggests that the reference to Trebur could be a confused reference to the Council of Trulla (692), the council that sanctioned clerical marriage for the eastern church (*Saint Peter Damian*, no. 193, p. 100).

68. Damian's writings against clerical marriage have attracted considerable attention. See Jean de Chasteigner, "Le Célibat sacerdotal dans les écrits de saint Pierre Damien," *Doctor Communis* 24 (1971): 169–83; Pietro Palazzini, "S. Pier Damiani e la polemica anticelibataria," *Divinitas* 14 (1970): 127–33; Barstow, *Married Priests*, pp. 58–64; Carlo Mazzotti, "Il celibato e la castità del clero in S. Pier Damiani," *San Pier Damiano*, pp. 343–56; and Fliche, *La Réforme grégorienne*, 1: 206–13. My contribution is to focus on some of the imagistic underpinnings of Damian's rhetoric.

69. "Uxor presbyteri officio functa est sacerdotis, dum et maternum ad pietatem mollivit affectum," John of Lodi, *Vita S. Petri Damiani* c. 1, *PL* 144, cols. 115–16; also see n. 2. Cf. Lester K. Little, "The Personal Development of Peter Damian," in *Order and Innovation in the Middle Ages: Essays in Honor of Joseph R. Strayer*, ed. William C. Jordan et al. (Princeton, N.J.: Princeton University Press, 1976), pp. 322, 323–24. On John of Lodi, his vita, sources, and the manuscript tradition, see Lucchesi, "Per una Vita di San Pier Damiani," in *San Pier Damiano*, 4: 7–66, esp. 8–22.

70. Ep. 70, To Landulf Cotta of Milan, *Die Briefe*, ed. Reindel, 2: 320; trans. Blum, *Letters*, 3: 110. The letter was written to this particular Milanese reformer, a member of the lower clergy, to remind him of his unfulfilled vow to become a priest.

71. Ibid. Also see Little, "Personal Development of Peter Damian," pp. 319–21, 333.

72. See, for example, the popular *passio* of Daria and Chrysanthus: "They were made companions in blood in their passion, just as they had been husband and wife in mind; as if in one bed, so they remained in one pit" ("Facti sunt in passione sociati sanguine, sicut fuerant etiam mente coniuges; quasi in uno lectulo, ita in una fovea durantes," *AA SS,* October, 11: 483); on this motif see Elliott, *Spiritual Marriage,* pp. 69–70. Cf. Damian's sermon on the martyrs St. Vitalis and his wife, Valeria, of Ravenna. He argues that since the city possesses the husband's relics, it must necessarily possess the wife's because a married couple who were two in one flesh would likewise be buried together ("Nam, si beata Valeria cum uiro suo, Scriptura teste, fuit *in carne una* [Gen. 2.24], necessario sequitur ut unius carnis una sit sepultura," Serm. 17, 1, c. 8, *Sermones,* ed. Lucchesi, *CCCM,* 57, p. 91). He extends this argument to include their two martyred sons, Gervasius and Protasius, who were mystically present in the body of their progenitor, Vitalis, though separated by burial sites.

73. Ep. 143, To Countess Guilla, *Die Briefe,* ed. Reindel, 3: 522; also see his letter on anger, which concludes with the admission of his own tendency toward anger and his ongoing struggle against lust (Ep. 80, To an Unidentified Bishop, *Die Briefe,* ed. Reindel, 2: 416; trans. Blum, *Letters,* 3: 200–201). These letters were written in 1067 and 1060 respectively, when Damian was well into his fifties—elderly by medieval standards. On Damian's relations with women, see Jean Leclercq, "S. Pierre Damien et les femmes," *Studia monastica* 15 (1973): 43–55; also see Little, "Personal Development of Peter Damian," pp. 333, 335.

74. His monastic conversion occurred in 1035, and the usual date given for his birth is 1007. Little, however, contests this second date and other aspects of the traditional chronology given for Damian's life (see Little, "Personal Development of Peter Damian," pp. 318–21; also see Blum's introduction to *Letters,* 1: 4–5).

75. Ep. 62, To Bishop Theodosius of Senigallia, and Bishop Rudolphus of Gubbio, *Die Briefe,* ed. Reindel, 2: 219–20; trans. Blum, *Letters,* 3: 14. He goes on to ask that these two men read his works carefully and censor anything inappropriate. Fortunately, his request seems to have gone unheeded—or perhaps his censors were not very censorious.

76. Ep. 138, To His Brother Damian, *Die Briefe,* ed. Reindel, 3: 474. See his panegyric in praise of flagellation, Ep. 161, To the Monks of Monte Cassino, *Die Briefe,* ed. Reindel, 4: 135–44. Also see his concern over light and frivolous speech in Ep. 56, To Petrus Cerebrosus, *Die Briefe,* ed. Reindel, 2: 154; trans. Blum, *Letters,* 2: 361–62. Elsewhere, he argues that the hermitage is a cure for the vice of scurrility (Ep. 28, To Leo of Sitria, *Die Briefe,* ed. Reindel, 1: 276; trans. Blum, *Letters,* 1: 285. See Little, "Personal Development of Peter Damian," pp. 335–37, 340).

77. Damian, Serm. 4, c. 1, *Sermones,* ed. Lucchesi, *CCCM,* 57, pp. 16–17.

78. Ibid., c. 2, p. 17.

79. Ibid., c. 2, p. 18.

80. Ibid.

81. "Antiquus enim hostis, quem non de paupertatis inopia, non de assidui laboris afflictione, non de inhonestarum uestium deformitate, prouocare ad inpa-

tientiam potuit, ad irrogandam uerborum contumeliam mentem uxoris accendit, et eius linguam ad iniuriam mordacis obiurgationis exacuit," ibid., c. 3, p. 19.

82. Ibid.

83. "Antiquus itaque hostis ab Adam in officina lanisterii perdidit, qui Adam in paradiso superauit; atque adiutricem suam mulierem, dum ad contumeliam amarae correptionis accendit, ad exemplum potius discendae patientiae nesciens detinauit," ibid., c. 4, p. 19.

84. Ibid., c. 5, pp. 20–21.

85. "Verumtamen non idcirco ista dicimus, ut beati uiri uxorem perisse cum reprobis mulieribus asseramus. Si enim ab electorum sorte exclusam esse cognosceret, nequaquam uir sancto repletus Spiritu unum cum ea sepulchrum habere uoluisset. Communis igitur sepultura corporum indicat quod beatorum coniugum animas meritorum uarietas non discernat," ibid., p. 21.

86. Ibid., c. 8, p. 30.

87. See n. 13, above. On Damian's contempt for lay life and his attitudes toward marriage, see Robert Bultot, *Christianisme et valeurs humaines. A. La doctrine du mépris du monde, en Occident, de S. Ambroise à Innocent III*, vol. 4, *Le XIe siècle:* 1. *Pierre Damien* (Louvain: Nauwelaerts, 1963), pp. 53–62, 100–111. Also see Walter Ferretti, "Il posto dei laici nella Chiesa secondo S. Pier Damiani," *San Pier Damiano*, 2: 246–47; and Owen J. Blum, *St. Peter Damian* (Washington, D.C.: Catholic University Press, 1947), pp. 91–97. Both of these authors point out that Damian in no way encouraged laypersons to aspire to higher levels of spirituality, reserving those heights for religious personnel.

88. "O lepores clericorum, pulpamenta diaboli, proiectio paradisi, virus mentium, gladius animarum, aconita bibentium, toxica convivarum, materia peccandi, occasio pereundi. Vos, inquam, alloquor ginecea hostis antiqui, upupae, ululae, noctuae, lupae, sanguisugae. . . . scorta, prostibula, savia, volutabra porcorum pinguium, cubilia spirituum immundorum, nimphae, sirenae, lamiae, dianae," Damian, Ep. 112, To Bishop Cunibert of Turin, *Die Briefe*, ed. Reindel, 3: 278. Barstow translates this and several of Damian's other lurid invectives in *Married Priests*, pp. 60–61.

89. "Ex vobis enim diabolus tanquam delicatis dapibus pascitur, vestrae libidinis exuberantia saginatur," Damian, Ep. 112, To Bishop Cunibert of Turin, *Die Briefe*, ed. Reindel, 3: 278.

90. Ibid. In Damian's own bestiary, the tigress may be tricked out of pursuit if hunters throw a glass ball in front of her, since she is liable to mistake her own reflection for that of her cub. He then continues to argue that the tigress is the devil. Humanity can throw off pursuit by showing the devil his true followers in the glass. These followers would be individuals who reflect the devil's own image and worship the beast (Rev. 14.9; Damian, Ep. 86, To Desiderius, Abbot of Monte Cassino, *Die Briefe*, ed. Reindel, 2: 476–78). On Damian and the bestiary tradition, see Leclercq, *Saint Pierre Damien*, pp. 83–92.

91. Damian goes on to say that the children thus engendered gnaw through the mother's sides, killing her as they are being born, concluding, "and so they were parricides before they were offspring" (Ep. 86, To Desiderius, Abbot of Monte Cassino, *Die Briefe*, ed. Reindel, 2: 490–91; trans. Blum, *Letters*, 3: 284–85). Cf.

Isidore of Seville, *Etymologiae* 12.4.10–11, *PL* 82, col. 413. Damian is also aware of the tradition whereby the male viper seeks illicit sexual union with the sea eel (murena), remarking that "the qualities of another strain are bred into the offspring of this venomous beast" (Ep. 86, To Desiderius, Abbot of Monte Cassino, *Die Briefe,* ed. Reindel, 2: 493; trans. Blum, *Letters,* 3: 286). On the murena, see Isidore, *Etymologiae* 12.4.43, *PL* 82, col. 455. The twelfth-century bestiarist relays all of the above information in his discussion of the viper and moralizes the male viper's defection from his violent wife in favor of the more accommodating murena into a warning to unruly wives (trans. T. H. White, *The Bestiary: A Book of Beasts* [New York: Putnam, 1954; Capricorn Books ed., 1960], p. 171).

92. " . . . viperae furiosae, quae prae inpatientis ardore libidinis Christum, qui caput est clericorum, vestris amatoribus detruncatis," Damian, Ep. 112, To Bishop Cunibert of Turin, *Die Briefe,* ed. Reindel, 3: 279.

93. " . . . infideles homines de sacrosancti altaris ministerio quo fungebantur avellitis ut, in lubrico vestri amoris glutino suffocetis," ibid.

94. "Sic a vobis ex universa humani generis multitudine illi tantummodo sunt electi, qui penitus ab omni muliebris affectus sunt confoederatione prohibiti. . . . Dum antiquus hostis per vos invadere castitatis aecclesiasticae cacumen anhelat. Vos plane non inmerito, fatear, dipsades vel cerastes, quae miseris et incautis hominibus sic sanguinem sugitis, ut loetale virus eorum visceribius influatis. . . . Et qua mentis audacia non perhorrescitis contrectare manus sacrosancto crismate vel oleo delibutas, sive etiam evangelicis vel apostolicis paginis assuetas? Dicit de maligno hoste scriptura, quia esca eius electa. Per vos ergo diabolus electam escam devorat, dum sanctiora membra aecclesiae suggestionis ac delectationis velut utriusque molae dentibus attertit, et dum vobis iungit, eos in sua viscera quasi traiciendo convertit," ibid., pp. 279–80.

95. "Aequitatis scilicet iure ut quae sacris altaribus rapuisse servorum Dei convincuntur obsequium, ipsae hoc saltim episcopo per diminuti capitis sui suppleant famulatum," ibid., p. 281.

96. See Mary Douglas, *Purity and Danger,* pp. 49–52.

97. Damian, Ep. 40, To Archbishop Henry of Ravenna, *Die Briefe,* ed. Reindel, 1: 411–12; trans. Blum, *Letters,* 1: 130. Humbert of Silva Candida's *Libri III adversus simoniacos* is cited above. On the contested relation between these two adversial works, see Damian, *Die Briefe,* ed. Reindel, 1: 432–33, n. 82. For an analysis of Damian's attitude toward simony, see Fliche, *La Réforme grégorienne,* 1: 214–30.

98. Damian, Ep. 40, To Archbishop Henry of Ravenna, *Die Briefe,* ed. Reindel, 1: 439; trans. Blum, *Letters,* 1: 154.

99. Damian, Ep. 31, To Leo IX, *Die Briefe,* ed. Reindel, 1: 284–330; trans. Blum, *Letters,* 2: 3–53. On Leo IX's tepid reception of this work, see John Boswell, *Christianity, Social Tolerance, and Homosexuality: Gay People in Western Europe from the Beginning of the Christian Era to the Fourteenth Century* (Chicago: University of Chicago Press, 1980), pp. 210–12; and Blum, *St. Peter Damian,* pp. 20–21. Also see his concern with masturbation, discussed in Chap. 1, p. 32, above, and Chap. 2 n. 53, above. Cf. Chap. 1, n. 83. Damian was also extremely concerned that the utensils used for celebrating Mass were clean. See Ep. 47, To an Unidentified Bishop, *Die Briefe,* ed. Reindel, 2:46–47; trans. Blum, *Letters,* 2: 255–56.

100. See Chap. 5, p. 110, below.

101. Barstow argues, with reason, that Damian prioritized the problem of clerical purity over simony (*Married Priests,* p. 52). On Damian's relative indifference to lay investiture, see Fliche, *La Réforme grégorienne,* 1: 256. Cf. Conrad Leyser, who argues that Damian's focus on sexual purity was conditioned by his calculation that the war against simony was both quixotic and destructive to the church, in "Peter Damian's 'Book of Gomorrah,'" *Romantic Review* 86 (1995): 206.

102. References to this biblical passage are especially apparent in Damian's *Liber gratissimus* (Ep. 40, To Archbishop Henry of Ravenna, *Die Briefe,* ed. Reindel, 1: 404, 412, 413, 453; trans. Blum, *Letters,* 2: 124, 131, 132, 167). In the context of the *Liber gratissimus,* however, Damian is ultimately applying the text to a different purpose, arguing for the efficacy of the sacrament in spite of an unworthy celebrant and the possible punishment he might incur for partaking undeservedly. The Pauline passage was the basis for the Eucharist as a form of ordeal. See H. C. Lea, *Superstition and Force: Essays on the Wager of Law — the Wager of Battle — the Ordeal — Torture,* 4th rev. ed. (Philadelphia: Lea Bros., 1892), pp. 344–51.

103. Damian, Ep. 61, To Nicholas II, *Die Briefe,* ed. Reindel, 2: 214; trans. Blum, *Letters,* 3: 10–11; cf. Ep. 162, To Archpriest Peter, *Die Briefe,* ed. Reindel, 4: 146, and Ep. 47, To an Unidentified Bishop, *Die Briefe,* ed. Reindel, 2: 45–46; trans. Blum, *Letters,* 2: 254–55.

104. Francis L. Filas, *Joseph: The Man Closest to Jesus* (Boston: St. Paul Editions, 1962) p. 99.

105. Damian, Serm. 45, c. 8, *Sermones,* ed. Lucchesi, *CCCM,* 57, p. 269; Ep. 162, To Archpriest Peter, *Die Briefe,* ed. Reindel, 4: 146.

106. Damian, Ep. 112, To Bishop Cunibert of Turin, *Die Briefe,* ed. Reindel, 3: 271.

107. Damian, Ep. 61, To Nicholas II, *Die Briefe,* ed. Reindel, 2: 215–16; trans. Blum, *Letters,* 3: 11.

108. Damian, Ep. 31, To Leo IX, *Die Briefe,* ed. Reindel, 1: 316; trans. Blum, *Letters,* 2: 38. On the priest's responsibility for the people and the grievousness of celebrating unworthily, also see Chasteigner, "Le Célibat sacerdotal," pp. 175–77.

109. See Lambert's discussion of the kind of spiritual paranoia endemic to this group (*Medieval Heresy,* pp. 107–8). The Cathars are further discussed in the section entitled "'Demons Our Brothers': An Alternative Cosmology," in Chap. 6, below.

110. Damian, Ep. 112, To Bishop Cunibert of Turin, *Die Briefe,* ed. Reindel, 3: 272; Ep. 31, To Leo IX, *Die Briefe,* ed. Reindel, 1: 317; trans. Blum, *Letters,* 2: 39.

111. Damian, Ep. 162, To Archpriest Peter, *Die Briefe,* ed. Reindel, 4: 153.

112. Damian, Ep. 47, To an Unidentified Bishop, *Die Briefe,* ed. Reindel, 2: 50; trans. Blum, *Letters,* 2: 260.

113. See Lea, *History of Sacerdotal Celibacy,* 1: 194–96, 227, 256; Fliche, *La Réforme grégorienne,* 2: 139–40; and Barstow, *Married Priests,* pp. 53, 57. On the resistance to the lay boycott, see Barstow, *Married Priests,* pp. 118, 133, 149–50; and Lea, *History of Sacerdotal Celibacy,* 1: 296, 308.

114. ". . . tractare non metuunt obscoenitates et spurca contagia mulierum. . . . Caelum aperitur, summa simul in unum et ima concurrunt, et se sordidus quilibet audacter ingerere non veretur. Postestates angelicae trementes assistunt, inter offerentium manus virtus divina descendit, donum sancti Spiritus influit, pontifex ille, quem adorant angeli, a sui corporis et sanguinis hostia non recedit, et adesse

non trepidat, quem tartareae libidinis estus inflammat," Damian, Ep. 162, To Archpriest Peter, *Die Briefe,* ed. Reindel, 4: 156.

115. I am influenced here by Slavoj Žižek's analysis of the skinheads' demonization of outsiders. This is motivated by a sense that the other "appears to entertain a privileged relationship to the object—the other either possesses the object-treasure, having snatched it away from us (which is why we don't have it), or poses a threat to our possession of the object. In short, the skinheads' 'intolerance' of the other cannot be adequately conceived without a reference to the object-cause of desire that is, by definition, missing," *The Metastases of Enjoyment: Six Essays on Woman and Causality* (London: Verso, 1994), p. 71. See Landulf the Senior's description of the mob violence against married priests in *Mediolanensis historiae libri quatuor* 3.10, p. 93.

5. Avatars of the Priest's Wife

I would like to thank the North Carolina Research Group on Medieval and Early Modern Women for their comments on this chapter.

1. *Don Juan Manuel: El Conde Lucanor* c. 43, ed. Alfonso I. Sotelo (Madrid: Alianza Editorial, 1995), p. 184; trans. John E. Keller and L. Clark Keating, *The Book of Count Lucanor and Patronio* (Lexington: University Press of Kentucky, 1977), pp. 158–59. I am particularly indebted to Meg Greer for bringing this passage to my attention.

2. The immediate impetus was Radbertus's quarrel with his confrère Ratramnus, another monk at Corbie. See E. Ann Matter's introduction to her edition of *De partu virginis, CCCM,* 56c (Turnhout: Brepols, 1985), pp. 12–13.

3. See Dominique Iogna-Prat, "Le Culte de la Vierge sous le règne de Charles le Chauve," in *Marie: le culte de la Vierge dans la société médiévale,* ed. Dominique Iogna-Prat et al. (Paris: Beauchesne, 1996), pp. 65–98. Charles the Bald encouraged his circle of scholars, which included Radbertus, to turn their attention to questions of Mariology (p. 70).

4. Radbertus, *De corpore et sanguine Domini* c. 1, 4, 7, 11, ed. Bede Paulus, *CCCM,* 16 (Turnhout: Brepols, 1969), pp. 15, 30, 38, 73; also see his letter to Fredugard (ca. 856), which defends these views (printed in the appendix of this edition, pp. 145, 149, 159, 162, 170). For dating, see Paulus's introduction, pp. viii–ix.

5. See Luke 2.22–23 for the purification/presentation. The former emphasis on Christ's presentation is in accordance with the Greek church, where the Marian feasts originated. These feasts were introduced into the West in the time of Pope Sergius (687–701). On the change in emphasis in the Carolingian period, see I Deug-Su, "La festa della purificazione in Occidente (secoli IV–VIII)," *Studi Medievali* ser. 3, 15, 1 (1974): 194–213; Iogna-Prat, "Le Culte de la Vierge," pp. 82–89; and Eric Palazzo and Ann-Katrin Johansson, "Jalons liturgiques pour une histoire du culte de la Vierge dans l'Occident (Ve–XIe siècles)," in *Marie: le culte de la Vierge,* ed. Iogna-Prat et al., pp. 23–32.

6. According to Matter, the treatise—written for a community of nuns who had asked Radbertus about Mary's perpetual virginity—was produced after his second and final redaction of *De corpore et sanguine Domini,* which was presented to

Charles the Bald in 844 (intro., pp. 11, 13). On Radbertus's other Marian writings, see p. 10, n. 8.

7. Mary's perpetual virginity, challenged by Helvidius, was successfully defended by Jerome in the late fourth century. See Dyan Elliott, *Spiritual Marriage: Sexual Abstinence in Medieval Wedlock* (Princeton, N.J.: Princeton University Press), p. 44.

8. "Et ideo, ista communis lex nascendi non naturae est, sed corruptionis et uitii," Radbertus, *De partu virginis* bk. 1, ed. Matter, *CCCM,* 56c, p. 49; cf. bk. 1, pp. 52, 55, 56, etc.

9. " . . . qui dicunt ostia uentris et uuluae eum aperuisse et colluuionem sanguinis, ut caeteri omnes, et secundarum spurcitias post se traxisse, in quibus omnibus *gemitus et dolor multiplicatur, tristitia et aerumnae* augentur ut nemo sine his pariat filium," ibid., p. 54.

10. " . . . beata et intemerata uirginitas inmaculata et incorrupta permansit," ibid., p. 59.

11. "Et ideo alia erat purgatio illa feminarum, in qua purgabantur non munus [sic] delicta animarum quam et uitia corporum, et alia purgatio Mariae, in qua non ob aliud quam pro mysterio consuetudo legis seruatur, quia nullis egebat purgamentis, quae Deum de se omnium purificatorem genuit incarnatum," ibid., p. 60.

12. "At uero beata Maria licet ipsa de *carne peccati* sit nata et procreata, ipsaque quamuis caro peccati fuerit, non tunc iam quando praeueniente Spiritus Sancti gratia ab angelo prae omnibus *mulieribus benedicta* uocatur. *Spiritus Sanctus* inquit *superueniet in te et uirtus Altissimi obumbrabit tibi,*" ibid., p. 52. Cf. bk. 1, p. 53, where the author reiterates that the angelic salutation implies that she was already full of grace.

13. "Nunc autem, quia ex auctoritate totius ecclesiae ueneratur, constat eam ab omni originali peccato inmunem fuisse, per quam non solum maledictio matris Euae soluta est, uerum etiam et benedictio omnibus condonatur," ibid., p. 53. Radbertus reached this conclusion by arguing backward from the fact that the church celebrates the nativity of Mary. Only the nativities of Christ and John the Baptist receive a parallel observance, and John was said to have been sanctified in his mother's womb. Radbertus then urges that the same privilege must thus extend to Mary—otherwise the church would hardly honor her nativity.

14. Alternatively, Radbertus does say that when the Holy Spirit came upon Mary, "it purified from filth and cooked the entire virgin" ("totam defaecauit a sordibus uirginem et decoxit," ibid., p. 54). On these ambiguities, see Carlo Balić, "The Mediaeval Controversy over the Immaculate Conception up to the Death of Scotus," in *The Dogma of the Immaculate Conception: History and Significance,* ed. Edward Dennis O'Connor (Notre Dame, Ind.: University of Notre Dame Press, 1958), pp. 163–65. For a brief overview of the controversy surrounding Mary's conception until the end of the fifteenth century, see Jaroslav Pelikan, *Mary Through the Centuries: Her Place in History* (New Haven, Conn.: Yale University Press, 1996), pp. 189–200.

15. On Damian's eucharistic views, see Jean de Montclos, *Lanfranc et Bérenger: la controverse eucharistique du XIe siècle,* Spicilegium Sacrum Lovaniense, Etudes et documents, fasc. 37 (Louvain: Spicilegium Sacrum Lovaniense, 1971), pp. 206–7, 223–24; Lanfranc's position is described in detail on pp. 341–32. Also see Gary

Macy, *The Theologies of the Eucharist in the Early Scholastic Period: A Study of the Salvific Function of the Sacrament According to Theologians c. 1080–c. 1220* (Oxford: Clarendon Press, 1984), pp. 35–43. For the increasing emphasis on the material presence, see Bynum, *Holy Feast and Holy Fast,* pp. 50–54.

16. Damian, Ep. 123, To His Nephew, *Die Briefe des Petrus Damiani,* ed. Kurt Reindel, *MGH, Die Briefe der deutschen Kaiserzeit,* 4 (Munich: *MGH,* 1989), 3: 402.

17. "Quatinus quae purum panem, ut videbatur, ante credebat, verae carnis speciem cerneret, sicque sacrilegam coepti sceleris audaciam suo ipsa iudicio condemnaret," Damian, Ep. 102, To Abbot Desiderius and the Monks of Monte Cassino, *Die Briefe,* ed. Reindel, 3: 119.

18. "O beata ubera, quae dum tenue lac puerilibus labris infundunt, angelorum cibum et hominum pascunt. . . . Manat liquor ex uberibus Virginis, et in carnem uertitur Saluatoris. . . . Illud siquidem corpus Christi quod beatissima Virgo genuit, quod in gremio fouit, . . . illud inquam, absque ulla dubietate, non aliud, nunc de sacro altari percipimus, et eius sanguinem in sacramentum nostrae redemptionis haurimus," Damian, Serm. 45, c. 4, *Sermones,* ed. Giovanni Lucchesi, *CCCM,* 57 (Turnhout: Brepols, 1983), p. 267. See Miri Rubin, *Corpus Christi: The Eucharist in Late Medieval Culture* (Cambridge: Cambridge University Press, 1991), p. 22; Bynum, "The Body of Christ in the Later Middle Ages: A Reply to Leo Steinberg," in *Fragmentation and Redemption: Essays on Gender and the Human Body in Medieval Religion* (New York: Zone Books, 1991), pp. 100–101; and eadem, "The Female Body and Religious Practice in the Later Middle Ages," in ibid., pp. 210–12. The theological and psychic emphasis on Mary's breasts is discussed later in the chapter.

19. On the office of the Virgin, see his Ep. 166, To Stephen the Monk, *Die Briefe,* ed. Reindel, 4: 230–34. He also suggested that the canticle of the Virgin be added to Vespers (Ep. 17, To T., an Anonymous Nobleman of Ravenna, *Die Briefe,* ed. Reindel, 1: 161–62; trans. Blum, *Letters,* 1: 152). On Damian's liturgical promotion of the Virgin, see Edmund Bishop, *Liturgica Historica* (Oxford: Clarendon Press, 1918), pp. 226–27.

20. See esp. Ep. 102, To Abbot Desiderius and the Monks of Monte Cassino, *Die Briefe,* ed. Reindel, 3: 171–74, 174, 177–78; Ep. 168, To Archbishop Alfonse of Salerno, 4: 242–43, 243–44, 246, 247. In Ep. 17 (To T., an Anonymous Nobleman of Ravenna), Damian describes how a sinful cleric, guilty of many breaches of chastity, was forgiven his sins on his deathbed due to his careful observance of the Virgin's office (*Die Briefe,* ed. Reindel, 1: 166–67; trans. Blum, *Letters,* 1: 157–58). Clarissa Atkinson also notes the correlation between the Gregorian Reform and the rise of Mariology (*The Oldest Vocation: Christian Motherhood in the Middle Ages* [Ithaca, N.Y.: Cornell University Press, 1991], pp. 116–19).

21. Gregory also promoted the laity's active participation in the Mass, generally. See Enrico Cattaneo, "La liturgia nella reforma gregoriana," in *Chiesa e riforma nella spiritualità del sec. XI,* Convegni del Centro di Studi sulla Spiritualità Medievale 6 (Todi: Presso l'Accademia Tudertina, 1968), pp. 188–89. Cattaneo cites the pertinent part of Gregory's letter to Mathilda on p. 188, n. 43. On Anselm's devotion to the Virgin, see R. W. Southern, *Saint Anselm and His Biographer: A Study of Monastic Life and Thought, 1059–c. 1130* (Cambridge: Cambridge University Press, 1963), p. 288.

22. David Russo, "Les Répresentations mariales dans l'art d'Occident du

Moyen Age: essai sur la formation d'une tradition iconographique," in *Marie: le culte de la Vierge*, ed. Iogna-Prat et al., p. 237.

23. S. J. P. Van Dijk refers to this possibility, which he says he has not been able to follow up, but cites no source for it. (It is not contained in the remaining *acta* for the council.) On the other hand, he thinks it possible that Leo IX did have some contact with Byzantium and may have learned of the feast in this way. See "The Origin of the Latin Feast of the Conception of the Blessed Virgin Mary," *Dublin Review* 228 (1954): 266. For fragmentary evidence in Byzantine and central Italy for an earlier period, see Cornelius A. Bouman, "The Immaculate Conception in the Liturgy," in *The Dogma of the Immaculate Conception*, ed. O'Connor, pp. 123–24; and Bishop, *Liturgica Historica*, pp. 256–58.

24. See Van Dijk, "Origin of the Latin Feast," pp. 253–55; Bishop, *Liturgica Historica*, pp. 239–41; and Southern, *Saint Anselm and His Biographer*, pp. 290–92.

25. See Van Dijk, "Origin of the Latin Feast," pp. 263–64. On the celebration of the Byzantine feast, see Bouman, "Immaculate Conception in the Liturgy," pp. 114–20. For an overview of Mary's life in the apocrypha, see Marina Warner, *Alone of All Her Sex: The Myth and the Cult of the Virgin Mary* (New York: Knopf, 1976), pp. 25–33, esp. p. 26.

26. See Southern, *Saint Anselm and His Biographer*, p. 293; and Van Dijk, "Origin of the Latin Feast," p. 429.

27. See Southern, *Saint Anselm and His Biographer*, pp. 294–95. Southern notes that in Eadmer's earlier writings on the Virgin, however, he does acknowledge that she was born in original sin. For Eadmer and other twelfth-century defenders of the feast, see Balić, "Mediaeval Controversy over the Immaculate Conception," pp. 171–83.

28. Eadmer, *Tractatus de conceptione B. Mariae Virginis*, *PL* 159, col. 305; Southern, *Saint Anselm and His Biographer*, p. 295.

29. See Balić, "Mediaeval Controversy over the Immaculate Conception," pp. 204–10, esp. p. 204.

30. Southern posits that, although the spread of the feast is often attributed to the continental visits of Anselm and his monks during their exile, the feast probably arrived later (ca. 1123). See "The English Origins of the 'Miracles of the Virgin,'" *Mediaeval and Renaissance Studies* 4 (1958): 198.

31. See, for example, Pelikan, *Mary Through the Centuries*, pp. 192–93, 195.

32. "Unde ergo conceptionis sanctitas? An dicitur sanctificatione praeventa, quatenus jam sancta conciperetur, ac per hoc sanctus fuerit et conceptus; quemadmodum sanctificata jam in utero dicitur, ut sanctus consequeretur et ortus? . . . An forte inter amplexus maritales sanctitas se ipsi conceptioni immiscuit, ut simul et sanctificata fuerit, et concepta?" Bernard of Clairvaux, Ep. 134, To the Canons of Lyons, c. 7, *PL* 182, col. 335. He was, however, prepared to acknowledge her sanctification in the uterus at some unspecified point (c. 7, col. 336). Bernard was sufficiently prescient to recognize that once the process got underway, efforts to sanctify Mary would not stop with her conception but would reach back to her parents and grandparents ad infinitum (c. 6, col. 334). These concerns were to some extent vindicated in the later Middle Ages by the burgeoning cult of St. Anne, the Virgin's mother, and a preoccupation with Mary's holy genealogy. See the collection edited by Kathleen Ashley and Pamela Sheingorn, *Interpreting Cultural Symbols:*

Saint Anne in Late Medieval Culture (Athens: University of Georgia Press, 1990), esp. Sheingorn's essay, "Appropriating the Holy Kinship: Gender and Family History," pp. 169–98.

33. Thomas Aquinas allows that Mary was sanctified before birth but denies that she was sanctified before animation (*Summa theologiae* 3a, q. 27, arts. 1–2, ed. and trans. Fathers of the English Dominican Province [London: Blackfriars, 1969] 51: 4–15). He does, somewhat begrudgingly, acknowledge that the church tolerates the observance of the feast in certain locales, but says that it is really the feast of her sanctification that is honored on the supposed feast of her conception (3a, q. 27, art. 2, resp. ad obj. 3, 51: 12–15). Also see the quodlibetical question in which he asks whether it is licit to celebrate the feast of the conception (quodlib. 6, q. 5, art. 7, in *Opera omnia* [Parma: Petrus Fiaccadori, 1859; rprt. Musurgia, 1949], 9: 545–46; cf. Stephen of Bourbon's solution, discussed in n. 38, below). On a devotional level, however, Thomas may have been sympathetic to the Immaculate Conception, as evidenced by a report of a sermon he preached on the angelic salutation in 1273. This *reportatio* is translated in the appendix to *Summa theologiae,* 51: 100–101. But Thomas's formal theological position posits that she underwent three spiritual purifications: her sanctification in the womb, which freed her from original sin, a greater sanctification in the birth of Christ, and a final one when she rose to glory in her assumption (3a, q. 27, art. 6, resp. ad 2, 51: 28–29). Both Albert the Great and Bonaventure were in essential agreement with Thomas, likewise denying that Mary was conceived without sin (Balić, "Mediaeval Controversy over the Immaculate Conception," pp. 204–10). Interestingly, Aquinas also used his Aristotelian-inflected arguments concerning Mary's physiology to argue that women, passive in generation, did not transmit original sin—a passivity that may have advantages in this context. See Prudence Allen, *The Concept of Woman: The Aristotelian Revolution, 750 BC–AD 1250* (Montreal: Eden Press, 1985), pp. 396–98. But also see Allen's discussion of Albert the Great, who, despite his conviction that Mary was possessed of every branch of higher learning, used the passivity of her conception and the equally passive way she was infused with knowledge to restrict women from attending universities (pp. 376–83).

34. This is in spite of the fact that aspects of the rhetoric surrounding the feast had subversive potential in the purification of conjugal sex. Nicholas of St. Albans, for example, fashions an impassioned response to Bernard's rhetorical gauntlet, "Wherein lies sanctity in conception?"—arguing that if God did not think that postlapsarian sex could be achieved without sin, he would never have ordered humanity to "be fruitful and multiply" (*De celebranda concepcione beate Marie contra beatum Bernardum,* ed. C. H. Talbot, as "Nicholas of St. Albans and Saint Bernard," *Revue Bénédictine* 64 [1954]: 102). The Virgin's marriage to Joseph is deployed in a novel way to buttress this contention: since a person cannot commit sin without the knowledge of the devil, the Virgin Mary's completely chaste and sinless union would provide no concealment from diabolical machinations (as was traditionally understood to be the function of the union) if there were not other couples who paid the conjugal debt and managed to remain sinless (pp. 102–3). Nicholas likens the involuntary subjection of the flesh to concupiscence with natural hunger and fatigue (both of which Christ endured in his human condition) and to the death of martyrs. Thus concupiscence, like death, can likewise be put to good use (pp. 103–

5). Gregory the Great's begrudging concession that a select few might be free from excessive concupiscence during conjugal intercourse and hence not be liable to the ritual washing and the respectful interlude before seeking admission to a church is resourcefully used to argue in favor of the chastity of Mary's parents. Nicholas even urges the probability that the Virgin's father was entirely chaste, not only waking but sleeping, and was not aware that he had experienced a nocturnal emission until he awoke (pp. 106–7, 108, 109; for the argument that Mary was conceived without any lust, see Balić, "Mediaeval Controversy of the Immaculate Conception," p. 183). The example of Nicholas suggests some ways in which the impulse to purify the Virgin could wobble dangerously out of control, cleansing her parents, and hence conjugal sex, to a degree that might open the way for clerical wives to return to their reluctantly relinquished beds. Yet clerical reform was sufficiently successful that no advocate for clerical marriage seems to have exploited the window of opportunity opened up by the discussion of Mary's conception. Nicholas's position is safeguarded by his discussion of a woman's postpartum purification. If the sole reason for this ritual was due to the excess sinfulness of the sex act, men would likewise be subject to purification. Thus Nicholas acknowledges that another unnamed reason must be assigned to this rite (*De celebranda*, p. 107). By this distinction, Nicholas emerges as somewhat more punctilious than Radbertus, who tends to assimilate the need for postpartum purification with active sinfulness. This kind of conflation would continue to loom especially large in the period of the Gregorian Reform and its aftermath, since the reformers' rhetoric had done so much to associate ritual pollution (which, while abominable, was morally neutral) with active sinfulness.

35. This move was anticipated by Radbertus (*De partu virginis* bk. 1, ed. Matter, *CCCM*, 56c, pp. 49, 52, 56). On the polarization of Mary and Eve, see Pelikan, *Mary Through the Centuries*, pp. 42–44, 52. The Eve/Mary dichotomy was also an essential component in the liturgy of the feast of the conception. Thus the twelfth-century Fécamp Missal extols the Virgin and disparages Eve by contrasting carefully shaded words that subtly call to mind the image of Damian's demonic concubine: "Eve the mother of the human race corrupted by the mind of a viper [*corrupta mente vipero*] succumbed [*succubuit*] to malice, Mary the bearer of the savior of the world, sealed by chastity, threatened his [the serpent's] head" ("Mater humani generis eva corrupta mente vipereo livori succubuit, genetrix salvatoris mundi maria signato pudore caput eius comminuit," as cited by Bouman, "Immaculate Conception in the Liturgy," p. 142; translation mine.) For dating, see V. Leroquais, *Les Sacramentaires et les missels manuscrits* (Paris: s.n., 1924), 1: 195–96.

36. "Tu autem miserrime seducta, et e vestigio multiplici perversarum cupiditatum semine imbuta, illecebrosa facundia illum ad tibi consentiendum illexisti, praesignans in hoc opere tuo veram fore futuram sententiam viri Dei, mulieres scilicet apostatare facere etiam sapientes," Eadmer, *De conceptione B. Mariae Virginis*, *PL* 159, col. 312.

37. Ibid., col. 314.

38. As R. W. Southern has shown, this miracle was enhanced by a fair degree of historicity ("English Origins," pp. 194–98). The story of Elsinus was extremely widespread. Certain renditions of it, moreover, demonstrate how intensely individuals struggled to accommodate the feast in the face of official disapproval. Thus when the Dominican Stephen of Bourbon relates the tale of Elsinus, he prefaces it

with the official view of his order that Mary was conceived in sin and that Bernard had demonstrated the feast should not be celebrated. Yet he argues that at the time of her ensoulment (around the fortieth day) she was sanctified in her mother's womb. Those wishing to honor her should remember this "secret conception" (*Anecdotes historiques, légendes et apologues tirés du recueil inédit d'Etienne de Bourbon,* ed. A. Lecoy de la Marche [Paris: Renouard, 1877], no. 106, pp. 93–95; cf. Thomas Aquinas's solution in n. 33, above). The anonymous twelfth-century sermon advocating the feast likewise suggests that her spiritual, not carnal, conception be honored (*Sermo de conceptione Beatae Mariae, PL* 159, col. 322). This sermon was probably written at the end of the twelfth century, but could be earlier. It is included in the works of Anselm. See Southern, "English Origins," p. 195, n. 1.

39. Anonymous, *Sermo de conceptione Beatae Mariae, PL* 159, cols. 319–20. This sermon has been translated in the appendix of *The Dogma of the Immaculate Conception,* ed. O'Connor, pp. 522–27.

40. Anonymous, *Sermo de conceptione Beatae Mariae, PL* 159, cols. 320–21.

41. See Warner, *Alone of All Her Sex,* pp. 156–58; Atkinson, *Oldest Vocation,* pp. 140–41; and Elliott, *Spiritual Marriage,* pp. 180–81.

42. See Bertrand of Pontigny, *Vita beati Edmundi Cantuariensis archiepiscopi* c. 10, in *Thesaurus Novus Anecdotorum,* ed. E. Martène and U. Durand (Paris: Lutetia, 1717; rprt. New York: Burt Franklin, 1968), vol. 3, cols. 1782–83. Cf. Vincent of Beauvais's account in his epitome of Edmund's life, *Speculum historiale* 30.70, in *Speculum quadruplex; sive Speculum maius* (Douai: B. Belleri, 1624), 4: 1309. Note that Vincent includes a less specific (and more marvelous) deployment of this anecdote among his assortment of Marian miracles (7.87, 4: 253). Cf. the visionary marriage of Hermann Joseph (d. 1241), who, as his name suggests, appropriates the biblical Joseph's role of husband. See the contemporary life by a member of Hermann Joseph's community at Steinfeld in *AA SS,* April, 1: 692.

43. On this concept, see Chap. 1, pp. 31–32, above.

44. Charles Wood, "The Doctors' Dilemma: Sin, Salvation, and the Menstrual Cycle," *Speculum* 56 (1981): 719–21; also see Atkinson, *Oldest Vocation,* p. 58. Mary's breasts are already explicitly referred to in this context by Radbertus when interpreting the words of scripture: "And lest we were to imagine that [Christ] was a phantasm, as many heretics said, [the psalmist] added *My hope is in my mother's breasts.* Therefore when my mother and breasts are proclaimed, the truth of flesh, and not phantasm, are proclaimed" ("Et ne putaremur phantasma fuisse, ut multi haereticorum dixerunt, addidit: *Spes mea ab uberibus matris meae.* Ergo ubi mater et ubera narrantur, ueritas carnis et non phantasma praedicatur," Radbertus, *De partu virginis* bk. 1, ed. Matter, *CCCM,* 56c, p. 57). The emphasis on her breasts is at one with the theological tendency to raise Mary's generative functions to a higher place in her body. This latter proclivity is discussed in the Introduction, above.

45. Elise F. Dexter, ed., *Miracula sanctae Virginis Mariae,* University of Wisconsin Studies in the Social Sciences and History, no. 12 (Madison: University of Wisconsin, 1927), no. 34, pp. 55–56. The monk was a special servant of Mary who, until his illness, conscientiously recited her hours. On the English provenance of these earliest collections, which were written between 1100 and 1140, see Southern, "English Origins," pp. 176–216.

46. See Caroline Walker Bynum, *Jesus as Mother: Studies in the Spirituality of the*

High Middle Ages (Berkeley: University of California Press, 1982), pp. 132–33; and Atkinson, *Oldest Vocation,* pp. 121, 142.

47. See Bynum, *Jesus as Mother,* pp. 113 ff., 154–59. Bynum notes that "to Bernard, the maternal image is almost without exception elaborated not as giving birth or even as conceiving or sheltering in a womb but as nurturing, particularly suckling" (p. 115). On the much less frequent use of womb or birthing imagery, see pp. 121–22, 124.

48. See Introduction, pp. 6–7, above; and Chap. 1, pp. 28–29, above.

49. "Sed attende quo cibo conceptus nutriatur in utero. Profecto sanguine menstruo, qui cessat ex femina post conceptum, ut ex eo conceptus nutriatur in femina. Qui fertur esse tam detestabilis et immundus, ut ex ejus contactu fruges non germinent, arescant arbusta, moriantur herbae, amittant arbores foetus, et si canes inde comederint in rabiem efferantur. Concepti fetus vitium seminis contrahunt, ita ut leprosi et elephantici ex hac corruptione nascantur. Unde secundum legem Mosaicam, mulier quae menstruum patitur, reputatur, immunda; et si quis ad menstruum patitur, reputatur, immunda; et si quis ad menstruatam accesserit, jubetur interfici. Ac propter immunditiam menstruorum praecipitur, ut mulier si masculum pareret quadraginta, si vero feminam, octoginta diebus a templi cessaret ingressu," Lothario dei Segni (Innocent III), *De contemptu mundi sive de miseria conditionis humanae* 1.5, *PL* 217, col. 704 (note that the biblical references cited in Migne's text are incorrect but have been corrected in my translation). Also see 1.3–4 regarding the inherent sinfulness of conception (cols. 703–4). In a later work, Lothario (now Innocent III) does raise the question of the whereabouts of Christ's umbilical cord and foreskin in the context of Christ's resurrection. Innocent then proceeds to claim that the foreskin was in the church of the Lateran, though he admits that some allege it was carried off to Charlemagne by an angel (*De sacro altaris mysterio* 4.30, *PL* 217, cols. 876–77). While not presenting the same threat as polluting afterbirth (from which, of course, Mary was spared), the question of the umbilical cord could still be perceived as a potentially dangerous move to Mary's lower body as the locus of veneration. Not surprisingly, Innocent chooses to assimilate the umbilical cord with Christ as opposed to the Virgin. On the cult of the holy foreskin, see *AA SS,* January, 1: 2–8; Bynum, "Female Body," in *Fragmentation and Redemption,* p. 186; and eadem, "Bodily Miracles in the High Middle Ages," in *Belief in History: Innovative Approaches to European and American Religion,* ed. Thomas Kselman (Notre Dame, Ind.: University of Notre Dame Press, 1991), p. 72. To my knowledge, no cult developed around the umbilical cord.

50. Archadale A. King, *Eucharistic Reservation in the Western Church* (New York: Sheed and Ward, 1964), pp. 12–13.

51. See Bynum, *Holy Feast and Holy Fast,* pp. 54–55; and Rubin, *Corpus Christi,* pp. 49–63, esp. pp. 49–50. On twelfth-century theological discussions surrounding the Eucharist, see Macy, *Theologies of the Eucharist,* chaps. 2–4.

52. "His body and blood are truly contained in the sacrament of the altar under the forms of bread and wine, the bread and wine having been changed in substance, by God's power, into his body and blood [*transsubstantiatis pane in corpus et vino in sanguinem potestate divina*]," Lateran IV, const. 1, in Norman P. Tanner et al., ed. and trans., *Decrees of the Ecumenical Councils,* original text established by G. Alberigo et al. (London: Sheed and Ward; Washington, D.C.: Georgetown University Press,

1990), 1: 230. See Bynum, *Holy Feast and Holy Fast,* pp. 50–53. The formal decree regarding the elevation of the Host occurred soon after Lateran IV. See V. L. Kennedy, "The Date of the Parisian Decree of the Elevation of the Host," *Mediaeval Studies* 8 (1946): 87–96; and idem, "The Moment of Consecration and the Elevation of the Host," *Mediaeval Studies* 6 (1944): 121–50. For the implementation of eucharistic legislation in the papal court, see S. J. P. Van Dijk and J. Hazeldon Walker, *The Origins of the Modern Roman Liturgy: The Liturgy of the Papal Court and the Franciscan Order in the Thirteenth Century* (Westminster, Md:: Newman Press; London: Darton, Longman, and Todd, 1960), pp. 361–70. About the problems and the evolution of the term "transubstantiation," see Gary Macy, "The Dogma of Transubstantiation in the Middle Ages," *Journal of Ecclesiastical History* 45 (1994): 11–41. Macy demonstrates that there was never any consensus surrounding the definition of the term, arguing convincingly that there was no "dogma" of transubstantiation.

53. See Rubin, *Corpus Christi,* pp. 131–32.

54. Lateran II, c. 6, in Tanner, ed. and trans., *Decrees of the Ecumenical Councils,* 1: 198. I have altered Tanner's translation slightly to convey a more literal sense.

55. Lateran II, c. 7, in ibid., 1: 198. This canon also reissued the lay boycott of masses. Also see C. 27 q. 1 c. 40; X.3.3.1; X.4.6.1–3.

56. Lateran IV, const. 14, 31, in Tanner, ed. and trans., *Decrees of the Ecumenical Council,* 1: 242, 249. As H. C. Lea points out, Lateran IV's contribution was in no way innovative but is symbolically important because of the general authority of the council and its further consolidation of the work of the reform (*A History of Sacerdotal Celibacy,* 2d ed. [Boston: Houghton Mifflin, 1884], pp. 327–28).

57. See James Brundage, *Law, Sex, and Christian Society in Medieval Europe* (Chicago: University of Chicago Press, 1987), pp. 401–5, 474–77; and Lea, *History of Sacerdotal Celibacy,* pp. 270, 283–90, 293–94, 330–33. Members of the clergy were also known to frequent brothels. See Ruth Mazo Karras, *Common Women: Prostitution and Sexuality in Medieval England* (New York: Oxford University Press, 1996), pp. 77–78.

58. Brundage, *Law, Sex, and Christian Society,* pp. 403, 475.

59. Gratian, though condemning the ordination of clerical bastards and even reiterating the canon that such offspring should be enslaved, nevertheless permitted the ordination of children born prior to the father's ordination. The later decretists, however, were considerably more rigid in this respect (D. 56 c. 1 and dpc; D. 56 c. 13 and dpc; C. 15 q. 8 c. 3; see Brundage, *Law, Sex, and Christian Society,* pp. 251–52, 318; cf. X.1.17.1–4). Nevertheless, the son's de facto inheritance of benefices was more widespread in some areas than others. In thirteenth-century Wales, for example, sons seemed routinely to follow in their fathers' footsteps. The pragmatic emperor Frederick II, yielding to necessity, legislated that the offspring of clerical marriages must be provided for from their parents' estates (Lea, *History of Sacerdotal Celibacy,* pp. 285, 335).

60. See X.1.17.9, X.1.17.17–18, as well as Hostiensis's discussion of dispensations for this kind of irregularity in birth in his *Summa* (Lyons: Iacobus Giunta, 1537; rprt. Aalen: Scientia, 1962), fols. 37v–38r. Also see the dispensations included in H. C. Lea's edition of *A Formulary of the Papal Penitentiary in the Thirteenth Century* (Philadelphia: Lea Brothers, 1892), nos. 141, 143, pp. 140–41, 142–43. Cf. no. 142, which concerns a son assisting his father in religious services (pp. 141–42).

This formulary, which Lea attributed to Cardinal Thomas of Capua (ca. 1216), is now thought to be the work of Cardinal Giacomo Tommasini Caetani (1295–1300). See Leonard Boyle, *A Survey of the Vatican Archives and Its Medieval Holdings* (Toronto: Pontifical Institute of Mediaeval Studies, 1972), p. 93.

61. See, for example, one of Stephen of Bourbon's exempla in which a Cathar brings the concubinage of a parish priest to the attention of Francis of Assisi in a vain effort to convert him (*Anecdotes historiques,* no. 316, pp. 264–65).

62. On eucharistic devotion as a confirmation of orthodoxy and response to heresy, see Bynum, *Holy Feast and Holy Fast,* pp. 64, 329, n. 139; and Rubin, *Corpus Christi,* pp. 168–72. Also see Bynum, "Female Body," in *Fragmentation and Redemption,* p. 195.

63. James of Vitry, *Vita B. Mariae Oigniacensis,* prologue, c. 8, *AA SS,* June, 5: 548; trans. Margot King, *The Life of Marie d'Oignies by Jacques de Vitry* (Saskatoon, Sask.: Peregrina Publishing, 1984), p. 8; on Mary's own cycle of fasting and eucharistic feasting, see 2.23–25, *AA SS,* June, 5: 552; trans. King, pp. 23–25.

64. On the difference between imitating the saints and admiring them, see Richard Kieckhefer, *Unquiet Souls: Fourteenth-Century Saints and Their Religious Milieu* (Chicago: University of Chicago Press, 1984), pp. 12–14.

65. Again, James of Vitry is at the forefront of the new interest in preaching, creating one of the first *ad status* collections of sermons for circulation among preachers. Mary of Oignies, in particular, was the subject of a series of illustrative tales that circulated widely. See Frederic C. Tubach, *Index Exemplorum: A Handbook of Medieval Religious Tales,* Folklore Fellows Communications, no. 204 (Helsinki: Suomalainen Tiedeakatemia, 1969), nos. 3201–4.

66. Caesarius of Heisterbach, *Dialogus miraculorum* 7.46, ed. Joseph Strange (Cologne: J. M. Heberle, 1851), 2: 65–66; trans. H. Von E. Scott and C. C. Swinton Bland, *Dialogue on Miracles* (London: Routledge, 1929), 2: 529–30. Cf. 9.2, ed. Strange, 2: 167–68; trans. Scott and Bland, 2: 108–9. Also see the vision of Adolphus discussed below. Note, however, that too close an assimilation of Mary with the divinity of Christ was ideologically suspect. This was the case with Richard of St. Laurent's *De laudibus B. Mariae Virginis,* wrongly attributed for a time to Albert the Great. See Allen, *Concept of Woman,* p. 384.

67. Radbertus, *De corpore et sanguine Domini* bk. 9, ed. Paulus, *CCCM,* 16, pp. 60–61; Honorius Augustodunensis, *In purificatione sanctae Mariae,* in *Speculum ecclesiae, PL* 172, col. 852. For its inclusion in the very earliest collections of Marian miracles, see Southern, "English Origins," pp. 186, 191–92.

68. For these very common motifs, see Tubach, *Index Exemplorum,* nos. 2689b, 2689, 2689c, 2662, 2668. For a discussion of such eucharistic miracles, see Rubin, *Corpus Christi,* pp. 108–29; and Bynum, *Holy Feast and Holy Fast,* pp. 63–64. Miri Rubin has recently completed a book on Host desecration and its links with anti-Semitism entitled *Gentile Tales* (London, Conn.: Yale University Press, forthcoming 1999).

69. Caesarius of Heisterbach, *Dialogus miraculorum* 9.53, ed. Strange, 2: 208; trans. Scott and Bland, 2: 157–58.

70. See Caesarius of Heisterbach, *Dialogus miraculorum* 2.5, 9.58, ed. Strange, 1: 64–66, 2: 210–11; trans. Scott and Bland, 1: 70–72, 2: 161–62.

71. Caesarius of Heisterbach, *Dialogus miraculorum* 9.3, ed. Strange, 2: 169;

trans. Scott and Bland, 2: 110–11. This, of course, led to his reform, whereby he placed his concubine in a monastery. Caesarius does say that the priest was not able to see the vision clearly or joyfully due to the sinful nature of his life. This point is blurred in the translation as the priest, named Adolphus, is wrongly called by the name Gotteschalk — who is the cleric in the previous vision.

72. "'Quomodo de manu leprosa vis aquam recipere qui a malis sacerdotibus dedignaris accipere sacramenta?'" James of Vitry, *The Exempla or Illustrative Stories from the Sermones Vulgares of Jacques de Vitry,* ed. Thomas Frederick Crane, Folk-Lore Society Publications, 26 (London: Folk-Lore Society, 1890; rprt. Nendeln, Liechtenstein: Kraus, 1967), no. 155, p. 68. This was a popular motif that was translated and repeated in many other important collections such as the English *An Alphabet of Tales: An English 15th Century Translation of the "Alphabetum narrationum" of Etienne de Besançon,* ed. M. M. Banks, *EETS,* o.s., nos. 126–27 (London: Kegan Paul, Trench, and Trübner, 1904 and 1905; rprt. as one volume Millwood, N.Y.: Kraus, 1987), no. 687, pp. 460–61. See Tubach, *Index Exemplorum,* no. 2672.

73. See Stephen of Bourbon, *Anecdotes historiques* no. 347, pp. 304–5. Also see n. 61, above.

74. The lay boycott of masses was reiterated by Gratian (D. 32 c. 6). Thomas Aquinas attempts to come to grips with his own time's less stringent application in one of his quodlibetical questions, where he poses the problem of whether it is a mortal sin to hear the Mass of a fornicating priest in light of the church sanction. He reconciles present practice with past tradition by reducing the possibility for sin into two basic contentions. First, although the priest undoubtedly sins mortally in celebrating, an individual who hears the Mass only sins in the event that he or she had encouraged the priest to say Mass when he was in a state of mortal sin. Second, Thomas further avers that the lay boycott only pertains to a priest who is a public fornicator and has been officially judged and sentenced as such (quodlib. 11, q. 8, art. 8, in *Opera omnia,* Parma edition, 9: 617).

75. In other nonsacramental contexts, a condition of her appearance might be her annihilation. Thus Caesarius of Heisterbach relates how a naive priest's concubine asked a cleric who had preached on hell what would become of clerical concubines. He, in turn, acquainted with the woman's simplicity, answered that such a woman must first pass through the fires of a furnace. The woman, accordingly, threw herself in the fire, and a dove was seen to issue from the flames (Caesarius of Heisterbach, *Dialogus miraculorum* 6.35, ed. Strange, 1: 387–88; trans. Scott and Bland, 1: 448–49). Cf. Beatrix de Ecclesia's similar conviction that a woman who sleeps with a priest cannot see the face of God — a view that she expressed to Petrus Clergus when he was attempting to seduce her (Jean Duvernoy, ed., *Le Registre d'inquisition de Jacques Fournier, évêque de Pamiers (1318–1325)* [Toulouse: Edouard Privat, 1965], 1: 224).

76. "Vere infelices et vecordes qui magis student cadavera concubinarum exornare quam Christi altaria. Subtilius et nitidius est peplum meretricis quam palle altaris, subtilior et preciosior est camisia concubine meretricis quam suppellicium sacerdotis. Immo tantum expendunt in vestimentis concubinarum quod pauperes afficiuntur et vilibus induuntur. Unde quidam solebat dicere quod optime inter alios sacerdotes sciret cognoscere qui haberent concubinas, et inspiciebat illos qui manicas ad cubitum perforatas habebant. In quibusdam autem regionibus ita abhomi-

nantur hujusmodi sacerdotisse quod illis in ecclesia nolunt pacem dare nec ab illis pacis osculum recipere. Opinio enim communis est eorum quod, si sacerdotum concubinas ad pacis osculum reciperent, partem in missa non haberent. Unde ad earum derisionem solent dicere vulgariter quasi quamdam carminationem qua mures carminati a segetibus eorum arceantur sub hiis verbis:
Je vos convie sorriz et raz,
Que vos n'aies part en ces tas,
Ne plus que n'a part en la messe,
Cil qui prent puis a la presteresse.
Quod est: 'Adjuro vos mures et rati, quod non habeatis partem in hac collectione manipulorum, vel in hoc acervo granorum, sicut non habet partem in missa qui osculum pacis accipit a sacerdotissa.' Et tenent quod mures postea manipulos vel grana non tangunt," James of Vitry, *Exempla,* no. 242, p. 101. See Tubach, *Index exemplorum,* nos. 2925, 3951. I am grateful to Douglas Browne for bringing this anecdote to my attention. Also see Stephen of Bourbon's remarks comparing the *sacerdotisse* to foxes who, once expelled, return at night and rob the henhouse. Therefore, once the bishop expels these women from sacerdotal homes, they return by stealth to carry off whatever they can (*Anecdotes historiques* no. 452, pp. 390–91). Note the fox is a standard metaphor for heretics in this period.

77. On the devolution of these terms in the high Middle Ages, see René Metz, "Le statut de la femme en droit canonique médiéval," *Recueils de Société Jean Bodin pour l'histoire comparative des institutions* 12 (1962): 98 and n. 2.

78. On myths concerning menstruation, see Introduction, pp. 5–6, above, and Chap. 6, p. 155, below.

79. As Miri Rubin indicates, in Enns in 1421 the sacristan's wife sold the Host directly to the Jews. In Breslau in 1453, a sacristan, approached by the Jews, consulted his wife and then agreed to the sale. In Mecklenburg in 1492, a priest's former concubine also pressured him into selling the Host (forthcoming in *Gentile Tales*). I am grateful to Rubin for sharing her findings with me prior to the publication of her book.

80. Efforts to perform sorcery with the Host were hardly new, as is clear from the eucharistic miracle related by Peter Damian, described above. But the concern certainly escalated in the thirteenth century, as is demonstrated in many different venues. Stephen of Bourbon denounces those who perform witchcraft (*sortilegia*) with sacraments and tells of a woman who steals a Host for this purpose (*Anecdotes historiques* no. 371, pp. 328–29). The vita of Margaret of Cortona reports that one day she was given an unconsecrated Host absent-mindedly, since consecrated Hosts (presumably reserved ones) were kept at the priests' home on account of witches (*AA SS,* February, 3: 343; Margaret's life was written by her confessor, Giunta Bevegnati). Inquisitor Bernard Gui considered such thefts, whether for witchcraft or other abuses, a heresy. Thus his inquisitional manual includes a *forma* for the sentencing of the crime's perpetrators: the offender should be made to wear a yellow Host on the back and front of his / her clothing and endure perpetual imprisonment. The *forma* further denies that the Host would even be magically efficacious, as such powers would be contrary to grace and salvation. See *Practica inquisitionis heretice pravitatis* pt. 3, no. 43, ed. Célestin Douais (Paris: Alphonse Picard, 1886), pp. 158–59. For the full-blown charges linking witches, now largely believed to be female, to

outrages against the sacrament, see Henry Kramer and James Sprenger, *Malleus maleficarum 1487,* photographic facsimile of the first edition (Hildesheim: Georg Olms, 1992), pt. 2, q. 1, c. 5, fol. 57r; trans. Montague Summers (London: John Rodker, 1928; rprt. New York: Dover, 1971), pp. 116–17.

81. Kramer and Sprenger, *Malleus maleficarum 1487,* pt. 2, q. 1, c. 2, fol. 48v; trans. Summers, p. 99.

82. Peter Dinzelbacher presents a series of holy women through which he demonstrates the parallels between these two seeming polarities in *Heilige oder Hexen? Schicksale auffälliger Frauen in Mittelalter und Frühneuzeit* (Munich: Artemis and Winkler, 1995). For the parallel fascination with the Host apparent in both saint and witch, see pp. 241–44. Also see Richard Kieckhefer, "The Holy and the Unholy: Sainthood, Witchcraft, and Magic in Late Medieval Europe," *Journal of Medieval and Renaissance Studies* 24 (1994): 355–85; Gabriella Zarri, *Le sante vive: cultura e religiosità femminile nella prima età moderna* (Turin: Rosenberg and Sellier, 1990), p. 118; and Bynum, *Holy Feast and Holy Fast,* p. 23.

83. Bynum, *Holy Feast and Holy Fast,* pp. 118, 128–29, 230.

84. Cf. ibid., pp. 123–24. For a sensitive discussion of some of these intense relationships, see John Coakley's "Friars as Confidants of Holy Women in Medieval Dominican Hagiography," in *Images of Sainthood in Medieval Europe,* ed. Renate Blumenfeld-Kosinski and Timea Szell (Ithaca, N.Y.: Cornell University Press, 1991), pp. 222–46. One might also argue that, while putting aside their wives, the clergy were nevertheless required to assume the spiritual direction of women—a fact reflected in Francis's acerbic remark, "'God has taken away our wives, and now the devil gives us sisters'" (as cited by Brenda M. Bolton, "*Mulieres sanctae,*" in *Women in Medieval Society,* ed. Susan Mosher Stuard [Philadelphia: University of Pennsylvania Press, 1976], p. 150). Many of these relations also had explicitly matrimonial overtones—imagistically as well as in terms of power relations. See the discussion of Dorothea of Montau's relationship with John of Marienwerder in Elliott, *Spiritual Marriage,* pp. 262–63; and eadem, "Authorizing a Life: The Collaboration of Dorothea of Montau and John Marienwerder," in *Gendered Voices: Medieval Saints and Their Interpreters,* ed. Catherine Mooney (Philadelphia: University of Pennsylvania Press, forthcoming 1999).

85. Bernard Pez, ed., *Ven. Agnetis Blannbekin, quae sub Rudolpho Habspurgico et Alberto I. Austriacis Impp. Wiennae floruit, Vita et Revelationes auctore anonymo ord. F.F. Min. è celebri conv. S. Crucis Wiennensis* c. 39 (Vienna: Petrum Conrad Monath, 1731), pp. 40–41. On Agnes, see Peter Dinzelbacher, "Die 'Vita et Revelationes' der Wiener Begine Agnes Blannbekin (†1315) im Rahmen der Viten- und Offenbarungsliteratur ihrer Zeit," in *Frauenmystik im Mittelalter,* ed. Peter Dinzelbacher and Dieter R. Bauer (Ostfildern bei Stuttgart: Schwabenverlag, 1985), pp. 152–77.

86. Pez, *Ven. Agnetis Blannbekin . . . Vita et Revelationes* c. 37, pp. 36–37; cf. Bynum, "Female Body," in *Fragmentation and Redemption,* pp. 185–86.

87. "Sacerdos vero, quando debuit sumere corpus, respexit hinc inde in altari sic, quasi aliquid amisisset," Pez, *Ven. Agnetis Blannbekin . . . Vita et Revelationes* c. 41, pp. 43–44. The priest some years later developed epilepsy and was appropriately humbled into penance. On the female mystic's role in the discernment of clerical impurity in a eucharistic context, see Bynum, *Holy Feast and Holy Fast,* pp. 227–29.

88. Pez, *Ven. Agnetis Blannbekin . . . Vita et Revelationes* c. 37, p. 37.

89. "Et flectens genua ibi coram altari sensit mox spiritus consolationem, et illa mentis conflictatio dimisit eam. Cumque surgeret, iterum dubitare coepit, utrum esset Corpus DOMINI, an non? Et ista conflictatio mentis fuit valde poenalis. Quotienscunque autem surgeret, illa tentatio invasit eam, et cum genua flecteret, dimisit eam," ibid. c. 153, pp. 85–86.

90. "Coepit quoque haec devota cogitare de Corpore DOMINI, cum irreverenter tractatur a veneficis, utrum sit ibi et maneat Corpus DOMINI? Cui interius divina inspiratio respondit: *Si Corpus Domini—cum pedibus conculcetur, non potest ipsum pes vel calceus attingere, nec quidquam pati potest, etiamsi projiciatur in cloacum:* Quia per passionem semel factum est impassible," ibid., pp. 185–86. Cf. a parallel, but less ambiguous, scenario in which Agnes finds herself compelled to bow at the entrance of a certain cellar she frequently passed on the street, only later to learn that a witch had hidden a consecrated Host there (c. 44, pp. 47–8; see Dinzelbacher, *Heilige oder Hexen?*, p. 243).

91. See Bynum, *Holy Feast and Holy Fast,* pp. 128–29, 141, 228. Also see nn. 80, 87, above.

6. Angelic Disembodiment and Purity of Demons

1. "Cum masculo non commiscearis coitu femineo, quia abominatio est. Cum omni pecore non coibis, nec maculaberis cum eo. Mulier non succumbet jumento, nec miscebitur ei: quia scelus est. Nec polluamini in omnibus his, quibus contaminatae sunt universae gentes, quas ego ejiciam ante conspectum vestrum, Et quibus polluta est terra: cujus ego scelera visitabo, ut evomat habitatores suos. . . . Omnes enim execrationes istas fecerunt accolae terrae, qui fuerunt ante vos, et polluerunt eam," Lev. 18.22–25; 27 (my translation).

2. Lev. 18.24, marginal, ad v. *Contaminate sunt gentes vniuerse, etc.:* "Demones: qui propter multitudinem dicuntur gentes vniuerse. Qui cum omni peccato gaudeant: praecipue tamen fornicatione et idolatria: quia in his et corpus et anima maculatur: et totus homo qui terra dicitur. Sed visitauit deus terram id est hominum genus" (*Textus Biblie cum glosa ordinaria, Nicholai de Lyra postilla, moralitatibus eiusdem* [Basel: Johannes Petri et Johannes Frobenium, 1506], vol. 1, fol. 246r). This reading corresponds with the interlinear gloss while imposing some kind of order on its rather unruly exegesis. The interlinear gloss, for example, clearly associates the evil inhabitants with demons, at one point linking them with the demons that Christ sent into the herd of pigs in Matt. 8.31 (ad v. *habitores*). The relative antiquity of demons strengthens their identification with the earlier inhabitants of the land: "demons are of a very ancient condition" (interlinear, ad v. *accole:* "demones qui antiquiores sunt conditione"). And yet the gloss also links the wicked things God visited on the demonic inhabitants with the evils of pollution, hence making pollution the punishment for pollution (interlinear, ad v. *scelera*). One of the purges let loose on the evil people, moreover, is *scabrones*—a term used for unclean spirits (interlinear, ad v. *euomat*). What seems to be occurring is that the evil people of the world are simultaneously identified with earlier demonic inhabitants and with humanity's current sinfulness.

3. Lev. 18.29, marginal gloss, ad v. *omnis anima etc.*: "Qui enim post euangelicam praedicationem talia committunt: aliam mali medicinam non inueniunt: nec in sorte hominum sed demonum erunt," in *Glossa ordinaria,* vol. 1, in *Textus Biblie* fol. 246r.

4. On the Book of Enoch, see Bernard J. Bamberger, *Fallen Angels* (Philadelphia: Jewish Publication Society of America, 1952), pp. 16–35; and Norman Powell Williams, *Ideas of the Fall and of Original Sin: A Historical and Critical Study* (London: Longmans, Green, 1927), pp. 20–35. For an overview of patristic angelology, see G. Bareille, "Angélologie d'après les Pères, *DTC,* 1,1, cols. 1192–1222; E. Mangenot, "Démon d'après les Pères," ibid., 4,1, cols. 339–84; and J. Turmel, "Histoire de l'angélologie: des temps apostoliques à la fin du Ve siècle," *Revue d'Histoire et de Littérature Religieuse* 3 (1898): 289–308 (but note Mangenot's warning regarding Turmel's suspect reading of angelic interbreeding, "Démon," cols. 375–76). Also see the historical background in Edward J. Montano, *The Sin of the Angels: Aspects of the Teaching of St. Thomas* (Washington, D.C.: Catholic University of America Press, 1955), pp. 1–47. Palémon Glorieux has collected key passages on angelic bodies ranging from scripture to Aquinas, with the greatest emphasis on the patristic period, in *Autour de la spiritualité des anges* (Tournai: Desclée, 1959).

5. Augustine touched on the question of angelic and demonic bodies frequently. See especially *De Genesi ad litteram libri duodecim* 3.10, where he says, "demons are living beings inhabiting the air" ("daemones aeria sunt animalia"), whose composition makes them susceptible to suffering from the other elements, especially fire. He tentatively describes a mutation in their originally celestial bodies and their punishment as follows: "Now, if the rebel angels before their fall had bodies of a celestial nature, there is no cause for wonder if these bodies in punishment were changed into the element of air so that they might undergo suffering from the element of fire, which is an element of a superior nature. They were then permitted to occupy not the pure realm of air above but this misty air near earth, and this is a sort of prison house for them, in keeping with their nature, until the day of judgment" ("Si autem transgressores illi, antequam transgrederentur, caelestia corpora gerebant, neque hoc mirum est, si conuersa sunt ex poena in aeriam qualitatem, ut iam possint ab igne, id est ab elemento naturae superioris aliquid pati; nec aeris saltem spatia superiora atque puriora, sed ista caliginosa tenere permissa sunt, qui eis pro suo genere quidam quasi carcer est usque ad tempus iudicii," ed. Joseph Zycha, *CSEL,* 28,1 [Vienna: F. Tempsky; Leipzig: G. Freytag, 1894], pp. 72, 74; trans. John Hammond Taylor, *The Literal Meaning of Genesis, ACW,* no. 41 [New York: Newman Press, 1982], 1: 83, 84). Cf. his letter to Nebridius, which describes the angels and demons who invade our bodies and affect our thoughts and dreams as aerial or ethereal beings ("aeriis aetheriisue animantibus") and who in aerial or ethereal bodies ("aerio uel aetherio corpore") act on our bodies (Ep. 9, *Epistolae,* ed. A. Goldbacher, *CSEL,* 34, 1 [Vienna: F. Tempsky; Leipzig: G. Freytag, 1895], p. 21. This letter is translated by Wilfrid Parsons, *Letters, FC,* vol. 12 [New York: Fathers of the Church, 1951], pp. 21–23. The pertinent parts are not particularly literal, however). Also see *Contra academicos* 1.7.20 (ed. W. M. Green, *CCSL,* 29 [Turnhout: Brepols, 1970], p. 14; trans. Denis J. Kavanagh, *Answer to Skeptics, FC,* vol. 5 [New York: Cima Publishing, 1942], p. 127). In *De civitate dei* 8.15, he again states that demons inhabit the air (ed. Bernardus Dombart and Alphonsus Kalb, *CCSL,* 47

[Turnhout: Brepols, 1955], p. 232; trans. Gerald G. Walsh et al., *City of God, FC,* vol. 14 [New York: Fathers of the Church, 1952], p. 48). At a later place in the same work, the demonic body is adduced from the sufferings the demons experience in hell, which would be less plausible without bodies: "It may be, as scholars have speculated, that the demons have bodies of their own, composed of the kind of dense moist air which we feel, by impact, when the wind is blowing" ("Nisi quia sunt quaedam sua etiam daemonibus corpora, sicut doctis hominibus uisum est, ex isto aere crasso atque umido, cuius inpulsus uento flante sentitur"). Although acknowledging the possibility that demons have no bodies, he nevertheless argues that they would still feel these fires in some way (*De civitate dei* 21.10, ed. Dombart and Kalb, *CCSL,* 48, p. 776; trans. Walsh, *City of God, FC,* vol. 24, p. 366). Augustine also uses the angelic body as a possible model for what we can expect from our glorified bodies after the resurrection (*De civitate dei* 22.29, ed. Dombart and Kalb, *CCSL,* 48, pp. 856–57, trans. Walsh, *City of God, FC,* vol. 24, pp. 496–97; *De diversis quaestionibus octoginta tribus* c. 47, ed. Almut Mutzenbecher, *CCSL,* 44a [Turnhout: Brepols, 1975], p. 74; trans. David L. Mosher, *Eighty-Three Different Questions, FC,* vol. 70 [Washington, D.C.: Catholic University Press, 1982], p. 82; and Serm. 277, in which he discusses the astonishing speed of the "corpus angelicum" in this context [c. 9, *PL* 38, col. 1262]). In his *Retractiones* 1.25, Augustine conditions that angelic bodies—which are "very lucid and ethereal" ("lucidissima atque aetheria")—should not be confused with flesh (ed. P. Knöll, *CSEL,* 36, 2 [Vienna: F. Tempsky; Leipzig: G. Freytag, 1902], p. 121; trans. Mary Inez Bogan, *The Retractions, FC,* vol. 60 [Washington, D.C.: Catholic University of America Press, 1968], p. 110).

6. See Chap. 2, pp. 52–53, above.

7. "Praesertim constet eos libidinum sordibus admodum delectari, quas procul dubio per semet ipsos exercere quam per homines mallent, si id ullo modo posset impleri," Cassian, *Conférences* 8.21, ed. E. Pichery, *SC,* no. 54 (Paris: Editions du Cerf, 1958), 2:28. For the way demons interact with humans in Cassian, see Philip Rousseau, "Cassian, Contemplation, and the Coenobitic Life," *Journal of Ecclesiastical History* 26 (1975): 120. Cassian likewise preserves pure incorporeality for God, who alone can penetrate all spiritual and intellectual substances—i.e., souls and angels (*Conférences* 7.13, ed. Pichery, *SC,* no. 42, 1: 257).

8. "Confidant sibi angelorum exempla conducere. nos iam non ualent flectere, qui nouimus et angelos cum feminis cecidisse," Ps.-Cyprian, *De singularitate clericorum, CSEL,* 3, 3, ed. G. Hartel (Vienna: C. Geroldi Filium Bibliopolam Academiae, 1871), p. 204. This practice of same-sex, chaste cohabitation was condemned at the Council of Nicaea in 325 (Nicaea I, c. 3, in Norman P. Tanner et al., ed. and trans., *Decrees of the Ecumenical Councils,* original text established by G. Alberigo et al. (London: Sheed and Ward; Washington, D.C.: Georgetown University Press, 1990), 1: 7. For the struggle against syneisaktism, which continued after this condemnation, see Elizabeth A. Clark, "John Chrysostom and the *Subintroductae,*" *Church History* 46 (1977): 171–85; and Dyan Elliott, *Spiritual Marriage: Sexual Abstinence in Medieval Wedlock* (Princeton, N.J.: Princeton University Press, 1993), pp. 32–38.

9. See the Introduction, above, for Nicholas of Lyre's reading. Also see Chap. 2, nn. 85, 100.

10. "But one had the covering of flesh, the other carried no weakness from the

flesh. For the Angel is spirit alone, but a human is spirit and flesh" ("Sed una tegmen carnis habuit, alia uero nil infirmum de carne gestauit. Angelus namque solummodo spiritus, homo uero est spiritus et caro"), Gregory the Great, *Moralia in Iob* 4.3.4, ed. Marcus Adriaen, *CCSL,* 143 (Turnhout: Brepols, 1979), p. 168. "Therefore he [God] was mindful that they [the transgressing angels] were robust because, since they were created without any infirmity of the flesh, an attached weakness did not hinder their depraved exertions" ("Quos idcirco robustos memorat quia dum absque carnis infirmitate sunt conditi, prauis eorum adnisibus imbecillitas adiuncta non obuiat," 7.34.50, p. 371).

11. "Sicut et ipsi illorum spiritus comparatione quidem nostrorum corporum, spiritus sunt sed comparatione summi et incircumscripti spiritus, corpus," ibid., 2.3.3, p. 61.

12. "Lapsi vero in aeream qualitatem conversi sunt," Isidore of Seville, *Etymologiae* 8.11.17, *PL* 82, col. 316. Cf. "Lapsi vero in aethercam qualitatem conversi sunt," Hrabanus Maurus, *De universo* 22.6, *PL* 111, col. 427.

13. On demonology in the high Middle Ages, see Jeffrey Burton Russell, *Lucifer: The Devil in the Middle Ages* (Ithaca, N.Y.: Cornell University Press, 1984), pp. 159–207; James, *Fallen Angels,* pp. 201–8; T. Ortolan, "Démon d'après les scolastiques et les théologiens postérieurs," *DTC,* 4.1, cols. 384–407; A. Vacant, "Angélologie dans l'église latine depuis le temps des Pères jusqu'à saint Thomas d'Aquin," *DTC,* 1,1, cols. 1222–28; and idem, "Angélologie de saint Thomas d'Aquin et des scolastiques postérieurs," *DTC,* 1,1, cols. 1228–48.

14. "Utrum angeli omnes corporei sint: quod quibusdam visum est, quibus Augustinus consentire videtur, dicens omnes angelos ante casum habuisse corpora tenuia et spiritualia, sed in casu mutata in deterius malorum corpora ut in eis possent pati," Peter Lombard, *Sententiae in IV libris distinctae* bk. 2, dist. 8, c. 1,1, ed. Fathers of the College of St. Bonaventure ad Claras Aquas, 3d ed. (Rome: College of St. Bonaventure, 1971), 1,2: 365.

15. Ibid., bk. 2, dist. 8, c. 1,1; 1,2: 365–66.

16. "Daemones aëria dicuntur animalia," ibid. bk. 2, dist. 8, c. 1,3; 1,2: 366. See 1,2: 366, n. 1, and 1,2: 367, n. 1. Cf. Augustine, *De Genesi ad litteram libri duodecim* 3.10, cited above in n. 5; and *Glossa ordinaria,* Gen. 1.20, marginal, ad v. *sub firmamento,* in *Textus Biblie,* vol. 1, fol. 27r.

17. "Quibusdam videtur Augustinus illud non ita sentiendo dixisse, sed opinionem referendo," Peter Lombard, *Sententiae* bk. 2, dist. 8, c. 1,3; 1,2: 367.

18. "Dicunt quoque plurimos catholicos tractatores in hoc convenisse atque id concorditer docuisse, quod angeli incorporei sunt, nec corpora habent sibi unita; assumunt autem aliquando corpora, Deo praeparante, ad impletionem ministerii sibi a Deo iniuncti, eademque post expletionem deponunt," ibid. bk. 2, dist. 8, c. 1,3; 1,2: 367.

19. Ibid. bk. 2, dist. 8, c. 2,1; 1,2: 367. Cf. Augustine, *De Trinitate* 2.7–18, 3.11.

20. "'Utrum in illis corporalibus apparitionibus creatura aliqua crearetur ad illud opus tantum, in qua Deus hominibus appareret; an angeli qui ante erant ita mitterentur, ut manentes in suis spiritalibus corporibus, assumerent ex corpulenta inferiorum elementorum materia aliquam speciem corporalem, quam coaptatam quasi aliquam vestem mutarent in quaslibet species corporales, veras quidem; an

corpus suum proprium verterent in species aptas actionibus suis per virtutem sibi a Deo datum.'" Peter Lombard, *Sententiae* bk. 2, dist. 8, c. 3,2; 1,2: 367–68; citing Augustine, *De Trinitate* 2.7.13. Peter's next chapter continues in the same vein, extending these questions through his citation of Augustine (bk. 2, dist. 8, c. 3,3; 1,2: 368; see Augustine, *De Trinitate,* proemium, nn. 3–4).

21. Peter Lombard, *Sententiae* bk. 2, dist. 8, c. 2,4; 1,2: 368. In this article, Peter continues to follow Augustine's *De Trinitate,* proemium, n. 5.

22. "In quibus verbis videtur Augustinus attestari angelos esse corporeos, ac propria et spiritalia habere corpora," Peter Lombard, *Sententiae* bk. 2, dist. 8, c. 2,5; 1,2: 368.

23. "Because all that is is one and simple and undivided and immaterial," Hugh of St. Victor, *De sacramentis Christianae fidei* 1.5.7, *PL* 176, col. 249; trans. Roy J. Deferrari, *On the Sacraments of the Christian Faith* (Cambridge, Mass.: Medieval Academy of America, 1951), p. 78; "If anyone, therefore, should ask of what character spiritual nature was made or founded in its beginning, these are the four things which we have proposed and have said were attributed to the angels at their foundation, namely: first, a simple and immaterial substance; second, distinction of person; third, a rational form of wisdom and understanding; but fourth, the free power of inclining their will and choice either to good or to evil," *De sacramentis* 1.5.8, *PL* 176, col. 250; trans. Deferrari, *On the Sacraments,* p. 78. The anonymous author of the *Summa sententiarum* makes similar points: "In the first condition there seem to be three attributes; an indivisible and immaterial essence, and therefore not lacking naturally in innate reason; a spiritual intelligence; and also free judgment by which it was able to be turned without violence to anything it chose by its own will" ("In prima conditionne [sic] tria videntur esse attributa; essentia indivisibilis et immaterialis, et ideo indeficiens per rationem naturaliter insitam; intelligentia spiritualis; liberum quo que arbitrium quo poterat sine violentia ad utrumlibet propria voluntate deflecti," 2.2, *PL* 176, col. 81). Marcel Chossat argues that this work, which had wrongfully been attributed to Hugh of St. Victor, was the creation of Hugh of Mortagne, writing ca. 1155. See *La Somme des sentences: oeuvre de Hughes de Mortagne,* Spicilegium Sacrum Lovaniense, Etudes et Documents, fasc. 5 (Louvain: Spicilegium Sacrum Lovaniense; Paris: Honoré Champion, 1923), esp. pp. 63–90, 171–79.

24. Rupert of Deutz, *De sancta Trinitate et operibus eius* 1.10, ed. Hraban Haacke, *CCCM,* 21 (Turnhout: Brepols, 1971), p. 138; cf. 9.21, *CCCM,* 24, p. 2123. On Rupert's life and works, see John Van Engen's *Rupert of Deutz* (Berkeley: University of California Press, 1983), esp. pp. 216–18 regarding angels.

25. "Verum pars eiusdem creaturae vero lumini Deo per humilitatem subiecta meruit fieri uel permanere lux per gratiam ejus, diabolus autem et angeli eius, quia rebelles exstiterunt, ab illa gratia exciderunt, factique sunt tenebrae, et non lux," Rupert of Deutz, *De sancta Trinitate et operibus eius,* 9.21, ed. Haacke, *CCCM,* 24, pp. 2122–23; cf. ibid. 1.9, ed. Haacke, *CCCM,* 21, pp. 136–37; and idem, *De victoria verbi Dei* 1.27, ed. Hraban Haacke, *MGH, Die deutschen Geschichtsquellen des Mittelalters,* 5 (Weimar: Hermann Böhlaus, 1970), p. 41. For Augustine's view that the creation of the angels corresponded to the words "Fiat lux," see *De Genesi ad litteram libri duodecim* 1.9, 4.32, ed. Zycha, *CSEL,* 28,1, pp. 11–13, 129–31; trans. Taylor, *The*

Literal Meaning of Genesis, 1: 27–29, 139–41. This was a widely adopted opinion. Cf. Isidore of Seville, *Sententiae* 1.3, *PL* 83, col. 554; and *Glossa ordinaria,* Gen. 1.3, marginal, ad v. *Fiat lux,* in *Textus Biblie,* vol. 1, fol. 24r.

26. "Quod si quaeritur, unde sint facti, qui tam gloriosi sunt et splendidi, responderi utcumque potest, quod de aeris substantia facti sunt. Habent enim, et a doctoribus tacitum non est eos habere, corpora aeria, quae tamen in sanctis angelis feliciter immutata sunt, ut dicantur et sint corpora caelestia. Porro apostatae angeli ab illa felicitate lapsi rursus in aeriam qualitatem conversi sunt, nec aeris illius puriora spatia, sed caliginosa ista tenere sunt permissi, qui eis quasi carcer est usque ad diem judicii," *De victoria verbi Dei* 1.28, ed. Haacke, p. 42. This passage in particular is heavily indebted to Augustine's *De Genesi ad litteram libri duodecim.* See n. 5, above.

27. Rupert of Deutz, *De victoria verbi Dei* 1.28, ed. Haacke, pp. 42–43.

28. "Quod Deus, et animae, et angeli, non habeant corpora, sicut justitia, et sapientia, et quod sola mente videantur," Honorius Augustodunensis, *Liber duodecim quaestionum* c. 9, *PL* 172, col. 1182. Little is known about Honorius. According to Valerie Flint, the *Liber duodecim quaestionum* and the *Libellus octo quaestionum* were early works—before the *Elucidarium,* which was probably written prior to 1100. The belief in angelic bodies also holds true for Honorius's later *Clavis physicae,* which was written after 1120. See Paolo Lucentini's edition, Temi e Testi, 21 (Rome: Edizione de Storia e Letteratura, 1974), c. 92, p. 67. Honorius maintained this view in spite of the spiritualizing influence of John Scotus Eriugena, which, as Caroline Walker Bynum notes, had the effect of altering Honorius's earlier thought—particularly his very corporeal view of the resurrection of the body. See Bynum, *The Resurrection of the Body in Western Christianity, 200–1336* (New York: Columbia University Press, 1995), pp. 146–50. For dating, see Valerie Flint, "The Chronology of the Works of Honorius Augustodunensis," *Revue Benedictine* 82 (1972): 215–42; rprt. in *Ideas in the Medieval West: Texts and Their Contexts* (London: Variorum Reprints, 1988).

29. "Sicut homines possunt sua corpora decolorare, videlicet dealbare, et denigrare aut aliqua veste contegere: ita possunt daemones sua corpora in varias formas transfigurare, aut splendida ad decipiendum, aut tetra ad terrendum demonstrare," Honorius Augustodunensis, *Liber duodecim quaestionum* c. 11, *PL* 172, col. 1183.

30. Honorius Augustodunensis, *Liber duodecium quaestionum* c. 11, *PL* 172, col. 1183.

31. "Spiritum de corpore creari dicere insani capitis est, corpus vero de corporibus vel de elementis dicere creari assertio veritatis est. Angelici spiritus, et humanae animae, et informis materia mundi ex nihilo creata sunt. . . . Corpora vero omnia ex quatuor elementis formata sunt, scilicet unumquodque corpus illi elemento specialiter attribuitur, quod in eo plus abundat. . . . Corpora autem angelicorum spirituum sunt ignea, dicente Scriptura: *Qui facit angelos suos spiritus, et ministros suos flammam ignis;* quod est dicere, angelicos spiritus ex nihilo fecit Deus; corpora vero eorum ex igne creavit. De quorum creatione dicit Scriptura: *Dixit Deus: Fiat lux.* . . . Sicut enim rationalis anima corpore vestita dicitur homo, ita intellectualis Spiritus corpore vestitus dicitur angelus. Angeli non alienis corporibus, sed in propriis olim apparuerunt hominibus, quibus locuti sunt," Honorius

Augustodunensis, *Libellus octo quaestionum: de angelis et homine* c. 3, *PL* 172, cols. 1188–89. Honorius's position introduces the possibility of a lag between the dual creation of spirit and body—one that he neither acknowledges nor attempts to fill, merely commenting that Genesis says nothing about the creation of spirits, as it is more usual to report visible things than invisible (col. 1189). Cf. his similar emphasis on the words "Let there be light," in *Liber duodecim quaestionum* c. 11, *PL* 172, col. 1183, and *L'Elucidarium et les Lucidaires* 1.27, ed. Yves Lèfevre (Paris: E. de Boccard, 1954), p. 36. Also see Lèfevre's commentary on the angelic doctrine in the *Elucidarium*, pp. 110–14.

32. *Glossa ordinaria*, Gen. 1.20, marginal, ad v. *sub firmamento*, in *Textus Biblie*, vol. 1, fol. 27r. The passage is from Augustine's *De Genesi ad litteram libri duodecim* 3.10, cited above in n. 5, where Augustine likewise introduces demons in the context of their habitat.

33. C. 26 q. 3 and 4 c. 2. The passage ultimately originates with Augustine's *De divinatione demonum* c. 3. But Gratian's editor, Friedberg, notes that Gratian derived the text via Hrabanus Maurus's *De magicis artibus* (*PL* 110, cols. 1101–2). It was also used by Ivo of Chartres (*Panormia* 8.68, *PL* 161, col. 1322).

34. "Ad praedictorum intelligentiam notandum est, quod circa istam quaestionem dubitaverunt aliquando magni doctores, utrum scilicet Angeli habeant corpora naturaliter sibi unita; unde super hoc dubie loquitur tam Augustinus quam Bernardus. Sed nunc satis certitudinaliter tenetur, et Richardus affirmat, quod *Angeli* sunt naturaliter incorporei, nec habeant corpora naturaliter sibi unita," Bonaventure, *Commentaria in quatuor libros sententiarum* bk. 2, dist. 8, pt. 1, art. 1, q. 1, resp., in *Opera omnia*, ed. Fathers of the College of St. Bonaventure ad Claras Aquas (Florence: College of St. Bonaventure, 1885), 2: 211. For Bernard of Clairvaux's views, see *Sermones super cantica canticorum* 5.2, ed. Jean Leclercq et al., *SC*, no. 414 (Paris: Editions du Cerf, 1990), pp. 124–25. For Richard of St. Victor, see *De Trinitate* 4.25, ed. Gaston Salet, *SC*, no. 63 (Paris: Editions du Cerf, 1959), pp. 288–91.

35. Bonaventure, *Commentaria in quatuor libros sententiarum* bk. 2, dist. 8, pt. 1, art. 1, q. 1, resp. ad oppositum 1 and 2, in *Opera omnia*, 2: 211.

36. Ibid. bk. 2, dist. 8, pt. 1, art. 1, q. 1, ad oppositum 3 and 4, resp. ad oppositum 3 and 4, 2: 210, 211. On the angel's assumed body as a response to humanity's need, also see bk. 2, dist. 8, pt. 1, q. 1, art. 2, q. 2, resp. ad oppositum 1, 2: 218.

37. Ibid. bk. 2, dist. 8, pt. 1, art. 2, q. 2, ad oppositum 1–6, 2: 217. Note that no. 6 debunks the idea of angels assuming celestial bodies, pointing out that demons also have assumed bodies but would be incapable of climbing to the heavens to don their borrowed bodies.

38. Ibid. bk. 2, dist. 8, pt. 1, art. 2, q. 2, resp., 2: 217.

39. Ibid.

40. Ibid., 2: 218.

41. Ibid. bk. 2, dist. 8, pt. 1, art. 2, q. 2, resp. ad oppositum 6, 2: 218.

42. Ibid. bk. 2, dist. 3, pt. 1, art. 1, q. 1, resp., 2: 90–91. Others scholars also maintained this distinction. See, for example, Alexander of Hales, *Quaestiones disputatae "antequam esset frater,"* ed. Fathers of the College of St. Bonaventure, Bibliotheca Franciscana Scholastica Medii Aevi, 21 (Florence: College of St. Bonaventure, 1960), app. 2, q. 1, resp. ad obj., 14, 3: 1457. Augustine implies the existence of

spiritual matter in *De Genesi ad litteram libri duodecim* 1.1 (ed. Zycha, *CSEL,* 28,1, pp. 4–5; trans. Taylor, *The Literal Meaning of Genesis,* 1: 20), as Alexander himself notes. For a full exposition of this slippery distinction, see the editor's note in Bonaventure's *Commentaria in quatuor libros sententiarum,* 2: 92–94.

43. Aquinas's output on angels was nothing short of astonishing; he often returned to the subject of angelic bodies in the course of his various works. See particularly his *Commentum in quatuor libros sententiarum,* written between 1252 and 1256 (bk. 2, dist. 8, q. un., arts. 1–3, in *Opera omnia* [Parma: Petrus Fiaccadori, 1856; rprt. New York: Musurgia, 1950], 6: 453–57); *Summa theologiae,* written between 1265 and 1273, though the *prima pars* was completed by 1268 (1a, q. 50, arts. 1–2; q. 51, arts. 1–3, ed. and trans. Fathers of the English Dominican Province [London: Blackfriars, 1968], 9: 5–17; 31–43; this edition is a face-to-face translation); *De potentia,* written between 1265 and 1266 (q. 6, arts. 6–8, in *Opera omnia,* Parma edition, 8: 134–42, trans. English Dominican Fathers, *On the Power of God,* 3 vols. in 1 [Westminster, Md.: Newman Press, 1952]); *De spiritualibus creaturis,* written between 1267 and 1268 (art. 5, Parma edition, 8: 441–44, trans. Mary C. Fitzpatrick and John J. Wellmuth, *On Spiritual Creatures* [Milwaukee: Milwaukee University Press, 1949]); and *De malo,* written between 1268 and 1269 (q. 16, art. 1, in *Opera omnia,* Parma edition, 8: 388–92, trans. Jean T. Oesterle, *On Evil* [Notre Dame, Ind.: University of Notre Dame Press, 1995], pp. 441–52). I am relying on James A. Weisheipl's chronology in *Friar Thomas d'Aquino: His Life, Thought, and Works* (New York: Doubleday, 1974), pp. 355ff.

In his rejection of demonic corporeality, however, Thomas is clearly indebted to his teacher, Albert the Great, and employs many of the same authorities. See especially Albert's *Commentarii in II sententiarum* bk. 2, dist. 8, art. 1, in *Opera omnia,* ed. A. Borgnet (Paris: Vivès, 1894), 27: 166–72. Although he argues vigorously against corporeality, Albert does leave the door open for a kind of spiritual matter (albeit one that is likened to form) by the very way in which he poses the question of whether all spiritual and corporeal things are of the same matter—a question that is naturally resolved in the negative (bk. 2, dist. 2, art. 2, 27: 47–48). Both Albert and Thomas cite Dionysius the Pseudo-Areopagite (fl. 500) with approval at the turning point in their arguments when they refute the angelic body. Dionysius was an eastern mystical writer (hence, untrammeled by the authority of Augustine) who had argued forcefully that angels were spiritual and incorporeal intelligences (see his *De divinis nominibus* 4.1, *PG* 3, col. 693). Writers such as Hugh and Richard of St. Victor, who were both deeply influenced by the Pseudo-Dionysius, opt for unmitigated angelic incorporeality.

44. Thomas was helped by the fact that many of the authorities he used were Greek and Arab philosophers, who did not require such gentle treatment as his coreligionists. With patristic authors, Thomas was careful to point out when a past authority was simply citing a classical source or speaking metaphorically as opposed to literally. In his *Commentum in quatuor libros sententiarum,* for example, Thomas notes that Augustine was citing Apuleius in *De civitate dei* 7.16 and not expressing his own opinion "because he wanted to assert few things about angels" ("quia pauca de Angelis asserere voluit"; bk. 2, dist. 8, q. un., art. 1, resp. ad obj. 1, in *Opera omnia,* Parma edition, 6: 454). Cf. *De potentia,* where he points out that in *De civitate dei* 21.10, Augustine was simply expressing the views of the Platonists and not his

own. Likewise, when Gregory the Great referred to an angel as an animal, Thomas notes that he was speaking in the general sense of anything living (q. 6, art. 6, resp. ad obj. 1, in *Opera omnia,* Parma edition, 8: 137; trans. English Dominican Fathers, *On the Power of God,* 2: 198). But Thomas is also prepared to state explicitly when the authorities were wrong: "The early philosophers went wrong here, because they did not grasp the power of intelligence, and so failed to distinguish between sensation and understanding. They thought that nothing existed except what could be sensed or imagined" (*Summa theologiae* 1a, q. 50, resp., 9: 6, 7).

45. Aquinas, *Summa theologiae* 1a, q. 50, art. 2, resp., 9:10, 11; also see *De spiritualibus creaturis* art. 5, resp. ad obj. 10, in *Opera omnia,* Parma edition, 8: 444, trans. Fitzpatrick and Wellmuth, *On Spiritual Creatures,* p. 72; and *Commentum in quatuor libros sententiarum* bk. 2, dist. 3, q. 1, art. 1, solutio, in *Opera omnia,* Parma edition, 6: 411–12. See James Collins, *The Thomistic Philosophy of the Angels* (Washington, D.C.: Catholic University of America Press, 1947), esp. pp. 42–74.

46. Aquinas, *Summa theologiae* 1a, q. 51, art. 2, resp. ad obj. 1 and 3, 9: 36, 37; also see *Commentum in quatuor libros sententiarum* bk. 2, dist. 8, q. 1, art. 3, solutio, in *Opera omnia,* Parma edition, 6: 455.

47. See *Summa theologiae* 1a, q. 50, art. 1, resp. ad obj. 1, 9: 6–7; and *De spiritualibus creaturis* art. 5, resp., in *Opera omnia,* Parma edition, 8: 443, trans. Fitzpatrick and Wellmuth, *On Spiritual Creatures,* p. 69. Also see the quotation in the following note.

48. "There must be some incorporeal creatures, because what God chiefly intends in creation is to produce a goodness consisting in a likeness to himself. . . . God causes by his intellect and will . . . whence it follows that the universe would be incomplete without intellectual creatures. And since intellection cannot be the act of a body or of bodily energies—body as such being limited to the here and now—it follows that a complete universe must contain some incorporeal creature," Aquinas, *Summa theologiae* 1a, q. 50, art. 1, resp., 9: 4–7. Cf. *De spiritualibus creaturis* art. 5, resp., in *Opera omnia,* Parma edition, 8: 443; trans. Fitzpatrick and Wellmuth, *On Spiritual Creatures,* p. 70.

49. "Now an intelligible good must be incorporeal, since were it not devoid of matter it could not be an object of intelligence: wherefore it must needs be intelligent, seeing that a substance is intelligent through being free of matter," Aquinas, *De potentia* q. 6, art. 6, resp., in *Opera omnia,* Parma edition, 8: 136; trans. English Dominican Fathers, *On the Power of God,* 2: 194. "If a spiritual substance has no other powers besides intellect and will, it were useless for it to be united to a body, since these operations are performed independently of the body," *De potentia* q. 6, art. 6, resp. in *Opera omnia,* Parma edition, 8: 136; trans. English Dominican Fathers, *On the Power of God,* 2: 196. Cf. *De malo* q. 16, art. 1, resp. ad obj. 14, in *Opera omnia,* Parma edition, 8: 391; trans. Oesterle, *On Evil,* pp. 450–51.

50. This is not to say that others in the high Middle Ages had not described angels as intellectual beings prior to Thomas. Intelligence was an essential attribute of the angelic nature for Hugh of St. Victor and especially for the anonymous author of the *Summa sententiae,* both of whom were influenced by the Pseudo-Dionysius. See n. 43, above.

51. For a summary of authoritative views, see Peter Lombard, *Sententiae* bk. 2, dist. 5, c. 6; bk. 2, dist. 7, c. 1–2; 1, 2: 351, 359–60. The major exception here would

be Origen, who, as Thomas notes, was said to have argued that everything with free will can turn to evil and good, and this pertains to angels as well (*Summa theologiae* 1a, q. 64, art. 2, resp., 9: 288, 289; cf. *De malo* q. 16, art. 5, resp., in *Opera omnia,* Parma edition, 8: 404; trans. Oesterle, *On Evil,* pp. 483–84, and n. 84, below). On Origen's views, see nn. 67, 92, 105, below.

52. Aquinas, *Summa theologiae* 1a, q. 64, art. 2, resp. ad obj. 1–3, 9: 291; *De malo* q. 16, art. 5, resp. ad obj. 4 and 6, in *Opera omnia,* Parma edition, 8: 405–6, trans. Oesterle, *On Evil,* p. 486. See Montano, *Sin of the Angels,* pp. 89–93, 235–36. By the same token, angels cannot sin venially. See the discussion of this question by Thomas, who argues that the angelic intelligence is not discursive as is humanity's, the latter making a gradual transition from principles to solutions (*Summa theologiae* 1a 2ae, q. 89, art. 2, resp., 27: 86, 87). Also see Jacques Maritain, "Le Péché de l'Ange: essai de ré-interpretation des positions Thomistes," *Revue Thomiste* 64 (1956): 226, and Montano, *Sin of the Angels,* pp. 160–64.

53. "Nevertheless the devil is not ignorant of the interminability of his punishment. For this would lessen his misery; indeed just as certainty about the continual duration of glory pertains to the increase of the happiness of the blessed, so the certainty of unending misery pertains to the increase of the misery of the damned," Aquinas, *De malo* q. 16, art. 6, resp. ad obj. 1, in *Opera omnia,* Parma edition, 8: 408; trans. Oesterle, *On Evil,* p. 494. Cf. *Summa theologiae* 1a, q. 64, art. 1, resp., 9: 282, 283. See Montano, *Sin of the Angels,* pp. 295–331. Note, however, that this view would later be contested by others, particularly Duns Scotus (d. 1308), who was prepared to grant the devil some capacity to will good (although this capacity was ultimately dubious). Furthermore, Scotus did not think that the devil's will was necessarily irrevocably evil (see Montano, *Sin of the Angels,* pp. 286–87, 316–17, n. 138). By the same token, Scotus undermined the confirmation of the good angels. See D. E. Sharp, *Franciscan Philosophy at Oxford in the Thirteenth Century* (New York: Russell and Russell, 1964), pp. 349–50.

54. Aquinas, *Summa theologiae* 1a, q. 63, art. 2, ad obj. 1, 9: 250, 251.

55. Ibid. 1a, q. 63, art. 2, resp. ad obj. 1, 9: 252, 253.

56. Ibid. 1a, q. 63, art. 2, resp. ad obj. 3, 9: 254–55. Cf. *De potentia* q. 6, art. 6, resp. ad obj. 3, in *Opera omnia,* Parma edition, 8: 137, trans. English Dominican Fathers, *On the Power of God,* 2: 198–99; and *De malo* q. 16, art. 1, resp. ad obj. 3, in *Opera omnia,* Parma edition, 8: 391, trans. Oesterle, *On Evil,* p. 449.

57. See R. E. Marieb, "The Impeccability of the Angels regarding Their Natural End," *The Thomist* 28 (1964): 471–73.

58. See Gregory the Great's discussion of the angel as *signaculum* with respect to the passage in Ezech. 28.12 (*Homiliae XL in Evangelia,* bk. 2, hom. 34, c. 7, *PL* 76, col. 1250); cf. Isidore of Seville, *Sententiae* 1.10.6, *PL* 83, col. 555.

59. For humanity's role in completing the number of the angels, in fulfillment of Luke 20.36, see Augustine, *Enchiridion* 9.29, ed. E. Evans, *CCSL,* 46 (Turnhout: Brepols, 1969), p. 65, trans. Bernard M. Peebles, *Faith, Hope, and Charity, FC,* vol. 2 (New York: Cima, 1947), p. 394; and *De civitate dei* 22.1, ed. Dombart and Kalb, *CCSL,* 48, p. 807, trans. Walsh, *City of God, FC,* vol. 24, p. 417. Some writers, such as Gregory the Great, came very near to presenting the creation of humanity as something of an afterthought contingent on Lucifer's fall. Thus, when interpreting the story of the woman who lost one of her ten coins (Luke 15.8–10), he posits: "But so

that the number of the elect would be complete, humanity was created tenth" ("Sed ut compleretur electorum numerus, homo decimus est creatus," *Homiliae XL in Evangelia* bk. 2, hom. 34, c. 6, *PL* 76, col. 1249). For a contestation of this view, see Rupert of Deutz, *De glorificatione trinitatis et processione sancti spiritus* 3.20, *PL* 169, cols. 71–72 (Rupert mentions Gregory explicitly); Honorius Augustodunensis, *Liber duodecim quaestionum* c. 3, 5, *PL* 172, cols. 1179–80, 1180–81; and idem, *Libellus octo quaestionum: de angelis et homine* c. 1, *PL* 172, col. 1185. Also see Hugh of St. Victor, *De sacramentis* 1.5.30, *PL* 176, col. 260, trans. Deferrari, *On the Sacraments,* p. 91; and the anonymous *Summa sententiarum* 2.5, *PL* 176, col. 87.

60. "Centrum est dignius quam circulus: centrum enim immobile figitur, circulus vero mobilis volvitur. Terra enim centrum elementorum est fixa et stabilis: ignis est ut circulus motus instabilis. Et licet omnia elementa in dignitate conditionis sint aequalia; tamen in figuris secundum naturam centrum habet primatum. Terra est centrum mundi. . . . Duas rationales creaturas Deus incorporavit de primo et summo elemento, hominem de terra in seipso deificandum, angelum de igne in coelo glorificandum," Honorius Augustodunensis, *Libellus octo quaestionum: de angelis et homine* c. 4, *PL* 172, 1189–90.

61. "De quatuor elementis: unde et microcosmus, id est minor mundus dicitur," Honorius Augustodunensis, *Elucidiarium* 1.57, ed. Lèfevre, p. 371; cf. the optimistic rubric "All is for and in man" ("Totus propter hominem et in homine," *Clavis physicae* c. 261, ed. Lucentini, p. 212). On the theme of humanity as microcosm, see M.-D. Chenu, *Nature, Man, and Society in the Twelfth Century: Essays on New Theological Perspectives in the Latin West,* trans. Jerome Taylor and Lester K. Little (Chicago: University of Chicago Press, 1968), pp. 24–37, esp. p. 29.

62. Honorius Augustodunensis, *Clavis physicae* c. 99, ed. Lucentini, p. 71.

63. "Illic aeterna resurrectione beatificatus secundum corpus autem uescetur si uult omni ligno pulchro et suauissimo, non pro necessitate sed pro magna et ineffabili uoluptate," *De sancta Trinitate et operibus suis* 2.26, ed. Haacke, *CCCM,* 21, p. 214.

64. Despite the undeniably innovative nature of this work, R. W. Southern points out that the emphasis on God's deserts and honor is intensely feudal. He thus describes it as on the brink of a great transformation. See *Saint Anselm and His Biographer: A Study of Monastic Life and Thought* (Cambridge: Cambridge University Press, 1963), pp. 97–113.

65. See particularly Caroline Walker Bynum's *Holy Feast and Holy Fast: The Religious Significance of Food to Medieval Women* (Berkeley: University of California Press, 1987), esp. pp. 251–59; eadem, "The Female Body and Religious Practice in the Later Middle Ages," in *Fragmentation and Redemption: Essays on Gender and the Human Body in Medieval Religion* (New York: Zone Books, 1991), pp. 181–238, 365–93. Also note Bynum's discussion of the physicality of twelfth-century theologians in *Resurrection of the Body,* pp. 117–35. She notes, however, that this trend began to decline in the mid-thirteenth century. On the rise of the penitential movement, see André Vauchez, *La Sainteté en Occident aux derniers siècles du moyen âge d'après les procès de canonisation et les documents hagiographiques* (Rome: Ecole Française de Rome, 1981), pp. 410–12, 431–35; and idem, *The Laity in the Middle Ages: Religious Beliefs and Devotional Practices,* ed. Daniel Bornstein, trans. Margery Schneider (Notre Dame, Ind.: University of Notre Dame Press, 1993), pp. 119–27.

66. See Lateran IV, const. 13 and 21, in Tanner, ed. and trans., *Decrees of the Ecumenical Councils,* 1: 242, 245.

67. "Unum universorum principium, creator omnium invisibilium et visibilium, spiritualium et corporalium, qui sua omnipotenti virtute simul ab initio temporis, utramque de nihilo condidit creaturam, spiritualem et corporalem, angelicam videlicet et mundanam, ac deinde humanum quasi communem ex spiritu et corpore constitutam. Diabolus enim et daemones alii a Deo quidem natura creati sunt boni, sed ipsi per se facti sunt mali," Lateran IV, const. 1, in Tanner, ed. and trans., *Decrees of the Ecumenical Councils,* 1: 230. See Paul M. Quay's discussion in "Angels and Demons: The Teaching of IV Lateran," *Theological Studies* 42 (1981): 20–45. Quay, arguing against the modern view that the belief in angels and demons is not required by the Catholic faith, rightly recognizes that the council's statement presupposes that a belief in angels is common to orthodoxy and heterodoxy alike. Their differences lie in what exactly is believed about angels. Quay does not, however, stress the extent to which the decisive (as opposed to the vacillating) description of angels as purely spiritual creatures should be perceived as innovative. Lateran IV represents one of the very few times the church intervened conciliarly in these debates. A similar intervention occurred at the ecumenical Council of Constantinople (553), which condemned the Origenist belief that the souls of fallen demons would return to God after a series of incarnations—an opinion that, as we will see, would be endorsed by the Cathars. See E. Mangenot, "Démon d'après les decisions officielles de l'église," *DTC,* 4,1, cols. 408–9.

68. For Gregory the Great, see n. 10, above. Cf. Isidore of Seville's remarks: "Human wretchedness should learn that for that reason God is provoked more quickly to furnish pardon since he feels pity for infirm humanity because it drew the infirmity of sinning from its lower part—that is from the flesh—in which the enclosed soul is detained. The apostate angels on that account do not have pardon because they are weighed down by no carnal fragility to make them sin. . . . And thus due to the infirm condition of the flesh a return to salvation is open to humanity" ("Discat humana miseria quod ea causa citius provocetur Deus praestare veniam, dum infirmo compatitur homini, quia ipse traxit ex parte inferiori peccandi infirmitatem, hoc est, ex carne, qua inclusa anima detinetur. Apostatae angeli ideo non veniam habent, quia carnalis fragilitatis nulla infirmitate gravati sunt, ut peccarent. . . . ideoque pro infirma carnis conditione reditus patet homini ad salutem") *Sententiae* 1.10–11, *PL* 83, col. 555. This line of thinking is still present in Nicholas of Lyre's *Postilla* on Genesis 6.3, ad v. *Quia caro est*: "that [i.e., human incarnation] means having a propensity to sin because the flesh aggravates the soul: thus more ought to be excused to him by punishing him with temporal and not eternal punishment" ("id est habens pronitatem ad peccandum ex carne animam aggrauante: propter quod magis sibi parcendum puniendo eum poena temporali et non eterna," in *Textus Biblie,* vol. 1, fol. 50r). See Quay, "Angels and Demons," pp. 29–30.

69. "Suspiremus ergo ad eos de quibus loquimur, sed redeamus ad nos. Meminisse etenim debemus quia caro sumus. Taceamus interim de secretis coeli, sed ante conditoris oculos manu poenitentiae tergamus macula pulveris nostri," Gregory the Great, *Homiliae XL in Evangelia,* bk. 2, hom. 34, *PL* 76, cols. 1255–56.

70. Rupert of Deutz, *De glorificatione Trinitatis et processione sancti spiritus* 3.19, *PL* 169, col. 71.

71. See Aquinas's short and to the point treatment of this in quodlib. 12, q. 21, art. 32, in *Opera omnia,* Parma edition, 9: 630.

72. Anselm of Canterbury, *Cur Deus Homo* 2.21, in *Opera omnia,* ed. F. S. Schmitt (Edinburgh: Thomas Nelson, 1946), 2: 132; trans. Jasper Hopkins and Herbert Richardson in *Anselm of Canterbury* (Toronto: Edwin Mellen, 1976), 3: 136. Cf. 1.17, where the question is first broached (ed. Schmitt, 2: 75–76; trans. Hopkins and Richardson, 3: 75–76). Also see *De casu diaboli* c. 17–18, in *Opera omnia,* ed. Schmitt, 1: 262–63; trans. Hopkins and Richardson, 2: 162–63.

73. Honorius Augustodunensis, *Elucidarium* 1.44, ed. Lèfevre, p. 368. Honorius seems to have written his early works in England, where he was very much influenced by Anselm's personal presence as well as his writings. See Flint, "Works of Honorius Augustodunensis," pp. 219–24, 228–31, 240.

74. Caesarius of Heisterbach, *Dialogus miraculorum* 3.26, ed. Joseph Strange (Cologne: J. M. Heberle, 1851), 1: 143–44; trans. H. Von E. Scott and C. C. Swinton Bland, *The Dialogue on Miracles* (London: Routledge, 1929), 1: 161–62.

75. Caesarius of Heisterbach, *Dialogus miraculorum* 5.36, ed. Strange, 1: 320; trans. Scott and Bland, 1: 366–67. For other instances of demons as seeming agents for good, also see 5.37–38 (ed. Strange, 1: 321–24; trans. Scott and Bland, 1: 368–72).

76. " 'Miser, ut quid consentiendo Lucifero sic de gloria aeterna ruimus?' "; " 'Tace, poenitentia ista nimis est sera, redire non poteris,' " Caesarius of Heisterbach, *Dialogus miraculorum* 5.10, ed. Strange, 1: 290; trans. Scott and Bland, 1: 330.

77. Caesarius of Heisterbach, *Dialogus miraculorum* 5.9, ed. Strange, 1: 289–90; trans. Scott and Bland, 1: 330.

78. "Si esset . . . columna ferrea et ignita, rasoriis et laminis acutissimis armata, a terra usque ad coelum erecta, usque ad diem iudicii, etiam si carnem haberem, in qua pati possem, me per illam trahere vellem, nunc ascendendo, nunc descendendo, dummodo redire possem ad gloriam in qua fui," Caesarius of Heisterbach, *Dialogus miraculorum* 5.10, ed. Strange, 1: 290; trans. Scott and Bland, 1: 331. (I have altered the translation slightly to make it more literal.)

79. " 'O miseri! vos nescitis quid cantatis. Nescitis quam sublimes isti sunt, sed ego scio, qui de eorum consorcio cecidi; et cum non habeam carnem in qua possim facere penitenciam, non possum illuc ultra conscendere; sed certe, si tantum haberem de carne quantum est in pollice humano, tantum facerem in ea de penitencia, quod adhuc ad alciorem statum ascenderem,' " Stephen of Bourbon, *Anecdotes historiques, légendes et apologues tirés du recueil inédit d'Etienne de Bourbon,* ed. A. Lecoy de la Marche (Paris: Renouard, 1877), no. 189, p 165.

80. Caesarius of Heisterbach, *Dialogus miraculorum* 5.15, ed. Strange, 1: 293–94; trans. Scott and Bland, 1: 335. Cf. Cassian's view in n. 7, above.

81. Caesarius of Heisterbach, *Dialogus miraculorum* 3.6, 5.5, ed. Strange, 1: 118, 282; trans. Scott and Bland, 1: 132, 322.

82. See Aquinas, *Commentum in quatuor libros sententiarum* bk. 2, dist. 6, q. un., art. 3, resp. ad obj. 6 in *Opera omnia*, Parma edition, 6: 441; *Summa theologiae* 1a, q. 64, art. 4, resp. ad obj. 3, 9: 296–99. Thomas is not very successful in explaining this process, but one gets the sense that the activity of the fire is oblique, acting on the demons mysteriously from a distance.

83. See Jacques Le Goff's dazzling exposition of how purgatory was "born" to

meet the needs of sin arising from an increasingly complex society, particularly the pressures of a market economy involving usury, in *The Birth of Purgatory,* trans. Arthur Goldhammer (Chicago: University of Chicago Press, 1981), esp. pp. 209–34. For Aquinas's views, see pp. 266–78.

84. Note that in Aquinas's exegesis of the first constitution of Lateran IV he argues that the council's emphasis on the damned joining Satan eternally and the saved partaking of eternal glory with Christ is in response to the Origenist view that the punishment of both damned and saved was not perpetual (*In Decretalem I. expositio ad Archidiaconum Tridentinum,* in *Opera omnia,* Parma edition, 16: 305).

85. For a general introduction to the Cathar movement and the beliefs of its followers, see Malcolm Lambert, *Medieval Heresy: Popular Movements from the Gregorian Reform to the Reformation,* 2d ed. (Oxford: Blackwell, 1977; 2d ed., 1992), pp. 55–61, 105–46; idem, "The Motives of the Cathars: Some Reflections," in *Religious Motivation: Biographical and Sociological Problems for the Church Historian,* ed. Derek Baker, Ecclesiastical History Society, Studies in Church History, vol. 15 (Oxford: Blackwell, 1978), pp. 49–59.

86. There are undoubted borrowings between the two treatises. Scholars have assumed that Durand of Huesca's effort was indebted to Alan's work. Christine Thouzellier, however, notes that the derivations could just as plausibly have occurred the other way around. See her "Controverses vaudoises-cathares à la fin du XIIe siècle (d'après le livre II du *Liber antiheresis,* Ms Madrid 1114 et les sections correspondantes du Ms BN lat. 13446)," *Archives d'histoire doctrinale et littéraire du moyen âge* 35 (1960): 138–39. Book 2 of Durand's treatise has been edited by Thouzellier and is printed as an appendix to the article, pp. 206–27. This work will be cited as *Liber antiheresis.* The second book in particular was seminal for Durand's later and more comprehensive treatise, *Liber contra manicheos* (written after his reintegration into orthodoxy), which has been edited by Thouzellier under the title *Une Somme anti-cathare: le "Liber contra manicheos,"* Spicilegium Sacrum Lovaniense, Etudes et documents, fasc. 32 (Louvain: Spicilegium Sacrum Lovaniense, 1964). See the introduction to this edition, pp. 34–35. The parts of this latter work that reflect Cathar theology (and were accordingly documented by Durand for refutation) have been translated in Walter L. Wakefield and Austin P. Evans, *Heresies of the High Middle Ages* (New York: Columbia University Press, 1969), pp. 494–510.

87. See Alan of Lille, *De fide catholica contra haereticos sui temporis, praesertim albigenses* 1.2–3, *PL* 210, cols. 308–9; and Durand of Huesca, *Liber antiheresis* 2.2, p. 215. Durand also responds to these contentions at considerable length in his *Liber contra manicheos* (see particularly c. 5, pp. 135–46). On Cathar theology, see Raoul Manselli, "Eglises et théologies cathares," in *Cathares en Languedoc,* ed. Edouard Privat, Cahiers de Fanjeaux, 3 (Toulouse: Edouard Privat, 1963), pp. 136–53.

88. " . . . solos angelos apostatas qui de coelo ceciderunt corporibus humanis infundi Dei permissione, ut ibi valeant poenitentiam agere," Alan of Lille, *De fide catholica contra haereticos* 1.9, *PL* 210, col. 316; trans. Wakefield and Evans, *Heresies of the High Middle Ages,* p. 217.

89. According to Alan of Lille, they also allege that all of the angels fell with Lucifer, thus none remain in the sky (*De fide catholica contra haereticos* 1.9, *PL* 210, col. 316). For his rebuttal of this belief, see 1.14, cols. 318–19.

90. Alan of Lille, *De fide catholica contra haereticos* 1.9, *PL* 210, col. 316; for

Alan's orthodox refutation, see 1.17–18, cols. 320–21. Also see Innocent III's application of John 3.13 to the power of the Eucharist in *De sacro altaris mysterio* 4.64, *PL* 217, col. 886. The Cathar reading of the Johannine passage is particularly obscure. The chronicle of William of Puylaurens (written after 1249), a contemporary account of the various measures taken against the Albigensians in southern France in the first part of the century, sheds further light on Cathar exegesis. When Bishop Diego of Osma and St. Dominic ask a heretic how he interprets the passage, the heretic responds that it refers to "John" — the son of God (ed. Beyssier, "Guillaume de Puylaurens et sa chronique," in *Troisièmes mélanges d'histoire du moyen âge*, ed. A. Luchaire, Université de Paris, Bibliothèque de la Faculté des Lettres, XVIII [Paris: Félix Alcan, Ancienne Librairie Germer Baillière, 1904], c. 8, p. 127). This answer stems from the adoptionist view that God chose one of the unfallen angels as his son for the purpose of redeeming the others — a view that arises in the heretical trial of Arnaldus Cicredi (ed. Jean Duvernoy, *Le Registre d'inquisition de Jacques Fournier, évêque de Pamiers (1318–1325)* [Toulouse: Edouard Privat, 1965] 2: 45–46; henceforth cited as *Fournier*). Also see the notes in the French edition, trans. Duvernoy, *Le Registre d'inquisition de Jacques Fournier, évêque de Pamiers (1318–1325)* (Paris: Mouton, 1978), 3: 798, n. 53. Unless otherwise indicated, the Latin edition is the one referred to. Also see n. 109, below. Adoptionist views cropped up intermittently in learned circles. See D. W. Johnson, "Adoptionism," *DMA*, 1: 57–58. As one would suspect, there is no room in the Cathar system for anything approaching the resurrection of the body. Thus, after defending the human body against the suspicion of permanently playing host to an angelic parasite, both authors turn their efforts toward defending the doctrine of bodily resurrection. See Alan of Lille, *De fide catholica contra haereticos* 1.23–26, *PL* 210, cols. 324–27; and Durand of Huesca, *Liber antiheresis* 2.3–4, pp. 218–27.

91. ". . . quia angeli peccaverunt in spirituali natura, voluit eos Deus punire in corporali substantia, et ibi poenitentiam agere; non enim est eis ablata, ut dicunt, libertas arbitrii, nec potentia poenitendi; aliter, injuste ageretur cum eis," Alan of Lille, *De fide catholica contra haereticos* 1.11, *PL* 210, col. 317. Note, however, that the important Cathar treatise *Liber de duobus principiis* bitterly opposes this view, deducing from the angelic fall that there is no such thing as free will (ed. Christine Thouzellier, *Livre des deux principes*, *SC*, no. 198 [Paris: Editions du Cerf, 1973]), c. 10–11, 15–17, pp. 180–91, 202–17; trans. Wakefield and Evans, *Heresies of the High Middle Ages*, pp. 520–23, 526–31.

92. ". . . dicunt animas in mundi principio peccasse et de celis usque ad terras diversaque vincula corpora meruisse eaque causa factum esse mundum confitentes," Durand of Huesca, *Liber antiheresis* 2.1, p. 206. This offense is explicitly linked with the theologian Origen by Durand. Origen, who believed that the angelic fall was not dependent on sin but was the predictable and even necessary fall of spiritual substances, posited a possible return for the fallen angels. See Elizabeth A. Clark's cogent account of the patristic controversy over the extent of his errors in *The Origenist Controversy: The Cultural Construction of an Early Christian Debate* (Princeton, N.J.: Princeton University Press, 1992). For striking convergences between positions attributed to Origen and later Cathar ideology, see esp. pp. 11–12, 95–96, 108–9, 113, 123–24, 128–29, 133, 134–35, 177. Also see Peter Brown, *The Body and Society: Men, Women, and Sexual Renunciation in Early Christianity* (New York:

Columbia University Press, 1988), pp. 162–68; Williams, *Ideas of the Fall and of Original Sin,* pp. 210–17; and Claude Tresmontant, *La Métaphysique du Christianisme et la naissance de la philosophie chrétienne: problèmes de la creation et de l'anthropologie des origines à saint Augustin* (Paris: Editions du Seuil, 1961), pp. 395–451. Tresmontant also discusses the presence of parallel beliefs among the Cathars. For a discussion of Durand's treatment of the angels' fall, see Thouzellier, "Controverses vaudoises-cathares," pp. 166–75.

93. In fact, Durand provides many more contested biblical texts than does Alan. For Durand's discussion of the sheep of Israel, see *Liber antiheresis* 2.1, 2.2, pp. 206, 215. Also see his later *Liber contra manicheos* c. 18, pp. 286–97. For his explanation of John 3.13, see *Liber antiheresis* 2.1, p. 207.

94. "Et ipsum dicunt esse ingressum curiam Patris celestis, ad decipiendos angelos et quosdam fecisse fornicari credunt. Et ob hanc causam Patrem dicunt surrexisse contra eum, et eum de patria celesti depulisse et angelos quos seduxerat," Durand of Huesca, *Liber antiheresis* 2.2, pp. 215–16.

95. Thus in the opening statement of book 2, Durand says, "we ought to publish certain testimonies, showing that not one of them will ever be saved who fell from heaven by their own arrogance" ("debemus quedam testimonia intimare, ostendentes quod nullus eorum unquam salvabitur qui de celis sua arrogantia ceciderunt"). Likewise he concludes chap. 2, which deals explicitly with the fall of the angels, with this statement: "For by these [authorities] it is given to be understood that none of the spirits falling from heaven can be saved" ("Istis namque datur intelligi nullum spirituum de celo cadentium salvari posse," *Liber antiheresis* 2.1, 2.2, pp. 206, 218). One of the subjects proposed by a *summa* (written between 1225 and 1250) intended for the use of those preaching against heresy and providing appropriate biblical citations as proof of the said doctrine is that demons are damned absolutely. See Célestin Douais, ed., *La Somme des autorités à l'usage des prédicateurs méridionaux au XIIIe siècle* (Paris: Picard, 1896), c. 23, p. 47. Also see c. 19, p. 45 (that God infuses new souls into bodies) and c. 20, pp. 45–46 (that it is a soul and not an angel that animates the human body). To the set of biblical passages intended to support this second orthodox claim, the author adds his own rationale: if evil spirits were intended to be in human bodies, why did Christ cast them out via exorcism? The rubrics for the chapters are translated in Wakefield and Evans, *Heresies of the High Middle Ages,* pp. 297–99.

96. See Brown, *Body and Society,* pp. 336–37; Elaine Pagels, *Adam, Eve, and the Serpent* (New York: Random House, 1988), pp. 27–30, 93–94; and Elliott, *Spiritual Marriage,* pp. 30–31.

97. See the following orthodox writers: Bonacursus (a former member of the sect), *Vita haereticorum* (between 1176 and 1180), *PL* 204, cols. 775–76, trans. Wakefield and Evans, *Heresies of the High Middle Ages,* pp. 171–72; the anonymous *Disputatio inter catholicum et paterinum haereticum,* in *Thesaurus Novus Anecdotorum,* ed. E. Martène and U. Durand (Paris: Lutetia, 1717; rprt. New York: Burt Franklin, 1968), vol. 5, cols. 1710–11, trans. Wakefield and Evans, pp. 295–96; and Moneta of Cremona, *Adversus Catharos et Valdenses* (ca. 1241), trans. Wakefield and Evans, pp. 318–19, 321–22. Cf. the anonymous Bogomil treatise *Interrogatio Iohannis,* which was being disseminated in the West by the end of the twelfth century (ed. with French translation, Edina Bozóky, *Le Livre secret des cathares: "Interrogatio Io-*

hannis" [Paris: Beauchesne, 1980], pp. 58–63; trans. Wakefield and Evans, pp. 460–61). Note that Bozóky edits two different manuscripts of this text: one from Vienna and one from Dôle. The translation in Wakefield and Evans follows the former. This vision of the diabolical race of Cain concurs in a limited sense with the orthodox reading of Genesis 6.2, which identifies the sons of God with Seth's line and the daughters of men with Cain's. See the *Glossa ordinaria,* interlinear, ad v. *filii dei* and ad v. *filias hominum,* as well as the marginal gloss ad v. *Uidentes filii Dei,* in *Textus Biblie,* vol. 1, fol. 50r.

98. Cf. the anonymous *De heresi catharorum in Lombardia* (between 1200 and 1245, possibly written by a one-time member of the sect), edited as an appendix in Antoine Dondaine's "La hiérarchie cathare en Italie: I," *Archivum Fratrum Praedicatorum* 19 (1949): 310, trans. Wakefield and Evans, *Heresies of the High Middle Ages,* p. 165; Peter of Vaux-de-Cernay (ca. 1213), *Petri Vallium Sarnaii monachii Hystoria albigensis* c. 12, ed. Paschal Guébin and Ernest Lyon (Paris: Honoré Champion, 1926), 1: 13, trans. Wakefield and Evans, p. 239; and Moneta of Cremona, *Adversus catharos et valdenses,* trans. Wakefield and Evans, p. 310.

99. In addition to Caesarius's view on the varying degrees of demonic culpability, both Alan of Lille and Durand of Huesca acknowledged that this was believed to be the case by Cathars (*De fide catholica contra haereticos* 1.13, *PL* 210, col. 318; *Liber antiheresis* 2.2, p. 218). As was discussed above, this kind of speculation over differing degrees of demonic culpability would be necessarily foreclosed if one accepted Aquinas's articulation of the nature of angelic will, which left no gray areas in degree of consent. Also see Aquinas, *Summa theologiae* 1a, q. 63, art. 8, resp. ad obj. 3, 9: 274, 275.

100. As an introduction to the Fournier register, Emmanuel Le Roy Ladurie's groundbreaking *Montaillou, village occitan de 1294 à 1324* (Paris: Gallimard, 1975) is unrivaled. See particularly the introduction for a discussion of Jacques Fournier and his inquisitional protocol (esp. pp. 10–19). Also see Gabriel de Llobet, "Variété des croyances populaires au Comté de Foix au début du XIVe siècle d'après les enquêtes de Jacques Fournier," in *La Religion populaire en Languedoc du XIIIe siècle à la moitié du XIVe siècle,* ed. Edouard Privat, Cahiers de Fanjeaux, 11 (Toulouse: Edouard Privat, 1976), pp. 109–26; and Duvernoy's introduction to his French translation of the register, *Fournier,* 1: 1–16. On the bishop's career and writings, see P. Fournier, "Jacques Fournier (Benoît XII)," in *Histoire littéraire de la France* (Paris: Imprimerie Nationale, 1938), 38: 174–209. On inquisitional procedure, see Célestin Douais, *L'Inquisition: ses orgines, sa procédure* (Paris: Librairie Plon, 1906), pt. 2, esp. pp. 169–89; and Edward Peters, *Inquisition* (Berkeley: University of California Press, 1989), pp. 52–71.

101. The fullest versions of this myth are given by Arnaldus Cicredi (*Fournier,* 2: 33–34); Sybilia Petri, 2: 406–8; Arnaldus Baiuli (the inquisitor's nuncio reporting against Johannes Maurini), 2: 441–42; Johannes Maurini, 2: 489–90, 2: 508; and Petrus Maurini, 3: 130–32, 219–20. Cf. Hato de Las Lenas's testimony against Arnaldus Textoris (2: 199). I am deliberately leaving the names in the form in which they appear in the register to avoid confusion. The remainder of the paragraph following n. 101 in the text is a composite of their testimonies. See Le Roy Ladurie's summary of this myth in *Montaillou,* pp. 609–10; and Peter Dronke's translation of Sybilia Petri's testimony in *Women Writers of the Middle Ages: A Critical Study of Texts*

from Perpetua (d. 203) to Marguerite Porete (d. 1310) (Cambridge: Cambridge University Press, 1984), p. 211.

102. Certainly some of the witnesses were literate, however, and had access to heretical texts. See, for example, how in the notary Petrus de Galhaco's testimony against Arnaldus Textoris, Petrus admits that he surreptitiously flipped through a book containing a debate between Cathars and Catholics (refuting the Catholic position) while he was doing business in Arnaldus's house (*Fournier,* 2: 196–97). Duvernoy compares this text to Durand of Huesca's parallel anti-Cathar debates (*Fournier,* 2: 608, n. 6 of the French edition). See Peter Biller, "The Cathars of Languedoc and Written Materials," in *Heresy and Literacy, 1000–1530,* ed. Peter Biller and Anne Hudson (Cambridge: Cambridge University Press, 1994), pp. 61–82.

103. Johannes Maurini, in *Fournier,* 2: 489, 508; Arnaldus Cicredi, 2: 34; Arnaldus Baiuli, 2: 441–42. The transformation of woman into man parallels the kind of masculine model of humanity that was rampant in the early church, especially in gnosticism. See Elaine Pagels, *The Gnostic Gospels* (New York: Random House, 1979), pp. 66–67. In Petrus Maurini's retelling of the Bogomil *Vision of Isaiah,* which was extremely popular in Cathar circles, the angelic instructor claims that there is no difference between women and men except in the flesh—the work of Satan, which will eventually disappear (*Fournier,* 3: 201; also see 3: 223). Wakefield and Evans translate the *Vision of Isaiah* in *Heresies of the High Middle Ages,* pp. 449–56. Also see Arnaldus Cicredi's more condensed account of the vision (*Fournier,* 2: 50–51; trans. Wakefield and Evans, pp. 456–58).

104. "Penitentes quia dimiserant Patrem celestem, inceperunt cantare Cantica de canticis Syon, ut solebant cantare quando erant cum Patre celesti; quod audiens, Sathanas dixit eis: 'Et estis adhuc memores de canticis Syon?' Et ipsi responderunt quod sic, et tunc Sathanas dixit eis: 'Ego ponam vos in terra oblivionis in qua obliviscemini illa que dicebatis et habebatis in Syon!' Et tunc fecit eis tunicas, id est corpora de terra oblivionis [cf. Ps. 136.4]," Petrus Maurini, *Fournier,* 3: 132; also see 2: 220. Cf. Arnaldus Cicredi, 2: 35; Arnaldus Baiuli, 2: 441. Interestingly, in Sybilia Petri's account, however, the devil asks the mournful spirits and souls why they are not singing their usual song (perhaps attempting to cheer them up). They answer that they cannot sing the songs of the Lord in a strange land (*Fournier,* 2: 407). The image of service to a strange God in a strange land, indicating Satan's hegemony over the world, is frequently evoked in Cathar texts. See Thouzellier, *Liber de duobus principiis* c. 47, *SC,* no. 198, pp. 322–25; trans. Wakefield and Evans, *Heresies of the High Middle Ages,* p. 557. On the possible heterodox genealogy of the tunics, see the following note.

105. The phrase used by Petrus Maurini is "tunice oblivitionis inverse" (*Fournier,* 3: 220). As is clear from elsewhere in his testimony, inversion represents a movement away from God, while reversion is the movement back toward God. Hence God says to the fallen angels: "You others will have tunics that are inverted in many ways because you will go from one tunic to another until you will be reversed in the tunic in which you stood in justice and truth" ("Vos alii habebitis tunicas multimodas inversas, quia ibitis de tunica in aliam, quousque reversi fueritis in tunicam in qua stetistis in iusticia et veritate"), 3: 131. Regarding the number of incarnations a soul must undergo: some say nine (Beatrix de Ecclesia, 1: 229);

others say seven or nine (Guillelmus Austatz, 1: 207). Curiously, St. Paul was believed to have required as many as thirteen (Petrus Maurini, 3: 179–80, 220).

The view of the body as a tunic donned after the fall, inspired by the Genesis account of how God gave Adam and Eve "tunicas pelliceas" ("tunics of skin"), is again associated with the theologian Origen (see Duvernoy's notes to the French edition, *Fournier,* 3: 798, n. 38; and Tresmontant, *La Métaphysique,* p. 430 n. 88). Orthodoxy interpreted these tunics metaphorically. Thus the *Glossa ordinaria* interprets "tunics of skin" simply as a symbol of mortality and not the body itself. See *Glossa ordinaria,* Gen. 3.21, interlinear, ad v. *tunicas*: "through which death is signified which after sin was owed to nature" ("quibus significatur mors quam post peccatum debebatur nature"); ad v. *pelliceas:* "Because mortals [are] from mortal things" ("Quia mortales ex mortalibus," in *Textus Biblie,* vol. 1, fol. 43r). Even in the first half of the twelfth century, prior to any real awareness of Catharism, Rupert of Deutz had nevertheless still thought it necessary to deride the concept of tunics of flesh as indicating the human body, insisting on the body's priority in creation (*De sancta Trinitate et eius operibus,* 3.27, *CCCM,* 21, pp. 266–67).

106. Arnaldus Cicredi, *Fournier,* 2: 35; Beatrix de Ecclesia, 1: 228. See Le Roy Ladurie, *Montaillou,* pp. 453–55.

107. " . . . quia spiritus maligni qui stant in aere eum decoqunt," Petrus Maurini, *Fournier,* 3: 179. The heretical preacher responsible for this remark does seem to imply, however, that a truly strong person, "who stood in truth and justice, that nothing can destroy" ("qui steterit in veritate et iustitia, quod nulla res extimare potest") might be capable of withstanding the pressure to enter another body. Cf. 3: 221.

108. Naturally, the devil does his best to stop the body from receiving the *consolamentum* (see Petrus Maurini, *Fournier,* 3: 221). Note, however, that the Fournier register refers to this rite as heretication. On the ministry of the Perfect, see Y. Dossat, "Les cathares dans les documents de l'inquisition," in *Cathares en Languedoc,* pp. 82–89.

109. The adoption of the son of God, his mission on earth, and his institution of the *consolamentum* is described in detail by Arnaldus Cicredi, *Fournier,* 2: 45–51. According to this account, the gospel was written in the sky before the coming of the son. All of the angels had an opportunity to read the many heroic and difficult things that Christ would be expected to do on earth. Only one (named John) finally agreed to undertake these tasks, albeit reluctantly, first falling into a three-day faint. He was then adopted as the son of God. Petrus Maurini also associates scripture with the gift of remembering, provided by God to counteract the effect of the tunics of forgetfulness (3: 132). On adoptionism and this particular testimony, see n. 90, above. The angel named John is not to be confused with John the Baptist, whom the Cathars seemed universally to detest—partially because he asked Christ *if* he was the messiah (see Duvernoy's comment in his French edition of *Fournier,* 3: 798, n. 53). One of the proposed topics for orthodox preachers was to refute the Cathar contention that John the Baptist was evil (see Douais, *La Somme des autorités* c. 17, p. 44).

110. The term, generally "adumbravit" or "adumbratus fuit," appears in the testimony of Beatrix de Ecclesia, *Fournier,* 1: 230, 241. But others also believed that Christ had a phantasmic body and only pretended to be born of the Virgin (see

Ramandus Valsiera, 1: 282; Guillelma Beneti, 1: 473; Petrus Maurini, 3: 224–25; and Johannes Rocas, 2: 242). Note that one heretical preacher, however, argues that Mary simply represents good will and that it is unworthy to even think that Christ could be shadowed forth in something as vile as a woman (Sybilia Petri, 2: 409). Despite reinterpretations of the role of Mary, many Cathar sympathizers displayed remarkable reverence for her. See Le Roy Ladurie, *Montaillou*, pp. 487–94. Recently, however, Kathrin Utz Tremp has demonstrated that this veneration was restricted to women. She explains the male indifference to Mariology in terms of misogyny. See "'Parmi les hérétiques . . .': la Vierge Marie dans le registre d'inquisition de l'évêque Jacques Fournier de Pamiers (1317–1326)," in *Marie: le culte de la Vierge dans la société médiévale*, ed. Dominique Iogna-Prat et al. (Paris: Beauchesne, 1996), pp. 554–58.

111. For the Eucharist's traditional commemorative function, see Innocent III's *De sacro altaris mysterio* 4.43, *PL* 217, cols. 883–884; also see Miri Rubin's *Corpus Christi: The Eucharist in Late Medieval Culture* (Cambridge: Cambridge University Press, 1991), esp. pp. 298 ff.

112. See Bynum's *Resurrection of the Body,* which emphasizes throughout the extent to which bodily resurrection was linked with the concept of identity—especially indicated by orthodoxy's anxious concern that every particle of the body be resurrected. This preoccupation bespeaks the positive valence accorded the body.

113. Russell judiciously observes that the polarization of orthodoxy and Catharism grossly oversimplifies the respective positions: "the debate was not between two extremes but rather where on a spectrum between dualism and monism the truth lay. Orthodox Christianity is itself a quasi-dualist religion" (*Lucifer,* p. 185).

114. "And just as we don clothes from these or from those skins of animals at will, so the demons dress now in these or now in those shapes of beasts" ("Et ut nos pro voluntate vestes de illis vel de istis animalium velleribus induimus; sic daemones nunc illarum vel illarum bestiarum formas induunt"), Honorius Augustodunensis, *Liber duodecim quaestionum* c. 11, *PL* 172, col. 1183. Cf. n. 29, above. For Peter Lombard's discussion, see n. 20, above.

115. One Cathar account describes how the adopted son of God simulated his birth. Mary became big, as if pregnant, and the son of God suddenly appeared beside her as a newborn infant. Because she immediately returned to normal weight, people assumed that she had given birth (Arnaldus Cicredi, *Fournier,* 2: 46). Cf. the vision of the nativity received by one of Caesarius of Heisterbach's holy men in which the very discretion of the vision has parallels with heretical descriptions of the nativity. After hearing a voice announcing that the Virgin was about to give birth, the holy man responded doubtfully that Christ could not be born twice: "Scarcely had he finished speaking when behold! she without any pain brought forth a son, and held Him out wrapped in swaddling clothes to the monk," *Dialogus miraculorum* 8.2, ed. Strange, 2: 82; trans. Scott and Bland, 2: 3.

116. William of Auvergne, *De anima* pt. 34, in *Opera omnia* (Paris: A. Pralard, 1674; rprt. Frankfurt am Main: Minerva, 1963), 2: 194 (in vol. 2, suppl.); idem, *De universo* 3a 2ae, c. 21 (note that this chapter is mislabeled as 20 in this edition), in *Opera omnia,* 1: 1056–58. See Dyan Elliott, "The Physiology of Rapture and Female Spirituality," in *Medieval Theology and the Natural Body,* ed. Peter Biller and A. J.

Minnis (Woodbridge, Suffolk: York Medieval Press, in association with Boydell and Brewer, 1997), pp. 144–45.

117. One Perfect, present when some believers were congratulating themselves on a pilfered lamb they were eating, reprimanded them, saying that such an act was a bad example—though not exactly a sin. He also implied that such crimes slow down the process leading to the reception of the *consolamentum* (Petrus Maurini, *Fournier,* 3: 179; cf. 3: 132). Also see Johannes Maurini's testimony in n. 120, below. On Cathar attitudes toward sin and the contempt with which they were treated by orthodoxy, see M.-H. Vicaire, "Les cathares albigeois vus par les polémistes," in *Cathares en Languedoc*, pp. 125–27.

118. On reincarnation as penance, see Beatrix de Ecclesia, *Fournier,* 1: 228; Arnaldus Textoris, 2: 200; Sybilia Petri, 2: 407; and Arnaldus Cicredi, 3: 36.

119. Thus one Perfect describes how a believer had undergone an *endura*—the suicidal fast that occasionally was practiced after the reception of the *consolamentum* on the sickbed—but was still incapable of dying, since he had been wicked in his past life and must suffer this particular penance in his body (Petrus Maurini, *Fournier,* 3: 131). There is no question but that many Cathars had a strong sense of cumulative merit over the course of their incarnations, which would eventually permit them to be perfected. This is even acknowledged by Caesarius of Heisterbach in one of his antiheretical anecdotes. Thus a heretic professed that he gave alms and lived well in order that he might deserve a better body—a hope conveyed by Caesarius as simply the body of a wealthy man (*Dialogus miraculorum* 5.21, ed. Strange, 1: 301; trans. Scott and Bland, 1: 344). See the description of the Perfects' ascetic regime as relayed through a heretical preacher, who asserts that if the Perfect in question observes these strictures he or she will be received into heaven three days after his or her death (Johannes Maurini, *Fournier,* 2: 480). On the reception of the *consolamentum* and its significance, see Manselli, "Eglises et théologies cathares," in *Cathares en Languedoc*, pp. 154–61.

120. "Dyabolus nichil potest aufferre Deo, set bene retardabat," Johannes Maurini, *Fournier,* 2: 481.

121. The fact that the good, immaterial God would ultimately be dependent on despised matter for the return of his beloved spirits was something of a metaphysical glitch in the Cathar system—one that its adherents attempted to smooth over with yet another myth. Satan made the human body but could not make it walk or speak. The good, spiritual Father agreed to animate the body (which he did by breathing into it), provided that his contribution (the spirit) ultimately be returned to him. The devil would, in turn, possess the body (Beatrix de Ecclesia, *Fournier,* 1: 228; Sybilia Petri, 2: 407; Petrus Maurini, 3: 223–24). This myth, however, is not easily reconciled with the fall legend and the ensuing tunics of forgetfulness.

122. Arnaldus Textoris, *Fournier,* 2: 199–200.

123. Johannes Maurini, *Fournier,* 2: 489, 490, 508; but note how he qualifies this assessment below.

124. "'Eatis pro modo et per ia[m],'" Sybilia Petri, 2: 407; cf. Petrus Maurini, *Fournier,* 3: 220.

125. Petrus Maurini, *Fournier,* 3: 232–33. This seems to contradict this witness's earlier assertion that all of the fallen spirits would be saved (3: 220).

126. Johannes Maurini, *Fournier,* 2: 491. Note, however, that Beatrix de Ecclesia, coached by the priest Petrus Clerici, who had Cathar sympathies, testifies that Judas and the Jews that betrayed Christ were damned eternally (1: 229). Cf. Le Roy Ladurie, *Montaillou,* p. 605.

127. "Quando scilicet homo se desperat de Dei misercordia de qua nullus debet desperare; et, ut dicebat, gravius peccatum inter omnia erat desperationis," Johannes Maurini, *Fournier,* 2: 481. It is at this point that he proceeds to affirm that the devil can take nothing away from God but can only slow down the process of redemption by instigating sin. Note that Johannes's perception of the one unforgivable sin corresponds to the orthodox notion of *accidia*—a mortal sin consisting of a sadness that leads to a rejection of a spiritual good (see Aquinas, *De malo* q. 11, arts. 1–4, in *Opera omnia,* Parma edition, 8: 360; trans. Oesterle, *On Evil,* pp. 359–70).

128. Johannes Maurini, *Fournier,* 2: 480–81.

129. "Respondit quod audivit a dicto Guillelmo Belibasta heretico quod nullus de illis spiritibus qui consenserunt et crediderunt dyabolo expresse, quia facti sunt demones, nunquam revertantur ad celum vel usque ad diem iudicii, set si in die iudicii revertentur ad celum vel non, omnes vel eorum aliqui, nullus homo sciebat, quia hoc est unum de secretis Dei, et stabunt misercordie Dei et voluntati super hoc," Johannes Maurini, *Fournier,* 2: 490.

130. " . . . quia talem misericordiam homo debet habere ad hominem qualem volebat quod Deus haberet ad ipsum," Johannes Maurini, *Fournier,* 2: 516.

131. "Et sic videbantur dicere quod Sathanas, demones et spiritus mali hominum, illi qui de celo non descenderunt, non erant creature Dei patris.

Aliquando tamen videbantur dicere quod nullum opus dyaboli perseverabat, set desinebat esse, et sic si demones et mali spiritus erant facti per deum malum, opportebat quod desinerent esse et non perpetuo perdurarent, et sic non perpetuo possent vivere et esse in inferno. Quam tamen contrarietatem non audivit ipse loquens solvere vel declarare," Petrus Maurini, *Fournier,* 3: 222.

132. Johannes Rocas, *Fournier,* 2: 244.

133. "'Si ita est ut vos dicitis, non oportet nos timere de demonibus, cum fratres nostri sunt!' et tunc dictus Arnaldus respondit: 'Ecce ita se habet res'" Hato de Las Lenas testifying against Arnaldus Textoris, *Fournier,* 2: 200; cf. the account of Guillelmus Castelli, who was privy to this conversation (2: 194–95). Note, however, that according to Arnaldus's view of the fall, the spirits who had expressly consented to Satan were eternally damned (2: 199).

134. Thus Petrus Clerici, a Cathar sympathizer, argued that all animals demonstrate their rationality on the basis of their common instinct for self-preservation, "on account of which it is an equal sin to kill whatsoever brute animal as to kill a human because brutes have a rational and knowing spirit—just like humans" (" . . . propter quod equale peccatum est occidere quodcumque animal brutum sicut et interficere hominem, eo quod bruta sicut et homines spiritum racionabilem et scientem habent"), Beatrix de Ecclesia, *Fournier,* 1: 228.

135. Alan of Lille, *Liber de planctu Naturae, PL* 210, cols. 449–50; trans. James J. Sheridan, *The Plaint of Nature* (Toronto: Pontifical Institute of Mediaeval Studies, 1980), pp. 133–25. See Larry Scanlon, "Unspeakable Pleasures: Alain de Lille,

Sexual Regulation, and the Priesthood of Genius," *Romantic Review* 86 (1995): 213–38, esp. 218ff.

136. See John Boswell, *Christianity, Social Tolerance, and Homosexuality: Gay People in Western Europe from the Beginning of the Christian Era to the Fourteenth Century* (Chicago: University of Chicago Press, 1980), pp. 269–334. Boswell points out that Lateran III (1179) set a precedent in explicitly condemning sexual acts "against nature" and that Alan's work anticipated this decree by only a few years (pp. 277–78). Also see James Brundage, *Law, Sex, and Christian Society in Medieval Europe* (Chicago: University of Chicago Press, 1987), pp. 472–74, 533–35.

137. Sarah Blanshei, "Criminal Law and Politics in Medieval Bologna," *Criminal Justice History* 2 (1981): 11–12, 26 n. 47. See the recent edition of the inquisitional proceedings by Lorenzo Paolini and Raniero Orioli, *Acta S. Officii Bononie ab anno 1291 usque ad annum 1310,* Fonti per la Storia d'Italia, no. 106, 3 pts. (Rome: Palazzo Borromini, 1982–84).

138. Athanasius, *Vita S. Antonii* c. 6, *PG* 26, cols. 849–52; trans. Mary Emily Keenan, *The Life of St. Anthony,* in *Early Christian Biographies, FC,* vol. 15 (New York: Fathers of the Church, 1952), pp. 139–40. See Cassian, *Conférences* 5.11, 7.15, 7.17, ed. Pichery, *SC,* no. 42, 1: 200, 259, 260; Lactantius, *Divinae institutiones* 6.23, *PL* 6, col. 717; and John Climacus, *Scala paradisi* 4, 15, 29, *PG* 88, cols. 697–98, 886, 1147–50; trans. Colm Luibheid and Norman Russell, *The Ladder of Divine Ascent* (New York: Paulist Press, 1982), pp. 102, 174–75, 283. John Climacus further described the dangerous affection between two monks as resulting from the devil's malice. He was also of the view that the devil only pretended chastity in order to entrap souls that had temporarily relaxed their vigilance (*Scala paradisi* 15, 26, *PG* 88, cols. 883–84, 1065–66; trans. Luibheid and Russell, *Ladder of Divine Ascent,* pp. 173, 250).

139. Guibert of Nogent, *Autobiographie* 1.26, ed. Edmond-René Labande (Paris: Société d'Edition "Les Belles Lettres," 1981), pp. 202–5; trans. Paul J. Archambault, *A Monk's Confession: The Memoirs of Guibert of Nogent* (University Park: Pennsylvania State University Press, 1996), pp. 89–90.

140. This modesty seems to be related to the rise of a certain kind of exemplum in which a demon threatens to reveal unconfessed sins, particularly sins of the flesh. In Caesarius of Heisterbach's renditions, this is effected through a truth-telling demoniac who threatens the sinner with exposure (*Dialogus miraculorum* 3.2–3, 3.5, ed. Strange, 1: 112–14, 115; trans. Scott and Bland, 1: 125–28, 128–29). But in Stephen of Bourbon, the devil takes the form of a prosecutor, dutifully appearing at bishop's court, in order to accuse the culprit (*Anecdotes historiques,* no. 176, pp. 155–56; no. 178, pp. 156–57). For Stephen's emphasis on confession, see Jacques Berlioz, "'Quand dire c'est faire dire': exempla et confession chez Etienne de Bourbon," in *Faire Croire: modalités de la diffusion et de la réception des messages religieux du XIIe au XVe siècle,* Collection de l'Ecole Française de Rome, 51 (Rome: Ecole Française de Rome, 1981), pp. 299–35. Cf. Chaucer's *Friar's Tale,* in which the devil appears as the Summoner for the archdeacon's court. Also see Damian's parallel and earlier use of the demoniac as an instrument of exposure for sins in Chap. 1, n. 83, above. The later tales, however, are told to reinforce the miraculous powers of confession, since the evidence of the crime miraculously disappears when the guilty party confesses.

Such anecdotes are steeped in ambivalence because, in theory, demons can only act with God's permission and, hardened by malice, never wish to do good by their own volition. Their seeming good is thus invariably turned toward an evil end (Aquinas, *Summa theologiae* 1a, q. 64, art. 2, resp. ad obj. 5, 9: 290–93). What reins these stories into an orthodox conception of demonic protocol is the view that demons can be constrained in various ways by God—though it hardly explains why their "virtuous" actions are depicted as villainous. For this kind of ambivalence in the behavior of saints and demons, see Aron Gurevich, "Santi iracondi e demoni buoni negli 'Exempla,'" in *Santi e demoni nell'alto medioevo occidentale (secoli V–XI)*, Settimane di studio del Centro italiano di studi sull'alto medioevo, 36 (Spoleto: Presso la Sede del Centro, 1989), 2: 1045–63.

141. "Erubescunt daemones de vicio contra naturam," Thomas of Cantimpré, *Bonum universale de apibus* 2.30.2 (Douai: B. Belleri, 1627), p. 329 (hereafter cited as *De apibus*). Thomas cites the *Glossa ordinaria* on Ezech. 16.27: "I give you into the hands of the Philistines—that is the demons—who also blush at your wicked path, understanding here the vice against nature" ("Dabo te in manus Palaestinorum, id est daemonum, qui etiam erubescunt de via tua scelerata, vicium contra naturam intelligens"). The original biblical passage says nothing about demons; instead, the sinners are given into the hands of the daughters of the Philistines. The gloss does interpret these figures as demons but makes no mention of sins against nature, which seems to be Thomas's own reading (*Glossa ordinaria,* marginal, ad. v. *Extendam manum meam super te,* in *Textus Biblie,* vol. 4, fol. 22v).

142. See Chap. 2, pp. 46–47, above.

143. "Nullum animale eijict semen extra nisi homo: et in hoc ordinationi nature contrarius est plus quam pecus," Thomas of Cantimpré, *De apibus* 2.30.7, p. 323. There is a possible conflation in this chapter between masturbation and same-sex intercourse (and the reference to the sodomites is by no means definitive in this context). But the following exemplum about a young cleric who was corrupted by his master—one assumes through same-sex intercourse rather than masturbation—completes the transition (*De apibus* 2.30.8, pp. 323–24; cf. 2.30.9, pp. 324–25). Also note that Thomas had announced earlier that he was going to discuss unnatural vices—first as perpetrated by oneself and second with another (2.30.1, p. 320).

144. Ibid. 2.30.10, 2.30.12, pp. 325, 326.

145. Ibid. 2.30.11, p. 325.

146. This event occurred while Thomas was working in the episcopal camera. In order to avoid an interview with the bishop, an expedient urged by Thomas, a former penitent who had relapsed into homosexual activity begged Thomas to absolve him again, calling down God's vengeance on himself should he fail in his resolve. He died crying that the vengeance of God was upon him (ibid. 2.30.9, pp. 324–25). Cf. the terrible death of Thomas's charming school companion, allegedly punished for a parallel offense (2.30.8, pp. 323–24).

147. Although William of Auvergne refers to angels as incorporeal substances, he also argues that demons are subject to the passions and capable of feeling (*De universo* 3a 2ae, c. 23; 2a 2ae, c. 40–41, in *Opera omnia,* 1: 884–85, 1062).

148. "Si tanto ardore libidinis insanirent, quomodo a sodomitica libidine immunes essent, ut non vel in viros nostros, vel in masculos suos concupiscentia

insanirent. Benedictus autem altissimus, qui virilem speciem in hominibus a flagitiis eorum usque hodie sic servavit, ut nullus virorum ista nefaria libidine pollutus adhuc auditus sit. Nec igitur praetereundum est, quod nec ipsi invicem istam abominationem, videlicet sodomiticam exercere, vel unquam exercuisse, dicti sunt. In quo non mediocriter confunditur sodomitarum flagitiositas, cum ab ea se contineant ipsi maligni spiritus, qui ad faedandam humanam naturam totis studiis invigilant, et totis viribus elaborant," William of Auvergne, *De universo* 3a 2ae, c. 25, in *Opera omnia,* 1: 1070–71; also see 3a 2ae, c. 2, pp. 1017–18. Similarly, in William's efforts to rationalize the Judaic conception of abomination, he interprets the interdict on the crossbreeding of animals (Lev. 19.19) in terms of a commendation of the order of nature and a condemnation of sodomy (*De legibus* c. 12, in *Opera omnia,* 1: 43). He further associates the offspring of these unions with idolatry (particularly the cults of Venus and Priapus) and alleges that the dung produced from crossbred animals was used for witchcraft in ancient times.

149. "Neque ad hominem quando fornicatus est accedunt maxime prima die vel secunda, propter peccati recentiam," John Nider, *Formicarium* 5.5 (Douai: B. Belleri, 1602), p. 366. Note that, following the lead of Thomas of Cantimpré, John also cites the suggestive passage from Ezech. 16.27 regarding demons blushing at human ways (see n. 141, above). Also see John's recycling of William of Auvergne's views concerning the demons' freedom from all feelings of carnal lust as well as from the vice of sodomy (5.10, p. 401). John's statement that demons are repelled by even simple fornication is at odds with his claims that demons pollute primarily through fornication and idolatry—thus making use of the *Glossa ordinaria*'s commentary on Leviticus, cited at the opening of this chapter (5.9, pp. 397–98).

150. For Thomas Aquinas, see Chap. 1, pp. 33, above; and Chap. 2, pp. 57, 58, above; Bonaventure, *Commentaria in quatuor libros sententiarum* bk. 2, dist. 8, pt. 1, art. 3, q. 1, resp. ad oppositum 4–6, *Opera omnia,* 2: 220.

151. Henry Kramer and James Sprenger, *Malleus maleficarum 1487,* photographic facsimile of the first edition (Hildesheim: Georg Olms, 1992), pt. 1, q. 3, fol. 13r; trans. Montague Summers (London: John Rodker, 1928; rprt. New York: Dover, 1971), p. 26; cf. pt. 2, q. 1, c. 4, *Malleus maleficarum 1487,* fol. 55r; trans. Summers, p. 112. The authors also allege that a demon can invisibly interpose itself between the woman and her husband, thereby corrupting the husband's seed with the seed of another. The belief that every individual is assigned a personal angel is very ancient (see Bareille, "Angélologie d'après les Pères," cols. 1216–19).

152. R. I. Moore, *The Formation of a Persecuting Society: Power and Deviance in Western Europe, 950–1250* (Oxford: Blackwell, 1987), esp. pp. 21 ff. Caesarius of Heisterbach, for example, consciously includes his discussion of heresy in the chapter on demons. In the first of these stories, the heretics perform miracles because they have amulets, signs of indenture to the devil, sewn into their flesh (*Dialogus miraculorum* 5.18, ed. Strange, 1: 296–98; trans. Scott and Bland, 1: 338–41). For the early development of this nexus of associations, see Peter Brown, "Sorcery, Demons, and the Rise of Christianity," in *Witchcraft Confessions and Accusations,* ed. Mary Douglas (London: Tavistock, 1970), pp. 35–36; and André Vauchez, "Diables et hérétiques: les réactions de l'église et de la société en occident face aux mouvements religieux dissidents, de la fin du Xe au début du XIIe siècle," in *Santi e demoni,* 2: 573–601. Although this demonizing rhetoric may have been in place,

David Nirenberg rightly cautions that a reasoned understanding of each instance of persecution must be assessed and interpreted in terms of its specific historical context. See his superb *Communities of Violence: Persecution of Minorities in the Middle Ages* (Princeton, N.J.: Princeton University Press, 1996).

153. See Nider's description of the sexual debauchery of heretics, in *Formicarium* 3.5–6, pp. 209–23. As suggested above with respect to Bologna, heretics were also frequently associated with the vice of sodomy. On this association, see Brundage, *Law, Sex, and Christian Society,* p. 473; and Moore, *Formation of a Persecuting Society,* p. 94.

154. With the new initiative against heresy, for example, such a charge became one of only three canonistic grounds for a legal separation from a spouse (the other two being cruelty and adultery). See X.4.19.2 (Alexander III, 1172 or 1173), X.4.19.7 (Innocent III, 1199). The term *fornicatio spiritualis* is not in either decretal proper but is used in the rubric. Note, however, that there was some contestation over the legitimacy of heresy as grounds for separation, since other authorities held that both parties were still bound to render the conjugal debt. See A. Esmein, *Le Mariage en droit canonique* (Paris: Larose et Forcel, 1891; rprt. New York: Burt Franklin, 1968), 2: 92–93, 95. Also see the *Glossa ordinaria*'s use of this term in Ezech. 16.28, marginal, ad v. *Et fornicata es,* in *Textus Biblie,* vol. 4, fol. 232v (in this instance, citing Jerome).

155. Kramer and Sprenger, *Malleus maleficarum 1487* pt. 1, q. 2, fol. 7v; trans. Summers, p. 12.

156. See Aristotle's *De somniis* for a description of the poisonous miasma a woman exudes from her eyes as a result of menstruation (*On Dreams,* in *Aristotle VIII: On the Soul, Parva Naturalia, On Breath,* ed. and trans. W. S. Hett, Loeb Classical Library [Cambridge: Mass.: Harvard University Press; London: William Heinemann, 1975], pp. 356–59). Also see Pseudo-Aquinas's commentary on this same treatise (*De somniis* c. 3, in Aquinas, *Opera omnia,* Parma edition, 20: 234). But Aquinas was also aware of this tradition himself. See *De malo* q. 16, art. 9, resp. ad obj. 13, in *Opera omnia,* Parma edition, 8: 418; trans. Oesterle, *On Evil,* p. 520. Also see Danielle Jacquart and Claude Thomasset, *Sexuality and Medicine in the Middle Ages,* trans. Matthew Adamson (Princeton, N.J.: Princeton University Press, 1985), pp. 74–75.

157. Kramer and Sprenger, *Malleus maleficarum 1487* pt. 1, q. 2, fols. 7v–9v; trans. Summers, pp. 12–18. They posit that this is particularly true of children, who are extremely impressionable (*Malleus maleficarum 1487,* fol. 9r–9v; trans. Summers, pp. 17–18).

158. On the transition between medieval witchcraft and the full-blown witchcraft charges of the early modern period, see Robin Briggs, *Witches and Neighbors: The Social and Cultural Context of European Witchcraft* (New York: Viking, 1996), pp. 33–35. For the influence of *Malleus maleficarum* on Renaissance thought, see G. S. Williams, "The Woman / the Witch: Variations on a Sixteenth-Century Theme (Paracelsus, Wier, Bodin)," in *The Crannied Wall: Woman, Religion, and the Arts in Early Modern Europe,* ed. C. A. Monson (Ann Arbor: University of Michigan Press, 1992), pp. 119–37.

159. Sylvester Prieras (d. 1523) explicitly contested the view that demons are

repelled by unnatural vice, arguing instead that witches are abused by demons with bifurcated penises, so that they are simultaneously corrupted anally and vaginally (H. C. Lea, *Materials Toward a History of Witchcraft,* ed. Arthur C. Howland [Philadelphia: University of Pennsylvania Press, 1939], 1: 161). According to Lyndal Roper, "sodomy" became something of a catchall term to describe the sexual activities of the witches' sabbath (*Oedipus and the Devil: Witchcraft, Sexuality, and Religion in Early Modern Europe* [London: Routledge, 1994] p. 25).

160. Cardinal Thomas de Vio Cajetan (d. 1534), although defending the views of Thomas Aquinas in most of his writings, nevertheless attempted this reversal (see Ortolan, "Démon d'après les scolastiques," cols. 402–3). Cajetan seems to have been an anomaly among professional theologians in endorsing demonic corporeality. But Enrico V. Maltese also argues that the rise of witchcraft charges (particularly the emphasis on ritualized intercourse with the devil) spawned a corporeal and anthropomorphized devil among demonologists, partially owing to the influence of the eleventh-century Byzantine demonologist Michael Psellos. See "'Natura daemonum . . . habet corpus et versatur circa corpora': una lezione di demonologia dal medioevo greco," in *Il demonio e i suoi complici: dottrine e credenze demonologiche nella Tarda Antichità,* ed. Salvatore Pricoco (Soveria Mannelli and Messina: Rubbettino, 1995), pp. 265–84.

Afterword

1. "Sacerdos: Ad menstruatam acessisti, vel praegnantem vel nondum purificatam?

Poenitens: Saepe. . . .

Sacerdos: Cum masculo peccasti?

Poenitens: Cum multis.

Sacerdos: Umquam aliquem innocentem introduxisti ad hoc?

Poenitens: Tres scholares et subdiaconum.

Sacerdos: Dic quot tu es abusus et quotiens et ordinem tuum et ordines illorum. . . .

Poenitens: Tribus subdiaconis et ego subdiaconus per dimidium annum, uno uxorato semel. . . .

Sacerdos: Nocturnam pollutionem passus es?

Poenitens: Frequenter. . . .

Sacerdos: Umquam in loco sacro peccasti?

Poenitens: Non. . . .

Sacerdos: Post istas enormitates umquam accessisti ad altare ad celebrandum inconfessus?

Poenitens: Numquam,"

Anonymous form 1, in Robert of Flamborough, *Liber poenitentialis,* ed. J. J. Francis Firth (Toronto: Pontifical Institute of Mediaeval Studies, 1971), app. B, pp. 297–99. Cf. the similar dialogue in the manual proper, 4.222–30, pp. 195–200.

2. For Robert of Flamborough's recognition of the current view of the subdiaconate, see ibid., 2.23, p. 70. For dating, see Firth's introduction, p. 8.

3. "Caveat autem sacerdos in inquirendo ne aliquid ignotum confitenti inquirat, ne ex mentione illius peccati occasionem peccandi poenitens accipiat, quod frequenter fit," Anonymous form 1, in ibid., app. B, p. 296.

4. Ibid., 4.224, p. 196.

5. See Chap. 1, p. 24, above.

6. See J. L. Austin, "Performative Utterances," in *The Philosophy of Language*, ed. A. P. Martinich (New York: Oxford University Press, 1996), pp. 120–29; and idem, *How to Do Things with Words*, 2d ed. (Cambridge, Mass.: Harvard University Press, 1962; rprt. 1975), pp. 99–100, 116–17.

7. Nietzsche as cited by Peter Jelavich, "Contemporary Literary Theory: From Deconstruction Back to History," *Central European History* 22 (1989): 366.

8. Henry Kramer and James Sprenger, *Malleus maleficarum 1487*, photographic facsimile of the first edition (Hildesheim: Georg Olms, 1992), pt. 1, q. 1; pt. 2, q. 1, c. 4. fols. 4r–7r, 54v; trans. Montague Summers (London: John Rodker, 1928; rprt. New York: Dover, 1971), pp. 1–11, 111.

9. See Chap. 6, n. 92, above.

Bibliography

Primary Sources

Abelard, Peter. *Peter Abelard's "Ethics".* Ed. and trans. D. E. Luscombe. Oxford: Clarendon, 1971.

———. *Sic et non.* Ed. Blanche B. Boyer and Richard McKeon. Chicago: University of Chicago Press, 1976–77.

Abelard, Peter and Heloise. "The Personal Letters Between Abelard and Heloise," ed. J. T. Muckle. *Mediaeval Studies* 15 (1953): 47–94. Trans. Betty Radice, *The Letters of Abelard and Heloise.* Harmondsworth: Penguin, 1974.

Aelred of Rievaulx. *De institutione inclusarum. CCCM,* 1, ed. C. H. Talbot, 635–82. In *Opera omnia,* ed. A. Hoste and C. H. Talbot. Brepols: Turnhout, 1971.

Agnellus. *Liber pontificalis. MGH, Scriptores Rerum Langobardicarum et Italicarum, saec. VI–IX,* ed. O. Holder-Egger, 275–391. Hanover: Impensis Bibliopolii Hahniani, 1878.

———. *Liber pontificalis.* Ed. Alessandro Testi Rasponi. In *Raccolta degli Storici Italiani,* 2, 3, ed. L. A. Muratori. Bologna: Nicola Zanichelli, 1924.

Alan of Lille. *De fide catholica contra haereticos sui temporis, praesertim albigenses. PL* 210, cols. 305–430.

———. *Liber de planctu Naturae. PL* 210, cols. 429–82. Trans. James J. Sheridan, *The Plaint of Nature.* Toronto: Pontifical Institute of Mediaeval Studies, 1980.

Albert the Great. *Animalium libri XXVI.* In *Opera omnia,* ed. A. Borgnet. Vols. 11–12. Paris: Vivès, 1890–99.

———. *De bono.* Ed. Heinrich Kühle et al. In *Opera omnia,* ed. Bernhard Geyer. Vol. 28. Aschendorff: Monasterium Westfalorum, 1951.

———. *Commentarii in I–IV sententiarum.* In *Opera omnia,* ed. A. Borgnet. Vols. 25–30. Paris: Vivès, 1890–99.

Ps.-Albert the Great. *Women's Secrets: A Translation of Pseudo-Albertus Magnus's "De secretis mulierum" with Commentaries.* Trans. Helen Rodnite Lemay. Albany: State University of New York Press, 1992.

Alcher of Clairvaux. *Liber de anima et spiritu. PL* 40, cols. 779–832.

Alcuin. *Carmina. PL* 101, cols. 723–848.

Alexander of Hales. *Quaestiones disputatae "antequam esset frater."* Ed. Fathers of the College of St. Bonaventure ad Claras Aquas. 3 vols. Bibliotheca Franciscana Scholastica Medii Aevi, 19–21. Florence: College of St. Bonaventure, 1960.

———. *Summa theologica.* Ed. Fathers of the College of St. Bonaventure ad Claras Aquas. 4 vols. in 5. Florence: College of St. Bonaventure, 1924–48.

Andrew of Strumi. *Vita sancti Arialdi. MGH, Scrip.* 30, 2, ed. F. Baethgen, 1047–75. Leipzig: Karl W. Hiersemann, 1934.

Andrieu, M., ed. *Le Pontifical romain du XIIe siècle.* Vol. 1 of *Le Pontifical romain au moyen-âge.* Studi e Testi, 86. Vatican City: Biblioteca Apostolica Vaticana, 1938.

Anselm of Canterbury. *De casu diaboli.* In *Opera omnia,* ed. F. S. Schmitt, 1: 227–76. Edinburgh: Thomas Nelson, 1946. Trans. Jasper Hopkins and Herbert Richardson, in *Anselm of Canterbury,* 2: 127–77. Toronto: Edwin Mellen, 1976.

——. *Cur Deus Homo.* In *Opera omnia,* ed. F. S. Schmitt, 2: 37–133. Edinburgh: Thomas Nelson, 1946. Trans. Jasper Hopkins and Herbert Richardson, in *Anselm of Canterbury,* 3: 39–137. Toronto: Edwin Mellen, 1976.

Ps.-Anselm of Canterbury. *Sermo de conceptione Beate Mariae. PL* 159, cols. 319–24. Translated in the appendix of *The Dogma of the Immaculate Conception: History and Significance,* ed. Edward Dennis O'Connor, 522–27. Notre Dame, Ind.: University of Notre Dame Press, 1958.

Anselm of Lucca. *Collectio canonum una cum collectione minore.* Ed. F. Thaner. Innsbruck: Libraria Academicae Wagnerianae, 1906–15.

Aristotle. *On Dreams.* In *Aristotle VIII: On the Soul, Parva Naturalia, On Breath,* ed. and trans. W. S. Hett, 347–81. Loeb Classical Library. Cambridge, Mass.: Harvard University Press; London: William Heinemann, 1975.

Athanasius. *Epistola ad Amun. PG* 26, cols. 1169–76. Trans. A. Robertson. In *St. Athanasius: Select Works and Letters,* ed. P. Schaff and Henry Wace, 556–57. *LNPNFC* 2d ser., vol. 4. Rprt. Grand Rapids, Mich.: Eerdmans, 1987.

——. *Vita S. Antonii. PG* 26, cols. 631–1164. Trans. Mary Emily Keenan, *The Life of St. Anthony.* In *Early Christian Biographies,* 133–216. *FC,* vol. 15. New York: *FC,* 1952.

Augustine. *De bono conjugali. CSEL,* 41, ed. Joseph Zycha, 185–231. Vienna: F. Tempsky; Leipzig: G. Freytag, 1900. Trans. Charles T. Wilcox, *The Good of Marriage.* In *Saint Augustine: Treatises on Marriage and Other Subjects,* 9–51. *FC,* vol. 27. New York: *FC,* 1955.

——. *De civitate dei.* Ed. Bernardus Dombart and Alphonsus Kalb. 2 vols. *CCSL,* 47, 48. Turnhout: Brepols, 1955. Trans. Gerald G. Walsh et al., *City of God.* 3 vols. *FC,* vols. 8, 14, 24. New York: Fathers of the Church, 1950, 1952, 1954.

——. *Confessionum libri XIII.* Ed. Lucas Verheijen. *CCSL,* 27. Turnhout: Brepols, 1981. Trans. R. S. Pine-Coffin, *Confessions.* Harmondsworth: Penguin, 1961; rprt. 1979.

——. *Contra academicos. CCSL,* 29, ed. W. M. Green, 1–61. Turnhout: Brepols, 1970. Trans. Denis J. Kavanagh, *Answer to Skeptics,* 103–233. *FC,* vol. 5. New York: Cima, 1942.

——. *De cura pro mortuis gerenda. CSEL,* 41, ed. Joseph Zycha, 619–60. Vienna: F. Tempsky; Leipzig: G. Freytag, 1900. Trans. H. Browne, *On Care to Be Had for the Dead.* In *St. Augustin: On the Holy Trinity, Doctrinal Treatises, Moral Treatises,* 539–51. *LNPNFC* 1st ser., vol. 3. Grand Rapids, Mich.: Eerdmans; rprt. 1978.

——. *De diversis quaestionibus octoginta tribus. CCSL,* 44a, ed. Almut Mutzenbecher, 1–249. Turnhout: Brepols, 1975. Trans. David L. Mosher, *Eighty-Three Different Questions. FC,* vol. 70. Washington, D.C.: Catholic University of America Press, 1982.

——. *De diuinatione daemonum*. *CSEL,* 41, ed. Joseph Zycha, 597–618. Vienna: F. Tempsky; Leipzig: G. Freytag, 1900. Trans. R. W. Brown, *The Divination of Demons*. In *Saint Augustine: Treatises on Marriage and Other Subjects,* 421–40. *FC,* vol. 27. New York: Fathers of the Church, 1955.

——. *Enchiridion*. *CCSL,* 46, ed. E. Evans, 49–114. Turnhout: Brepols, 1969. Trans. Bernard M. Peebles, *Faith, Hope, and Charity,* 369–472. *FC,* vol. 2. New York: Cima Publications, 1947.

——. *Epistolae*. Ed. A. Goldbacher and J. Divjak. *CSEL,* vols. 34 (pts. 1 and 2), 44, 47, 58, 88. Vienna: F. Tempsky; Leipzig: G. Freytag, 1895–1981. Trans. Wilfrid Parsons, *Saint Augustine: Letters*. *FC,* vols. 12, 18, 20, 30, 32. New York: Fathers of the Church, 1951–56.

——. *De Genesi ad litteram libri duodecim*. *CSEL,* 28, 1, ed. Joseph Zycha, 1–435. Vienna: F. Tempsky; Leipzig: G. Freytag, 1894. Trans. John Hammond Taylor, *The Literal Meaning of Genesis*. *ACW,* nos. 41–42. New York: Newman Press, 1982.

——. *Quaestionum in Heptateuchum libri VII*. Ed. I. Fraipont. *CCSL,* 33. Turnhout: Brepols, 1958.

——. *Retractiones*. Ed. P. Knöll. *CSEL,* 36, 2. Vienna: F. Tempsky; Leipzig: G. Freytag, 1902. Trans. Mary Inez Bogan, *The Retractions*. *FC,* vol. 60. Washington, D.C.: Catholic University of America Press, 1968.

Banks, M. M., ed. *An Alphabet of Tales: An English 15th Century Translation of the "Alphabetum narrationum" of Etienne de Besançon*. 2 vols. *EETS,* o.s., nos. 126–27. London: Kegan Paul, Trench, Trübner, 1904 and 1905; rprt. as one volume Millwood, N.Y.: Kraus, 1987.

Bede. *Ecclesiastical History of the English People*. Ed. and trans. Bertram Colgrave and R. A. B. Mynors. Oxford: Clarendon Press, 1969.

Benedict of Nursia. *Benedicta Regula*. Ed. Rudolph Hanslik. Rev. ed. *CSEL,* 75. Vienna: Hoelder, Pichler, Tempsky, 1977. Trans. Anthony Meisel and M. C. del Mastro, *The Rule of St. Benedict*. New York: Doubleday, 1975.

Bernard of Clairvaux. Ep. 174. *Ad canonicos Lugdunenses, de conceptione S. Mariae*. *PL* 182, cols. 331–36.

——. *Sermones super cantica canticorum*. Ed. Jean Leclercq et al. *SC,* no. 414. Paris: Editions du Cerf, 1990.

Bernardino of Siena. *Opera omnia*. Ed. Fathers of the College of St. Bonaventure ad Claras Aquas. 7 vols. Florence: College of St. Bonaventure, 1950.

——. *Le prediche volgari di San Bernardino da Siena, dette nella Piazza del Campo l'anno MCCCCXXVII*. Ed. L. Banchi. 3 vols. Siena: Edit. all'inseg. di S. Bernardino, 1880–88.

——. *San Bernardino da Siena: le prediche volgari*. Ed. C. Cannarozzi. 3 vols. Pistoia: Alberto Pacinotti, 1934.

Bertrand of Pontigny. *Vita beati Edmundi Cantuariensis archiepiscopi*. In *Thesaurus Novus Anecdotorum,* ed. E. Martène and U. Durand, vol. 3, cols. 1775–1826. Paris: Lutetia, 1717; rprt. New York: Burt Franklin, 1968.

Bonacursus. *Vita haereticorum*. *PL* 204, cols. 775–92. Sections translated in Walter L. Wakefield and Austin P. Evans, *Heresies of the High Middle Ages,* 171–73. New York: Columbia University Press, 1969.

Bonaventure. *Commentaria in quatuor libros sententiarum.* In *Opera omnia,* ed. Fathers of the College of St. Bonaventure ad Claras Aquas. Vols. 1–4. Florence: College of St. Bonaventure, 1882–1902.

Bozóky, Edina, ed. *Le Livre secret des cathares: "Interrogatio Iohannis".* Paris: Beauchesne, 1980. Sections translated in Walter L. Wakefield and Austin P. Evans, *Heresies of the High Middle Ages,* 458–65. New York: Columbia University Press, 1969.

Burchard of Worms. *Decretum. PL* 140, cols. 537–1058.

Caesarius of Heisterbach. *Dialogus miraculorum.* Ed. Joseph Strange. 2 vols. Cologne: J. M. Heberle, 1851. Trans. H. Von E. Scott and C. C. Swinton Bland, *The Dialogue on Miracles.* 2 vols. London: Routledge, 1929.

Canonum prisca collectio (= *The Collection in Nine Books*). *PL* 138, cols. 397–442.

Cassian, John. *Conférences.* Ed. and trans. E. Pichery. 3 vols. *SC,* nos. 42, 54, 64. Paris: Editions du Cerf, 1955–59.

———. *Institutions cénobitiques.* Ed. and trans. Jean-Claude Guy. *SC,* no. 109. Paris: Editions du Cerf, 1965.

Chaucer, Geoffrey. *The Riverside Chaucer.* Ed. Larry D. Benson. 3d ed. Boston: Houghton Mifflin, 1987.

Cherubino of Spoleto. *Regole della vita matrimoniale.* Ed. Francesco Zambrini and Carlo Negroni. Scelta di curiosita letterarie inedite o rare del secolo XIII al XVII, Dispensa 128. Bologna: Romagnoli-dall'Acqua, 1888.

Collijn, Isak, ed. *Acta et processus canonizacionis Beate Birgitte.* Uppsala: Almqvist and Wiksells, 1924–31.

Constantine the African. "Constantinus Africanus' *De coitu:* A Translation." Trans. Paul Delany. *Chaucer Review* 4 (1969): 55–65.

Ps.-Cyprian. *De singularitate clericorum. CSEL,* 3, 3, ed. G. Hartel, 173–220. Vienna: C. Geroldi Filium Bibliopolam Academiae, 1871.

Damian, Peter. *Die Briefe des Petrus Damiani.* Ed. Kurt Reindel. 4 vols. *MGH, Die Briefe der deutschen Kaiserzeit,* 4. Munich: *MGH,* 1983, 1988, 1989, 1993. Trans. Owen J. Blum, *Letters. FC,* Mediaeval Continuation, vols. 1–3. Washington, D.C.: Catholic University of America Press, 1989–92.

———. *Sermones.* Ed. Giovanni Lucchesi. *CCCM,* 57. Turnhout: Brepols, 1983.

———. *Vita beati Romualdi.* Ed. Giovanni Tabacco. Instituto Storico Italiano per il medio evo. Rome: nella Sede dell'Instituto, Palazzo Borromini, 1957.

Denis the Carthusian. "De laudabili vita conjugatorum." In *Opera minora,* 6: 57–117, ed. The Monks of the Sacred Order of the Carthusians. Vol. 38 of *Opera omnia.* Tournai: Typis Cartusiae S. M. de Pratis, 1909, p. 102.

Dexter, Elise F., ed. *Miracula sanctae Virginis Mariae.* University of Wisconsin Studies in the Social Sciences and History, no. 12. Madison: University of Wisconsin, 1927.

Dionysius the Ps.-Areopagite. *De divinis nominibus. PG* 3, cols. 585–996.

Dondaine, Antoine, ed. *De heresi catharorum in Lombardia.* In "La hiérarchie cathare en Italie: I." *Archivum Fratrum Praedicatorum* 19 (1949): 300–312. Trans. Walter L. Wakefield and Austin P. Evans, *Heresies of the High Middle Ages,* 160–67. New York: Columbia University Press, 1969.

Douais, Célestin, ed. *La Somme des autorités à l'usage des prédicateurs méridionaux au XIIIe siècle.* Paris: Picard, 1896.

Durand of Huesca. *Liber antiheresis* (bk. 2). Ed. Christine Thouzellier. "Controverses vaudoises-cathares à la fin du XIIe siècle (d'après le livre II du *Liber antiheresis,* Ms. Madrid 1114 et les sections correspondantes du ms. BN. lat. 13446)." *Archives d'histoire doctrinale et littéraire du moyen âge* 35 (1960): 206–27.

——. *Une Somme anti-cathare: le "Liber contra manicheos."* Ed. Christine Thouzellier. Spicilegium Sacrum Lovaniense, Etudes et documents, fasc. 32. Louvain: Spicilegium Sacrum Lovaniense, 1964.

Durandus, William. *Le Pontifical de Guillaume Durand.* Ed. M. Andrieu. Vol. 3 of *Le Pontifical romain au moyen-âge.* Studi e Testi, 88. Vatican City: Biblioteca Apostolica Vaticana, 1940.

Duvernoy, Jean, ed. *Le Registre d'inquisition de Jacques Fournier, évêque de Pamiers (1318–1325).* 3 vols. Toulouse: Edouard Privat, 1965.

——, ed. and trans. *Le Registre d'inquisition de Jacques Fournier, évêque de Pamiers (1318–1325).* 3 vols. Paris: Mouton, 1978.

Eadmer. *Tractatus de conceptione B. Mariae Virginis. PL* 159, cols. 302–18.

Ernaldus, Abbot of Bona-Vallis et al. *S. Bernardi vita et res gestae. PL* 185, cols. 225–466.

Fornasari, M., ed. *Collectio canonum in V libris. CCCM,* 6. Turnhout: Brepols, 1970.

Franz, Adolph, ed. "Die Benedictio post partum," "Die Benedictio ad introducendam mulierem in ecclesiam." In *Die kirchlichen Benediktionen im Mittelalter,* 2: 208–13; 213–40. Freiburg im Breisgau: Herder, 1909.

Gaiffier, B. de, ed. "Vita Beati Raimundi Lulli." *AB* 48 (1930): 130–78.

Gerson, John. *Oeuvres complètes.* Ed. Palémon Glorieux. 10 vols. in 11. Paris: Desclée, 1960–73.

Glorieux, Palémon, ed. *Autour de la spiritualité des anges.* Tournai: Desclée, 1959.

Glossa ordinaria (biblical). In *Textus Biblie cum glosa ordinaria, Nicholai de Lyra postilla, moralitatibus eiusdem.* 6 vols. in 5. Basel: Johannes Petri et Johannes Frobenium, 1506–8.

Gratian. *Decretum Magistri Gratiani.* Ed. A. Friedberg. In *Corpus Iuris Canonici.* 2d ed. Vol. 1. Leipzig: B. Tauchnitz, 1879; rprt. Graz: Akademische Druck-U. Verlagsanstalt, 1955.

Gregory I (the Great). *Dialogues.* Ed. Adalbert de Vogüé. Trans. Paul Antin. 3 vols. *SC,* nos. 251, 260, 265. Paris: Editions du Cerf, 1978–80. Trans. Odo John Zimmerman, *Dialogues. FC,* vol. 39. Washington, D.C.: Catholic University of America Press, 1959.

——. *Homiliae XL in Evangelia. PL* 76, cols. 1075–1312.

——. *Homiliae in Hiezechihelem prophetam.* Ed. Marcus Adriaen. *CCSL,* 142. Turnhout: Brepols, 1971.

——. *Moralia in Iob.* Ed. Marcus Adriaen. 3 vols. *CCSL,* 143, 143a, 143b. Turnhout: Brepols, 1979–85.

Gregory VII. *Epistolae Collectae.* Ed. P. Jaffé. In *Monumenta Gregoriana, Bibliotheca Rerum Germanicarum.* Berlin, 1865; rprt. Aalen: Scientia, 1964.

Gregory IX et al. *Decretalium Collectiones.* Ed. A. Friedberg. In *Corpus Iuris Canonici.* 2d ed. Vol. 2. Leipzig: B. Tauchnitz, 1879; rprt. Graz: Akademische Druck-U. Verlagsanstalt, 1955.

Grimald of St. Gall. *Liber sacramentorum. PL* 121, cols. 797–926.

Gui, Bernard. *Practica inquisitionis heretice pravitatis*. Ed. Célestin Douais. Paris: Alphonse Picard, 1886.

Guibert of Nogent. *Autobiographie*. Ed. Edmond-René Labande. Paris: Société d'Edition "Les Belles Lettres," 1981. Trans. Paul J. Archambault, *A Monk's Confession: The Memoirs of Guibert of Nogent*. University Park: Pennsylvania State University Press, 1996.

Hellman, Robert and Richard O'Gorman, trans. *Fabliaux: Ribald Tales from the Old French*. New York: Thomas Y. Crowell, 1965.

Hildegard of Bingen. *Causae et curae*. Ed. Paul Kaiser. Leipzig: B. G. Teubner, 1903.

———. *Scivias*. Ed. Adelgundis Führkötter and Angela Carlevaris. 2 vols. *CCCM*, 43, 43a. Turnhout: Brepols, 1978. Trans. Columba Hart. New York: Paulist Press, 1990.

Honorius Augustodunensis. *Clavis physicae*. Ed. Paolo Lucentini. Temi e Testi, 21. Rome: Edizione de Storia e Letteratura, 1974.

———. *L'Elucidarium et les Lucidaires*. Ed. Yves Lèfevre. Paris: E. de Boccard, 1954.

———. *Libellus Honorii Augustodunensis presbyteri et scholastici*. *MGH, Libelli de lite imperatorum et pontificum, saec. XI et XII*, 3, ed. J. Dieterich, 34–80. Hanover: Impensis Bibliopolii Hahniani, 1897.

———. *Libellus octo quaestionum: de angelis et homine*. *PL* 172, cols. 1185–92.

———. *Liber duodecim quaestionum*. *PL* 172, cols. 1177–86.

———. *Speculum ecclesiae*. *PL* 172, cols. 807–1108.

Horstman, Carl, ed. "Vita Clitaucus." *Nova Legenda Anglie*, 1: 190–91. Oxford: Clarendon, 1901.

Hostiensis. *Summa*. Lyons: Iacobus Giunta, 1537; rprt. Aalen: Scientia, 1962.

Hrabanus Maurus. *De magicis artibus*. *PL* 110, cols. 1095–1110.

———. *De universo*. *PL* 111, cols. 9–614.

Hugh of St. Victor. *De sacramentis Christianae fidei*. *PL* 176, cols. 183–618. Trans. Roy J. Defarrari, *On the Sacraments of the Christian Faith*. Cambridge, Mass.: Medieval Academy of America, 1951.

Ps.-Hugh of St. Victor. *Summa sententiarum*. *PL* 176, cols. 41–174.

Humbert of Silva Candida. *Libri III adversus simoniacos*. *MGH, Libelli de lite*, 1, ed. F. Thaner, 100–253. Hanover: Impensis Biblipolii Hahniani, 1891.

Innocent III (Lothario de Segni). *De contemptu mundi sive de miseria conditionis humanae*. *PL* 217, cols. 701–46.

———. *De sacro altaris mysterio*. *PL* 217, cols. 773–916.

Isidore of Seville. *Etymologiae*. *PL* 82, cols. 73–728.

———. *Sententiae*. *PL* 83, cols. 537–738.

Ivo of Chartres. *Panormia*. *PL* 161, cols. 1041–1344.

James of Vitry. *The Exempla or Illustrative Stories from the Sermones Vulgares of Jacques de Vitry*. Ed. Thomas Frederick Crane. Folk-Lore Society Publications, 26. London: Folk-Lore Society, 1890; rprt. Nendeln, Liechtenstein: Kraus, 1967.

Jerome. *Adversus Jovinianum*. *PL* 23, cols. 221–352. Trans. W. H. Fremantle, *Against Jovinian*. In *St. Jerome: Letters and Select Works*, 346–416. *LNPNFC* 2d ser, vol. 6. Rprt. Grand Rapids, Mich.: Eerdmans, 1979.

———. Ep. 22. To Eustochium. In *Epistulae*. Rev. ed. *CSEL*, 54, ed. Isidore Hilberg, 143–211. Vienna: Verlag der österreichischen Akademie der Wissenschaften,

1996. Trans. W. H. Fremantle, in *St. Jerome: Letters and Select Works*, 22–41. *LNPNFC* 2d ser., vol. 6. Rprt. Grand Rapids, Mich.: Eerdmans, 1979.

Ps.-Jerome. *Liber de lapsu Susannae virginis consecratae*. *PL* 16, cols. 383–400.

John of Freiburg. *Summa confessorum*. Rome: s.n., 1518.

John of Lodi. *Vita S. Petri Damiani*. *PL* 144, cols. 113–46.

John Climacus. *Scala paradisi*. *PG* 88, cols. 631–1164. Trans. Colm Luibheid and Norman Russell, *The Ladder of Divine Ascent*. New York: Paulist Press, 1982.

Johnson, Charles, ed. *Registrum Hamonis Hetthe Diocesis Roffensis, A.D. 1319–1352*. Canterbury and York Society, vol. 49. Oxford: Oxford University Press, 1948.

Kempe, Margery. *The Book of Margery Kempe*. Ed. Sanford Meech Brown and Hope Emily Allen. *EETS*, o.s., no. 212. London: Oxford University Press, 1940; rprt. 1960.

Kramer, Henry, and James Sprenger. *Malleus maleficarum 1487*. Photographic facsimile of the first edition. Hildesheim: Georg Olms, 1992. Trans. Montague Summers, *Malleus maleficarum*. London: John Rodker, 1928; rprt. New York: Dover, 1971.

Lactantius. *Divinae Institutiones*. *PL* 6, cols. 111–822.

Landulf the Senior. *Mediolanensis historiae libri quatuor*. Ed. Alessandro Cutulo, *Rerum Italicarum Scriptores*, 4,2. Rev. ed. Bologna: Nicola Zanichelli, 1942.

Lea, H. C., ed. *A Formulary of the Papal Penitentiary in the Thirteenth Century*. Philadelphia: Lea Brothers, 1892.

Little, A. G., ed. *Liber exemplorum ad usum praedicantium*. Aberdeen: Typis Academicis, 1908.

McNeill, John T. and Helena M. Gamer, trans. *Medieval Handbooks of Penance: A Translation of the Principal "Libri poenitentiales"*. New York: Columbia University Press, 1938; rprt. 1990.

Macrobius. *Commentary on the Dream of Scipio*. Trans. William Harris Stahl. New York: Columbia University Press, 1952.

Mansi, G. D., ed. *Sacrorum conciliorum nova et amplissima collectio*. 53 vols. in 60. Paris: H. Welter, 1901–27.

Manuel, Don Juan. *Don Juan Manuel: El Conde Lucanor*. Ed. Alfonso I. Sotelo. Madrid: Alianza Editorial, 1995. Trans. John E. Keller and L. Clark Keating, *The Book of Count Lucanor and Patronio*. Lexington: University Press of Kentucky, 1977.

Marie de France. *The Lais of Marie de France*. Trans. Robert Hanning and Joan Ferrante. Durham, N.C.: Labyrinth, 1982.

Martène, Edmund, ed. *Ordines* 11–12, "De mulieribus post partum," and "De mulieribus post partum purificandis." In *De Antiquis Ecclesiae Ritibus*. Rev. ed. 1: 135–37. Venice: Redmondini, 1788.

Martène, E. and U. Durand, eds. *Disputatio inter catholicum et paterinum haereticum*. In *Thesaurus Novus Anecdotorum*, vol. 5, cols. 1705–11. Paris: Lutetia, 1717; rprt. New York: Burt Franklin, 1968.

Matthew of Cracow. *De modo confitendi et de puritate conscientie*. Paris: Guy Marchant for Denis Roce [?], before 1501.

Menestò, Enrico, ed. *Il processo di canonizzazione di Chiara da Montefalco*. Regione dell'Umbria: La Nuova Italia, 1984.

Montaiglon, Anatole de, ed. *Le Livre du Chevalier de la Tour Landry*. Paris: P. Jannet, 1854. Trans. William Caxton, *The Book of the Knight of the Tower.* Ed. M. Y. Offord. *EETS,* supp., no. 2. Oxford: Oxford University Press, 1971.

Nicholas of Lyre. *Postilla*. In *Textus Biblie cum glosa ordinaria, Nicolai de Lyra postilla, moralitatibus eiusdem*. 6 vols. in 5. Basel: Johannes Petri et Johannes Frobenius, 1506–8.

Nicholas of St. Albans. *De celebranda concepcione beate Marie contra beatum Bernardum*. Ed. C. H. Talbot as "Nicholas of St. Albans and Saint Bernard." *Revue Bénédictine* 64 (1954): 82–117.

Nider, John. *Formicarium*. Douai: B. Belleri, 1602.

——. *De morali lepra*. Louvain: Johann von Paderborn, 1481.

Paolini, Lorenzo and Raniero Orioli, eds. *Acta S. Officii Bononie ab anno 1291 usque ad annum 1310*. 2 vols. and index. Fonti per la Storia d'Italia, no. 106, 3 pts. Rome: Palazzo Borromini, 1982–84.

Pelagius and John, trans. (from the Greek). *Verba seniorum*. *PL* 73, cols. 851–1062.

Peter the Chanter. *Summa de sacramentis et animae consiliis*. Ed. Jean-Albert Dugauquier. 3 pts. in 5 vols. Analecta Mediaevalia Namurcensia, 4, 7, 11, 16, 21. Louvain: Nauwelaerts; Lille: Librairie Giard, 1954–67.

Peter Lombard. *Sententiae in IV libris distinctae*. Ed. Fathers of the College of St. Bonaventure ad Claras Aquas. 3d ed. 2 vols. Rome: College of St. Bonaventure, 1971–81.

Peter of Poitiers. *Summa de confessione: Compilatio praesens*. Ed. Jean Longère. *CCCM,* 51. Turnhout: Brepols, 1980.

Peter of Vaux-de-Cernay. *Petri Vallium Sarnaii monachi Hystoria albigensis*. Ed. Paschal Guébin and Ernest Lyon. 3 vols. Paris: Honoré Champion, 1926–1939. Sections translated in Walter L. Wakefield and Austin P. Evans, *Heresies of the High Middle Ages,* 236–41. New York: Columbia University Press, 1969.

Pez, Bernard, ed. *Ven. Agnetis Blannbekin, quae sub Rudolpho Habspurgico et Alberto I. Austriacis Impp. Wiennae floruit, Vita et Revelationes auctore anonymo ord. F. F. Min. è celebri conv. S. Crucis Wiennensis*. Vienna: Petrum Conrad Monath, 1731.

Pliny. *Natural History*. Ed. and trans. H. Rackham et al. 10 vols. Loeb Classical Library. Cambridge, Mass.: Harvard University Press; London: William Heinemann, 1938–62.

Pomponazzi, Peter. *De naturalium effectuum admirandorum causis sive de Incantationibus*. In *Opera,* 6–327. Basel: Henricpetrina, 1567.

Radbertus, Paschasius. *De corpore et sanguine Domini*. Ed. Bede Paulus. *CCCM,* 16. Turnhout: Brepols, 1969.

——. *De partu virginis*. *CCCM,* 56c, ed. E. Ann Matter, 47–89. Turnhout: Brepols, 1985.

Regino of Prüm. *De ecclesiasticis disciplinis et religione Christiana*. *PL* 132, cols. 187–370.

Richard of St. Victor. *De Trinitate*. Ed. Gaston Salet. *SC,* no. 63. Paris: Editions du Cerf, 1959.

Robert of Brunne. *Handlyng Synne*. Ed. Frederick J. Furnivall. *EETS,* o.s., nos. 119 and 123. London: Kegan Paul, Trench, and Trübner, 1901; rprt. Millwood, N.Y.: Kraus, 1975.

Robert of Flamborough. *Liber poenitentialis.* Ed. J. J. Francis Firth. Toronto: Pontifical Institute of Mediaeval Studies, 1971.

Rosenberg, Samuel, trans. *Lancelot-Grail: The Old French Arthurian Vulgate and Post-Vulgate in Translation.* Ed. Norris J. Lacey. New York: Garland, 1993.

Rudolf von Schlettstadt. *Historiae memorabiles: zur Dominikanerliteratur und Kulturgeschichte des 13. Jahrhunderts.* Ed. Erich Kleinschmidt. Cologne: Böhlau, 1974.

Rudolph of Bourges. *Capitula. PL* 119, cols. 703–26.

Rupert of Deutz. *De glorificatione trinitatis et processione sancti spiritus. PL* 169, cols. 13–202.

———. *De sancta Trinitate et operibus eius.* Ed. Hraban Haacke. *CCCM,* 21–24. Turnhout: Brepols, 1971–72.

———. *De victoria verbi Dei.* Ed. Hraban Haacke. *MGH, Die deutschen Geschichtsquellen des Mittelalters,* v. 5. Weimar: Hermann Böhlaus, 1970.

Saxo Grammaticus. *Danorum regum heroumque historia: The Text of the First Edition with Translation and Commentary.* Trans. Eric Christiansen. 3 vols. Oxford: B. A. R., 1981.

Schmitz, J. H., ed. *Die Bussbücher und die Bussdisciplin der Kirche nach handschriftlichen Quellen dargestellt.* Vol. 1. Mainz: Franz Kirchheim, 1883.

———, ed. *Die Bussbücher und das kanonische Bussverfahren nach handschriftlichen Quellen dargestellt.* Vol. 2. Düsseldorf: L. Schwann, 1898.

Soranus. *Gynecology.* Trans. Owsi Temkin. Baltimore: Johns Hopkins University Press, 1956; rprt. 1991.

Stephen of Bourbon. *Anecdotes historiques, légendes et apologues tirés du recueil inédit d'Etienne de Bourbon.* Ed. A. Lecoy de la Marche. Paris: Renouard, 1877.

Tanner, Norman P. et al., ed. and trans. *Decrees of the Ecumenical Councils.* Original text established by G. Alberigo et al. 2 vols. London: Sheed and Ward; Washington, D.C.: Georgetown University Press, 1990.

Theodulf of Orleans. *Theodulfi capitulare ad eosdem [i.e., ad presbyteros parochiae suae] (Second Diocesan Statute). PL* 105, cols. 207–24.

Thomas Aquinas. *Commentum in quatuor libros sententiarum.* In *Opera omnia,* vols. 6, 7 (pts. 1 and 2). Parma: Petrus Fiaccadori, 1852–73; rprt. New York: Musurgia, 1948–50.

———. *In Decretalem I. expositio ad Archidiaconum Tridentinum.* In *Opera omnia,* Parma edition, 16: 300–306.

———. *De malo.* In *Opera omnia,* Parma edition, 8: 219–424. Trans. Jean Oesterle, *On Evil.* Notre Dame, Ind.: University of Notre Dame Press, 1995.

———. *De potentia.* In *Opera omnia,* Parma edition, 8: 1–218. Trans. English Dominican Fathers, *On the Power of God.* 3 vols. in 1. Westminster, Md.: Newman Press, 1952.

———. *Quaestiones quodlibetales.* In *Opera omnia,* Parma edition, 9: 439–631.

———. *De spiritualibus creaturis.* In *Opera omnia,* Parma edition, 8: 425–64. Trans. Mary C. Fitzpatrick and John J. Wellmuth. *On Spiritual Creatures.* Milwaukee, Wisconsin: Milwaukee University Press, 1949.

———. *Summa theologiae.* Ed. and trans. Fathers of the English Dominican Province. 61 vols. London: Blackfriars, 1964–81.

Ps.-Aquinas. *De somniis*. In *Opera omnia*, Parma edition, 20: 229–38.
Thomas of Cantimpré. *Bonum universale de apibus*. Douai: B. Belleri, 1627.
——. *Liber de natura rerum*. Vol. 1. Ed. H. Boese. Berlin: Walter de Gruyter, 1973.
Thomas of Chobham. *Summa confessorum*. Ed. F. Broomfield. Analecta Mediaevalia Namurcensia, 25. Louvain: Nauwelaerts, 1968.
Thouzellier, Christine, ed. *Livre des deux principes*. *SC*, no. 198. Paris: Editions du Cerf, 1973.
Vincent of Beauvais. *Speculum quadruplex; sive Speculum maius*. 4 vols. (Vol. 1: *Speculum naturale;* Vol. 2: *Speculum doctrinale;* Vol. 3: *Speculum morale;* Vol. 4: *Speculum historiale*.) Douai: B. Belleri, 1624.
Vogel, Cyrille, and Reinhard Elze, eds. *Le Pontifical romano-germanique du dixième siècle*. 3 vols. Studi e Testi, 226–27, 269. Vatican City: Biblioteca Apostolica Vaticana, 1963, 1972.
Wakefield, Walter L. and Austin P. Evans, eds. and trans. *Heresies of the High Middle Ages*. New York: Columbia University Press, 1969.
Wasserschleben, F. W., ed. *Die Bussordnungen der aberländischen Kirche*. Halle: Graeger, 1851.
White, Hugh, trans. *Ancrene Wisse: A Guide for Anchoresses*. Harmondsworth: Penguin, 1993.
White, T. H., trans. *The Bestiary: A Book of Beasts*. New York: Putnam, 1954; Capricorn Books ed., 1960.
William de Nangis. *Continuatio chronici*. Ed. Danou and Naudet. In *Recueil des historiens des Gaules et de la France*, 20: 583–646. Paris: Imprimerie Royale, 1840.
William of Auvergne. *Opera omnia*. 2 vols. Paris: A. Pralard, 1674; rprt. Frankfurt am Main: Minerva, 1963.
William of Puylaurens. "Guillaume de Puylaurens et sa chronique." Ed. Beyssier. In *Troisièmes mélanges d'histoire du moyen âge*, ed. A. Luchaire, 85–175. Université de Paris, Bibliothèque de la Faculté des Lettres, XVIII. Paris: Félix Alcan, Ancienne Librairie Germer Baill., 1904.
William of Rennes. Glosses for the *Summa sancti Raymundi Peniafort de poenitentia, et matrimonio*. Rome: Sumptibus Joanni Tallini, 1603.
Zeydel, Edwin H., ed. and trans. *Ruodlieb: The Earliest Courtly Novel [After 1050]*. University of North Carolina Studies in the Germanic Languages and Literatures, no. 23. Chapel Hill: University of North Carolina Press, 1959.

Hagiographical Materials from *AA SS*

Ailly, Peter. *Vita S. Petri Coelestini*. May, 4: 486–500.
Anonymous contemporary at Steinfeld. *Vita B. Hermanni Josephi*. April, 1: 683–707.
Anonymous. *Vita S. Severi Episcopi Ravenn*. February, 1: 82–87.
Anselm of ?. *Acta de S. Fingare sive Guignerio, S. Piala virgine et sociis martyribus in Britannia*. March, 3: 454–57.
Bevegnati, Giunta. *Vita B. Margaritae de Cortona*. February, 3: 304–63.
Celestine V (Petrus Coelestinus). *Confessio*. May, 4: 421–25.
James of Vitry. *Vita B. Mariae Oigniacensis*. June, 5: 547–72. Trans. Margot King,

The Life of Marie d'Oignies by Jacques de Vitry. Saskatoon, Sask.: Peregrina Publishing, 1984.

Liudolf. *Vita alia S. Severi Episcopi Ravenn.* February, 1: 88–91.

Rosweydus, Herbertus, ed. *Commemoratio sacrosancti praeputii Christi.* January, 1: 3–8.

Thomas of Cantimpré. *Vita S. Lutgardis.* June, 4: 189–210. Trans. Margot King, *The Life of Lutgard of Aywières.* Saskatoon, Sask.: Peregrina Publishing, 1987.

Selected Secondary Sources

Allen, Prudence. *The Concept of Woman: The Aristotelian Revolution, 750 BC–AD 1250.* Montreal: Eden Press, 1985.

Arx, Walter von. "La Bénédiction de la mère après la naissance: histoire et signification." *Concilium* 132 (1978): 81–92.

Atkinson, Clarissa. *The Oldest Vocation: Christian Motherhood in the Middle Ages.* Ithaca, N.Y.: Cornell University Press, 1991.

———. "'Precious Balsam in a Fragile Glass': The Ideology of Virginity in the Later Middle Ages." *Journal of Family History* 8 (1983): 131–43.

Baldwin, John. *The Language of Sex: Five Voices from Northern France Around 1200.* Chicago: University of Chicago Press, 1994.

Balić, Carlo. "The Mediaeval Controversy over the Immaculate Conception up to the Death of Scotus." In *The Dogma of the Immaculate Conception: History and Significance*, ed. Edward Dennis O'Connor, 161–212. Notre Dame, Ind.: University of Notre Dame Press, 1958.

Bamberger, Bernard J. *Fallen Angels.* Philadelphia: Jewish Publication Society of America, 1952.

Bareille, G. "Angélologie d'après les Pères." *DTC*, vol. 1, 1, cols. 1192–1222.

Barstow, Anne Llewellyn. *Married Priests and the Reforming Papacy: The Eleventh-Century Debates.* Texts and Studies in Religion, vol. 12. New York: Edwin Mellen, 1982.

Benedictow, Ole Jørgen. "On the Origin and Spread of the Notion That Breast-Feeding Women Should Abstain from Sexual Intercourse." *Scandinavian Journal of History* 27, 1 (1992): 65–76.

Bhabha, Homi. "Signs Taken for Wonders: Questions of Ambivalence and Authority Under a Tree Outside Delhi, May 1817." *Critical Inquiry* 12 (1985): 144–65.

Biale, David. *Eros and the Jews: From Biblical Israel to Contemporary America.* New York: Basic Books, 1992.

Biller, Peter. "The Cathars of Languedoc and Written Materials." In *Heresy and Literacy, 1000–1530*, ed. Peter Biller and Anne Hudson, 61–82. Cambridge: Cambridge University Press, 1994.

Bishop, Edmund. *Liturgica Historica.* Oxford: Clarendon Press, 1918.

Blanshei, Sarah. "Criminal Law and Politics in Medieval Bologna." *Criminal Justice History* 2 (1981): 1–30.

Blomme, Robert. *La Doctrine du péché dans les écoles théologiques de la première moitié du XIIe siècle.* Louvain: Universitaires de Louvain; Gembloux: J. Duculot, 1958.

Blum, Owen J. *St. Peter Damian.* Washington, D.C.: Catholic University of America Press, 1947.

Blumenfeld-Kosinski, Renate. *Not of Woman Born: Representations of Caesarean Birth in Medieval and Renaissance Culture.* Ithaca, N.Y.: Cornell University Press, 1990.

Bolton, Brenda M. "*Mulieres sanctae.*" In *Women in Medieval Society,* ed. Susan Mosher Stuard, 141–58. Philadelphia: University of Pennsylvania Press, 1976.

Boswell, John. *Christianity, Social Tolerance, and Homosexuality: Gay People in Western Europe from the Beginning of the Christian Era to the Fourteenth Century.* Chicago: University of Chicago Press, 1980.

Bouman, Cornelius A. "The Immaculate Conception in the Liturgy." In *The Dogma of the Immaculate Conception: History and Significance,* ed. Edward Dennis O'Connor, 114–59. Notre Dame, Ind.: University of Notre Dame Press, 1958.

Bouwsma, William. "Anxiety and the Formation of Early Modern Culture." In *After the Reformation: Essays in Honor of J. H. Hexter,* ed. Barbara C. Malament, 215–46. Philadelphia: University of Pennsylvania Press, 1980.

Boyarin, Daniel. *Carnal Israel: Reading Sex in Talmudic Culture.* Berkeley: University of California Press, 1993.

Brakke, David. "The Problematization of Nocturnal Emissions in Early Christian Syria, Egypt, and Gaul." *Journal of Early Christian Studies* 3 (1995): 419–60.

Brennan, Brian. "'Episcopae': Bishops' Wives Viewed in Sixth-Century Gaul." *Church History* 54 (1985): 311–23.

Briggs, Robin. *Witches and Neighbors: The Social and Cultural Context of European Witchcraft.* New York: Viking, 1996.

Brooke, Christopher. "Gregorian Reform in Action: Clerical Marriage in England, 1050–1200." *Cambridge Historical Journal* 12, 1 (1956): 1–21, app. in 12, 2 (1956): 187–88.

Brown, Judith. *Immodest Acts: The Life of a Lesbian Nun in Renaissance Italy.* New York: Oxford University Press, 1986.

Brown, Peter. *The Body and Society: Men, Women, and Sexual Renunciation in Early Christianity.* New York: Columbia University Press, 1988.

———. *Society and the Holy in Late Antiquity.* London: Faber and Faber, 1982.

———. "Sorcery, Demons, and the Rise of Christianity." In *Witchcraft Confessions and Accusations,* ed. Mary Douglas, 17–45. London: Tavistock, 1970.

Brown, T. S. *Gentlemen and Officers: Imperial Administration and Aristocratic Power in Byzantine Italy, A.D. 554–800.* Hertford: printed by Stephen Austin and Sons for the British School at Rome, 1984.

Brundage, James. *Law, Sex, and Christian Society in Medieval Europe.* Chicago: University of Chicago Press, 1987.

Bultot, Robert. *Christianisme et valeurs humaines. A: La doctrine du mépris du monde, en Occident de S. Ambroise à Innocent III.* Vol. 4. *Le XIe siècle: 1. Pierre Damien.* Louvain: Nauwelaerts, 1963.

Butler, Judith. *Gender Trouble: Feminism and the Subversion of Identity.* New York: Routledge, 1990.

Bynum, Caroline Walker. "Bodily Miracles in the High Middle Ages." In *Belief in History: Innovative Approaches to European and American Religion,* ed. Thomas Kselman, 68–106. Notre Dame, Ind.: University of Notre Dame Press, 1991.

———. *Fragmentation and Redemption: Essays on Gender and the Human Body in Medieval Religion*. New York: Zone Books, 1991.

———. *Holy Feast and Holy Fast: The Religious Significance of Food to Medieval Women*. Berkeley: University of California Press, 1987.

———. *Jesus as Mother: Studies in the Spirituality of the High Middle Ages*. Berkeley: University of California Press, 1982.

———. *The Resurrection of the Body in Western Christianity, 200–1336*. New York: Columbia University Press, 1995.

Cadden, Joan. *The Meanings of Sex Difference in the Middle Ages: Medicine, Science, and Culture*. Cambridge: Cambridge University Press, 1993.

Cardman, Francine. "The Medieval Question of Women and Orders." *The Thomist* 42 (1978): 582–99.

Carroll, Michael. *Madonnas That Maim: Popular Catholicism in Italy Since the Fifteenth Century*. Baltimore: Johns Hopkins University Press, 1992.

Carruthers, Mary. *The Book of Memory: A Study of Memory in Medieval Culture*. Cambridge: Cambridge University Press, 1990.

Cattaneo, Enrico. "La liturgia nella reforma gregoriana." In *Chiesa e riforma nella spiritualità del sec. XI*, 171–90. Convegni del Centro di studi sulla spiritualità medievale 6. Todi: Presso l'Accademia Tudertina, 1968.

Chartier, Roger. *Cultural History: Between Practices and Representations*. Trans. Lydia Cochrane. Oxford: Polity Press, 1988.

Chasteigner, Jean de. "Le célibat sacerdotal dans les écrits de saint Pierre Damien." *Doctor Communis* 24 (1971): 169–83.

Chenu, M.-D. *Nature, Man, and Society in the Twelfth Century: Essays on New Theological Perspectives in the Latin West*. Trans. Jerome Taylor and Lester K. Little. Chicago: University of Chicago Press, 1968.

Clark, Elizabeth A. "John Chrysostom and the *Subintroductae*." *Church History* 46 (1977): 171–85.

———. *The Origenist Controversy: The Cultural Construction of an Early Christian Debate*. Princeton, N.J.: Princeton University Press, 1992.

Coakley, John. "Friars as Confidants of Holy Women in Medieval Dominican Hagiography." In *Images of Sainthood in Medieval Europe*, ed. Renate Blumenfeld-Kosinski and Timea Szell, 222–46. Ithaca, N.Y.: Cornell University Press, 1991.

Cohen, Shaye J. D. "Menstruants and the Sacred in Judaism and Christianity." In *Women's History and Ancient History*, ed. Sarah B. Pomeroy, 273–99. Chapel Hill: University of North Carolina Press, 1991.

Cohn, Norman. *Europe's Inner Demons: An Enquiry Inspired by the Great Witch-Hunt*. New York: Basic Books, 1975.

Cowdrey, H. E. J. "The Papacy, the Patarenes, and the Church of Milan." *Transactions of the Royal Historical Society* ser. 5, 18 (1986): 25–48.

Cressy, David. "Purification, Thanksgiving, and the Churching of Women in Post-Reformation England." *Past and Present* 14 (1993): 106–46.

Crouzel, Henri. *Virginité et mariage selon Origène*. Museum Lessianum, section théologique, no. 58. Paris: Desclée de Brouwer, 1963.

Dean-Jones, Lesley. "The Cultural Construct of the Female Body in Classical Greek Science." In *Women's History and Ancient History*, ed. Sarah B. Pomeroy, 111–37. Chapel Hill: University of North Carolina Press, 1991.

———. "The Politics of Pleasure: Female Sexual Appetite in the Hippocratic Tradition." *Helios* 19 (1992): 72–91.

Derrida, Jacques. *Limited Inc.* Trans. Samuel Weber. Evanston, Ill.: Northwestern University Press, 1988.

Deug-Su, I. "La festa della purificazione in Occidente (secoli IV–VIII)." *Studi Medievali* ser. 3, 15, 1 (1974): 143–216.

Dinzelbacher, Peter. *Heilige oder Hexen? Schicksale auffälliger Frauen in Mittelalter und Frühneuzeit.* Munich: Artemis and Winkler, 1995.

———. "Die 'Vita et Revelationes' der Wiener Begine Agnes Blannbekin († 1315) im Rahmen der Viten und Offenbarungsliteratur ihrer Zeit." In *Frauenmystik im Mittelalter,* ed. Peter Dinzelbacher and Dieter R. Bauer, 152–77. Ostfildern bei Stuttgart: Schwabenverlag, 1985.

Dondaine, Antoine. "La hiérarchie cathare en Italie: I." *Archivum Fratrum Praedicatorum* 19 (1949): 280–312.

Dortel-Claudot, M. "Le Prêtre et le mariage: évolution de la législation canonique des origines au XIIe siècle." *L'Année canonique* 17 (1973): 319–44.

Dossat, Y. "Les cathares dans les documents de l'inquisition." In *Cathares en Languedoc,* ed. Edouard Privat, 82–104. Cahiers de Fanjeaux, 3. Toulouse: Edouard Privat, 1963.

Douais, Célestin. *L'Inquisition: ses orgines, sa procédure.* Paris: Librairie Plon, 1906.

Douglas, Mary. *Purity and Danger: An Analysis of the Concept of Pollution and Taboo.* London: Routledge and Kegan Paul; Ark Paperbacks, 1966; rprt. 1988.

Dronke, Peter. *Women Writers of the Middle Ages: A Critical Study of Texts from Perpetua (d. 203) to Marguerite of Porete (d. 1310).* Cambridge: Cambridge University Press, 1984.

Eilberg-Schwartz, Howard. *The Savage in Judaism: An Anthropology of Israelite Religion and Ancient Judaism.* Bloomington: Indiana University Press, 1990.

Elliott, Dyan. "Bernardino of Siena versus the Marriage Debt." In *Desire and Discipline: Sex and Sexuality in Premodern Europe,* ed. Jacqueline Murray and Konrad Eisenbichler, 168–200. Toronto: University of Toronto Press, 1996.

———. "The Physiology of Rapture and Female Spirituality." In *Medieval Theology and the Natural Body,* ed. Peter Biller and A. J. Minnis, 141–73. Woodbridge, Suffolk: York Medieval Press, in association with Boydell and Brewer, 1997.

———. *Spiritual Marriage: Sexual Abstinence in Medieval Wedlock.* Princeton, N.J.: Princeton University Press, 1993.

Emmerson, Richard Kenneth. *Antichrist in the Middle Ages: A Study of Medieval Apocalypticism, Art, and Literature.* Seattle: University of Washington Press, 1981.

Esmein, A. *Le Mariage en droit canonique.* 2 vols. Paris: Larose et Forcel, 1891; rprt. New York: Burt Franklin, 1968.

Ferretti, Walter. "Il posto dei laici nella Chiesa secondo S. Pier Damiani." In *San Pier Damiano nel IX centenario della morte (1072–1972),* 2: 233–77. Cesena: Centro Studi e Richerche sulla Antica Provincia Ecclesiastica Ravennate, 1972.

Fliche, Augustin. *La Réforme grégorienne.* 3 vols. Spicilegium Sacrum Lovaniense, fascs. 6, 9, 16. Louvain: Spicilegium Sacrum Lovaniense, 1924–37.

Flint, Valerie. "The Chronology of the Works of Honorius Augustodunensis." *Re-*

vue Benedictine 82 (1972): 215–42. Rprt. in *Ideas in the Medieval West: Texts and Their Contexts*. London: Variorum Reprints, 1988.

Foucault, Michel. "The Battle for Chastity." In *Western Sexuality: Practice and Precept in Past and Present Times,* ed. Philippe Ariès and André Béjin, 14–25. Trans. Anthony Forster. Oxford: Blackwell, 1985.

——. *The History of Sexuality*. Trans. Robert Hurley. 3 vols. New York: Vintage, 1978–86.

Franz, Adolph. *Die kirchlichen Benediktionen im Mittelalter.* 2 vols. Freiburg im Breisgau: Herder, 1909.

Freud, Sigmund. *Instincts and Their Vicissitudes*. In *The Standard Edition of the Complete Psychological Works of Sigmund Freud,* ed. James Strachey, 14: 117–40. London: Hogarth Press, 1953–74.

——. *Negation*. In ibid., 19: 235–39.

——. *Notes upon a Case of Obsessional Neurosis* (i.e., "Rat Man"). In ibid., 10: 155–249.

——. *On Narcissism: An Introduction*. In ibid., 14: 73–102.

——. *Repression*. In ibid., 14: 146–58.

——. *Three Essays on Sexuality*. In ibid., 7: 130–243.

——. *The Uncanny*. In ibid., 17: 219–56.

——. *The Unconscious*. In ibid., 14: 166–215.

Frugoni, Chiara. "Female Mystics, Visions, and Iconography." In *Women and Religion in Medieval and Renaissance Italy,* ed. Daniel Bornstein and Roberto Rusconi, 130–64. Trans. Margery J. Schneider. Chicago: University of Chicago Press, 1996.

Gazaeus, Alardus. Commentary on Cassian's *Collationes*. *PL* 49, cols. 477–1328.

Geary, Patrick. *Furta Sacra: Thefts of Relics in the Central Middle Ages*. Princeton, N.J.: Princeton University Press, 1978.

Gibson, Gail McMurray. "Blessing from Sun and Moon: Church as Women's Theater." In *Bodies and Disciplines: Intersections of Literature and History in Fifteenth-Century England,* ed. Barbara Hanawalt and David Wallace, 139–54. Minneapolis: University of Minnesota Press, 1996.

Goering, Joseph. "The Invention of Transubstantiation." *Traditio* 46 (1991): 147–70.

Gravdal, Kathryn. *Ravishing Maidens: Writing Rape in Medieval French Literature and Law*. Philadelphia: University of Pennsylvania Press, 1991.

Gurevich, Aron. *Medieval Popular Culture: Problems of Belief and Perception*. Trans. János M. Bak and Paul A. Hollingsworth. Cambridge: Cambridge University Press; Paris: Editions de la Maison des Sciences de l'Homme, 1988.

——. "Santi iracondi e demoni buoni negli 'Exempla.'" In *Santi e demoni nell'alto medioevo occidentale (secoli V–XI),* 2: 1045–63. Settimane di studio del Centro italiano di studi sull'alto medioevo, 36. Spoleto: Presso la Sede del Centro, 1989.

Hanson, Ann Ellis. "Conception, Gestation, and the Origin of Female Nature in the *Corpus Hippocraticum*." *Helios* 19 (1992): 31–71.

Hasenohr, Geneviève. "La Vie quotidienne de la femme vue par l'église: l'enseignement des 'journées chrétiennes' de la fin du moyen-âge." *Frau und spätmittelalterlicher Alltag,* 19–101. Internationaler Kongress Krems an der Donau 2. bis 5. Oktober 1984, Veröffentlichungen des Instituts für mittelalterliche Realienkunde Österreichs, no. 9. Vienna: Österreichische Akademie der Wissenschaften, 1986.

Hewson, M. A. *Giles of Rome and the Medieval Theory of Conception.* London: Athlone Press, 1975.

Hodgkin, Thomas. *Italy and Her Invaders.* 2d ed. 8 vols. in 9. Oxford: Clarendon, 1885–99.

Iogna-Prat, Dominique. "Le Culte de la Vierge sous le règne de Charles le Chauve." In *Marie: le culte de la Vierge dans la société médiévale,* ed. Dominique Iogna-Prat et al., 65–98. Paris: Beauchesne, 1996.

Jacquart, Danielle, and Claude Thomasset. *Sexuality and Medicine in the Middle Ages.* Trans. Matthew Adamson. Princeton, N.J.: Princeton University Press, 1988.

Karras, Ruth Mazo. *Common Women: Prostitution and Sexuality in Medieval England.* New York: Oxford University Press, 1996.

Kieckhefer, Richard. "The Holy and the Unholy: Sainthood, Witchcraft, and Magic in Late Medieval Europe." *Journal of Medieval and Renaissance Studies* 24 (1994): 355–85.

———. *Unquiet Souls: Fourteenth-Century Saints and Their Religious Milieu.* Chicago: University of Chicago Press, 1984.

Kiessling, Nicolas. *The Incubus in English Literature: Provenance and Progeny.* Pullman: Washington State University Press, 1977.

Klapisch-Zuber, Christiane. *Women, Family, and Ritual in Renaissance Italy.* Trans. Lydia Cochrane. Chicago: University of Chicago Press, 1985.

Klein, Melanie. *The Selected Melanie Klein.* Ed. Juliet Mitchell. New York: Free Press, 1987.

Kruger, Steven F. *Dreaming in the Middle Ages.* Cambridge: Cambridge University Press, 1992.

Kudlien, Fridolf. "The Seven Cells of the Uterus: The Doctrine and Its Roots." *Bulletin of the History of Medicine* 39 (1965): 415–23.

Lambert, Malcolm. *Medieval Heresy: Popular Movements from the Gregorian Reform to the Reformation.* Oxford: Blackwell, 1977; 2d ed., 1992.

———. "The Motives of the Cathars: Some Reflections." In *Religious Motivation: Biographical and Sociological Problems for the Church Historian,* ed. Derek Baker, 49–59. Ecclesiastical History Society, Studies in Church History, vol. 15. Oxford: Blackwell, 1978.

Laqueur, Thomas. *Making Sex: Body and Gender from the Greeks to Freud.* Cambridge, Mass.: Harvard University Press, 1990.

Lea, H. C. *A History of Sacerdotal Celibacy.* 2d ed. Boston: Houghton Mifflin, 1884.

———. *Materials Toward a History of Witchcraft.* Ed. Arthur C. Howland. 3 vols. Philadelphia: University of Pennsylvania Press, 1939.

Leclerq, Jean. *Saint Pierre Damien: ermite et homme d'église.* Uomini e dottrine, 8. Rome: Edizione di storia et letteratura, 1960.

Le Goff, Jacques. *The Birth of Purgatory.* Trans. Arthur Goldhammer. Chicago: University of Chicago Press, 1981.

———. *The Medieval Imagination.* Trans. Arthur Goldhammer. Chicago: University of Chicago Press, 1988.

Le Roy Ladurie, Emmanuel. *Montaillou, village occitan de 1294 à 1324.* Paris: Gallimard, 1975.

Little, Lester K. "The Personal Development of Peter Damian." In *Order and Innovation in the Middle Ages: Essays in Honor of Joseph R. Strayer,* ed. William C. Jordan et al., 317–41. Princeton, N.J.: Princeton University Press, 1976.

Llobet, Gabrielle de. "Variété des croyances populaires au Comté de Foix au début du XIVe siècle d'après les enquêtes de Jacques Fournier." In *La Religion populaire en Languedoc du XIIIe siècle à la moitié du XIVe siècle,* ed. Edouard Privat, 109–26. Cahiers de Fanjeaux, 11. Toulouse: Edouard Privat, 1976.

Lottin, Odon. *Psychologie et morale aux XIIe et XIIIe siècles.* 2d ed. 5 vols. Louvain: Abbaye du Mont César; Gembloux: J. Duclot, 1948–59.

Lucchesi, Giovanni. "Clavis S. Petri Damiani." In *Studi su S. Pier Damiano in onore del Cardinale Amleto Giovanni Cicognani,* 1–215. Biblioteca Cardinale Gaetano Cicognani, 5. Faenza: Seminario Vescovile Pio XII, 1970.

———. "Per una Vita di San Pier Damiani." In *San Pier Damiano nel IX centenario della morte (1072–1972),* 1: 13–179; 2: 13–160. Cesena: Centro studi e richerche sulla antica provincia ecclesiastica Ravennate, 1972.

———. "Il Sermonario di S. Pier Damiani." In *Studi Gregoriani per la storia della "Libertas Ecclesiae,"* ed. Alfonso M. Stickler et al., 9–67. Rome: Libreria Ateneo Salesiano, 1975.

Lukacher, Ned. *The Primal Scenes: Literature, Philosophy, and Psychoanalysis.* Ithaca, N.Y.: Cornell University Press, 1986.

Maclean, Ian. *The Renaissance Notion of Woman: A Study in the Fortunes of Scholasticism and Medical Science in European Intellectual Life.* Cambridge: Cambridge University Press, 1980.

McNamara, Jo Ann. "Canossa and the Ungendering of the Public Man." In *Render unto Caesar: The Religious Sphere in the World of Politics,* ed. Sabrina Petra Ramet and Donald W. Treadgold, 131–50. Washington, D.C.: American University Press, 1995.

———. "Chaste Marriage and Clerical Celibacy." In *Sexual Practices and the Medieval Church,* ed. Vern Bullough and James Brundage, 22–33, 231–35. Buffalo, N.Y.: Prometheus, 1982.

———. "The *Herrenfrage:* The Restructuring of the Gender System, 1050–1150." In *Medieval Masculinities: Regarding Men in the Middle Ages,* ed. Clare Lees, 3–29. Minneapolis: University of Minnesota Press, 1994.

Macy, Gary. "The Dogma of Transubstantiation in the Middle Ages." *Journal of Ecclesiastical History* 45 (1994): 11–41.

———. *Theologies of the Eucharist in the Early Scholastic Period: A Study of the Salvific Function of the Sacrament According to Theologians c. 1080–c. 1220.* Oxford: Clarendon Press, 1984.

Maltese, Enrico V. "'Natura daemonum . . . habet corpus et versatur circa corpora': una lezione di demonologia dal medioevo greco." In *Il demonio e i suoi complici: dottrine e credenze demonologiche nella Tarda Antichità,* ed. Salvatore Pricoco, 265–84. Soveria Mannelli and Messina: Rubbettino, 1995.

Mangenot, E. "Démon d'après les Pères." *DTC,* vol. 4,1, cols. 339–84.

Manselli, Raoul. "Eglises et théologies cathares." In *Cathares en Languedoc,* ed. Edouard Privat, 129–76. Cahiers de Fanjeaux, 3. Toulouse: Edouard Privat, 1963.

Maritain, Jacques. "Le Péché de l'Ange: essai de ré-interpretation des positions Thomistes." *Revue Thomiste* 64 (1956): 197–239.

Martin, Dale B. *The Corinthian Body*. New Haven, Conn.: Yale University Press, 1996.

Mazzotti, Carlo. "Il celibato e la castità del clero in S. Pier Damiani." *San Pier Damiano nel IX centenario della morte (1072–1972)*, 343–56. Cesena: Centro studi e richerche sulla antica provincia ecclesiastica Ravennate, 1972.

Meersseman, G. G. "Chiesa e 'Ordo laicorum' nel sec. XI." In *Chiesa e riforma nella spiritualità del sec. XI*, 39–74. Convegni del Centro di studi sulla spiritualità medievale, 6. Todi: Presso l'Accademia Tudertina, 1968.

Metz, René. "Le statut de la femme en droit canonique médiéval." *Recueils de Société Jean Bodin pour l'Histoire Comparative des Institutions* 12 (1962): 59–113.

Michaud-Quantin, Pierre. "A propos des premières *Summae confessorum*." *Recherches de Théologie Ancienne et Médiévale* 26 (1959): 264–306.

Montano, Edward J. *The Sin of the Angels: Aspects of the Teaching of St. Thomas*. Washington, D.C.: Catholic University of America Press, 1955.

Montclos, Jean de. *Lanfranc et Bérenger: la controverse eucharistique du XIe siècle*. Spicilegium Sacrum Lovaniense, Etudes et documents, fasc. 37. Louvain: Spicilegium Sacrum Lovaniense, 1971.

Moore, R. I. "Family, Community, and Cult on the Eve of the Gregorian Reform." *Transactions of the Royal Historical Society* 5th ser., 30 (1980): 49–69.

———. *The Formation of a Persecuting Society: Power and Deviance in Western Europe, 950–1250*. Oxford: Blackwell, 1987.

———. *The Origins of European Dissent*. New York: St. Martin's Press, 1977.

———. "The Origins of Medieval Heresy." *History* 55 (1970): 21–36.

Morris, Colin. *The Discovery of the Individual, 1050–1200*. New York: Harper and Row, 1972.

Morse, Ruth. "Telling the Truth with Authority: From Richard II to *Richard II*." *Common Knowledge* 4 (1995): 111–28.

Nelson, Janet. "Society, Theodicy, and the Origins of Heresy: Towards an Assessment of the Medieval Evidence." In *Schism, Heresy, and Religious Protest*, ed. Derek Baker, 65–77. Studies in Church History, 9. Cambridge: Cambridge University Press, 1972.

Newman, Barbara. *From Virile Woman to WomanChrist: Studies in Medieval Religion and Literature*. Philadelphia: University of Pennsylvania Press, 1995.

Nirenberg, David. *Communities of Violence: Persecution of Minorities in the Middle Ages*. Princeton, N.J.: Princeton University Press, 1996.

Noonan, John T. "Power to Choose." *Viator* 4 (1973): 419–34.

Palazzini, Pietro. "S. Pier Damiani e la polemica anticelibataria." *Divinitas* 14 (1970): 127–33.

Palazzo, Eric and Ann-Katrin Johansson. "Jalons liturgiques pour une histoire du culte de la Vierge dans l'Occident (Ve–XIe siècles)." In *Marie: le culte de la Vierge dans la société médiévale*, ed. Dominique Iogna-Prat et al., 23–32. Paris: Beauchesne, 1996.

Parks, Katherine. "The Criminal and the Saintly Body: Autopsy and Dissection in Renaissance Italy." *Renaissance Quarterly* 47 (1994): 1–33.

Payer, Pierre J.. *The Bridling of Desire: Ideas of Sex in the Later Middle Ages.* Toronto: University of Toronto Press, 1993.

——. *Sex and the Penitentials: The Development of a Sexual Code, 550–1150.* Toronto: University of Toronto Press, 1984.

Pelikan, Jaroslav. *Mary Through the Centuries: Her Place in History.* New Haven, Conn.: Yale University Press, 1996.

Pine, Martin L. *Pietro Pomponazzi: Radical Philosopher of the Renaissance.* Padua: Editrice Antenore, 1986.

Preus, Anthony. "Galen's Criticism of Aristotle's Conception Theory." *Journal of the History of Biology* 10 (1977): 65–85.

Quay, Paul M. "Angels and Demons: The Teaching of IV Lateran." *Theological Studies* 42 (1981): 20–45.

Roper, Lyndal. *Oedipus and the Devil: Witchcraft, Sexuality, and Religion in Early Modern Europe.* London: Routledge, 1994.

Rousselle, Aline. *Porneia: On Desire and the Body in Antiquity.* Trans. Felicia Pheasant. Oxford: Blackwell, 1988.

Rubin, Miri. *Corpus Christi: The Eucharist in Late Medieval Culture.* Cambridge: Cambridge University Press, 1991.

Ruggiero, Guido. *The Boundaries of Eros: Sex Crime and Sexuality in Renaissance Venice.* New York: Oxford University Press, 1985.

Russell, Jeffrey Burton. *Lucifer: The Devil in the Middle Ages.* Ithaca, N.Y.: Cornell University Press, 1984.

——. *Witchcraft in the Middle Ages.* Ithaca, N.Y.: Cornell University Press, 1972.

Russo, David. "Les Répresentations mariales dans l'art d'Occident du Moyen Age: essai sur la formation d'une tradition iconographique." In *Marie: le culte de la Vierge dans la société médiévale,* ed. Dominique Iogna-Prat et al., 173–291. Paris: Beauchesne, 1996.

Ryan, J. Joseph. *Saint Peter Damiani and His Canonical Sources: A Preliminary Study in the Antecedents of the Gregorian Reform.* Studies and Texts, 2. Toronto: Pontifical Institute of Mediaeval Studies, 1956.

Salisbury, Joyce. *Medieval Sexuality: A Research Guide.* New York: Garland, 1990.

Schulenburg, Jane Tibbetts. "The Heroics of Virginity: Brides of Christ and Sacrificial Mutilation." In *Women in the Middle Ages and Renaissance: Literary and Historical Perspectives,* ed. Mary Beth Rose, 29–72. Syracuse, N.Y.: Syracuse University Press, 1986.

——. "Sexism and the Celestial Gynaeceum, from 500–1200." *Journal of Medieval History* 4 (1978): 117–33.

Sedgwick, Eve Kosofsky. "Queer Performativity: Henry James's *The Art of the Novel.*" *GLQ* 1,1 (1993): 1–16.

——. *Tendencies.* Durham, N.C.: Duke University Press, 1993.

Sheingorn, Pamela. "Appropriating the Holy Kinship: Gender and Family History." In *Interpreting Cultural Symbols: Saint Anne in Late Medieval Culture,* ed. Kathleen Ashley and Pamela Sheingorn, 169–98. Athens: University of Georgia Press, 1990.

Simons, W., and J. E. Ziegler. "Phenomenal Religion in the Thirteenth Century and Its Image: Elisabeth of Spalbeek and the Passion Cult." In *Women in the*

Church, ed. W. J. Sheils and Diana Wood, 117–26. Studies in Church History, 27. Oxford: Blackwell, 1990.

Somigli, Constanzo. "San Pier Damiano e la Pataria." In *San Pier Damiano nel IX centenario della morte (1072–1972),* 3: 193–206. Cesena: Centro Studi e Richerche sulla Antica Provincia Ecclesiastica Ravennate, 1972.

Southern, R. W. "The English Origins of the 'Miracles of the Virgin.'" *Mediaeval and Renaissance Studies* 4 (1958): 176–216.

———. *Saint Anselm and His Biographer: A Study of Monastic Life and Thought, 1059–c. 1130.* Cambridge: Cambridge University Press, 1963.

Staden, Heinrich von. "Women and Dirt." *Helios* 19 (1992): 7–30.

Stoller, Michael. "Eight Anti-Gregorian Councils." *Annuarium Historiae Conciliorum* 17,2 (1985): 252–321.

Tentler, Thomas N. *Sin and Confession on the Eve of the Reformation.* Princeton, N.J.: Princeton University Press, 1977.

Thomasset, Claude. "La répresentation de la sexualité et la génération dans la pensée scientifique médiévale." In *Love and Marriage in the Twelfth Century,* ed. Willy Van Hoecke and Andries Welkenhuysen, 1–17. Louvain: Louvain University Press, 1981.

Thouzellier, Christine. "Controverses vaudoises-cathares à la fin du XIIe siècle (d'après le livre II du *Liber antiheresis,* Ms Madrid 1114 et les sections correspondantes du Ms BN lat. 13446)." *Archives d'histoire doctrinale et littéraire du moyen âge* 35 (1960): 137–227.

Tremp, Kathrin Utz. "'Parmi les hérétiques . . .': la Vierge Marie dans le registre d'inquisition de l'évêque Jacques Fournier de Pamiers (1317–1326)." In *Marie: le culte de la Vierge dans la société médiévale,* ed. Dominique Iogna-Prat et al., 533–60. Paris: Beauchesne, 1996.

Tresmontant, Claude. *La Métaphysique du Christianisme et la naissance de la philosophie chrétienne: problèmes de la creation et de l'anthropologie des origines à saint Augustin.* Paris: Editions du Seuil, 1961.

Tubach, Frederic C. *Index Exemplorum: A Handbook of Medieval Religious Tales.* Folklore Fellows Communications, no. 204. Helsinki: Suomalainen Tiedeakatemia, 1969.

Turmel, J. "Histoire de l'angélologie: des temps apostoliques à la fin du Ve siècle." *Revue d'Histoire et de Littérature Religieuse* 3 (1898): 289–308.

Vacant, A. "Angélologie dans l'église latine depuis le temps des Pères jusqu'à saint Thomas d'Aquin." *DTC,* 1,1, cols. 1222–27.

———. "Angélologie de saint Thomas d'Aquin et des scolastiques postérieurs." *DTC,* 1,1, cols. 1228–48.

Van Dijk, S. J. P. "The Origin of the Latin Feast of the Conception of the Blessed Virgin Mary." *Dublin Review* 228 (1954): 251–67.

Vauchez, André. "Diables et hérétiques: les réactions de l'église et de la société en Occident face aux mouvements religieux dissidents, de la fin du Xe au début du XIIe siècle." In *Santi e demoni nell'alto medioevo occidentale (secoli V–XI),* 2: 573–601. Settimane di studio del Centro italiano di studi sull'alto medioevo, 36. Spoleto: Presso la Sede del Centro, 1989.

———. *The Laity in the Middle Ages: Religious Beliefs and Devotional Practices.* Ed.

Daniel Bornstein, trans. Margery Schneider. Notre Dame, Ind.: University of Notre Dame Press, 1993.

———. *La Sainteté en Occident aux derniers siècles du moyen âge d'après les procès de canonisation et les documents hagiographiques.* Rome: Ecole Française de Rome, 1981.

———. *La Spiritualité du moyen âge occidental, VIIIe–XIIe siècles.* Collection Sup., L'historien, 19. Rome: Presses Universitaires de France, 1975.

Vicaire, M.-H. "Les cathares albigeois vus par les polémistes." In *Cathares en Languedoc,* ed. Edouard Privat, 105–27. Cahiers de Fanjeaux, 3. Toulouse: Edouard Privat, 1963.

Warner, Marina. *Alone of All Her Sex: The Myth and the Cult of the Virgin Mary.* New York: Knopf, 1976.

Weinstein, Donald, and Rudolph M. Bell. *Saints and Society: The Two Worlds of Western Christendom, 1000–1700.* Chicago: University of Chicago Press, 1982.

Wemple, Suzanne F. *Women in Frankish Society: Marriage and the Cloister, 500 to 900.* Philadelphia: University of Pennsylvania Press, 1985.

Williams, G. S. "The Woman / the Witch: Variations on a Sixteenth-Century Theme (Paracelsus, Wier, Bodin)." In *The Crannied Wall: Woman, Religion, and the Arts in Early Modern Europe,* ed. Craig A. Monson, 119–37. Ann Arbor: University of Michigan Press, 1992.

Williams, Norman Powell. *The Ideas of the Fall and of Original Sin: A Historical and Critical Study.* London: Longmans, Green, 1927.

Young, Robert. *White Mythologies: Writing History and the West.* London: Routledge, 1990.

Zarri, Gabriella, ed. *Finzione e santità tra medioevo ed età moderna.* Turin: Rosenberg and Sellier, 1991.

———. *Le Sante vive: cultura e religiosità femminile nella prima età moderna.* Turin: Rosenberg and Sellier, 1990.

Žižek, Slavoj. *Looking Awry: An Introduction to Jacques Lacan through Popular Culture.* Cambridge, Mass.: MIT Press, 1991.

———. *The Metastases of Enjoyment: Six Essays on Woman and Causality.* London: Verso Books, 1994.

———. *The Sublime Object of Ideology.* London: Verso, 1989.

Index

Printed in the United States
121154LV00003B/155/A

9 780812 216653